The Nazi War on Cancer

ROBERT N. PROCTOR

Princeton University Press, Princeton, N.J.

Library of Congress Cataloging-in-Publication Data

Proctor, Robert, 1954–
The Nazi war on cancer / Robert N. Proctor.
p.   cm.
Includes bibliographical references and index.
ISBN 0-691-00196-0 (cloth : alk. paper)
1. Cancer—Prevention—Government policy—Germany—History—
20th century.   2. Public health—Germany—History—20th century.
3. Health care reform—Germany—History—20th century.
4. National socialism.   I. Title.
RC268.P77   1999
362.1'96994'0094309043—dc21   98-49405

This book has been composed in Palatino

http://pup.princeton.edu

Printed in the United States of America

10 9 8 7 6 5 4 3 2

For Stephen Jay Gould, Richard Lewontin,
Ruth Hubbard, Richard Levins,
and the rest of the Bio 106 gang.

CONTENTS

ILLUSTRATIONS

THE NAZI WAR ON CANCER

PROLOGUE

At 3:30 A.M. on the morning of June 22, 1941, German armed forces invaded the Soviet Union along a two-thousand-mile front, beginning the largest and deadliest military campaign in history. Within a matter of weeks, more than a million Soviet men, women, and children would be killed. The campaign would eventually stall, Napoleon-like, in the bitter winter outside Stalingrad, but not before many millions more had died.

Hitler had been rather jittery in the weeks leading up to operation *Barbarossa*. In his diary entry for the morning of the invasion, Joseph Goebbels, the Third Reich's minister of popular enlightenment and propaganda, wrote that only after the invasion had begun would the Führer again become calm, as if a burden had been lifted from his shoulders. Goebbels was very close to Hitler, delighting in the precious hours he spent "eye to eye" with the man he called "a genius" and "the greatest commander of all time." The propaganda minister stayed up late with his beloved Führer that predawn morning, pacing back and forth for hours in the huge salon of the Reichskanzlei.

What did these two men talk about, only hours before the beginning of the operation designed to reduce Slavs to slaves and to acquire *Lebensraum* for Germans in the depopulated East? Goebbels's diary reveals that the two men worked on Hitler's speech announcing the invasion and debated also the precise timing of its broadcast (final decision: 5:30 A.M. that morning). Both lamented the treachery of Rudolf Hess, the Führer's former deputy and successor, who only weeks before had parachuted into England to try to bargain a separate peace with Churchill. Both men marveled at the historic magnitude of the imminent invasion, the explosive surge that would redraw the map of Europe and extirpate the "cancerous tumor" of communism.[1]

But Hitler and Goebbels discussed other things that night. They discussed the importance of English pacifism for the Nazi cause, and the political situation in Italy. And shortly before they separated—only an hour before the invasion—they discussed recent advances in cancer research, including the work of a certain Hans Auler, professor of medicine in Berlin and one of several up-and-coming stars of German cancer research. We don't know exactly what was said (the trail is strong enough to allow some plausible inferences), but the fact that cancer was even broached seems puzzling. How did Germany's political leaders find the time—hours before a major invasion—to discuss cancer and cancer research? Was this idle chitchat, designed to ease the tension, or was there something more at stake? What was cancer in the Thousand Year Reich that set it apart from other health obsessions of the hour?

THIS is a book about fascism, and a book about science. We think we know a lot about both topics, and many of the most horrific images are surely familiar: bodies being bulldozed into pits, gold being stolen from human teeth and buried in Swiss vaults, human hair bundled for recycling, scattered ashes, shattered families. The twisted science of the time is no less notorious: the horrific experiments in the camps; the Luftwaffe killing dozens of men by subjecting them to icy cold or very low pressure; SS doctors like Josef Mengele in Auschwitz injecting dyes into living eyes to see whether brown eyes could be changed into blue.

How many of us know, though, that Dachau prisoners produced organic honey, or that Nazi health activists launched the world's most powerful antismoking campaign? How many of us know that the Nazi war on cancer was the most aggressive in the world, encompassing restrictions on the use of asbestos, bans on tobacco, and bans on carcinogenic pesticides and food dyes? How many of us know that soybeans were declared "Nazi beans," or that Nazi bakeries were required by law to produce whole-grain bread?

This is a book about the history of medicine, but it is also about body politics: Nazi body politics, concepts of health and disease that flourished in the Nazi era, Nazi plots to fight disease. It is about conceptions of health, but it is also about health itself, including who suffered and how much, and why. It addresses the *complicity* of science under fascism but also the *complexity* of science within fascism. It is about how fascism suppressed certain kinds of science—by expelling Jews and communists, for example—but it is also about how fascist ideals fostered research directions and lifestyle fashions that look strikingly like those we today might embrace.

Books about Nazism are almost always designed to shock or disturb; the brute facts lend themselves to this treatment. The distress I would like to evoke, however, is different from that of most recent histories of Nazi medicine, or the Holocaust more generally. There is a by-now-conventional narrative of sorts that treats medicine of the era as an unfolding monstrosity—from racial hygiene, sterilization, and racial exclusion to euthanasia, abusive experimentation, and the Final Solution. The participation of doctors in Nazi racial crimes is disturbing, but it is equally disturbing that Nazi doctors and public health activists were also involved in work that we, today, might regard as "progressive" or even socially responsible—and that some of that work was a direct outgrowth of Nazi ideology. Nazi nutritionists stressed the importance of a diet free of petrochemical dyes and preservatives; Nazi health activists stressed the virtues of whole-grain bread and foods high in vitamins and fiber. Many Nazis were environmentalists; many were vegetarians. Species protection was a going concern, as was animal welfare.[2] Nazi doctors worried about overmedication and the overzealous use of X-rays; Nazi doctors cautioned against an unhealthy workplace and the failure of physicians to be honest with their patients—allowing momentous exclusions, of course, for the "racially unfit" or undeserving.

What are we to make of the Nazi antitobacco campaign or the public health initiatives launched to control cancer? How do we understand the efforts to curb asbestos exposure or exposures to X-rays and radium—or the campaign to secure food quality and "truth in advertising"? Did the Nazis do good work? Was some of that good work motivated by Nazi ideals?

It is difficult to write on this topic without participating in a kind of moral drama—the sort that boils down to questions such as whether "good can come from evil." I am always troubled by such questions, because they seem to stem from a kind of scarecrow image of fascism and a wooden, ahistorical image of science. I should make clear at the outset that it is not at all my goal to *praise* those scientists who, despite obstacles, managed to continue scientific work throughout the Nazi era. There is a tendency in Nazi science historiography to treat the survival of science—such as there was—as proof of the indomitable spirit of the intellect, but my concern is more to ask: what is science that it so easily flourished under fascism? What was it about German fascism that encouraged the progress of (certain kinds of) science, and why has this part of the story been lost to historical memory?

There is an image we have of fascism as a totalizing ideology: Nazi rhetoric and values are seen as having penetrated every crevice of German intellectual life. But that is a misconception, at least in part. Science was often tolerated as a faithful and neutral servant, an engine of economic and military power, blind to politics. Many fields of scholarship did turn out cheering squads for fascism, but just as frightening are the legions of subservients who continued to work quietly, reassured by the myth of cloistered neutrality. Through this lens, the "good science" of the Reich becomes evidence not of heroic ideological innocence but of a blind-eyed failure to reflect and resist—"irresponsible purity" in Herbert Mehrtens's aptly crafted phrase.[3]

I am one of those who believe it is important for scholars to be able to defend their choice of research projects. I should note that I would never have written the present book had I not already explored the more heinous aspects of Nazi medical crime in my first book, *Racial Hygiene: Medicine under the Nazis* (Cambridge: Harvard University Press, 1988), which can be regarded as a kind of prolegomenon to the present book. There I showed that many of the most brutal health initiatives came from physicians, that physicians were never coerced into collaborating with the regime, that doctors were not pawns but pioneers when it came to Nazi policies of racial extermination.

My focus here is less on Nazi racial crime than on the activities of health activists lost to memory by virtue of their association with this terrible time. The point is not to rescue lost gems of wisdom or to exploit the past for the present, but rather to explore the troubling phenomenon of "quality science" under Nazism: science that we might well celebrate as pathbreaking were the circumstances of its origins peeled away, but also run-of-the-mill science that, like Hitler's watercolors,[4] is not obviously and indelibly a Nazi product.

Do we look at history differently when we learn that Nazi leaders opposed tobacco, or that Nazi health officials worried about asbestos-induced lung cancer? I think we do. We learn that Nazism was a more subtle phenomenon than we commonly imagine, more seductive, more plausible. We learn that the barriers which separate "us" from "them" are not as high as some would like to imagine. We learn that there are chilling parallels between those times and ours. But we also get a better sense of why so many Germans—and especially German doctors—welcomed the Nazi movement. Nazism was not about just Nordic supremacy or humiliating and then killing the handicapped; it was not only about territorial expansion or murdering Jews and Gypsies. It was all of these things in spades, but it was also about making jobs and cleaning up the streets and long-term care for the "German germ plasm."

Nothing in this excuses or balances—and if I thought it did, I would not have written this book. Nazism rightly stands as the low-water mark in twentieth-century moral culture, the ultimate refutation to ethical relativism and solipsistic egoism. Nothing anyone can say will change this. What I do hope to show, however, is that fascism is nuanced and complex, and that its appeal went deeper than we are usually willing to admit, and in different directions. Nazism was popular not just because Germans hated Jews. Antisemitism was central to Nazi ideology, but it was not the only or even the main reason people flocked to the cause. People saw the movement as a source of rejuvenation—in public health and in other spheres as well. People looked to Nazism as a great and radical surgery or cleansing, and not always in ways that are abhorrent, even with the privilege of hindsight.

I HAVE chosen cancer as an organizing theme, because cancer gives us a window onto broader aspects of culture. Cancer has always been a frustrating disease, given both the insidious nature of its growth and its notorious resistance to therapeutic onslaughts. Cancer was on the rise in the 1920s and 1930s, and the millenarian leaders of the Thousand Year Reich wanted to know why. Cancer was a difficult symbol: a disease of civilization, of modernity; a not-yet-conquered foe. We shall be looking at these symbolic resonances, especially at how the language of cancer (tumors as Jews, Jews as tumors) expressed larger cultural idioms. Cancer becomes a metaphor for all that was seen as wrong with society, and not just in Germany (recall Nuremberg prosecutor Telford Taylor's postwar characterization of Nazism itself as "a spreading cancer in the breast of humanity"). Cancer gets attention, and cancer gets neglected, in ways that reveal deep struggles over the nature of disease and how it should be confronted.

The first two chapters look at the background to German cancer campaigns, including the extraordinary efforts made in the Wilhelmine and Weimar eras, when German medicine and public health became the envy of the world. We look at the *Gleichschaltung* (Nazification) of German cancer institutions and the fates of Jewish cancer researchers; we also explore the centrality of prevention in Nazi cancer ideology. The language of cancer is held up for scrutiny—the effort to replace foreign by Germanized technical terminology, for example, but also the push for public "enlightenment" concerning the value of early detection. We look at the muscular, problem-solving rhetoric of Nazi medicine, including calls for "final solutions" to diverse problems circa 1941—to the "bread" and "tobacco questions," just to name a couple of the lesser known.

Chapters 3 and 4 turn to genetic and racial theories of cancer, the persecution of Jewish cancer researchers, and the pioneering work done to identify workplace carcinogens. Readers may be surprised to find that German cancer theorists recognized that few cancers are heritable in any simple sense and that many (and perhaps even most) are caused by external irritations like tar, soot, asbestos fibers, and tobacco smoke. Radiation was a particularly feared source of malignancy, and at the same time that monuments were made to "martyrs to radiation" (almost always scientists, rarely technicians, never patients), lists of women and girls exposed to radiation (to induce abortion, for example) were drawn up to identify carriers of genetic damage. Germans in the 1930s become leaders in the identification of radon-induced lung cancer (especially among uranium miners) and lung cancers associated with asbestosis. New workplace hazards are identified, but usually in the context of what has been called *Selektionsmedizin*—the idea being that workers should be adapted to the workplace, and not just vice versa. Workers were screened en masse for early signs of lung or skin disease, and efforts were launched to protect women from cancer and reproductive hazards. Slave labor was eventually used to perform the dirtiest jobs, as a dual system of worker health and safety emerged—involving strict precautions for "healthy" citizens and precarious, life-threatening pollution for foreigners and *Untermenschen*.

Nazi food and body politics is the subject of chapter 5, where I examine what Hitler ate and why, and how the Führer's body became a propaganda tool to inculcate a healthy lifestyle among the masses. I look at the banning of the food dye known as "butter yellow," and the much-debated questions of whether things like meat, fat, and saccharine could cause cancer. I look at debates over food stockpiling, where militarists demanding large canned reserves ran afoul of organicists extolling the virtues of fresh fruits and vegetables. Alcohol, coffee, and tea, and much else, become the object of ideological struggle, especially as romantic concerns clashed with wartime urgencies.

Tobacco is the focus of the longest chapter in the book, a focus justified by the startling fact—heretofore unnoticed—that Nazi

Germany had the world's strongest antismoking campaign and the world's most sophisticated tobacco disease epidemiology. Nazi medical and military leaders worried that tobacco might prove a "hazard to the race," and Hitler intervened personally at several points to combat the hazard. Antitobacco activists pointed to the fact that while Churchill, Stalin, and Roosevelt were all fond of to-bacco, the three major fascist leaders of Europe—Hitler, Mussolini, and Franco—were all nonsmokers. Hitler was the most adamant of the lot, characterizing tobacco as "the wrath of the Red Man against the White Man, vengeance for having been given hard liq-uor." The Führer even suggested that Nazism might never have triumphed in Germany had he not given up smoking! German epidemiologists meanwhile managed to prove, securely and for the first time anywhere, that smoking was the major cause of lung cancer. This, along with its subsequent neglect by chroniclers of medical history, is surely one of the most astonishing aspects of the Nazi war on cancer.

The final chapter looks at wartime and postwar science, the main point being that wartime urgencies compromised much of the public health optimism of the early Nazi era. Organic impulses (e.g., the push for whole-grain foods and natural herbal medicines) were justified as economical and therefore war-worthy—but long-term public health concerns of nearly every sort were placed on back burners (a notable exception being the killing of "racial infe-riors," which continued unabated throughout the war). Here we also explore the mysterious case of the Reich Institute for Cancer Research established near Posen in occupied Poland in 1942: no one knows exactly what went on there, but there is evidence that the institute functioned as the nerve center of Hitler's biological warfare program, a sop thrown to the army's general staff to com-pensate for the emasculation of the atom bomb project.

I should note that I have organized the chapters loosely around the kinds of things that we today recognize as causes of cancer (genetics, radiation, diet, alcohol, and tobacco, etc.), well aware that some of my more puritanical colleagues may accuse me of "Whiggism"—reading the future into the past. I do this, I hope, not out of any subconscious desire to inflate the intellectual achievements of my native informants—a common seduction among ethnographers—but rather from a desire to say something about what cancer itself was really like at this time (and after). Did the Nazi war on cancer influence German cancer rates? Were some strategies more successful than others? When was Nazism carcinogenic, and when did it manage to prevent some cancers?

ONE thing historians do is look for patterns in jarring juxtapositions; out-of-place oddities can be keys to larger truths.* My focus is therefore not so much on Nazi horrors (though there are several we shall have to face) as on substances and practices we do not normally associate with fascism: food and drink, chemicals and radiation, efforts to clean up factories and to detoxify the German lifestyle. This is the lesser-known "flip side" of fascism—the side that gave us struggles against smoking, campaigns for cleaner food and water, for exercise and preventive medicine.

Nazism itself I will be treating as an experiment of sorts—a vast hygienic experiment designed to bring about an exclusionist sanitary utopia. That sanitary utopia was a vision not unconnected with fascism's more familiar genocidal aspects: asbestos and lead were to be cleansed from Germany's factory air and water, much as Jews were to be swept from the German body politic. Nazi ideology linked the purification of the German body politic from environmental toxins and the purification of the German body from "racial aliens." Accurate and absurd fears blended promiscuously in the Nazi view of the world: there is a kind of *homeopathic paranoia* pervading the Nazi body ethos, a fear of tiny but powerful agents corroding the German body, a fear that is sometimes cruel and vicious, sometimes eerily on target.

This jarring mix of the sensible and the insane is surely one of

---

* Not every oddity is significant: surely one of the strangest is the fact that, in October of 1919, the *American Hebrew* decried the "holocaust" of "six million men and women." The oddity has been exploited by Holocaust deniers but is simply a remarkable coincidence and nothing more; see Martin H. Glynn, "The Crucifixion of Jews Must Stop!" *American Hebrew*, October 31, 1919, p. 582.

the most disturbing aspects of Nazism, but it also provides another key, I think, to understanding the Holocaust. Historians and social philosophers have for many years tried to reduce the sadder sides of fascism to capitalism, totalitarianism, militarism, antisemitism, or "the authoritarian personality"—all of which are central, though none is all-explaining. I tend to agree with Omer Bartov that the Holocaust is a kind of idiot's tale we can understand only in parts, never altogether;[5] but perhaps this quest for a sanitary utopia can help us bridge the discomforting gap between the horrific crimes of the era and its pioneering—if reclusive and now forgotten—feats in the sphere of public health.

One final note on a possible misinterpretation of this book. Those who point to Nazi environmentalism sometimes extract from this the message that there is a fascist danger inherent in any state-sponsored public or environmental health protection. Antitobacco advocates have been labeled "health fascists" and "Nico-Nazis," the rather contrived point being that since the Nazis were purists, purists today must be Nazis.[6] There is a Latin name for such a fallacy, the logical error is so simple. Tobacco does cause 80–90 percent of all First World lung cancers, and none of this is diminished by the fact that Nazi-era scientists were the first to prove the point. It is wise to cut down on sugar, fat, and foods preserved with chemicals, even though Nazi nutritionists issued similar recommendations.

We may be surprised by such things, but surely we cannot let them influence us in our choices of how to eat or work today. Or perhaps we should? I must admit that one reason I decided to write this book was to try to come up with an answer. Perhaps what is needed is a severing of the already frayed ties that once were said to conjoin technical and moral virtues; I'm not really sure. I am not usually one to claim that science is or even should be value-free, but I do think that if the Nazis were pioneers in cancer research, we need to know how this came about and what it means.

1

Hueper's Secret

Of course! There is a great deal being done for cancer research in Germany. In every part of the Reich there are
magnificent institutes, for which the Führer has provided
large sums of money.

Adolf Butenandt, Germany's postwar president of the
Max Planck Gesellschaft, in a 1941 radio interview

ON September 28, 1933, Dr. Wilhelm Hueper, chief pathologist at
the University of Pennsylvania's Cancer Research Laboratory,
wrote to the Nazi minister of culture, Bernhard Rust, inquiring
into the possibility of an academic or hospital appointment in the
new Germany. Hueper had emigrated to the United States in 1923,
and we know from his unpublished autobiography that he had
worn the swastika on his Freikorps helmet as early as 1919. Now,
only months after the *Machtergreifung* (Nazi seizure of power), the
young pathologist was petitioning Nazi authorities to allow him
to return to Germany to restore his bonds to German culture
(*deutsches Volks- und Kulturgut*).[1]

It is not always easy to distinguish between conviction and op-
portunism in such matters. And though the distinction may not be
as crucial as we like to think, Hueper's apparent support for the
Nazi regime (he ends his letter with an enthusiastic "Heil Hitler!")
still comes as a shock to anyone unfamiliar with the political landscape of European cancer activism in the 1930s (see fig. 1.1). The
story is a disturbing one, one that seems to violate some of our
most cherished political prejudices. Hueper, after all, went on to

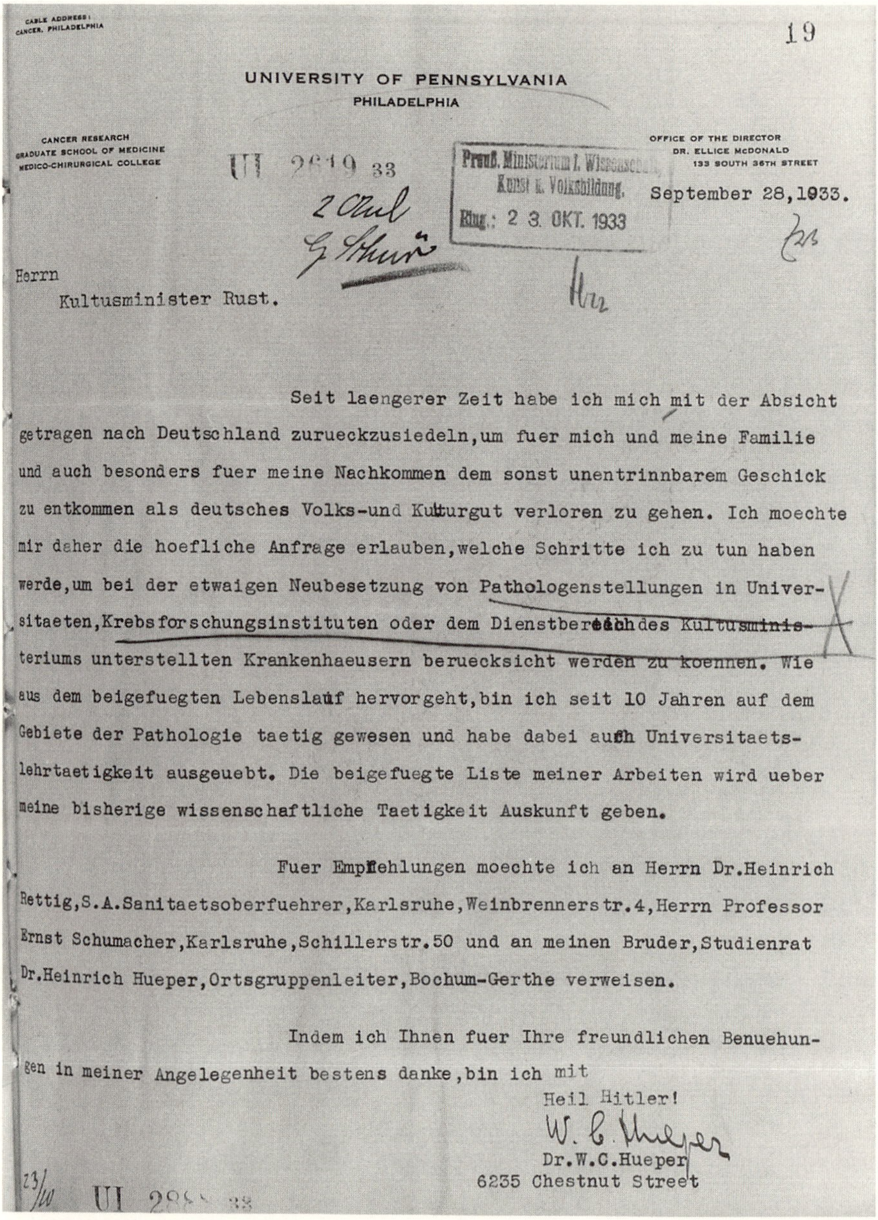

CABLE ADDRESS: CANCER, PHILADELPHIA

19

UNIVERSITY OF PENNSYLVANIA
PHILADELPHIA

CANCER RESEARCH
GRADUATE SCHOOL OF MEDICINE
MEDICO-CHIRURGICAL COLLEGE

UI 2619 33

Preuß. Ministerium f. Wissensch., Kunst u. Volksbildung.
Eing.: 23. OKT. 1933

OFFICE OF THE DIRECTOR
DR. ELLICE McDONALD
133 SOUTH 36TH STREET

September 28,1933.

Herrn
Kultusminister Rust.

Seit laengerer Zeit habe ich mich mit der Absicht getragen nach Deutschland zurueckzusiedeln,um fuer mich und meine Familie und auch besonders fuer meine Nachkommen dem sonst unentrinnbarem Geschick zu entkommen als deutsches Volks-und Kulturgut verloren zu gehen. Ich moechte mir daher die hoefliche Anfrage erlauben,welche Schritte ich zu tun haben werde,um bei der etwaigen Neubesetzung von Pathologenstellungen in Universitaeten,Krebsforschungsinstituten oder dem Dienstbereich des Kultusministeriums unterstellten Krankenhaeusern beruecksicht werden zu koennen. Wie aus dem beigefuegten Lebenslauf hervorgeht,bin ich seit 10 Jahren auf dem Gebiete der Pathologie taetig gewesen und habe dabei auch Universitaetslehrtaetigkeit ausgeuebt. Die beigefuegte Liste meiner Arbeiten wird ueber meine bisherige wissenschaftliche Taetigkeit Auskunft geben.

Fuer Empfehlungen moechte ich an Herrn Dr.Heinrich Rettig,S.A.Sanitaetsoberfuehrer,Karlsruhe,Weinbrennerstr.4,Herrn Professor Ernst Schumacher,Karlsruhe,Schillerstr.50 und an meinen Bruder,Studienrat Dr.Heinrich Hueper,Ortsgruppenleiter,Bochum-Gerthe verweisen.

Indem ich Ihnen fuer Ihre freundlichen Benuehungen in meiner Angelegenheit bestens danke,bin ich mit

Heil Hitler!
W. C. Hueper
Dr.W.C.Hueper
6235 Chestnut Street

23/10 UI 288 33

FIG. 1.1. Letter of September 28, 1933, from Wilhelm Hueper to Nazi culture minister Bernhard Rust, requesting an academic position in the new Reich. Hueper is widely regarded as the "father of American occupational carcinogenesis" and the inspiration for the cancer chapter in Rachel Carson's famous *Silent Spring*. Note the "Heil Hitler" above the signature. Source: Geheimes Staatsarchiv, Preussischer Kulturbesitz, Berlin-Dahlem, Rep. 76 Va Sekt.1 Tit. IV, #5, vol. 27, p. 19, with thanks to Michael Hubenstorf.

become "the father of American occupational carcinogenesis," the man who tried to alert medical officials to the hazards of unventilated uranium mining, and the man who, more than any other, brought the cancer hazards of pollutants in our food, air, and water to scientific attention. Hueper was the guiding light behind the ominous cancer chapter in Rachel Carson's *Silent Spring* (titled "One in Every Four"), and it was Hueper who, only months before his death in 1979, was showered with honors for his work on occupational and environmental cancer.[2]

How could the hero of *Silent Spring* have found hope in the Nazi movement? What were German fascists saying and doing about cancer that might have led a man such as Hueper to bet his future on the Thousand Year Reich?

TRIUMPHS OF THE INTELLECT

A great deal is known about science and medicine in the Nazi era. We know that while certain kinds of science were destroyed, others flourished. Sciences of an applied nature were especially encouraged, as were sciences that fit within the larger program of Nazi segregation and extermination.[3] We know that physicians joined the Nazi party in very large numbers, that about 60 percent of all biologists joined the party,[4] and that roughly 80 percent of all professors of anthropology—most of whom were physicians—were members.[5] We know that the Nazi regime maintained a large medical surveillance capacity, as part of its program to "improve the strength of the German nation";[6] we know that there is a curious blend of the modern and the romantic in Nazi culture—a blend Jeffrey Herf has characterized as "reactionary modernism."[7]

Part of our story has to be understood in light of the fact that Nazism took root in the world's most powerful scientific culture, boasting half of the world's Nobel Prizes and a sizable fraction of the world's patents. German science and medicine were the envy of the world, and it was to Germany—the "land of scholars and poets"—that many academic hopefuls flocked to cut their scientific teeth.

The Third Reich itself cannot be thought of as an icebound retreat into intellectual slumber: think of television, jet-propelled aircraft, guided missiles, electronic computers, the electron microscope, atomic fission, data processing, industrial murder factories, and racial research—all of which either were first developed in Nazi Germany or reached their high point at that time. (The recent sci-fi film *Contact*, based on Carl Sagan's novel, reminds us that the first television broadcast strong enough to escape the planet featured Hitler's speech at the opening of the 1936 Berlin Olympics.) There are innovations in the area of basic physics (nuclear fission, discovered by Otto Hahn and Lise Meitner in 1938), hormone and vitamin research, automotive engineering (the Volkswagen was supposed to be the "people's car"), pharmacology, and synthetic gasoline and rubber (I. G. Farben in 1942 controlled more than 90 percent of the world's synthetic rubber production).[8] The nerve gas sarin and the chemical warfare agent tabun are both I. G. Farben inventions of Third Reich vintage—as is the opiate methadone, synthesized in 1941, and Demerol, created about this time with the name "pethidine."[9]

There are many other examples. Nazi aeronautic engineers designed the first intercontinental ballistic missiles—never actually assembled—and it was Germans in the 1940s who built the first jet ejection seat. German engineers built the world's first autobahns, and the world's first magnetic tape recording is of a speech by Hitler. American military leaders knew that German scientists had not slept through the Hitler era, and after the war commissioned dozens of leading scholars to write book-length summaries of their fields, a veritable *Encyclopedia Naziana* with entries on everything from biophysics to tropical medicine. It is interesting what fields they chose to ignore: occupational health and antitobacco research, for example.[10]

It is therefore surely not enough to say that the human inventive spirit was suppressed or even that it survived as "pockets of innovation" immune to Nazi influence.[11] The story of science under German fascism must be more than a narrative of suppression and survival; we have to find out how and why Nazi ideology *promoted* certain areas of inquiry, how research was turned and twisted, how projects and policies came and went with the movement of political forces. If we find that certain sciences flourished, we then have to ask: What was science that it so easily adapted to fascist politics?

Little has been written on Nazi cancer research and policy,[12] and there are interesting reasons for the neglect. Historians who have focused on Nazi medicine have tended to concentrate either on political and racial ideology, or on the complicity of physicians in Nazi campaigns of sterilization, segregation, and medicalized killing (e.g., the "euthanasia" operation).[13] These deadly aspects of medicine under fascism are far better known than many other aspects—addiction or vitamin research, for example—that were also woven into Nazi ideology. Public health professionals have paid little attention, both because of the distance of history and because little might appear to be gained by pointing to Nazi success in fighting food dyes, tobacco, or occupational dust. The forgetfulness is especially strong in Germany itself, where the predictable ahistoricity of cancer researchers is compounded by their unstudied aversion toward anything that went on in the 1930s and 1940s. Nazism, for many Germans, is still a dirty word.

The topic is sobering, given that Nazi health activists may well have developed the most aggressive and successful cancer prevention program of the era. This should not be too surprising, since German cancer research—and medical research more generally—was the most advanced in the world by the time of the *Machtergreifung* (1933). German scientists were the first to discover skin cancers caused by coal tar distillates, and the first to show that uranium mining could cause lung cancer (both in the 1870s). Germans were the first to identify a bladder cancer hazard of aniline dye manufacture (in 1895),[14] a lung cancer hazard from chromate manufacture (1911),[15] and a skin cancer hazard of sunlight exposure (1894).[16] German physicians were the first to diagnose an X-ray-induced cancer (in 1902) and the first to prove, by animal experimentation, that X-rays could cause leukemia (1906). They were even the first to suggest that domestic indoor radon might prove to be a health hazard, in 1907.[17]

There are many other examples one can name[18]—and in the

interest of completeness (and at the risk of tedium), I shall continue. Johannes Müller in the 1830s pioneered the microscopic analysis of malignancies, identifying tumors as composed of cells, and Rudolf Virchow in Berlin in the 1860s developed the theory of cancer as caused by local "irritations."[19] Germans were pioneers of cancer transplant research,[20] and early in the development of the theory of dose-response latency (*Latenzzeit*).[21] Germans were among the first to propose a major role for hormones in carcinogenesis[22] and were early on aware of what is sometimes today called the "xenoestrogen hypothesis"—the idea that powerful petrochemical carcinogens such as methylcholanthrene may work by mimicking the body's natural hormones.[23] It was a Munich pathologist (Max Borst) who first classified tumors according to their histogenesis, the method used today by the World Health Organization to classify cancers.[24]

The list goes on: Germans were the first to utilize tissue stains as chemotherapeutic agents (in 1922),[25] and were the first to inject thorotrast (thorium dioxide) into patients to improve the contrast in X-ray photographic plates (1928).[26] German geneticists were the first to show that colon cancer could be inherited as a dominant trait, and it was a German zoologist—Theodor H. Boveri—who first proposed that chromosomal abnormalities might be responsible for the onset of malignancies (1902).[27] Germany was the site of the first international congress of cancer research (Heidelberg and Frankfurt, in 1906)[28] and the first country to establish a permanent journal devoted exclusively to cancer research.[29] Germany pioneered the optical diagnosis of cancer, being home to the development of not just X-rays and the colposcope but also the rectal endoscope—a candlelit version of which was introduced in Frankfurt in 1807.[30] German was arguably, at least for a time, the *language* of international cancer research: in 1915, for example, when Katsusaburo Yamagiwa and Koichi Ichikawa announced their experimental production of coal tar cancer in laboratory animals, they published it *auf Deutsch*.[31] Germans were also apparently the first to suggest that secondhand tobacco smoke might be a cause of lung cancer—in 1928.[32]

German scientists in the mid-1930s elaborated on this scientific base. The Reich Anticancer Committee (Reichsausschuss für Krebsbekämpfung) established in 1931 was enlarged, and an ambitious new journal, the *Monatsschrift für Krebsbekämpfung* (Monthly journal for the struggle against cancer), published by the notoriously antisemitic J. F. Lehmann publishing house, was launched in 1933 to coordinate the anticancer effort. More than a thousand medical doctoral theses explored cancer in one form or another in the twelve years of Nazi rule; only diseases of the blood attracted more attention.[33] Cancer registries were established, including the first German registries to record cancer morbidity (incidence) and not just mortality (deaths). Efforts were made to strengthen prevention-oriented public health measures, including occupational safeguards, laws against the adulteration of food and drugs, bans on smoking, and programs to reduce the use of cancer-causing cosmetics, to name only a few.

Could Nazi anticancer measures have influenced postwar German cancer rates? The question is intriguing, given that Germany shows a fairly clear-cut decline in overall age-adjusted cancer mortality since the 1950s, when one would first expect the policies and practices of the 1930s to show up in cancer mortality and morbidity statistics. It is also possible, though, that measures taken with the goal of improving general health—the support for female athletics, for example, or the campaign to increase the consumption of whole-grain bread—may have had unintentional anticancer consequences. Other steps taken in consequence of Nazi goals may have had anticancer effects—the pronatalist movement, for example, which increased the number of women having babies and lowered the average age of conception—though the biggest factor of all may have been the war itself, as tobacco rationing and low-fat, near starvation diets became the order of the day, along with other "lifestyle" changes now known to reduce cancer risk.

How does one interpret such possibilities? Could one of the most murderous regimes in history actually have succeeded in lowering cancer rates for certain segments of its population? Who benefited from such policies and who suffered?

"The Number One Enemy of the State"

The strength of German interest in cancer must be understood in light of the fact that Germany by the beginning of the twentieth century was a wealthy, highly industrialized nation with one of the highest cancer rates in the world. German labor unions and socialist parties had begun to emphasize occupational health and safety in the final decades of the previous century, an era of dramatic innovations in social medicine—including the world's most elaborate social welfare system, launched in 1883 in response to socialist demands. German medicine was powerful and politicized, and Berlin was one of the world's strongest centers for medical research.[34] Germany also had a strong "back to nature" (*Lebensreform*) movement that saw cancer as an unhealthy expression of the distance humans had traveled from their organic origins. Given that the insurance bureaucracy saw prevention as more cost-effective than curative medicine, it is perhaps not surprising that Germans in the 1930s took steps to combat cancer.

The *kinds* of cancers focused on must also be understood against the backdrop of Germany's unique professional, ideological, and technological history. Aniline dye cancer was discovered in Germany in the 1890s, largely because Germany by this time was the world's leading producer of synthetic colorings.[35] German professional societies were the first to establish informal standards for radiation protection,[36] not just because X-rays were discovered in Germany, but also because the professional societies in that country were large and influential. Germans were early to perceive the cancer hazards of tar, asbestos, and radium, prompted by the strength of the union movement and the political parties representing workers' interests. (Germany was the first nation to recognize lung cancer as a compensable occupational disease for uranium miners—in 1926—and by 1934 was the envy of American industrial toxicologists wanting to emulate its practice of closed-system manufacture to prevent dye-related bladder cancer.)[37] Germans formed organizations to combat alcohol and tobacco, because these were seen as violating the organic integrity of the German body—a concern that informed both the racial hygiene and *Lebensreform* (organic health) movement.

Recognition of a steadily growing cancer incidence was one reason German physicians launched the world's first state-supported anticancer agency, the Central Committee for Cancer Research and Cancer Combat (Zentralkomitee zur Erforschung und Bekämpfung der Krebskrankheit), founded in 1900.[38] Increasing cancer rates had been observed in Germany since the end of the nineteenth century, and by the 1920s these escalating rates had become a major scandal.[39] Cancer surpassed tuberculosis as the nation's second-most common cause of death in 1928; cancer was declared "the number one enemy of the state" (*Staatsfeind Nummer Eins*), surpassing even the major form of heart attack.[40] (All forms of heart attack combined, however, were still the number one cause of death.) A hundred thousand Germans died of cancer every year in the 1930s; another half a million lived and suffered with the disease.[41] Germany by this time had one of the highest cancer rates in the world—owing to the longevity of its populace and its cancer-inducing habits—and one of the most elaborate medical organizations struggling to deal with it. It also had a health-conscious political party with unprecedented police powers allowing it to combat the growing threat.

One of the more arresting features of the Nazi anticancer effort was its emphasis on prevention. Prevention fit with the Nazi approach to many other problems: racial hygiene, for example, was supposed to provide long-term care for the German germ plasm, by contrast with more traditional social or personal hygiene.[42] The emphasis was not, of course, entirely new: socialist and communist physicians had long stressed prevention, and Nazi physicians could even cite Plato's admonishment that "care of the body" was better than the healing art, since "the former makes the latter superfluous."[43] The Weimar period saw several important moves in this direction, reflected in the establishment of statistical offices, propaganda campaigns to stress early detection, and legislation to protect occupational health and safety. What was new in the Nazi

period were augmented police and legislative powers to implement broad preventive measures, and the much-touted "political
will" to deploy those powers to strengthen the health of the nation.

Erwin Liek and the Ideology of Prevention

The Danzig surgeon Erwin Liek (1878–1935) was one of the more
vocal heralds of the Nazi approach to cancer. Liek is a complex and
fascinating person whom we shall reencounter in our discussion of
Nazi food fashions (see chapter 5). He is widely reviled today as
the "father of Nazi medicine"; yet he was also a cosmopolitan
world traveler who managed to publish kind words of praise for
Freud as late as 1934.[44] In his thirty-year professional career he
produced writings on a broad range of topics—including a stirring
attack on overzealous human experimentation[45]—but he was best
known for his critique of the "spiritual crisis" of modern medicine,
medicine enervated by specialization, bureaucratization, and sci-
entization, warped by greed and myopia but also by its failure to
appreciate the natural capacity of the body to heal itself. Liek was
a hands-on practitioner but also something of a romantic, yearning
after simpler times when science was not the be-all and end-all of
medicine, when the doctor-patient relationship was (purportedly)
intimate and sacred. As founding editor of *Hippokrates*, a magazine of general health interest with strong ties to homeopathy
and the natural foods movement, he helped to usher in a broader
and more holistic medicine of the sort embraced by many Nazi
leaders—medical men like Kurt Klare, Karl Kötschau, Walter
Schultze, and Ernst Günther Schenck, but also high-placed politicos like Heinrich Himmler, Julius Streicher, Rudolf Hess, and even
Hitler himself.[46]

Liek is difficult to pigeonhole, however, and his attitude toward
Nazism was, at least for a time, ambivalent. He never joined the
party but was nonetheless apparently offered—prior to 1933 and
by Hitler himself—the position of Reich Physicians' Führer (eventually assumed by his admirer, Gerhard Wagner; Liek's failing

health precluded his appointment).[47] By 1933 he was clearer in his praise for the Nazi movement. In an essay that year titled *The World of the Physician*, he applauded Hitler for "destroying Marxism, rejecting the delusions of equality (*Gleichheitswahn*), defeating the party system, silencing the do-nothing chitchat parliament (*Schwatzparlament*), unifying the German people, reducing unemployment," and much else. Nazism represented the "dawn of freedom" (*Aufbruch zur Freiheit*) and the cleansing of Germany's "Augean stables."[48]

There is little evidence of overt antisemitism in Liek's many published works, but there are oblique insinuations that are hard to misinterpret—his assault on analytic laboratory methods, for example. Even his attack on human experimentation has an antisemitic resonance, given the degree to which "Jewish excesses" in this area had been publicized. (In the most notorious case, the dermatologist Albert Neisser in 1895 had injected young prostitutes—the youngest being only ten—with a syphilis serum, hoping to confer immunity; many instead contracted a full-blown case of the disease, prompting a widespread debate on the ethics of human experimentation and the world's stiffest restrictions against experimental abuse—Prussia's famous 1900 Code.)[49] We know that he privately lamented the "jewification" (*Verjüdung*) of German medicine—in letters to his close friend and publisher, Julius F. Lehmann, for example—blaming Jews for overvaluing exactitude and for bringing a certain superficiality and "showmanship" into science. Liek became friends with the Munich-based Lehmann, Germany's leading medical publisher and an ardent Nazi,[50] after Lehmann printed his first and most successful book, *Der Arzt und seine Sendung* (1926), which went through many editions and sold more than a hundred thousand copies (mostly after 1933). Liek professed to sympathize with the publisher's concern for "the frightening influence of the Jews" in medicine; he agreed that the "Jewish-dominated Weimar Republic" was an era of "spiritual poverty," and hoped that the nation's new leaders would resurrect German honor, morality, and selflessness. Liek's wife later praised him as an "early struggler for Nazi ideals."[51] He might more properly be described as a kind of medical Nietzsche, Germany's

Frederick Hoffman,[52] if not its Rachel Carson (for his critique of environmental degradation).

Liek wrote two books on cancer. In his 1932 volume on "The Spread, Prevention, and Control of Cancer," the Danzig surgeon argued that cancer was a disease of civilization, a "cultural disease" whose incidence was on the rise. A natural way of life was the best protection: "the simpler and more natural one's way of life, the rarer is cancer."[53] Liek endorsed the view that cancer was rare among the primitive races of the world, a view dating back at least to the 1840s and subsequently upheld by people like Frederick Hoffman, the American insurance agent, and Vilhjalmur Stefansson, the Arctic explorer.[54] Liek was convinced that the growth of cancer could be traced to things like arsenic pesticides, artificial fertilizers, excessive smoking and drinking, and sexual promiscuity. People were getting too many X-rays, and stress from the rapid pace of modern life was weakening our overall bodily resistance, making us vulnerable to cancer.

Faulty nutrition, in Liek's view, was the single most important cause of cancer. Japan's high rate of stomach cancer, for example, must have something to do with their consumption of "enormous quantities" of spicy foods, compounded by their infrequent consumption of meat. In Germany, the pumping of massive quantities of petrochemical preservatives and colorings into foods must play a role. Vegetables, Liek complained, were too often "greened" with copper sulfate (one hundred milligrams per kilogram was the legal limit in his day), while sugar was routinely "blued" with a dye known as "ultramarine" (a sulfated sodium aluminum silicate—later replaced by the coal tar derivative indanthrene). Bread was regularly bleached with benzoyl peroxide after many of the natural vitamins and fibers found in traditional whole-grain breads had been destroyed by overprocessing.[55] All of these things, in Liek's view, contributed to the cancer burden.

In his second book on this topic—*The Struggle against Cancer*, published in 1934—Liek admitted exaggerations on the part of some food critics. He did not believe, for example, that aluminum pans were a cause of cancer (a near-hysterical fear in the late 1920s), and he questioned whether the dangers of lead or mercury had been exaggerated (fears of poisoning from dental fillings had already begun to be raised). He also corrected certain errors in his 1932 book—that raw sugar was superior to refined, for example, and that the most common "blueing" agent of sugar was a coal tar derivative (the coal tar product was introduced later).[56] The larger point was still valid, however, he maintained: cancer could be prevented. If lifestyle degradations were behind the increase, then lifestyle changes could reverse the trend. What was needed was a reorientation of medicine from cure and care to prevention: *Fürsorge* and *Nachsorge* (comfort and care) were to be complemented by an increased attention to *Vorsorge* (taking precautions).[57]

Liek was well aware that powerful financial interests would resist efforts to remove carcinogens from the environment—suppliers of alcohol, food products, and pharmaceuticals, for example, who made it their business to convince the public that beer was food, that tin cans were a convenience, and that Brand X toothpaste would fight cavities. He pointed out that resistance was to be expected from such companies; he also pointed out, though, that new political winds were blowing which might change all this. (He doesn't actually mention Nazism, but that is clearly implied). It had taken ten years for his critique of surgery to be taken seriously, he says, but his cancer complaints were likely to gain a sympathetic hearing sooner. Universities (e.g., the University of Vienna) were establishing cancer clinics featuring dietary therapeutics, and cancer journals (e.g., the *Zeitschrift für Krebsforschung*) were recommending nutritional expertise as a requirement for directors of German cancer clinics. Germans were preparing, he says, to move from "care for the individual" to "cancer prevention on a large scale—for the entire people."[58]

Liek's was not the only voice from the political right-of-center advocating prevention. A broad range of Nazi officials—from Gauleiter Julius Streicher to Reich Health Führer Leonardo Conti—championed a renewed focus on preventive medicine.[59] The *Monatsschrift für Krebsbekämpfung* adopted the motto: "The earlier a tumor is treated, the better the likelihood of a cure." The *Zeitschrift für Krebsforschung* announced that "prevention is the best therapy."[60] The ideology of prevention merged with the ideology of "one for all and all for one" (*Gemeinnutz geht vor Eigennutz*) that was yet another hallmark of Nazi thought: as one antitobacco activist put it, nicotine damages not just the individual but the population as a whole.[61]

Cancer prevention also fit with the Nazi emphasis on nature and natural modes of living.[62] Hitler, we should recall, was a vegetarian and did not smoke or drink; nor would he allow anyone else to do so in his presence—excepting the occasional woman.[63] (As already noted: Benito Mussolini of Italy and Generalissimo Franco of Spain were also nonsmokers, a point not lost in Nazi health propaganda; attention was also drawn to the fact that Roosevelt and Stalin smoked cigarettes, while Churchill smoked cigars.)[64] Vegetarianism got a boost: more than one writer for *Hippokrates* revived Friedrich Beneke's nineteenth-century recommendation that cancer patients adopt a vegetarian diet.[65] Karl Kötschau, professor of "organic medicine" at Jena since 1934 and chief spokesman for the natural healing movement, launched a tirade against the lead arsenate pesticides used on wine grapes,[66] and Weimar-era worries over the health effects of lead from water pipes and toothpaste tubes were revived. Efforts were made to control food additives and to limit the oversalting of prepared foods.[67]

This emphasis on a return to nature led to some curious alliances. German Seventh-Day Adventists with their theology of health reform endorsed the regime in the summer of 1933, rejoicing in the fact that the nation was now in the hands of a man "who has his office from the hand of God, and who knows himself to be responsible to Him. As an anti-alcoholic, non-smoker, and vegetarian, he is closer to our own view of health reform than anybody else." The Adventist stress on temperance and healthful living seemed to fit with the new swing of things, though their aversion to pork must have raised some eyebrows. The sect was banned on November 26, 1933, and it took some clever politicking by its leader, Hulda Jost, to produce a reversal.[68]

Homeopaths likewise joined with Nazi enthusiasts to argue that mercury could cause memory loss and that arsenic could cause depression. The homeopathic stress on the potency of rare (or absent!) trace elements fit well with the idea that powerful bodily disturbances were likely to come from our surrounding ourselves with exotic substances like mercury, lead, and arsenic. The idea of prevention fit well with this notion that health could be restored by avoiding exposure to rare but powerful agents corroding the German *Volkskörper*.

EARLY DETECTION AND MASS SCREENING

The emphasis on prevention gave the Nazi war on cancer new hope: there is an *optimism* to the anticancer effort that distinguishes it from programs of the Weimar era (see fig. 1.2). Felix Grüneisen, general secretary of the Reich Anticancer Committee, in 1933 hailed a coming era of "planned cancer combat" on an unprecedented scale.[69] Nazi officials rejected the timid, "ostrich-like" approach of previous efforts and promised renewed strength in this area.[70] Medical journals cited the Führer's brag that *impossible* was simply not a word in the proper Nazi's vocabulary.

Early detection was a centerpiece of Nazi-era cancer propaganda. Physicians lamented the number of late-stage cancers presented in their offices—especially among women, given the growing conviction that tumors of the uterus or breast found early stood a much greater chance of being healed. The claims made for early detection sometimes sound grandiose: Hans Hinselmann, inventor of the colposcope (an illuminated optical device used to screen for uterine and cervical cancer), predicted in 1938 that if his device were widely used, mortality from these diseases would virtually disappear. He also cautioned that physicians who failed to use it were complicit in the annual deaths of 400,000 women from uterine and cervical cancer worldwide.[71]

Calls for early detection were not, of course, entirely new in the Nazi period. Georg Winter, chief physician at the University of Berlin's Women's Clinic, had noticed around the turn of the century that nearly three-quarters of the women seeking treatment for uterine cancer at his office were showing up too late to be helped. In December of 1902 he launched a campaign in Königsberg (where he was now director of the university women's clinic)

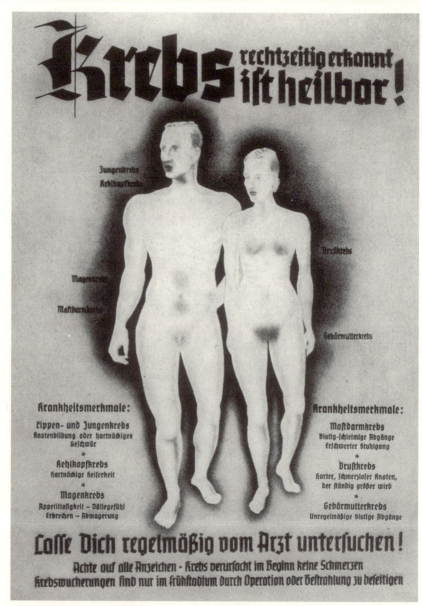

Fig. 1.2. "Cancer can be cured, if detected early!" The Nazis launched mass campaigns to encourage early screening; this poster gives some of the early warning signs for cancer and urges the public to consult their physicians regularly. Source: Friedrich Kortenhaus, "Krebs," in *Deutsches Gold: Gesundes Leben—Frohes Schaffen*, ed. Hans Reiter and Johannes Breger (Munich: Röhrig, 1942), p. 439.

to encourage early detection, sending 1,200 brochures to physicians, plus 1,100 copies of a handbill to midwives advertising the value of early detection. He also published a popular article, printed in every regional newspaper, alerting women to the early signs of the disease and the need for prompt diagnosis. Winter in 1933 celebrated his efforts as "the first organized campaign against cancer."[72]

In the Nazi era, the propaganda designed to encourage (especially) women to consult their physicians was kicked up several notches. Radio and newspaper announcements urged women to submit to annual or even biannual cancer exams, while men were advised to check up on their colons as often as they would check out the engine of their car (see fig. 1.3). "Cancer counseling centers" were established in most German cities, both to popularize the value of early detection and to advise people with cancer of their therapeutic options.[73] Leaflets were also distributed to alert physicians to the value of early detection. Hans Auler helped produce a propaganda film stressing the value of early diagnosis and the curability of cancer; the film's very title (*Jeder Achte*) cautioned that "one in eight" Germans would eventually succumb to cancer[74]—a rhetorical device Rachel Carson would later introduce to American readers.[75] Women were instructed in how to examine their own breasts for cancer (see fig. 1.4; Germans seem to have been the first in the world to take this step (American physicians would not issue comparable instructions until the 1960s).

Hundreds of thousands of women were probed for cancer in this period. In Königsberg alone, 25,000 women had submitted to such exams by 1942, which resulted in the discovery of 129 previously undetected cancers.[76] The massive propaganda for early detection subsided somewhat after 1938, the "peak year" for such propaganda by many accounts. The war put a damper on such efforts, though hopes remained bright in the eyes of some. In a 1942 article on "cancer campaigns of the future," gynecologist Georg Winter looked forward to a time when propaganda (*Aufklärung*) would be combined with mass screening. Radio propaganda was to a play a key role, as was the example of the cured cancer patient ("a patient freed from cancer is a good propagandist"). Physicians

Jeder Mensch über **40** Jahre
sollte sich im Jahre einmal **gründlich**
untersuchen lassen.

Jedes Auto wird regelmäßig
durchgesehen; das findet jeder
selbstverständlich.

WARUM

findet er es nicht selbstverständlich,
daß die viel kompliziertere Maschine
seines Körpers nachgesehen wird?

Fig. 1.3. Early detection is as important as care for your car. Middle and bottom captions read: "Every automobile gets a regular checkup; that is obvious. Shouldn't the much more complicated machine of the human body also get regular checkups?" From Kortenhaus, "Krebs," p. 437; first published in the exhibition catalog of the Deutsches Hygiene-Museum, *Kampf dem Krebs*, by Bruno Gebhard (Dresden: Deutscher Verlag für Volkswohlfahrt, 1933), p. 45.

Kennzeichen des Krebses

Brustdrüse:

Bildung eines harten, <u>schmerzlosen</u> Knotens, der langsam größer wird und mit der Haut oder mit der Unterlage (Brustkorb) verwachsen kann. Einziehung der Haut und blaurote Verfärbung an dieser Stelle.

Alle über 35 Jahre alten Frauen sollen daher alle 4 Wochen ihre Brust auf das Vorhandensein von <u>schmerzlosen,</u> harten Knoten abtasten.

Gebärmutter:

Er äußert sich durch u n r e g e l - m ä ß i g e Blutungen und Absonderung fleischwasserähnlichen Ausflusses, Mattigkeit, später durch Kreuzschmerzen, Blasenschmerzen, Stuhlverstopfung und ausstrahlende Schmerzen in die Oberschenkel.

Jede Frau kann sich hinsichtlich der Blutungen durch Eintragung in einen Kalender kontrollieren.

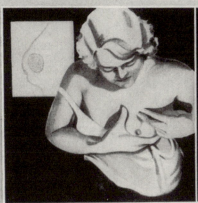 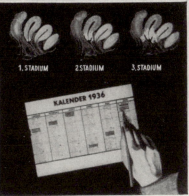

Die einzig wirksamen Waffen im Kampf gegen den Krebs sind die Operation und Bestrahlung; hinzu kommt eine zusätzliche Behandlung durch D i ä t, Hormone und andere Stoffe, welche die Abwehr des Körpers gegen den Krebs steigern. Schlecht heilende Geschwüre der Haut, besonders im Gesicht, an der Nase, an den Lippen und Augenlidern sind k r e b s v e r d ä c h t i g und bedürfen der ärztlichen Behandlung. Appetitlosigkeit, plötzlich einsetzende Abmagerung, häufig auftretendes Brechen (kaffeesatzbraune Farbe) sind Zeichen, daß im Magen-Darmkanal eine Krebsgeschwulst vorhanden sein kann. Hartnäckige Schwellungen am Zahnfleisch, in der Zunge, am Zungenrand und Zungengrund müssen dem Arzt gezeigt werden. Wer an sich einen h a r t e n, s c h m e r z l o s e n Knoten, der langsam größer wird, bemerkt, muß den Arzt aufsuchen.

K r e b s h e i l t n i e v o n a l l e i n! Je früher eine Krebsgeschwulst fachärztlich behandelt wird, um so wahrscheinlicher ist eine Befreiung des krebskranken Menschen von seinen Leiden!

Urheber: Deutsches Hygiene-Museum, Dresden

FIG. 1.4. Breast self-examination instruction, circa 1936. The Deutsches Hygiene-Museum in Dresden urged women to examine their breasts to detect tumors at an early stage; Germany's seems to have been the first such campaign anywhere in the world (comparable American campaigns did not begin until thirty years later). Women were also urged to track their menstrual cycles to look for anomalies that might indicate cancer. Top captions read "The Signs of Cancer," and "Breast" and "Uterus." Source: Kortenhaus, "Krebs," p. 431.

would have to learn to combat cancer fear, a special weakness "of the female sex." Winter predicted that cancer physicians of the future would move through the countryside in autos specially equipped with X-ray and other diagnostic equipment, ferreting out uterine and cervical cancers. He also proposed two annual "cancer awareness months," perhaps March and September, during which women would be urged to submit to cancer exams. The campaigns would begin with a barrage of publicity—including lectures, radio announcements, and articles in local newspapers—during which time clinics, hospitals, and counseling stations would gear up for the flood of examinations. Persons found afflicted would immediately be sent to a hospital for treatment, free of charge.[77]

There were many in the German medical community who took this need for early diagnosis quite seriously. A 1939 article in the Viennese medical weekly, by the antitobacco misogynist Robert Hofstätter, argued that all German women over the age of thirty should be required to undergo a semiannual gynecologic cancer exam. Hofstätter reported that a nationwide cancer-screening program of this sort would require a staff of 5,760 physicians at a cost of 35 million reichsmarks per year, a significant but tolerable sum. He also claimed that women who failed to submit to such exams should be punished for placing an extra financial burden on the insurance bureaucracy. Women who refused the exams and chose to "go it alone" were to be awarded only half the normal insurance coverage in the event that they became sick from cancer.[78] Hofstätter, I might note, was not particularly astute when it came to political timing: he joined the Nazi party in August of 1944, only months before the collapse of Nazi rule in Austria. His party number—10,078,751—put him near the last in that long line of infamy.[79]

Despite general agreement on the need for screening, opinions differed on the utility of the various techniques to be used. Most radiologists supported the mass use of X-rays, but there were also those—notably Fritz König, head of the Reich Anticancer Committee's science advisory board—who argued that the value of the rays had been exaggerated.[80] There was also a great deal of debate over the value of colposcopy for cervical cancer screening. At a 1937 meeting in Berlin, a number of gynecologists suggested that the device was superfluous, given that the experienced specialist could identify suspicious cervical changes using only a speculum and the unaided eye. A more common objection was that proper use of the device took a great deal of time. The cervix had to be examined both before and after it was bathed with iodine and acetic acid if precancerous growths were to be detected. In the most commonly expressed view, the colposcope could be profitably used in cases already identified as suspicious but was inappropriate for mass screening.[81]

Criticisms of this sort may be one reason Hinselmann collaborated with Auschwitz physicians in a project to test how well his beloved (and much-hyped) colposcope might serve in detecting cervical cancer at a very early stage. Hinselmann was assisted in this project by Eduard Wirths, the physician-commandant of Auschwitz, who had studied gynecology with Hinselmann. Eduard and his brother, Helmut, a gynecologist colleague of Hinselmann's in Hamburg-Altona, used the colposcope to collect samples of cervical tissues from camp inmates, which were then sent back to Hamburg for examination by Hinselmann and Helmut.[82] The exact purpose of the experiments is not yet clear (postwar testimony suggested Helmut was the instigator), but the studies may have been part of an effort to bolster the reputation of colposcopy for identifying early-stage cancers. The experimenters may have caused the deaths of several Auschwitz inmates, since the entire cervix was generally removed, even in ambiguous cases where cancer was not obvious, causing not infrequent bleeding or infection. After the war, a physician formerly imprisoned in the camp characterized the Hinselmann experiments as equal in brutality to many of the more notorious experiments at the camp.[83]

NAZISM was supposed to set the world in motion, to redraw the map of Europe in harmony with the German-imposed "New World Order." The spirit of the times was utopian and millenarian, but it was also pragmatic in the sense that things were supposed to get done. "Positive thinking" was the order of the day, designed to replace the sullen "critical/Jewish" spirit of the Weimar era. Aggressive measures in the field of public health would usher in a new era of healthy, happy Germans, united by race and common outlook, cleansed of alien environmental toxins, freed from the previous era's plague of cancers, both literal and figurative.

2

The *Gleichschaltung* of German Cancer Research

> We Germans stand at an important turning point: new
> men are shaping the destiny of our fatherland, new laws
> are being created, new measures put into place, new
> forces awakened. The struggle touches on everything
> that has been and is unclean.
>
> *Prof. Dr. Immanuel Gonser, a leading antialcohol activist,*
> *in 1933*

THE Nazification of German cancer research meant, first and foremost, the exclusion of Jews and communists from governmental research and teaching positions. According to the Civil Service Law of April 7, 1933, all persons of "Jewish or related blood" were no longer entitled to work for the state. The consequences for cancer research were profound. At Berlin's famous Charité Hospital Cancer Institute alone, twelve of thirteen cancer researchers lost their jobs.[1] The only scientist to survive the purge—Hans Auler—took over as director of the *entjudetes* (dejewified) institute after Ferdinand Blumenthal, general secretary of the Central Committee since 1919 and vice chairman of the Reich Anticancer Committee since 1931, was forced to resign.[2] The Charité never again attained its former glory, as the core of Berlin's cancer research shifted to a "General Institute against Tumorous Diseases," erected in 1935 with financial support directly from the Führer at the new Rudolf Virchow Hospital in Berlin. Heinrich Cramer, the radiologist named to head the new institute, trumpeted the beginning of a "centralization" of German cancer research,[3] but in many areas—notably immunology, histology, and other fields in which Jews had been prominent—basic cancer research had suffered a blow from which it would never recover.

Basic and applied cancer research are two different things, however; the Nazi war on cancer, as we shall see, was waged more on the basis of prevention than on cure. One way to look at the Nazi period, in fact, is as a time when the political center of gravity tilted slightly away from academic medicine in favor of a more public health–oriented approach to disease. One gets two very different pictures of how to control cancer when one contrasts the research projects funded by the German Research Council, for example, with those funded by the Reich Health Office or the Public Health Office of the NSDAP or Jena's Institute for Tobacco Hazards Research (see chapter 6). As callous as this may seem, the loss of many cancer scientists arguably did not hamstring the campaign to conquer cancer—conceived as a campaign to curtail smoking, to encourage early detection, and to improve the diet of large masses of people. But first, some words on victims.

THE FATES OF JEWISH SCIENTISTS

It would be impossible, of course, to trace the fates of all of those who suffered—but the experiences of a few may give a glimpse of what happened. Hans Sachs (1877–1945) worked in the area of immunology and serology at Heidelberg's Institute for Experimental Cancer Research, where he also coedited the *Zeitschrift für Immunitätsforschung*. He lost his Heidelberg position in 1935, emigrated to Oxford in 1938, and died in Dublin in 1945. Richard V. Werner (1875–1943) directed both the Heidelberg institute and that city's Samaritan Hospital (from 1916 to April 1933) while serving as chair of Baden's Regional Cancer Committee and cofounding editor of *Strahlentherapie*, the nation's leading radiotherapy journal; he fled Germany in 1934 and established a private medical practice in a cancer clinic in Brno, Czechoslovakia, until 1942 when the clinic was taken over by Nazi authorities. Werner was fired and deported to Theresienstadt, where he died in 1943. Ernst Witebesky (1901–1969), a Heidelberg immunologist, was put on leave in April 1933; he fled to Switzerland and then, in 1934, to the United States, where he practiced medicine at Mt. Sinai Hospital in Manhattan and later taught bacteriology and immunology at the University of Buffalo. Wilhelm Liepmann, director of Berlin's Institut für Frauenkunde and the moving force behind the creation (in 1929) of a museum depicting the value of early detection for uterine cancer, was fired; he eventually obtained a position in Istanbul, where he remained until his death in 1939.[4] Those dismissed included several naturopathic physicians (doctors stressing natural herbs and low-tech medicines): Max Gerson, for example, famous for his dietary treatments of tuberculosis and cancer, was forced from his post at Munich's University Hospital, whereupon he fled to New York and established a private medical practice (in 1938).

The total number of cancer researchers who lost their jobs may be in excess of a hundred. Almost all, it seems, were "Jewish" in the Nazi definition of that term, which looked only to ancestry rather than culture or belief. One of the few Jewish cancer researchers of any note to remain at work in Germany was the Nobel laureate biochemist Otto Warburg, who continued to direct Berlin's Kaiser Wilhelm Institute for Cell Physiology throughout the period of Hitler's rule—surviving even a 1941 effort by the director of the Kaiser Wilhelm Gesellschaft to have him purged. (Viktor Brack and Philipp Bouhler, two of the most powerful men behind the so-called "euthanasia operation," apparently managed to have Warburg saved "for the world.")[5] Warburg's mother was "pure Aryan" but his father was Jewish; the most common explanation for his having been able to stay when most of the others in his situation were forced to leave has been that Hitler may have believed he was moving toward a cancer cure.[6] A more likely explanation, as noted by the historian Kristie Macrakis, is that Warburg's institute had been founded with heavy support from the Rockefeller Foundation and the Gradenwitz Fund, rendering him immune to the 1933 Civil Service Law, which barred Jews and communists from government employment. Intervention by

powerful friends in industry must also have helped, as did his ability to show that he had faithfully fought for the fatherland in the
First World War.[7]

The Reich Anticancer Committee, suitably aryanized, appeared
to support the Nazification of German cancer research. In its first
annual report after the *Machtergreifung* the committee declared itself eager to embrace the new regime:

> The year 1933 was a decisive one for the war against cancer: the national
> socialist revolution (*Umwälzung*) has created entirely new opportunities
> for sweeping measures in an area that until now has been rather lim-
> ited. . . . The energetic and unanimous engagement (*Einsatz*) of the med-
> ical profession has shown that new avenues have opened for the strug-
> gle against cancer in the new Germany.[8]

The *Zeitschrift für Krebsforschung* sounded similar themes,[9] and the
newly formed *Monatsschrift* announced its desire to provide anticancer activists with new "weapons" to continue their struggle. No
stone was to be left unturned.[10]

The Central Committee (Zentralkomitee) was dissolved in December of 1933; all cancer research within the borders of the Reich
was henceforth to be coordinated by the more activist and nationalist Reich Anticancer Committee. The elevation of this latter organization after 1933 signaled an effort to unify the heretofore scattered forces of the German anticancer effort; it also signaled a
move to favor practical measures such as early detection over basic
research initiatives.[11] The Reich Committee had emphasized since
its inception the value of preventive medicine (especially early detection), and post-1933 policies strengthened this emphasis.
Women over forty were urged to have an annual exam, and the
prevention-oriented cancer exhibit prepared at Dresden's Hygiene
Museum traveled all over Germany, attracting more than half a
million visitors.[12]

The expulsion of Jews and communists, in other words, was
only part of the *Gleichschaltung* (unification and purification) of
German cancer research. Nazi ideologues also emphasized the
need for a shift from "scientific abstractions" to more practical
approaches. The *Zeitschrift für Krebsforschung* announced that it

would henceforth publish less in the areas of basic biochemistry, tissue culture, and animal experimentation, and more on clinical observation, human tumor pathology, and statistics, consistent with Liek's critique of *Mäusedoktoren* ("mouse doctors"—by which he meant vivisectionists or laboratory cancer specialists more generally). The journal cautioned against an excessive focus on laboratory methods that "lose themselves in fruitless details" (a veiled antisemitic reference); the new focus was to be more statistical, allowing a better understanding of the distribution of cancer by race, social status, occupation, and the environmental factors that give rise to cancer in the first place.[13]

One surprising aspect of the Nazi turn in German science is that many Jewish scholars continued to be cited in German cancer journals. It is not yet clear how we should interpret this: it may suggest that German fascism was less "total" than is sometimes imagined (the system was polycentric, and sometimes "leaky"); it may also indicate that scientific citation did not have the significance that we today attach to it. There are scholars today who worry about the unreflective citation of "Nazi data" (Mengele's work on the genetics of cleft palate is still cited);[14] our present-day concerns with criminal scientific citation, however, may simply reflect the status we have invested in displays of debt and credit.

No one will ever be able to say what the loss of Jewish scientific talent meant for the course of German science. From a moral point of view, of course, the loss of talent is nothing compared to the loss of life. A thousand laments for Einstein sound hollow against the silence of the millions of lesser-knowns who perished.

It is also possible, though, as already noted, that the expulsion of Jewish scientists did relatively little to slow the German campaign against cancer—at least in the short run. If this is so, it is because basic science was not mainly what was needed in the war on cancer. It was already known that tobacco, soot, tar, asbestos, and radiation were causes of cancer, and that prevention of exposure to such agents could prevent a sizable fraction of all cancers. Successful anticancer campaigns seemed to require political and public health muscle more than scientific subtleties. That was not true in every instance—little was known about the molecular basis of carcinogenesis, and little was known about how to design effective therapeutics. Cancer to many seemed to be a political disease, requiring political solutions. Prevention of exposure to carcinogens seemed to require certain infringements of political and commercial liberties. Appreciating this, we can begin to see how cancer continued to be fought while many areas of "basic" science suffered.

REGISTRIES AND MEDICAL SURVEILLANCE

The Nazification of German science and medicine was accompanied by an increased focus on statistics. This is partly due to the elevation of the notion of "population" in the sciences of the time, but it also reflects the Nazi effort to monitor and manage hitherto uncontrolled spheres of human life. There was never a government as obsessed with counting, sorting, and sifting as was the Nazi regime. It is an era of mass screenings: of women for cervical and breast cancer, children for dental cavities, students for TB, factory workers for silicosis and lung cancer, pregnant women for health impairments, and so on. Genetic and racial maps are constructed, as are elaborate catalogs of the spatial distribution of genetic diseases. Germany becomes the most X-rayed nation in the world (see chapter 4), a nation obsessed with tracking, diagnosing, registering, grading, and selecting.

In the field of cancer, this push for statistical control was reflected in efforts to establish cancer registries. The scale of the efforts is impressive. Between October 1, 1933, and September 30, 1938, for example, private and hospital physicians in Göttingen, Halle, Kiel, and Nuremberg, as well as in the larger regions (*Landkreisen*) surrounding Neustadt, Burgdorf in Hanover, Hohenzollern, and Donaukreis (Württemberg) collaborated in an unprecedented project to register every case of cancer appearing in those areas. Standardized forms were provided to all physicians in these areas for this purpose.[15] Population-based registries were subsequently established for Mecklenburg (1937) and for Sachsen-

Anhalt, the Saarland, and Vienna (all in 1939). The University of Munich's Pathological Institute coordinated a statistical analysis of all cases of esophageal cancer at forty-four pathological institutes throughout the nation. Registration efforts were facilitated by the fact that, beginning in 1933, Germany's National Bureau of Statistics (Statistisches Amt) distinguished twelve different kinds of cancer death, in place of the previous six. This allowed a far more nuanced classification of deaths from tumors.[16]

One interesting aspect of these registries is that they sought to record not just cancer mortality but incidence.[17] Incidence registries are important because they tell you how often cancers are arising in a population, and not just how many people are dying from the disease. Incidence rates theoretically tell you whether cancer rates are on the rise or on the decline—regardless of how well you are doing in the realm of therapeutics. Incidence rates can also elucidate new kinds of causes and therefore new possibilities for prevention. Cancer officials had long hoped for data of this kind: the requirement to report not just mortality but also morbidity was hailed as the first such requirement "in Germany, if not in the world."[18]

The dead, of course, were not to be excluded from surveillance, and by the middle of the 1930s Germany had become perhaps the most autopsied nation in the world. Somewhere between 6 and 10 percent of all dead bodies were being subjected to autopsy, an extraordinary rate. As a result, statisticians had unprecedented opportunities to analyze cancer rates. In 1934, the Reich Anticancer Committee asked Professor Ernst Dormanns of Munich's Pathology Institute to compile all available autopsy data concerning cancer deaths among adult men for the period 1925–1933; the study, published in 1936, was apparently the largest of its kind anywhere in the world. Dormanns analyzed autopsy records for 125,000 males over the age of twenty performed at forty-two German pathology institutes between 1925 and 1933 and found that *18 percent* of the men—or one in six—had died from cancer of one sort or another. Given that 300,000 German men were dying in any given year, this meant that about a sixth of these—or 50,000—were dying from cancer. Dormanns's study also showed that the most common cause of cancer death was cancer of the stomach, which accounted for about a third of all male cancer deaths.[19]

One of the things revealed by such studies was that cancer was more common than had previously been recognized. Official mortality statistics for the mid-1930s indicated that only *13 percent* of all German deaths were from malignancies; Dormanns's and other investigations showed, however, that a substantial portion of the nation's cancers were going undiagnosed. Walther Fischer, a Rostock pathologist, claimed that a quarter of all cancers were not recognized during the lifetime of the patient—and that only about half were being diagnosed early enough to permit successful treatment. Hellmut Haubold, an influential Berlin cancer statistician and SS officer, proclaimed that cancer was actually Germany's leading cause of death, surpassing even the major forms of heart disease.[20] Rudolf Ramm in 1942 estimated an annual cancer death toll of 150,000 to 160,000 Germans,* not to mention the half a million people sick with the disease at any given time.[21]

Worries about the growing cancer mortality and the imperfections of diagnosis led a number of local cancer associations—in collaboration with the Nazi party's Office of Public Health—to implement mass screening programs. East Prussia's was one of the most ambitious. A 1937 meeting of an East Prussian Anticancer Working Group concluded that all German women over the age of thirty were to be regularly screened for breast and genital cancer. Breast and genital/uterine cancer were targeted since, as the Königsberg gynecologist Felix von Mikulicz-Radecki pointed out, these were among the most easily detected and treated. The screening program was voluntary, but exams were free of charge to encourage

* One of the interesting things about such figures is their deployment as part of a larger apocalyptic drama: alarming statistics of one sort or another were often put forward to stir up worries about a particular danger, the hope being to generate a sharp political response. One finds this in a number of areas of Nazi medicine: in eugenicists' discussions of the threat of genetic inferiors, for example, and in discussions of dire and imminent food shortages. Émigré critics like Martin Gumpert sometimes took such claims at face value—to vilify the regime—failing to understand their larger rhetorical function.

maximal compliance. Doctors' fees were covered by the local branch of the Nazi party's Office of Public Health, which also helped organize the exams. Poor as well as rich were said thereby to benefit equally from the screening process; radio and billboard propaganda encouraged women to visit the centers and newspaper articles extolled the sensibility of screening.

Propaganda was directed especially at women's groups.[22] Women from Nazi party organizations were supposed to be the first examined, the hope being that other women would follow in their footsteps. In the city of Königsberg, all public and private hospitals established screening centers, where surgeons looked for breast cancer and gynecologists looked for cancer of the uterine cervix. In 1937, each of the city's screening centers was examining thirty-five to sixty women on any given evening. Mikulicz-Radecki himself examined two thousand women that year, among whom he found three previously hidden cancers (a rectal cancer, an advanced cervical cancer, and an early-stage cervical tumor—plus a number of other disorders having nothing to do with cancer). The breast exam lasted an average of two minutes, the gynecologic exam an average of eight minutes. Organizers emphasized that the screening was supposed to be as pleasant as possible, performed in separate cubicles to give women the impression they were receiving individual attention. Care was taken to ensure that anticancer propaganda would not arouse undue cancer fears (*Krebsangst*); this was a commonly discussed difficulty—how to generate concern without generating panic.[23]

Early in the Nazi era, discussions were begun on how to construct a comprehensive Cancer Law (*Krebsgesetz*) involving mandatory registration of all cases of cancer, stronger safeguards against exposures to X-rays and radioactive materials, and limitations on publications by cancer quacks.[24] Despite great expectations, however, Germany as a whole never did get a Cancer Law. Only Danzig (now Gdansk, in Poland) passed such a law, on April 14, 1939. The Danzig law required that every case of the disease, and every suspicion of incidence, be reported within six days to state health authorities. It also gave women over the age of thirty and men over forty-five the right to an annual cancer screening

free of charge.[25] Danzig's Cancer Law was hailed as a model for all
of Germany,[26] though the exigencies of war appear to have prevented it from becoming widely emulated.

The establishment of registries, mass screenings, and the like
should be understood in the context of Nazi efforts to strengthen
medical surveillance. (Recall that the now-famous cancer registry
of Denmark was launched during the occupation of that country,
in 1942, though it is not yet clear whether Nazi policies played a
role in the establishment of that registry.)[27] Proposals in this area
were often ambitious, as when Rudolf Ramm, as deputy chief of
the Reich Anticancer Committee, called for an annual examination
of all German women aged thirty-five to sixty, and all German
men aged forty-five to sixty. The proposal was recognized as one
of "gigantic proportions," involving more than eighteen million
exams every year.[28] And though Ramm's and similar proposals
were only partially implemented, the period does see a substantial
increase in the number of people screened.

Germany's ambitious cancer registries were ultimately compromised by the antisemitic policies of the regime. In 1940, the director of the Nuremberg registry noted that the July 25, 1938, ban on
Jewish physicians' practicing medicine (except on other Jews) had
put a crimp in the collection of accurate cancer data. Roughly one
in eight German physicians was of Jewish ancestry, and the massive transfer of patients required by the ban seems to have interfered with both patient follow-up and other aspects of statistical
monitoring. The Nuremberg registry director noted that it would
be difficult to continue certain parts of the registry past 1938.[29]

Record keeping also took on a sinister air, as population surveys
were used to round up racial undesirables. The population census
of 1939, for example, was used to identify Jews for deportation.
Data-processing technologies were important in the Final Solution, a fact memorialized in the United States Holocaust Memorial
Museum in Washington, D.C., where Hollerith cards and a 1930s-
era IBM card-punch sorting machine are displayed to illustrate
some of the technologies used in the campaign of mass extermination.[30] The Nazi infatuation with registration and the murderous

use of medical surveillance appears to be a major reason many German intellectuals today are suspicious of plans to assemble cancer registries.[31]

The Rhetoric of Cancer Research

The doublespeak of totalitarian regimes is legendary. Nazi Germany is full of words cloaked in careful disguises, political "euphemisms" designed not to soften a blow but to deceive. Joseph Goebbels was the master of this art, barring words like *sabotage* and *assassination* that, from their very utterance, might give people the wrong kind of ideas:

> In wartime one should not speak of assassination either in a negative or an affirmative sense. There are certain words from which we should shrink as the devil does from Holy Water; among these are, for instance, the words "sabotage" and "assassination." One must not permit such terms to become part and parcel of everyday slang.[32]

Some examples are amusing: Germans were not supposed to use the traditional expression "catastrophe aid" but rather the more upbeat "first aid"; also barred was any media use of the expression "Yellow Peril," in deference to the Japanese.[33] There are efforts to modernize medical discourse: the shift from "cripple" (*Krüppel*) to "handicapped" (*Behinderte*) occurs in this period, for example, as does the shift from *idiot* and *asylum* to *retarded* and *clinic*. Strange as it may seem, both of these latter terms were introduced in the early 1940s by physicians orchestrating the "euthanasia" operation. The term "handicapped" (*Behinderte*), for example, was first used in 1940 by physicians and bureaucrats organizing the murder of the physically and mentally handicapped. Genocide was not a matter of public discourse (the word had not yet even been coined), so "special treatment" (*Sonderbehandlung*) became one of many code words for murder, along with *Abtransport, Desinfektion, Einschläferung, Endlösung, Erlösung, Euthanasie, Evakuierung, Gnadentod, Judenaktion, Liquidation, Reinigung, Selektion, Vergasung, Vernichtung,* and so forth, ad nauseam.[34] The Nazis ended up with as many words for murder as Eskimos (purportedly) have for snow.

Nazification was also accompanied, though, by sometimes-subtle changes in the language of cancer research. With cancer on the rise, it is perhaps not surprising that malignancy came to serve as a powerful metaphor, stigmatizing all that was undesirable in the Nazi scheme of things. Joseph Goebbels routinely castigated the objects of his contempt as "cancers" or "malignancies"—this included not just the Jews and homosexuals but the Foreign Office (*Auswärtiges Amt*) and Stalin's communist empire.[35] Germans were not alone, of course, in using this kind of rhetoric: an American eugenics catechism of 1935, for example, compared genetic defectives to "cancers in the body politic" and the eugenics society itself to a "Society for the Control of Social Cancer."[36]

Medical imagery was commonly used to dehumanize racio-political undesirables. In a 1936 lecture on radiotherapy in Frankfurt, the SS radiologist Prof. Dr. Hans Holfelder showed students in attendance—including the young Richard Doll from England—a slide in which cancer cells were portrayed as Jews (the same slide depicted the X-rays launched against these tumor-Jews as Nazi storm troopers).[37] Jews were often characterized as tumors within the German body, though bacteriologic and pathogenic images (Jew as bacillus, virus), or even older metaphors of plagues, vermin, parasites, "fungoid growths," and so forth, were actually somewhat more common[38]—possibly because cancer was not yet something over which health authorities were able to exercize a great deal of control. Infectious diseases had largely succumbed to public health reforms and the science-based therapies devised by Koch, Pasteur, and Ehrlich, but cancer was still on the rise—and this may be why pundits looked to an older era of medical horror for their invidious imagery.

Doctors were often the ones portraying Jews as cancers or tumors as Jews. What is also interesting, though, is that Nazi ideals penetrated the technical rhetoric of cancer research. Medical speech was supposed to be Germanized, clarified, and simplified. Foreign terms were to be abandoned in favor of homespun expressions (not *Allele* but rather *Anlagen-Partner*, not *Chromosom* but

Kernfaden, not *Bastard* but *Mischling*, etc.), and unclear bureaucratic language comes under attack (e.g., the legalese of the insurance industry).[39] Medical speech also sees an increased use of metaphors of racial struggle, the threat of political chaos, and the need for political unity. Bernhard Fischer-Wasels, the world-renowned father of experimental petrochemical carcinogenesis,[40] characterized the nascent tumor as "a new race of cells, distinct from the other cell races of the body"; the task of the cancer therapist was to destroy this pathological race (*vollständige Zerstörung der pathologischen Zellrasse*).[41] Cancer cells are elsewhere described as anarchists, spongers (*Schmarotzer*),[42] Bolshevists, breeders of chaos and rebellion, and the like. Hans Auler, a beneficiary of the *Gleichschaltung* of German cancer research, in 1937 characterized cancer cells as "revolutionary cells," perhaps deliberately poking fun at communist rhetoric, while Curt Thomalla of the Propaganda Ministry spoke of cancer cells' creating "a state within a state"[43]—a charge also leveled at Jews and homosexuals. The language of medicine was thus saturated with political ideology—sometimes consciously and deliberately, sometimes not.[44]

Linguistic cleansing and reversible images of racial inferiors as cancers (and vice versa) are not the only notable aspects of Nazi cancer language. Another is the widespread talk of "problem solving." Nazi medico-political leaders often spoke about finding "radical," "final," or "permanent" solutions to Germany's problems—especially in the early war years, when plans for the radical transformation of German society reached a fever pitch. The Final Solution (*Endlösung*) to the Jewish Question is the best known and most ghastly, but similar expressions were used for countless other problems. Nazi population policy was directed toward what Interior Minister Wilhelm Frick called "the solution to the woman question" (*Lösung der Frauenfrage*),[45] while the campaign to repopularize whole-grain bread was dubbed "the final solution to the bread question" (*Endlösung der Brotfrage*).[46] A medical thesis of 1940 called for a "solution to this difficult problem of smokers" (*Lösung dieses schweren Raucherproblems*),[47] and there was talk about finding a solution to the cancer question (*Lösung der Krebsbekämpfungsfrage*).[48] A spirit of millenarian social engineering infuses the era, accompanied by a sense that the New World Order will require the radical extirpation of the old. The transformation is cast in Nietzschean terms with the invocation of "twilight" metaphors: so we hear talk about the "twilight of tobacco" (*Tabakdämmerung*) or of race (Astel's 1935 *Rassendämmerung*), and so forth. The appeal to Nietzschean or Wagnerian imagery gave a poetic, one could say "operatic," flavor to Nazi racialist skulduggery.

An equally curious aspect of Nazi cancer language is its obsessive romance with "enlightenment." Enlightenment (*Aufklärung*) was a frequent element of Nazi rhetoric, conveying roughly what we today would call "education," "outreach," or "public indoctrination." The term was featured in the names of several party organizations: Walter Gross's Aufklärungsamt für Bevölkerungspolitik und Rassenpflege (Office of Population Policy and Racial Care) was a kind of news bureau designed to keep Nazi party bigwigs informed in matters of national and international racial policy (the office was later renamed the Rassenpolitisches Amt); recall also that Goebbels's propaganda ministry was actually called "The Ministry of Popular Enlightenment and Propaganda" (Ministerium für Volksaufklärung und Propaganda). Goebbels, Gross, and many other party officials characterized their work as *Aufklärungsarbeit*—literally "the work of enlightenment"—as did many health authorities at this time. The Reich Anticancer Committee identified one of its duties as *Publikumsaufklärung* (education of the public);[49] Brandenburg's Anticancer Committee professed an obligation to "enlighten" the population concerning the value of early detection.[50] Enlightenment had been a feature of leftist and Weimar-era rhetoric (calls for *Sexualaufklärung*, or sex education, for example), but the Nazis gave it new and more sinister nuances.

It is surprising, in retrospect, how pervasive this "enlightenment" talk was. Medical officials talked endlessly about the need for *Krebsaufklärung*, *Volksaufklärung über den Krebs*, or *Aufklärung der Volksgenossen* concerning the value of early detection. Nazi party officials showed *Aufklärungsfilme* (educational films), and antitobacco activists called for "aufklärende" articles to warn against the hazards of tobacco. One cancer office distinguished

Einzelaufklärung from *Volksaufklärung*—depending upon whether the enlightenment was directed toward the individual or the population. (Men were said to be particularly in need of enlightenment, since they were much less likely than women to visit a clinic for a routine cancer exam.)[51] The word "enlightenment" is probably used more in the Nazi period than at any other time, before or since.

What does *Aufklärung* mean in the Nazi era? The verb *aufklären* most commonly means to clarify, to clear up, to educate, to inform, to instruct, to solve, to set right; an *Aufklärer* was a scout or a reconnaissance pilot, but *Aufklärung* was (and is) also used as a term for sex education or criminal detective work. As originally popularized in the eighteenth century, the noun *Aufklärung* was intended to contrast the illuminating power of science against the dark forces of ignorance and superstition. In the Nazi period, use of the word was not consciously intended to evoke any reference to "the Enlightenment." (The French *lumière* was more often derided as an early ancestor of positivist apathy and the impoverished doctrine of "science for its own sake.") The images evoked are rather those of public education, public indoctrination—as when psychiatric authorities professed an *Aufklärungspflicht* to inform their patients they were about to be sterilized.[52] Enlightenment in the Nazi era was not something you yourself strived to attain, but rather something you did to other people or other people did to you. The idea of enlightenment as personal refinement—as in Kant's original sense of coming to maturity and making decisions for yourself—is replaced by a notion of state-directed indoctrination and state-serving elucidation. Nazi society was supposed to be transparent from above—a philosophy with far-reaching consequences, from pervasive eavesdropping to bans on attic storage.

The original notion of casting light is not entirely lost, however. An obsessive quest for clarity is apparent in the already-mentioned efforts to eliminate medical bureaucratese, and the quest for "clean speech" harmonized with the larger quest for bodily and political purity. Propaganda Minister Goebbels in March of 1942 took pride in announcing—at least to his diary—

that he and his fellow travelers were "carrying in our hands the torch that brings light to humanity."[53] *Aufklärung* in the Nazi period becomes another word for propaganda—a one-way flow of information, a vectored and extreme form of clarification (hence the odd-to-our-eyes amalgam *Aufklärungspropaganda*, commonly used in the Nazi era).[54] If I may generalize: enlightenment under conditions of fascism becomes a form of propaganda.[55] Recall also that the notorious burning of books at Alexanderplatz on the night of May 10, 1933, was characterized as a "campaign of enlightenment" (*Aufklärungsfeldzug*) to eliminate from German culture elements regarded as Jewish, pacifist, or Bolshevist.[56]

We should keep in mind that, when it came to cancer, many of those deploying the most colorful metaphors were not quacks but rather scholars familiar with state-of-the-art cancer research. This was the case, for example, with Karl H. Zinck, who in 1940 characterized cancerous growths as "revolutionary, anarchistic, and Bolshevistic, directing a civil war (*Bruderkampf*) against the body." Zinck was not a raving fool but a *habilitierter* professor of medicine (*Dozent*) at the University of Kiel, whose lecture was published in the most highly respected public health journal of the Nazi era.[57] Zinck was well versed in contemporary theories of cancer causation, judging from his recognition that most of the reported increase in cancer was due to the aging of the population, that lung cancer was the only clear-cut case where even age-adjusted rates were on the rise (a trend "according to some researchers" due to the growth of the tobacco habit), that paraffin could cause scrotal cancer, that abestos could cause (and had caused) lung cancers, and that aniline dyes could cause bladder cancer. Zinck knew that carcinogens targeted particular organs (the liver in the case of scarlet red; the kidney in the case of anthraquinone) because of how those carcinogens were metabolized; he felt that the significance of viruses and trauma had been exaggerated and that more attention needed to be paid to the role of hormones. He was aware that several rare cancers were heritable as simple Mendelian dominants (the best known being xeroderma pigmentosum, polyposis intestinii, and certain neuroblastomas), but he also knew that heredity did not play a major part in the development of most cancers.[58] His characterization of tumors as "Bolshevistic" must therefore be understood not as the product of crankish ignorance but as part of a larger medical currency circulating at this time.

ROMANCING NATURE AND THE QUESTION OF CANCER'S INCREASE

It is important to realize, of course, that even after the *Gleichschaltung* of German medicine[59] there was still a great deal of dispute over just what was wrong with German cancer policy and what should be done to fix it. Opinions remained divided over many basic questions of causation, treatment, and policy—and even over whether cancer was in fact on the rise. We have to understand these tensions in the context of ongoing feuds between orthodox and "alternative" organic traditions in German medicine— tensions that can be seen in the response to Liek's 1932 book on cancer.

Erwin Liek was widely read both inside and outside the medical community, but he was also sharply criticized by physicians who resented his emphasis on environmental carcinogenesis (especially industrial chemicals, but also food additives and polluted air and water) and personal habits (especially diet and exercise). Many of Germany's more conservative physicians scoffed at his advocacy of a more natural way of life and disputed his assertion that cancer was on the rise. Fischer-Wasels in the *Deutsches Ärzteblatt*, for example, asserted that Liek's 1932 book contained "neither a single new idea nor a single new fact." The Frankfurt pathologist labeled the book "a great failure" having "nothing to do with science."[60]

One of the issues dividing organicists such as Liek from their more conventional colleagues was this question of whether cancer was actually on the increase. Statistical evidence for an increase was strong and frequently cited in the organic medical press, but so, then, were the objections against the methods used to gather and interpret those statistics.[61] One common complaint was that the growth in reported cancer deaths might simply be due to the fact that many more cancers were being diagnosed—a result not

just of improved instrumentation but also of increasing hospital-
ization and the preparation of ever-more-accurate mortality tables.[62] Evidence for such a view came from the fact that techniques
of cancer diagnostics had improved enormously in the second half
of the nineteenth century. Prominent among these were medical
microscopy, cellular pathology, X-ray photography, and a host of
new devices designed to allow the viewing of the interior of the
body: illuminated rectoscopy, ureter cystoscopy, the laryngeal
mirror, the gastric tube, the bronchoscope, and so forth.[63] Further
evidence came from the circumstance that opportunities for diagnosing cancer were far greater than in previous years.[64]

Hellmut Haubold, the Berlin physician (and SS officer) who
wrote about cancer policy in France, Germany, and Japan, examined the question of increase in a 1937 article comparing cancer
rates in cities and farming regions. Since the 1830s, urban cancer
rates had been observed to be higher than rural rates—the presumption being that something about urban/industrial life (or
"civilization" more generally) was causing an upsurge in malignancies. Haubold argued that the lower cancer mortality in rural
areas was simply an artifact of the failure in those locales to record
accurately the causes of deaths. Support for this idea came from
the fact that deaths from "old age" or "undefined causes" were
invariably *high* in regions where cancer rates were *low*, and vice
versa. Statistics from various parts of the world showed that countries with high cancer rates invariably recorded few deaths from
"old age" or "cause unknown." Austria, for example, was home to
Europe's highest annual cancer mortality (161/100,000) but it also
recorded zero deaths from old age or unknown causes. Haubold
formulated this as a law: "the higher the death rate from cancer,
the fewer the deaths from old age and 'unknown causes.'"

Haubold also showed that, at least in the case of France, the reported cancer rate was rising somewhat more slowly than the rate
at which deaths from "old age" or "cause unknown" had been falling—suggesting that progress was being made against the disease.
He rejected the notion that people living in industrial nations were
more likely to die of cancer than were people in agricultural regions: cancer rates in industrial nations were often higher (one in

eight Austrians died of cancer in 1930 compared with only one in forty Lithuanians), but this was most likely a result of differences in the thoroughness with which such data were gathered. High cancer rates, when found with low rates of death from unknown or unspecified causes, were simply a measure of the reliability of a region's mortality statistics. Haubold concluded that "the primary and perhaps the only cause for the increase in Germany's cancer rate" was that Germans were now living twenty years longer than their counterparts half a century earlier.[65] This was not something taken lightly. The "aging" of the German population was a major fear of racial hygienists, to which now could be added the additional threat of cancer, notorious for striking down the elderly. Haubold cautioned that a nation losing its "will to bear children" (*Wille zum Kind*) would suffer higher and higher rates of tumorous malignancies.[66]

The question of whether "civilization" (modernity, luxury, industry, city life, etc.) was a major cause of cancer, and whether cancer was therefore on the increase, continued to divide German intellectuals—as it does to a certain extent today. The political valence of the dispute, however, was different from what it would become in the 1960s and 1970s, when the environmental Left began to warn against an "epidemic" of cancer caused by industrial pollution and diverse personal vices.[67] In Germany in the 1930s, the romantic Right was more likely to raise the specter of epidemic cancer than was the technocratic Left. The orthodox curative medical community (radiologists, for example) was more likely to argue that cancer was under control and that evidence for its increased incidence was illusory.[68] This was a common view in many of Germany's most influential pathological institutes: Hans Schwarz at the German university in Prague[69] doubted a genuine increase, as did Robert Rössle in Berlin and Bernhard Fischer-Wasels at Frankfurt.[70] The same was true of many industrial physicians. E. Pfeil, chief physician for the Ammoniawerk Merseburg and the man who, in 1911, first identified lung cancer among the chromate workers at Ludwigshafen, was convinced that lung cancer rates were not on the rise and that the disease was simply more likely to be diagnosed than in the era prior to X-rays. Lung cancers had once been commonly misdiagnosed as emphysema, tuberculosis, pleurisy, or chronic bronchitis, and it was only now, he claimed, in 1935, that cases were being properly identified.[71]

Part of what has to be understood in this context is the romantic Right's more general fear of "civilization." The racial hygienist Fritz Lenz had argued in a widely read essay of 1917 ("The Renewal of Ethics"—which he once claimed to have anticipated the leading elements of Nazi philosophy) that the growth of technology had brought with it an alienation from nature. Lenz felt that society's abundance of goods had only led to abuse; he cited Kant and Nietzsche in support of his thesis that suffering was an inevitable accompaniment of progress. Civilization was "merely technical"; culture, by contrast, was the patterning of human relationships according to values. Civilization had to do with means, culture with ends. Yet culture could not be the highest value; that honor went to biological "race"—hence the moral imperative of racial hygiene.[72]

Many of the attitudes toward health at this time can be seen as flowing from this distrust of "civilization." Reich Health Office president Hans Reiter pushed for the elimination of carcinogenic food dyes, urging a return to diet more closely approximating that to which our ancestors had adapted (see chapter 5). Reich Health Führer Leonardo Conti advocated the construction of Nordic-style saunas throughout the Reich, the purpose being to combat colds and other "diseases of civilization."[73] Civilization was blamed for nervousness, for the growing use of alcohol, tobacco, and illegal narcotics, for countless other diseases—including cancer.

The romantic Right was never able to gain exclusive control over German medicine, even at the height of Nazi power (see also chapters 5 and 7). This is no doubt one reason preventive health initiatives fell short of what many Nazi ideologues had once hoped. Alternative medical journals began to express some irritation at the slow pace of progress; one gets the sense in reading *Hippokrates*, for example, that interest in cancer in the late 1930s was not what it had been in previous years. Gearing up for war may have been one reason; Liek's death in 1935 also seems to have slowed the movement. A 1937 remembrance of Liek lamented a "notable stillness" surrounding the question of what causes cancer and what to do about it.[74]

One reason naturopathic healers were disappointed was that the orthodox medical community reasserted its power in the later years of the Nazi regime. Part of this has to do with the fact that the ambitious medical initiatives launched by the regime—mass X-ray screenings, sterilizations, racial surveys, vaccinations, the "euthanasia operation," just to name a few—required the talents and authority of orthodox practitioners. Alternative healers lost one of their major supporters in 1939, when Reich Physicians' Führer Gerhard Wagner died; the outbreak of war that same year also made it less fashionable to talk about the once-hailed "New German Science of Healing" (*Neue Deutsche Heilkunde*).[75] The alternative impulse was not lost, but naturopathic practices were henceforth more likely to be folded into the orthodox, allopathic, sphere rather than vice versa.

Yet another element slowing the spread of natural medicine was the Rudolf Hess *Fallschirm* fiasco, one of the oddest events of the oddity-filled Third Reich. Hess had been Hitler's right-hand man since the Nazi party's "time of struggle": it was he who, in Landsberg prison in 1923, had taken down the dictation that later became *Mein Kampf*, and the Führer had rewarded his secretary by naming him his second-in-command and successor. Hess had long been a follower of homeopathic methods, and his was the name given to the nation's most ambitious naturopathic hospital—the Rudolf Hess Krankenhaus, founded in Dresden in 1933. Hess had always fought to establish natural healing on a par with "academic" medicine, and many of the leaders of the natural health movement—Reich Physicians' Führer Gerhard Wagner, for example—owed at least some of their political success to his patronage.

Hitler's right-hand man had parachuted dramatically into England in the spring of 1941, apparently to try to negotiate some kind of end to the war with Churchill (he seems not to have had the Führer's permission—though the story remains somewhat mysterious). Hess was arrested and imprisoned in the Tower of London, and Germany's political elite were embarrassed, to say the least. Goebbels in his private diaries derided Hess as a "nut," a "morphine addict" and "the dupe of astrologers"; but the flight of the *Stellvertreter des Führers* also opened up an opportunity to attack medical quackery—and quackery more generally.[76] On June 12, 1941, the propaganda minister announced the arrest of "all astrologers, magnetopaths, anthroposophists, and so forth"; he also wryly noted that none of these purported "seers" (*Hellseher*) had managed to foresee their own arrest.[77] I do not want to leave the impression that alternative traditions disappeared from Germany or even went underground. Himmler continued to be a fan of organic medicine, sponsoring concentration camp experiments to test various folk and native remedies. (The Dachau concentration camp had several greenhouses in which various herbs and medicinal plants were grown both for experiments and for large-scale production.) Himmler remained enthusiastic about homeopathy, mesmerism, and the holistic traditions that went under the name of *Biochemie*. His belief that the "vital heat" of the human body was fundamentally different from ordinary mechanical heat led him to support the notorious experiments to determine whether pilots downed in the icy waters of the North Sea might be more rapidly warmed by human flesh than by conventional methods. At Dachau, naked women were forced to embrace the frozen, near-dead victims of hypothermia experiments, the theory being that their "organic" heat would prove more effective than, say, submersion in a bath of warm water.

After the war, a number of orthodox physicians accused of crimes against humanity cited Himmler's organic affinities in an effort to distance themselves from the Reichsführer's policies. SS Gruppenführer Karl Gebhardt, for example, who participated in several of the most notorious camp experiments, used Himmler's fondness for alternative medicine to argue that his own work bore no resemblance to that of the SS Reichsführer.[78] The ploy did not work, and Gebhardt—the last president of the German Red Cross in the Third Reich and a well-published medical professor—was executed by Allied authorities at Landsberg on June 2, 1948.

Ever since this time, the Nazi romance with nature has been used—especially in medical literature—to tar the regime as a kind of irrationalist backwater. Historians have shown the complexity

of the ideological struggles of the time, but the myth-making apparatus of the medical profession seems to prefer a more cardboard
image of the era: Nazis as fanatics, as antiscience. This serves, of
course, to distance the self-righteous "we" from the tainted "they";
perhaps it is comforting to believe that "Nazi doctors" were
quacks—and that since orthodox physicians were not quacks, they
could never have become implicated in such crimes as were common in the era.

What is important to recognize, however, is that naturopathic
medicine was only one of several ways stalwart Nazi doctors dealt
with illness. Nazism pervaded orthodox medicine as deeply as alternative traditions; academics were as eager as "quacks" to vilify
their Jewish colleagues, for example. The challenge of understanding Nazi medicine is to comprehend how terror crossed new
boundaries; how crime, callousness, and common sense came to
coexist in the country once hailed as "the land of thinkers and
poets." We shall return to the question of quackery in chapters 5
and 7—for there was no shortage of charlatans—but first some
words on the more familiar racial reductionism of the era, and one
of the lesser-known fertile facets of fascism: the push to explore
genotoxic hazards.

3

Genetic and Racial Theories

We have the duty, if necessary, to die for the Fatherland;
why should we not also have the duty to be healthy? Has
the Führer not explicitly demanded this?

Robert Hofstätter, antitobacco activist, 1939

BIOLOGICAL determinism was one of the pillars of Nazi ideology.
Nazi philosophers argued that biology is destiny and that "diseases" as diverse as diabetes and divorce are genetically anchored.
The Nazi imagination ran wild in this territory, claiming racial, genetic, or "constitutional" predispositions for every conceivable
human talent and disability. Criminality was said to be heritable—
and not just criminality, but specific forms of crime (rape, embez-
zlement, etc.). The racial zealot Hans F. K. Günther claimed that
the tendency to divorce was heritable, and Fritz Lenz of Munich
went so far as to argue that the tendency to believe in Lamarck-
ism—the doctrine of the inheritance of acquired characteristics—
was inborn. The most prominent Lamarckians were Jews, he suggested, in consequence of their inborn drive to assimilate, to blend
in—a kind of human variant of the "animal mimicry" common in
the rest of the animal kingdom.[1]

CANCER AND THE JEWISH QUESTION

Consistent with this ideology, a number of German physicians argued that cancer, too, was a genetic disease, a disease to which
different individuals and races were susceptible in differing de-

grees. The idea that cancer runs in families was already an old one, dating back at least to Friedrich Hoffmann's postulate, circa 1700, of a *haereditaria dispositio*.[2] Statistical explorations of cancer's heritability proliferated in the nineteenth century (always rather crude, one must say), and by the early years of the twentieth century, evidence had accumulated that certain cancers of the eye (retinoblastoma), colon cancers, and at least some breast cancers could be passed from parent to offspring via the germ cells.[3] Twin studies fueled the idea that at least some cancers might be heritable, and by the 1930s a multitude of such studies claimed to have proven a genetic predisposition.[4] Certain families were said to be immune: a 1938 study of one Croatian noble lineage claimed to have found that among 133 members of this well-documented family there was not a single instance of cancer over a period spanning nearly two hundred years.[5]

Early hints of the idea that chromosomal events might be involved in carcinogenesis began to be discussed in the 1910s and 1920s, following the rediscovery of Mendelian genetics in 1900 and the work of Theodor Boveri and others. Fritz Lenz, the Munich-based racial hygienist, suggested in 1921 that cancers must arise from the mutation of somatic cell tissues by external agents (X-rays and alcohol, for instance),[6] but the most important advocate of the mutation theory was a young Heidelberg surgeon by the name of Karl Heinrich Bauer—a man whose career reveals the forgotten but formative role played by eugenics in the progress of certain sciences.

Best known today as the first postwar president of the University of Heidelberg and founding director of Germany's National Cancer Institute (in Heidelberg in 1964), Bauer was also an avid and early supporter of eugenics, albeit of a fairly innocuous stripe. His 1926 book on racial hygiene called for sterilization of inferior stocks and marital bans, while opposing the "craziness of certain racial fanatics" who proposed the wholesale elimination of "lives unworthy of living."* He was not a big believer in cancer's

* Karl Heinrich Bauer, *Rassenhygiene: Ihre biologischen Grundlagen* (Leipzig: Quelle und Meyer, 1926), p. 207. Bauer was relatively modest in his earliest eugenic proposals: he followed Bonhoeffer, for example, in arguing that sterilization would be appropriate only for a "small circle of diseases"; compare also his opposition to

heritability, but his enthusiasm for more traditional eugenics—to combat the breeding of the feebleminded, for example—led him to coauthor the official technical manual for the Nazi-era Sterilization Law, published in 1936. His efforts in such areas later earned him the scorn of postwar student activists who occupied his Heidelberg office in 1968 and charged him with Nazi collaboration[7]—not entirely fairly, I would argue. Bauer never joined the Nazi party: he apparently could not have joined, given that his wife, the daughter of an admiral, was one-fourth Jewish, a particularity that also barred him from military service (and may have saved his postwar career).

In 1928, Bauer published the first book-length treatise postulating somatic mutation as the initial event in cancerous growth.[8] (Somatic mutation means changes in the body's nonreproductive cells—as opposed to changes in the "germ line" reproductive cells, like sperm and eggs.) The American geneticist Hermann J. Muller had recently shown that X-rays could cause mutations in the sperm cells of fruit flies, and Bauer used this to argue that since X-rays could cause cancer, then cancer, too, must be regarded as a product of mutation. Bauer's formulation was simple, and sweeping: "Any form of radiant energy capable of producing mutations

---

"dem Irrwahn gewisser Rassefanatiker, die da glauben, eine aktivistische eliminatorische Rassenhygiene erfordere spartanische Methoden; missbildete Kinder z. B. gehörten in die Schluchten des Taygetus oder lebensunwertes Leben, z. B. unheilbarer Geisteskranker, sei zu vernichten" (p. 207). Bauer cautioned that an overly aggressive eugenics might inadvertently prevent the birth of a future Wilhelm III of England (born premature), an Alexander von Humboldt (feeble at birth), or a Beethoven (pp. 207–8). Curiously, given his future career, there is no mention of cancer in this book. Bauer did become an avid supporter of the 1933 Sterilization Law, however. After the war, he was rehabilitated by the widely respected philosopher Karl Jaspers, who defended him to the Americans, which allowed him to become the University of Heidelberg's first postwar president. See Bernd Laufs, "Vom Umgang der Medizin mit ihrer Geschichte," in Hohendorf and Magull-Seltenreich, *Von der Heilkunde zur Massentötung*, pp. 237–41; Cornelia Girndt and Abraham Lauve, "Die vertanen Jahre," *Frankfurter Rundschau*, October 18, 1986. For a rather superficial evaluation of Bauer's life and work, see *In Memoriam Karl Heinrich Bauer*, ed. Fritz Linder (Berlin: Springer, 1992); compare also Karl Jaspers and K. H. Bauer, *Briefwechsel 1945–1968* (Berlin: Springer, 1983).

is also capable of causing cancer." His somatic mutation hypothesis was widely accepted by the late 1930s—especially among eugenicists; Otmar von Verschuer in his racial hygiene textbook, for example, stated bluntly that malignant tumors could be regarded as "somatic mutations."[9] The mutation theory was attractive to eugenicists worrying about the corruption of the human genetic stock; some of these concerns sound plausible and or even prescient to us today (worries about X-rays and tobacco, for example); others strike us as misconceived, if not horrific (genetic harms from racial intermixing, for example).

In the common understanding of the 1920s and 1930s, genetic variation implied racial variation. It is hardly surprising, therefore, that German scientists sometimes postulated racial predispositions to account for the fact that people in different parts of the world suffered from cancer in differing degrees. Germans, Jews, and Scandinavians, for example, were said to contract cancer more readily than Latins, Slavs, and Celts.[10] Differences in cancer rates among white and black Americans were already well known (the most common view being that blacks were more "resistant"),[11] but cancer rates were also said to vary between Jews and other European peoples. Cancer studies in the Ukraine in the early 1930s, for example, seemed to indicate that elderly Jews were more than twice as likely to die of cancer as elderly Ukrainians or Russians; Jews were found to suffer exceptionally high rates of stomach cancer and low rates of uterine, genital, and breast cancer.[12]

Results such as these were sometimes used as proof of Jewish bodily inferiority. We should recall this as a time of efforts to pathologize the Jewish body: Jews were said to have bad eyes, flat feet, and bad backs, along with high rates of mental infirmity, sexual deficiency, and homosexuality.[13] Jewish diseases were alternately said to be diseases of poverty or of wealth; Jewish stomach cancer, for example, was sometimes said to be a sign, as historian Sander Gilman has noted, of the Jews' "intense striving after wealth."[14] Nazi physicians selectively drew from those parts of this literature that could be used to establish Jewish physical and mental deficiency. This was one reason Germans and Jews were instructed not to intermarry: Reich Physicians' Führer Gerhard

Wagner claimed that the mixing of Jewish and non-Jewish blood would spread the "diseased genes" of the "bastardized" Jewish race into the "relatively pure" European stocks.[15]

Today, most of the world's variation in cancer rates is recognized as due either to some kind of reporting bias (people with poor access to health care often look as if they have low cancer rates, when in fact they simply do not get fully counted in statistical surveys) or to reseachers' failure to take into account age profiles;[16] alternatively, there may be something about dietary or tobacco habits or exposure to pathogens that would explain the difference. But in the hyperracialized biologism of an earlier age, geographic and ethnic variations were often taken as proof of inborn racial predispositions. Cesare Lombroso, the Italian father of criminal biology, claimed that the Jews of Verona were twice as likely to suffer from cancer as Veronese Christians. Many Americans regarded Negroes as relatively immune[17]—a consequence, it is now recognized, of the failure properly to count all the tumors in this population. At the First International Conference on Cancer in London in 1928, Alfredo Niceforo of Naples and Eugene Pittard of Geneva claimed that *Homo alpinus* and *Homo nordicus* (the Alpine and Nordic types) had the highest rates of cancer among the "native" anthropological types in Europe, owing to their higher cancer "receptivity."[18] Italians were sometimes said to be cancer resistant—an idea that led some Americans to argue that intermarriage with Italian women would confer cancer resistance on the offspring.[19] Jews were said to be particularly susceptible to tumors of the "neuromyo-arterial glomus," while at the same time being virtually immune to cancer of the penis.[20]

In Germany, opinions differed concerning whether Jews were more or less vulnerable to cancer. Berlin's mortality tables for 1905 showed that 8.6 percent of all Jewish deaths were from cancer, compared to only 6 percent for Christians, but faith in such data was not always strong, and evidence was also growing that for some kinds of cancer, Jews were actually less vulnerable. The requirement (circa 1900) that cause of cancer deaths be recorded according to site in the body (lung, stomach, etc.), prompted new speculation about who was vulnerable or immune to particular kinds of cancer. The gynecologist Adolf Theilhaber noted that Jewish men had higher rates of stomach and intestinal cancer, but very little penis cancer. The rarity of Jewish uterine cancer was most often attributed to the ritual practice of (male) circumcision, but the Jewish neurologist Leopold Löwenfeld offered a "constitutional" explanation: Jews began their menstrual periods earlier and therefore had more blood in the uterus and were less likely, as a result, to contract uterine cancer. This was typical, he claimed, of people of the "plethoric" constitutional type.[21]

Hints of racial propensities also came from laboratory studies, which had already shown by the 1920s that strains of mice could be bred that were more or less receptive to the uptake of cancer tissue transplants, or more or less vulnerable to the agency of carcinogens.[22] SS chief Heinrich Himmler was apparently intrigued by the prospect of breeding a race of cancer-prone rats: in a 1939 meeting with Sigmund Rascher, the notorious Dachau hypothermia experimenter, the SS Reichsführer proposed breeding such a race of rodents to be released in German cities to control the rat population. It is not yet clear how far such far-fetched plans were ever carried out.[23]

Animal experimental evidence was extrapolated to humans, bolstered by the ideological push to see all aspects of human behavior—including purported racial differences—as rooted in "blood," race, or genes. Otmar Freiherr von Verschuer, director of the Frankfurt Institute for Racial Hygiene and mentor to Dr. Josef Mengele of Auschwitz, argued that Jews suffer disproportionately not just from diabetes, flat feet, hemophilia, and deafness, but also from xeroderma pigmentosum, a heritable childhood disease that results in multiple cancers of the skin, and muscular tumors (the latter ailment shared also with "coloreds" [*Farbige*]). TB, interestingly, was the only disease Verschuer considered to be less frequent in Jews, a consequence, he claimed, of the "evolutionary adaptation" of Jews to urban life.[24]

Clear-cut evidence of cancer's heritability, however, turned out to be more elusive than many cancer researchers had hoped. Karl Heinrich Bauer in 1937 used twin studies to argue that cancer was overwhelmingly a disease of "external" environmental origins:

why else would identical twins so rarely have the same kind of cancer?[25] In 1940, Bauer argued that there were other reasons cancers should be regarded as exogenous in origins. For one thing, there was the fact that heritability was obvious in only a very few cancers. Xeroderma pigmentosum, neuroblastomas of the retina, and polyposis of the colon were well-known examples, but these were all quite rare. There was also the fact that men and women could have very different cancer rates. Cancer of the larynx, for example, was twenty times more common in men than in women, and lung cancer was five or ten times as likely to strike a man as a woman. Could male and female lungs really be so different—or were environmental influences involved? Lip and stomach cancers were also found more than twice as often among males, though with gallbladder cancer the ratios were reversed (women were six or seven times more likely to suffer the disease). It was hard to see how heredity could explain such differences. Male and female lungs and lips and stomachs were not obviously different in any relevant aspect; the more satisfactory explanation, Bauer suggested—correctly, as it turned out—was that something in the environments of the two sexes—smoking or drinking habits, for example—must be responsible for the differences. He also pointed out that cancer might well "run in families" for no other reason than that people in those families may be exposed to a common environment, as in the families of Schneeberg's uranium miners, longtime sufferers from lung cancer.[26]

"Lifestyle" theories of carcinogenesis were actually quite popular in the Nazi era—even among committed Nazis. In 1939, in a long review of world cancer trends, Arthur Hintze, a leading Berlin radiologist and professor of surgery, argued that dietary habits and religious practices were important in explaining cancer rates on different parts of the planet. Stomach cancer, for example, was the most common cause of cancer death in both Europe and Japan, but the same disease was rare in Calcutta, accounting for less than 1 percent of all malignancies. The difference in the Indian case seemed to have little to do with race; rather, it appeared to stem from economic constraints and religious practices that led local populations to consume very little alcohol and almost no meat.

Lifestyle factors also seemed to be at work in the rarity of stomach cancer among the Malays living in Java and Sumatra: one large autopsy study of 3,885 Malays in Batavia found only a single gastric malignancy, a fairly common disease among the Europeans and Chinese living in that part of the world. Hintze pointed out that most of the Malays were Muslims and therefore avoided alcohol and meat—habits which led to low stomach cancer rates also among the predominantly Buddhist Sinhalese of Ceylon. Lifestyle factors were similarly responsible for the high rates of genital and bladder cancers among Arabs in the Middle East, a situation that, he explained, following Sigismund Peller (a Jew whose books had been banned, interestingly), was most likely a consequence of infection by pathogens such as bilharzia and the syphilis spirochete.

Hintze did not deny that different individuals and perhaps even different races were unequally susceptible to the influence of carcinogens (he mentions the fact that light-skinned peoples are more vulnerable to sun-induced skin cancer); he simply claimed that environmental and lifestyle factors played a stronger role than was sometimes acknowledged. The upshot: we should not be fatalistic in thinking of cancer as an unavoidable accompaniment of civilization. Hintze also noted that demographic variables were the root cause of many "racial" variations: Africans, for example, were often observed to have high sarcoma rates—though part of the reason, he explained, was that these were cancers which most often struck at an early age. Africans did not live as long as some other peoples, giving rise to the (false) impression that sarcomas were a particular weakness of the Negro race. He also suggested that the idea that Africans were particularly vulnerable to benign tumors might have something to do with non-Africans' failure to appreciate the widespread cosmetic practice of ritual scarring.[27]

I don't want to leave the impression that Hintze was a flaming Boasian—he was not. He was a dedicated Nazi who profited directly from the expulsion of Jews at the Rudolf Virchow Hospital. Cancer was common among the young in certain populations, he speculated, because those populations were "closer to the youth of humanity"—meaning humans' evolutionary ancestors. He also disagreed with the American Frederick L. Hoffman's perception that cancer rates as a whole were on the rise in civilized nations. Hoffman, in his view, had failed to take into account the aging of the population, whereas properly age-adjusted cancer death rates (for Switzerland in the period 1901–1933, for instance) actually showed *falling* rates. Lung cancer was the only clear-cut exception, and its rise was more than balanced by declines in other kinds of tumors. Hintze could just as well have taken aim at Liek, but Hoffman was a safer target. Haubold—an SS man as well as a party member—was his ally in stating that cancer was not an ineluctable consequence of "culture" (or civilization). His upbeat conclusion: culture has been conquering and will continue to conquer cancer.[28]

Lifestyle cancer theories were put forward even by a number of men (and almost all were men) whose primary focus was on genetic (or "racial") disease. Otmar von Verschuer's 1941 racial hygiene textbook stated not just that cancers were "somatic mutations" but that heredity contributed only trivially to cross-cultural variations in cancer incidence. Clear-cut heritable cancer syndromes accounted for less than 1 percent of all cancers, in his view.[29] Even Jewish cancer inclinations were often explained by environmental etiologies. In 1940, Martin Staemmler and Edeltraut Bieneck—both influential Nazi physicians—noted that Jewish birthrates had declined considerably in recent years and that there was therefore a higher proportion of elderly among Jews than among non-Jews. This helped account for the higher Jewish mortality rates from disorders such as cancer, diabetes, and circulatory failure; it also helped explain their lower death rates for tuberculosis and other infectious diseases, ailments that most commonly struck the young.[30] The much-commented-upon rarity of Jewish penis and cervical cancer was sometimes given a racial explanation, though, as already noted, it was more often—and correctly— traced to the ritual practice of circumcision. (Penis cancer was also observed to be rare among Muslims who practiced ritual circumcision.) Hintze in 1939 went so far as to celebrate circumcision as "the only definite example" of how "cultural measures" could help prevent cancer; circumcision was a case where "culture has conquered cancer."[31]

How curious to hear a Nazi doctor in 1939 defending the health benefits of a Jewish ceremonial rite! Scientists at this time were in fact divided over what to attribute to nature, what to nurture—at least when it came to cancer. Generalizing, it seems that "nature" in the Nazi view of the world was looked to to explain diseases that seemed to appear in excess in Jews, while "nurture" was invoked to account for diseases from which Jews appeared to be exempt. When it came to cancer, however, opinions remained divided—for reasons I shall indicate in a moment.

More common than racial explanations were efforts to determine whether certain "constitutional body types" were predisposed to cancer, or cancer-causing behaviors—like smoking or alcohol abuse.[32] Fritz Lickint suggested that genetic factors might be involved in the addiction of certain people to tobacco or narcotics; Hans Weselmann postulated that the "vegetative-labile" type was less able to tolerate nicotine and was therefore less likely to smoke (and contract cancer).[33] Hofstätter in the 1920s put the matter bluntly, if anecdotally: "It seems to me that the Jewish race is more prone to nicotine addiction than the Aryan race. . . . Among the female smokers I know, those who smoke the most are three Jews and one Aryan woman. I know of no red-haired woman who smokes heavily, and only one blond."[34]

It was widely recognized by this time that darker skin pigmentation protected against sun-induced skin cancer; the Munich radiologist Friedrich Voltz, editor of the *Radiologische Rundschau*, took this further and proposed that the "red-blond constitutional type" was more vulnerable to cancers in general,[35] and even that the cancers of different races responded differently to X-ray therapeutics (he maintained that tumors in the "red-blond type" responded less favorably than did tumors in other races).[36] Robert Ritter, the Tübingen psychiatrist and Gypsy "expert" (read: murderer), wrote an entire essay on "red hair as a problem of racial hygiene," hinting at, among other things, a cancer predisposition.[37] The factory physician Wilhelm Hergt suggested that "blonds with delicate complexions" were more likely to fall victim to occupational cancers than were "stout and well-fed persons,"[38] and some physicians argued that the diverse races of the world harbored different predispositions to addictive drugs. Thus blacks were said to prefer hashish, Asians opium, and "Nordic" Europeans alcohol.[39] A 1940 medical thesis claimed that cigar smoking was most common among the "pyknic" and "sclerotic" types (Winston Churchill was the example given), while slender leptosomes—the typical Bavarian farmer—stood out among the users of snuff.[40]

The story of Jews and cancer is rather more subtle and scurrilous than what I have presented thus far: Jews were not just said to be either more or less prone to cancer; Jews were also said to be the *purveyors* of cancer, in various and sundry ways. The 1941 conference celebrating the founding of Jena's antitobacco institute (see chapter 6) blamed Jews for introducing tobacco into Germany, and Jews were charged with dominating the tobacco import centers of Amsterdam.[41] Jews were also said to trade in other dangerous products. Hugo Kleine in a popular book on nutrition blamed "capitalist special interests" and "masculinized Jewish half-women" (*jüdischer Emanzipierter und vermännlichter Halbweiber*) for the deterioration of German foods—one consequence of which was cancer.[42] Jews were not just disproportionately immune or susceptible to cancer; Jews were also accused of being one of its causes.

Selection and Sterilization

One should keep in mind, of course, that there were practical, one could say surgical, implications at this time for whether a particular disease was classed as heritable. The 1933 Sterilization Law (Gesetz zur Verhütung erbkranken Nachwuchses) provided for the sterilization of a broad class of genetic defectives, and familial cancers were sometimes categorized as falling under the rubric of the law.[43] Prof. Wilhelm Clausen of Halle, for example, in 1936 argued that children suffering from retinoblastoma, a familial cancer of the eye, should be sterilized. (He did not believe that people with lesser forms of hereditary blindness—such as color or night blindness or blindness in consequence of minor albinism—should be sterilized.)[44] Fischer-Wasels was another outspoken supporter of sterilization to prevent the breeding of cancerous human stocks. In a 1934 article in *Strahlentherapie*, the Frankfurt pathologist claimed that "much that is good" could be achieved "by removing the heavily burdened families from the reproductive community, by preventing the combination and expression of afflicted genes."[45] The cancers in question included tumors of the nerve and kidney stem cells, neuroblastomas of the adrenal gland and sympathetic nerves, and certain heritable kidney cancers (nephromas) and childhood cancers of the retina (retinoblastomas). These were by no means common cancers, but the fact that they were highly heritable and often killed at an early age mandated sterilization, in his view, to prevent their being passed on into future generations.[46]

There were also implications of a more subtle nature. We do not yet know whether the notion of "red-blond" types being more vulnerable to cancer led radiologists to be less prudent in their irradiation of darker-skinned individuals, but we do have evidence that the idea of differential racial susceptibility was used to screen workers in carcinogenic industries.[47] In November of 1934, for example, at a meeting of the German Society for Industrial Hygiene, Prof. Gunther Lehmann of Dortmund's Kaiser Wilhelm Institute for Labor Physiology found that workers differed substantially in how well their noses filtered out the silica (quartz) dust known to cause silicosis, a much-feared hazard of mining, foundry work, porcelain making, sandblasting, gem cutting, and other trades where large volumes of rock dust were inhaled (see also chapter 4). Lehmann constructed an apparatus by which dust could be blown into the upper air passages of a worker, retrieving it through the mouth to see how much had been filtered out (presumably avoiding lung contamination during the test).[48]

Lehmann found that while noses with "exceptionally good filtering capacity" were able to capture 60 percent or more of the dust introduced, there were also noses that allowed almost all of the dust to enter the lungs. He used his apparatus to examine several hundred miners and found that those who had remained healthy after sixteen years tended to have much better nasal filtration than those who had fallen ill from silicosis. He also found that "mouth breathers" were more likely to contract the disease than "nose breathers." The Dortmund professor concluded that nasal filtration was probably the single most important factor predisposing an individual to silicosis, and he recommended that only persons found to have good dust-capturing capacity be allowed to work in trades where silicosis was a danger.[49] The device was apparently widely used, though not everyone agreed on its ability to identify susceptible workers.[50]

There are many similar cases of predisposition screening from this era. In 1939, when scientists from Berlin's Institute for Radiological Research conducted experiments on the human response to ultraviolet radiation, they deliberately selected "darkly pigmented brunettes" on the grounds that such people would be less susceptible to the harmful effects of the rays.[51] Miners were regularly X-rayed for early signs of lung disease, and suspect workers were dismissed. This was consistent, as we shall see, with a paternalistic philosophy that saw workers as abstract inputs in the production process (see chapter 4). The point in most such efforts was to adapt the worker to the workplace, rather than vice versa.

Racism played an important role in conceptions of who was vulnerable to cancer and who was not—and not just in Germany. An idea commonly heard in occupational health circles even after the war was that people of darker complexion were better suited for work in cancerous industries. Wilhelm Hueper, the American pioneer of environmental carcinogenesis and a guiding light for Rachel Carson, suggested in his 1942 magnum opus that "colored races" were "markedly refractory to the carcinogenic effect exerted upon the skin by tar, pitch, and mineral oils." Hueper argued that "the natural oiliness of the skin of Negroes seems to protect their skin against the irritative and carcinogenic action of many industrially used chemicals, as occupational dermatitis and cutaneous cancer is rarely seen in Negroes." The German expatriate admitted that the entire question of "racial resistance" was controversial and in flux, illustrating this with the example of changing views on the rarity of penile cancer among Jews. While this had originally been considered a racial characteristic, the view now accepted by "the great majority of investigators" was that the rarity was the result of the practice of circumcision.[52] Hueper nonetheless remained convinced, however, that Africans were physically less vulnerable to occupational cancers of the skin. As late as 1956, he was claiming that dark-skinned persons were more appropriate choices for work in industries with a substantial cancer danger[53]—a view at odds with the increasingly antiracialist ideas of mainstream American social science. Hueper successfully defended himself against the charge that he was a Nazi—along with charges that he was a communist—but his views on race remained strikingly similar to those of his former compatriots across the Atlantic.

NAZISM transformed German cancer research and policy in many different spheres: in the language of research, in concepts of causality, in the bolstering or banishment of individuals and institutions, in the kinds of questions asked and the day-to-day ways patients interacted with their doctors. Nazism privileged the racial, the radical, and the rapid; Nazi policies would survey, sort, and screen to an extent never seen before, fighting carcinogens and cancer carriers and even "cancer fears" with the goal of creating a secure and sanitary utopia. Hans Auler, the Berlin professor who climbed in the cancer research ranks and managed to catch Goebbels's eye, saw the Nazi regime itself as anticarcinogenic:

> It is fortunate for German cancer patients, and for anyone threatened by cancer, that the Third Reich has grounded itself on the maintenance of German health. The most important measures of the government—in genetics, education, sports, postgraduate service, physical education in the Hitler Youth, SA, and SS, marital loans, home hygiene, settlements, work service, and so forth—can all be regarded as prophylactic measures against cancer.[54]

Small wonder that Auler captured the attention of Joseph Goebbels, who not only discussed his ideas with the Führer but also awarded him the hefty sum of RM 100,000 to carry on his studies.[55]

The horrendous outcomes of Nazi racial hygiene are well known, and well publicized. Less well publicized, however, is the fact that Nazi eugenics actually stimulated research into the toxic effects of mutagens and carcinogens—everything from alcohol and tobacco to workplace toxins and genotoxic contraceptives.[56] The next three chapters explore Nazi-era examples of research of this sort—in the areas of occupational health, food protection, and the aggressive war on tobacco. In each case, what we find is that Nazi ideology pushed and pulled on cancer research, sometimes for better, sometimes for worse.

4

Occupational Carcinogenesis

> The extraordinary powers exerted by a rising people can-
> not be maintained without some health dangers to the
> population.
>
> *Leonardo Conti, May 25, 1939*

ONE surprising aspect of the Nazi cancer program is its emphasis
on occupational carcinogenesis. German physicians had a long tradition of support for industrial hygiene,[1] and Nazi physicians continued this emphasis, though with contradictory agendas revealing tensions between ideology and *realpolitik*.[2] Many different
kinds of occupational cancers had been discovered by the 1930s,
the most important of these being skin, bone, and blood cancers
caused by X-rays, internal cancers caused by radium ingestion,
bladder cancers among dye workers, lung cancers caused by chromate exposure and uranium mining, the arsenic cancers occasionally found among vintners, glassworkers, and steelworkers,[3] and
the skin cancers caused by prolonged contact with paraffin, tar,
soot, and certain types of mineral oil.[4] The contribution of such
cancers to the overall burden was disputed (Fischer-Wasels in 1934
remarked that occupational cancers constituted only a "tiny fraction" of the overall cancer burden in Germany),[5] but their political
significance was magnified by virtue of their being, by almost all
accounts, preventable.

We begin with a general look at occupational health and safety
in the 1930s, turning then to an analysis of how Nazi authorities
dealt with the most notorious occupational carcinogens of the era:

X-ray cancers, radium and uranium cancers, arsenic, chromium, and asbestos cancers, and the chemical industry cancers associated with the production of aniline dyes. Each of these agents has a convoluted political history, as we shall see. In the Nazi period, health officials developed safeguards against exposure to deadly chemical toxins at the same time that efforts were also underway to use some of those very same toxins to kill millions of Jews and Gypsies.

HEALTH AND WORK IN THE REICH

Hitler assumed power in January of 1933, promising to put an end to Germany's joblessness and to diverse "malaises" identified with Weimar culture. Millions of laborers were out of work, and the promise struck a positive chord with many desperate people. The Communist party had grown in recent years, though internecine squabbling had kept the Left from forming a united front, giving Hitler and his acolytes their opening. Hitler's party did not scare off business as did the communists: when asked whether he would nationalize industry, Hitler replied: "why nationalize industry when you can nationalize the people?"

Labor projected a special, almost magical, aura for the Nazis. Art and literature celebrated the virtues of the workingman, echoing similar serenades by the Stakhanovites in Russia and the social realists in America (Edward Hopper, for example). The working-man was a hero, the nonworking man a degenerate asocial. Work was a "moral duty," an obligation comparable to military service or, for women, the bearing and rearing of children. People had not so much a right to work as a duty to work[6]—a change signaled also by the dissolution of the trade unions. In May of 1933 Robert Ley engineered a coup d'état against the unions, after which time all workers and employers were required to join the Nazi successor organization, the German Labor Front (DAF), a factory-policing agency with unprecedented powers over life in the workplace. Shirking in this climate becomes tantamount to treason, as people formerly not expected to work are pressed into service—first women, then people with tuberculosis, then the underage and elderly, and eventually millions of foreign and slave laborers from conquered territories. For people unfortunate enough to land in a concentration camp, inability to work becomes a virtual death sentence.

Hitler's mobilization dramatically increased the pace of work. Production of iron, steel, chemicals, machines, and agricultural products grew by leaps and bounds, as more and more people entered the labor force, working harder and for longer hours. Overtime became routine at iron- and other metalworks, in automobile and aircraft production, in work in the mining field and cement industry (the Nazis poured a lot of cement). In the summer of 1938, uniform makers were working twelve hours a day to fulfill military demands. The same was true for tank makers and manufacturers of explosives and ammunition—as in many other industries. Armaments workers often worked sixty hours a week, including Saturdays; similar schedules were kept by laborers erecting the massive fortifications along the French border known as the *Westwall* or Siegfried Line.

The rapid militarization of the German economy increased the number of accidents and injuries suffered by German workers. The rate of fatal accidents rose by 10 percent in the first four years of Nazi rule, an increase health officials openly traced to the escalating tempo of work.[7] (Brewery-workers suffered the highest accident rates, higher even than those of miners.)[8] The number of laborers forced to retire owing to injuries rose, from 4,000 in 1933 (excluding mining) to more than 6,000 three years later.[9] A 1938 propaganda campaign pointed out that 1.5 million Germans would suffer accidents or injuries at work that year; another 8,000 would die from injuries on the job. Two years later, the émigré physician Martin Gumpert predicted that if Germany's feverish work-frenzy did not slow down, the nation would suffer "a collapse much more dreadful than that of 1918."[10]

German labor officials worried about the growing number of accidents and illnesses. A dozen-odd journals published a steady stream of articles on threats to occupational health and safety, from the debilitating effects of asbestos to the hazards of zinc. The

Archiv für Gewerbepathologie und Gewerbehygiene published on carbon monoxide poisoning, while the *Zentralblatt für Gewerbehygiene und Unfallverhütung* published articles on dust control in the textile industry and radiation protection in the radium trades.[11] *Arbeitsphysiologie* published articles on work physiology, and the *Monatsschrift für Unfallheilkunde* published on industrial accidents and other concerns of insurance medicine. Other journals dealt with more specialized aspects of labor health and safety. *Gesundheitsingenieur* (Health engineer) covered health and safety engineering in the workplace (e.g., how to keep factory air clean), while *Die Ärztliche Sachverständigen-Zeitung* (Medical expert review) examined problems faced by factory physicians.[12] *Arbeitsschutz* published on general matters of protection against workplace hazards, while *Die Gasmaske*, issued by the Auergesellschaft of Berlin, a uranium producer, published on dust-control technologies. There are many other journals and several book-series devoted to occupational health in this period[13]—more, in fact, than were produced by any other nation in the world.

Nazi officials also put an unprecedented number of physicians on factory floors—the goal being partly to supervise worker health and safety, but also to certify who was sick enough to stay at home (and, of course, to identify shirkers). The number of "factory physicians" (*Betriebsärzte*) grew from only 467 in 1939 to an astonishing 8,000 in 1944. Most of these physicians had multiple duties, including maintaining labor discipline and doing whatever else was necessary to ensure optimal employee performance.[14]

National socialist attitudes toward worker health and safety have to be understood in several different contexts. For one thing, we should recall that much, but not everything, changed when the new regime seized power. A great deal of Nazi-era literature on industrial health can be regarded as a continuation of pre-Nazi concerns—including many of the prevention-oriented policies advocated by socialist or communist health officials (disease registration and health-oriented workplace engineering, for instance). The fact that Germany enjoyed a state-supported social insurance system was also important: the "sickness funds" (*Krankenkassen*) established in 1883 gave the state a strong interest in reducing medical costs, a key factor in the "euthanasia operation" (designed to reduce the financial burden imposed by "the unfit") but also part of the logic behind many occupational health reforms. Germans were early to discover many occupational hazards, because the national health care system required that work-related accidents and illnesses be registered and compensated—which also gave the state a strong incentive to reduce workplace accidents and illnesses.

A second consideration is that Nazi officials wanted productive, high-performance workers, free of sickness and full of love for their work. Many of the innovations of the 1930s and 1940s must be seen as part of this effort to engineer a high-achieving worker. The ambitious health reorganization plan (*Gesundheitswerk*) of Robert Ley's German Labor Front, for example, was supposed to make Germany "the healthiest high-performance people in the world."[15] "Performance medicine" (*Leistungsmedizin*) and "selection medicine" (*Selektionsmedizin*) were supposed to increase the labor pool's performance by improving the working environment and weeding out inferior personnel.[16] Much of this drive for performance was motivated by the war mobilization: the ambitious four-year plan announced in 1936 put all of German production on a military footing, increasing both the pace of work and the number of hours put in—including the hours spent on work performed at home.[17]

Nazi efforts in this area must also be understood in light of broader military and geopolitical events—especially the territorial aspirations of the regime and its massive and often murderous policy of using foreign and slave labor in German factories. Millions of foreigners were forced to toil in German industry and agriculture; tens of thousands perished in the process. Slave laborers from concentration camps were compelled to work in German factories, and prisoners of war were forced to serve as "subjects" in deadly concentration camp experiments—many of which can be viewed as efforts to enlarge the field of occupational health and safety. The freezing and low-pressure experiments conducted at Dachau, for example, were designed to advance the field of flight physiology (a branch of "military hygiene"), providing the knowledge base needed to rescue pilots exposed to icy cold air or water or the rapid decompression associated with high-altitude bailouts. German military authorities wanted to know whether a pilot downed in the North Sea and exposed to water at a temperature of, say, ten degrees Celsius for three hours might still be alive and worth a rescue effort. Many of the most notorious experiments were designed to answer practical questions of this sort.

Germany, in effect, had two systems of occupational health and safety: one for the racially desirable and one for the racially inferior. Most of the ordinances protecting "decent healthy Germans" were formalized by law; many of the abuses suffered by "racial inferiors" were perpetrated in a legal gray area confused by the exigencies of war and the disregard for international human rights (a concept not yet well developed). For upstanding healthy German males—that is, males with full citizenship rights judged racially unimpeachable—there were in fact a number of new legal protections (see table 4.1). New laws mandated compensation for illnesses acquired at work (cancers caused by asbestos or petrochemicals, for example) and restrictions on the hours worked by youth. New laws strengthened certain kinds of protections for mothers, children, and the "unborn." Restrictions were placed on the hours that women or children could work; mothers and/or children were also barred from exposure to certain substances or processes (see table 4.2).

Much of the interest in women's occupational health focused on threats to proper reproductive or sexual function. A 1941 medical thesis, for example, explored hazards of women's work in tobacco factories, looking at things like the effect of absorbed nicotine on menstrual disorders, age of menopause, ovarian and hormonal dysfunction, and so forth.[18] Paternalistic, pro-natalist concerns were clearly at the center of many rulings in this area—especially as the fraction of women employed in the workplace grew over time.

Foreign workers, of course, rarely benefited from such safeguards. Five million foreigners were forcibly brought into Germany to make up for labor shortages caused by the war; responsibility for organizing this gigantic task was in the hands of Fritz

TABLE 4.1
Occupational Health and Safety Regulations in Germany, 1933–1945

December 16, 1936	The Third Occupational Disease Ordinance adds several new diseases to the list of compensable occupational illnesses, including asbestosis, lung cancers from work with chromate, and bladder cancer from exposure to aromatic amines.[a]
1937	A "Cancer Commission" is established by the Deutsche Gesellschaft für Arbeitsschutz under the direction of Franz Koelsch.
October 30, 1939	The "Gesetz über die Heimarbeit" regulates health and safety conditions for work performed for employers in the home ("outwork").
May 23, 1940	Smoking is banned in the entryways and waiting rooms of factories in which there is a danger of fire (involving work with explosives, flammable liquids, etc.).[b]
February 7, 1941	Work involving exposure to X-rays is barred for anyone deemed unfit for such work by a state-certified occupational physician (*Gewerbearzt*). X-ray technicians must be examined for both local and general radiologic injuries at least twice yearly. Evidence of radiation injury is to be followed up by urine and blood analysis; radium workers evidencing injuries must have a close-up X-ray taken of their lungs.
August 6, 1942	Health and safety conditions are strengthened for lacquer and varnish workers.[c]
January 29, 1943	The Fourth Occupational Disease Ordinance requires compensation for employees suffering from asbestos-related lung cancer.[d]

[a] "Dritte Verordnung über Ausdehnung der Unfallversicherung auf Berufskrankheiten. Vom 16. Dezember 1936," *Reichsgesetzblatt* 1 (1936): 1117–20.

[b] "Rauchverbot in den Aufenthaltsräumen feuergefährdeter Betriebe," *Arbeitsschutz* 3 (1942): 99.

[c] "Richtlinien für den Gesundheitsschutz bei Lackier- und Anstricharbeiten," *Arbeitsschutz* 3 (1942): 297–98.

[d] "Vierte Verordnung zur Ausdehnung der Unfallversicherung auf Berufskrankheiten. Vom 29. Januar 1943," *Arbeitsschutz* 3 (1943): 65–67.

Sauckel, Thuringia's hard-line Gauleiter and, as of March 21, 1942, Plenipotentiary for the Mobilization of Labor (and a leading anti-tobacco activist—see chapter 6). The jobs worked by many of these men, women, and children were usually difficult or dirty; most such workers were paid, but few were free to leave their place of work or move about the countryside. The philosophy behind the

TABLE 4.2
Occupational Protections for Women, Children, and the Unborn in Germany, 1933–1945

April 30, 1938	"Youth Protection Law" bars child labor, excepting work in the home and in agriculture and forestry.[a]
August 1, 1940	Children under the age of 18 are barred from work with asbestos.[b]
January 20, 1941	Boys under the age of 18 and girls under 20 are barred from work with aromatic nitro-compounds and glyconitrates; nursing mothers and pregnant women also barred from work with such substances. Monthly exams required for all workers.[c]
May 17, 1942	"Maternal Protection Law" (*Mutterschutzgesetz*) bars pregnant women from any employment that may endanger either the mother or the child. The law specifically bars pregnant women from work involving: lifting or carrying loads heavier than 5 kg; long periods of standing; use of machines requiring foot control; exposure to occupational toxins or carcinogens (e.g., lead, mercury, benzene-related solvents, or halogenated hydrocarbons); work involving exposure to X-rays or radioactive substances; assembly-line work or piecework; and night-shift or holiday work. Pregnant women are henceforth not allowed to work from 6 weeks prior to delivery until 6 weeks after delivery; women also cannot be fired for being pregnant or for giving birth. Nursing mothers working more than 4½ hours must be given 45 minutes to nurse their infants; nursing mothers working 8-hour shifts must be given two 45-minute breaks. Pregnant and nursing mothers are not allowed to work more than 9 hours per day in agricultural work.[d]
December 2, 1942	Children under 18 are barred from work with cyanide; apprentices over 16 can be employed, but only if they are not involved in pouring off the crucible or cleaning the residue.
April 20, 1943	Women and girls working on streetcars are required to be at least 1.6 meters tall and between 18 and 40 years old. Work may be only during daylight hours. Women with goiter, hearing problems, cramps, or foot or leg ailments are barred.[e]
March 23, 1943	Women are permitted to drive trucks up to 3.5 tons, but only if they are over 21 years of age and not for more than 8 hours, and not after dark. Women are not, however, allowed to crank up the motor or to hand-carry heavy loads. Pregnant women are barred from all such work.

Note: These protections were not generally extended to foreign or slave laborers, of course, or to women in German concentration camps. Nor is it clear to what extent these regulations were enforced, especially in the final years of the war.

[a] "Verordnung über die Beschäftigung Jugendlicher in der Eisen schaffenden Industrie," *Reichs Gesundheitsblatt* 13 (1938): 226 ff.

[b] *Reichsarbeitsblatt* 3 (1940): 263.

[c] *Reichsarbeitsblatt* 1 (1941): 75.

[d] "Gesetz zum Schutze der erwerbstätigen Mutter (Mutterschutzgesetz)," *Arbeitsschutz* 3 (1942): 157–62.

[e] *Reichsarbeitsblatt* 1 (1943): 280 and 3 (1943): 141.

employment of these people was "to exploit them to the highest possible extent at the lowest conceivable degree of expenditure."[19] Official protections were not entirely absent,[20] but supervision was often lax or nil.

Early on in the war, most foreign laborers were Russian or Polish civilians. Soviet prisoners of war were "exempted" from such work, largely, it seems, on the basis of Hitler's fear that they would do more harm than good in German factories. Within a span of about three years, nearly two and a half million Soviets were allowed to starve to death in German POW camps. Late in the war, when the decision was finally made to put some of these men and women to work, food rations were meager and treatment was often less than humane. Russian workers received only about half the rations German workers did, and Sauckel's brutality earned him the death sentence at Nuremberg after the war.[21]

Even for "healthy" Germans, though, protections were eventually weakened to fulfill quotas required by the militarizing economy. A December 23, 1938, ruling, for example, required all unmarried women under the age of twenty-five to work a year on the land. That same day, the Youth Protection Law of April 1938 was amended to permit boys under the age of sixteen to work in steel mills until 9 P.M. in weekly rotations; young men over the age of sixteen were allowed to work all hours, including night shifts between the hours of 8 P.M. and 6 A.M. Similar amendments were drafted for work in other hazardous industries, like glassworks, and a 1939 ruling empowered the Ministry of Labor "to invalidate the provisions of the youth protection laws for other industries connected with armaments."[22] Backsliding such as this led Martin Gumpert to denounce the labor protection laws of the Reich: "Behind a propaganda facade of humaneness there is the most shameless exploitation of child and youth labour which any legislator has ever dared to institute."[23]

Most of the protections implemented at this time were designed to prevent accidents, though physical injuries were by no means the only dangers. The escalating pace of work seems to have caused a rash of nervous ailments—especially ulcers and other stomach disorders—though it is hard to say how many of these were real and how many were pretenses on the part of workers attempting to gain relief from onerous work. Stomach disorders were notoriously difficult to confirm, making this the ideal bodily organ from which to spring a phony illness. A great deal of research went into how to determine when such complaints were real and when the worker was "dissimulating." Ernst W. Baader, director of Berlin's prestigious University Institute for Occupational Disease and a Nazi party member since 1933, accused physicians and insurance officials of collaborating in "swindles" of this sort to keep workers off the job.[24] Many physicians were convinced, however, that the increase in stomach disorders was real and a consequence of the increased pace of work. Initiatives were launched to make the work environment more comfortable; one outcome was the DAF's ocean cruise vacations for workers, organized as part of the *Kraft durch Freude* (power through joy) movement.

The guiding principle informing many of these measures was the maintenance of a strong and healthy workforce. Maximization of labor potential had always been a focus of occupational medicine, but in the Nazi era keeping workers on the job was elevated to the be-all and end-all of the discipline. Calling in sick became a rather precarious process, requiring medical approval and—if any time was involved—medical certification. Physicians were instructed to approve such requests only in exceptional cases, and only if the worker in question was clearly unable to work. After the onset of the war, when foreigners were doing much of the work in German factories and on German farms, a work-threatening illness could result in a life-threatening transport to a concentration camp.

The focus on productivity helps us understand how it was that, though injuries were up in the early years of the regime, the fraction of workers receiving compensation was down—from 14 percent in 1933 to only 9 percent in 1936. The number of industrial workers employed in Germany increased dramatically in these early years—by 2.25 million—but the number obtaining pensions for work disability actually fell, from 633 per year to only 532.[25] Nazi leaders wanted a healthy workforce, but they were not always willing to help an injured worker.

It is in this context that the "progressive" measures of occupational medicine in the Third Reich must be situated. Nazi leaders
in many instances took steps to improve workers' health and
safety, though not everyone was equal when it came to obtaining
help. Being sick or injured became more and more dangerous. Inability to work could itself become a death sentence, especially if
there were doubts about your "racial fitness."

X-Rays and Radiation Martyrs

Though X-radiation was not discovered until 1895, by the turn of
the century the "wonder rays" had already found uses in hundreds of clinical settings against every imaginable kind of illness.
X-rays were used to combat hysteria and infertility; X-rays were
administered to children, for no other reason than to precipitate
hair loss so that other diseases (ringworm, for example) could be
treated. X-rays and radium implants became fashionable tools in
cancer treatment, joining surgery in the therapeutic arsenal (che-
motherapy, the other branch of the therapeutic triad, would not
become popular until the 1950s). A 1937 review suggested that radiation had already surpassed surgery as the favored treatment for
many malignancies.[26]

Knowledge of a cancer hazard from X-rays and radioactive
sources—as opposed to burns, hair loss, and other symptoms of
acute radiation poisoning—emerged in the first decade of the
twentieth century.[27] Skin cancers of the hand were the first to be
noticed (especially among X-ray technicians, who often tested
the rays with their hands); these were followed by leukemias, bone
cancers, and cancers at various other sites. German physicians
published evidence of X-ray-induced breast cancer in 1919, of
X-ray-induced uterine and cervical cancer in 1923, and of X-ray-
induced bone cancer in 1930.[28] By the end of the 1920s there was a
sizable scientific literature on radiation carcinogenesis, including a
large body of work based on animal experiments.[29] X-rays even
began to be blamed for the upsurge in lung cancer rates: the chest
was rapidly becoming the most often X-rayed part of the body (the

point being to diagnose tuberculosis and other lung diseases), and some physicians worried that this could have epidemic cancer consequences.[30]

The overly precise dates of discovery I have mentioned for this or that radiation/cancer link conceal the fact that people suffering from a radiogenic cancer might linger over a period of decades, as the disease spread from one part of the body to another. A laboratory assistant who began X-ray work in 1897 in a surgical clinic in Breslau, for example, developed chronic X-ray eczema on his hands in 1899, and in 1908 developed two small cancers on his left index finger. These were removed, but tumors continued to appear: in 1911 on the little finger of his right hand, and nine years later on the ring finger of his other hand. In 1923 he had tumors removed from his left hand, along with the lymph glands from below his shoulder. The cancer continued to spread, and in 1927 he lost his entire left arm to the disease. His shoulder was removed in 1930, and he probably lost his life to the disease, though the published account stops at this point.[31] Many other professionals suffered a similar fate—the noted roentgenologist Guido Holzknecht, for example, and countless patients and technicians whose names we will never know.

Reports that X-rays could cause genetic damage began to be taken seriously in the 1920s. Fears were especially strong among German eugenicists, terrified that radiation might harm the German germ plasm.[32] Experimental evidence that X-rays could cause sterility had been around since 1903, when Heinrich Albers-Schönberg in Hamburg showed that X-rays could induce impotence in male rabbits,[33] but human evidence was not long in coming. In 1908, another young German radiologist found severe chromosomal damage in the fetus of a woman X-rayed thirty-three times to induce abortion.[34] By the early 1920s, German human geneticists were aware that an unusually large number of X-ray workers—including therapists and technicians—were sterile, and that X-ray mutagenesis was the most likely cause.[35] Scientists in other countries were encountering similar horrors: French scientists in 1923 published their first case of an *enfant des rayons X* (born with a deformed head after fetal irradiation),[36] and an American textbook shortly thereafter cautioned that "fetal monsters" could result from the X-raying of pregnant women.[37]

The response by several of Germany's leading racial theorists was to caution that excessive exposure to ionizing radiation could jeopardize Germany's biological future. Fritz Lenz, Germany's first professor of racial hygiene (and a Nazi party member as of 1937), warned in his widely read 1921 textbook on human heredity that X-rays and radioactive sources might cause genetic damage.[38] Eugen Fischer, founding director of Berlin's Kaiser Wilhelm Institute for Anthropology, Human Genetics, and Eugenics, in 1929 and 1930 cautioned that while many substances were suspected of being genotoxic (alcohol, nicotine, mercury, lead, and arsenic, for example), only X-rays had been shown conclusively to have this power. Fischer cited H. J. Muller's well-known demonstration that X-rays could mutate the sperm cells of the fruit fly, *Drosophila* (in 1927); he also noted that Emmy Stein working with Erwin Baur had earlier shown that radium could cause heritable defects in snapdragons (in 1922, published in 1926).[39] By the end of the decade there were dozens of reports testifying to the power of the rays to cause congenital injuries.[40]

Continuing evidence of congenital deformities from X-rays led physicians to argue for stronger radiation safeguards and for limits on the marriageability of exposed persons—to prevent them from breeding. A 1927 report in Germany's leading pediatric journal reviewed twenty cases of birth defects caused by X-rays, including severe deformities such as fetal microcephaly. One year later, Germany's leading journal of X-ray therapeutics described a child born with limb deformities similar to those observed in the embryos of irradiated mice; the child had been X-rayed in utero, prompting the deduction that the rays were to blame for the handicap.[41] Concerns such as these led the Bavarian Society for Pediatrics and Gynecology in 1927 to adopt a resolution recommending that women receiving extensive X-ray treatments while pregnant should have their fetuses aborted.[42] Professional eugenicists responded with equally imaginative proposals. Eugen Fischer in 1930 warned that women exposed to X-rays should be permanently barred from bearing children.[43] X-raying a woman's ovaries had become a popular method of inducing temporary sterility, both in Germany and in the United States. Racial hygienists saw this as a source of potentially devastating mutations; Hans Luxenburger, a eugenicist at Fischer's institute, in 1932 proposed the construction of an "archive of irradiated girls and women" to identify such women so they could be counseled against having children.[44]

Eugenicists' worries over the health effects of radiation have to be understood in light of the fact that many of the physicians using X-rays and radium sources displayed a rather cavalier attitude toward radiation health and safety. With no formal guidelines on dosages, injuries were common—especially in the early 1920s, when high-dose irradiation became a fashionable means of treating cancer, skin diseases, and countless other ailments. According to Hermann Holthusen, an influential Hamburg radiologist, there was in the mid-1920s "not a major hospital in Germany without patients suffering from the delayed effects of radiation" applied in the early years after the First World War and prior to the establishment of accurate dosimetry and meaningful tolerances.[45] Radiologic negligence was propelled by the fact that the professional societies organized by radiologists and radiotherapists were far more interested in promoting the use of X-rays—primarily as a diagnostic tool—than in warning against a possible health hazard. The Bavarian Society for Roentgenology and Radiology, for example, was founded in 1931 "to represent the economic interests of radiologists" and "to promote roentgenology and radiology." Radiation health and safety were only secondary concerns.[46]

Indeed, when it came to the question of whether to warn the public about possible long-term genetic damage, professional radiological societies were very clearly opposed. In 1931, when the German Genetics Society and the German Society for Racial Hygiene issued a formal warning that X-rays could cause genetic damage, the Bavarian Society for Roentgenology and Radiology produced a sharply worded rebuttal, noting that the eugenicists had relied "exclusively on experimental studies of insects and plants" to arrive at their conclusions. The society cautioned that the animal studies in question (the reference is clearly to Muller's work with fruit flies) could not be extrapolated to humans. It was

furthermore "extremely dangerous"—according to these early radiologists—to raise the specter of radiation hazards, given that
one might thereby impede the advance of X-ray therapeutics and
diagnostics.[47]

Professional radiologists, interestingly, had allies on this question among the leaders of the Association of Socialist Physicians,
Germany's most prominent left-wing medical association (driven
into exile shortly after the Nazi seizure of power in 1933, since
most of its members were Jewish).[48] Socialist physicians were
among the earliest and most avid critics of both Nazism and racial
hygiene; what may seem strange to us today, however, is that
some socialists ridiculed the specter of long-term health damage
from X-rays as yet another instance of racial scaremongering.
Julian Marcuse, writing in 1932 in the association's journal, derided the Nazi distrust of X-rays as "racial fanaticism": this, oddly
enough, is one of the first uses—perhaps the very first—of this expression in Germany.[49]

The fact that Nazi racial hygienists came out on the "right" side
of the X-ray/genetic damage issue—and that socialists scoffed at
the danger—may be surprising, but one should also realize that
the eugenicists' desire to limit radioactive exposure was no match
for the power of professional radiologists. The Nazis were afraid of
cancer, but they were even more afraid of tuberculosis, the second
leading cause of death in Germany until the mid-1920s (when cancer moved into this spot). In the 1930s, mass X-ray screenings were
implemented—of everyone in a factory, for example, or an entire
student class—to identify potential carriers of the TB bacillus. On
August 5, 1933, the *Deutsches Ärzteblatt* reported on a new requirement at the University of Munich that all students be X-rayed. The
sixty students found to be infected and contagious (among a thousand screened) were barred from university classrooms.[50] Similar
exams were required at other German universities, and in many
other contexts (see fig. 4.1). At the Nuremberg party congress of
September 1938, assembled dignitaries and the public all lined up
to have themselves X-rayed. The SS roentgenologist Prof. Dr. Hans
Holfelder of Frankfurt personally administered 10,500 X-rays to
SS men over a six-day period, an "unprecedented achievement."[51]

ufn.: Koch & Sterzel, Dresden

Reihenuntersuchung.

FIG. 4.1. Mass X-ray screening for lung disease. Despite eugenicists' fears of radiation damage, Germany becomes the most X-rayed nation in the world. Here, members of the Hitler Youth line up to receive a chest X-ray. Note the swastika-like Koch & Sterzel logo; many companies (e.g., Siemens-Reiniger) adopted similar logos ("pseudoswastikas") after 1933. Source: Reiter and Breger, *Deutsches Gold*, p. 414.

Mobile X-ray units were also deployed at German factories to screen workers for silicosis, though health officials were often aware that X-ray photography was not usually sensitive enough to identify early signs of the disease.[52]

Despite warnings by racial hygienists such as Fischer and Lenz, the number of people X-rayed increased dramatically under the Nazis. Proposals were put forward that the entire German population be screened for tuberculosis, and in some parts of the country that goal was apparently achieved.[53] In the spring and summer of 1939, for example, thanks to the efforts of the "SS X-ray battalion" (*Röntgenreihenbildnertruppe der SS*) headed by Holfelder, the entire adult population of Mecklenburg and Pomerania—everyone aged sixteen and over, roughly 650,000 people—received a chest X-ray. Special X-ray bulbs and photographic films were designed for this gargantuan effort, and some of the most heavily used devices produced as many as 100,000 photos during the operation. (Organizers claimed that 600 people per hour could be X-rayed by the newly developed methods.) Physicians coordinating the operation thanked the "disciplined intervention of the party"—especially the Nazi welfare organization (NS-Volkswohlfahrt)—for instilling a "100 percent positive attitude in the population." Gauleiter Friedrich Hildebrandt's office assumed the bulk of the cost, though participants also contributed a nominal sum of fifty pfennigs. X-rayees were also given the opportunity to purchase, for an additional twenty pfennigs, an enlarged copy of their interior image.[54]

The growing use of X-rays was often cited as an index of medical progress: a 1943 overview of medical research during the war boasted that Munich's university women's clinic had administered 50 percent more X-rays in 1942 than in 1937 (11,617 versus 7,528).[55] Mass screenings were implemented not just for TB, cancer, and silicosis but also for heart disease, stomach ailments, asbestosis, circulatory problems, and other diseases.[56] The process took on a quasi-military character during the war, when medical authorities sought to identify infirm workers who might infect other workers. The army itself became a major promoter of the practice, as special "X-ray troops" of the military medical command (under Albert Speer in at least one instance) X-rayed soldiers and civilians on the eastern front, looking for signs of lung or heart disease.[57] Mass X-ray screenings were also used to identify tubercular Poles, the original design being to exterminate them as "ballast lives" of no use to the Reich (that plan was apparently never carried out).[58]

A particularly brutal use of X-rays emerged in Auschwitz, where scientists performed experiments to determine whether X-rays might be used to prevent the breeding of racial undesirables. Exploration of this possibility began in 1941, when plans were already underway to exterminate the Jews of eastern Europe. SS Oberführer Viktor Brack proposed the sterilization of Europe's Jewry in a letter to Himmler of June 23, 1942:

> Among 10 millions of Jews in Europe there are, I guess, at least 2–3 millions of men and women who are fit enough to work. Considering the

extraordinary difficulties the labor problem presents us with, I hold the view that those 2–3 millions should be specially selected and preserved. This can, however, only be done if at the same time they are rendered incapable to propagate. About a year ago I reported to you that agents of mine had completed the experiments necessary for this purpose. I would like to recall these facts once more. Sterilization, as normally performed on persons with hereditary diseases, is here out of the question, because it takes too long and is too expensive. Castration by X-ray however is not only relatively cheap, but can also be performed on many thousands in the shortest time.[59]

Brack had earlier proposed that X-ray sterilization (castration) could be done surreptitiously:

One practical way of proceeding would be, for instance, to let the persons to be treated approach a counter, where they could be asked to answer some questions or to fill in forms, which would take them 2 or 3 minutes. The official sitting behind the counter could operate the installation in such a way as to turn a switch which would activate the two valves simultaneously (since the radiation has to operate from both sides). With a two-valve installation about 150–200 persons could then be sterilized per day, and therefore, with 20 such installations as many as 3,000–4,000 persons per day.[60]

Brack's grandiose scheme was never implemented; a series of experiments at Auschwitz by the gynecologist Horst Schumann determined that the people sterilized by this method were burned so severely they were no longer capable of work. Nearly all of the subjects of these experiments—at least a hundred people—were later killed.[61]

Given the exposures used and the scale of the mass screenings, it is not hard to imagine that hundreds or even thousands of people may have eventually contracted cancer from the procedures. Cancers must also have been caused by the use of X-rays for purposes of eugenic sterilization. A February 25, 1936, amendment of the Nazi Sterilization Law allowed the use of X-rays to sterilize women over the age of thirty-eight and women for whom the stan-

dard tubal ligation might be dangerous.[62] Eugenicists had earlier objected to the use of radiation as a form of temporary birth
control; permanent sterilization, by contrast, seemed morally,
medically, and racially unobjectionable. No one can say how many
cancers may have been caused by such exposures, especially since
many of the people sterilized were later killed in the "euthanasia
operation."

One must realize that at the same time that X-rays were being
used en masse to screen and to sterilize, physicians continued to
caution against the mutagenic effects of radiation. *Volk und Rasse*,
a leading racial monthly, in 1935 warned that physicians should
use "extreme care" in treating patients with radium and X-rays,
given the possibility of genetic damage, even from vanishingly
minute levels of exposure.[63] As two radiologists/racial hygienists
put the matter, "there is no threshold below which radiation exposure can be considered safe." (These authors also warned that genetic damage accumulated with every exposure and could be
passed on to future generations.)[64] A 1938 overview summarized
the danger in no uncertain terms:

> Every new mutation weakens the genetic profile (*Erbbild*) of the people
> and increases the number of inferior genes that already exist in a popu-
> lation. Careful and responsible action can protect us from endangering
> healthy people with radiation. The steps we must take are clear: famili-
> arity with the harmful properties of X-rays and radium, conservative
> and expert judgment in their use in diagnostics and therapy, and ade-
> quate radiation protection for everyone exposed in medicine and in in-
> dustry can all help limit the ill-effects of radiation on the human genetic
> heritage (*Erbgut*).[65]

Practical steps were taken to limit harms from excess or unregu-
lated exposures, the most important measure being the "X-Ray
Ordinance" (*Röntgenverordnung*) issued by the Reich Labor Ministry on February 7, 1941. The ordinance established exposure limits similar to those being established by other countries at this
time: the occupational "tolerance dose" (*Toleranzdosis*) of 0.25
roentgen per day, for example, was roughly comparable to that

recommended in the United States, though Germany seems to have been unique in specifying a tolerance dose ten times stricter (0.025 roentgen per day) "when there is a possibility of (germ-line) genetic damage."[66] In 1942, special regulations were established to govern nonmedical uses of X-ray technologies—as, for example, in the construction industry, where the rays were used to locate flaws in metal castings and other materials.[67] German regulations may have been more strictly followed than those promulgated elsewhere, judging from the massive outpouring of compliance literature produced in the wake of the law, detailing optimal levels of lead shielding, control of beam coherence, and so forth.[68] Anyone wishing to install or operate an X-ray machine had to demonstrate compliance with these regulations.[69]

Efforts also continued to document radiogenic cancer. In 1937, the journal *Strahlentherapie* (X-ray therapy) published a report of a woman who developed cancer in her larynx twenty years after receiving X-ray treatments for a thyroid disease. In 1938, the *Klinische Wochenschrift* described the course of a leukemia contracted by an X-ray laboratory assistant exposed for many years to the rays. In 1944, the *Zeitschrift für Krebsforschung* published the case of a thirty-year-old man with thyroid cancer who, at the age of six, had been X-rayed as part of a treatment for scrofula.[70]

Of course, concerns about health effects were never distributed equally. Radiologists who suffered harms were elevated to the status of "martyrs to science," as in April of 1936, when Hamburg radiologists unveiled a monument to commemorate the physicians who had perished from work with radium and X-rays (the monument still stands outside the St. Georg Hospital). One year later, the journal *Strahlentherapie* published an "honor roll" of 169 "roentgenologists and radiologists of all nations" who had given their lives or limbs to the cause.[71] American radiologists published similar lists (e.g., Percy Brown's of 1936)[72]—though martyrdom by this time was beginning to shift to embarrassment, as evidenced by American characterizations of the 1937 Congress of Radiology as a "congress of cripples."[73] In neither Germany nor America were monuments ever erected to commemorate the much larger number of patients and technicians who must have suffered.

Let me end this section by pointing out that therapy, diagnostics, and sterilization were not the only uses for X-rays under the Nazis. During the Second World War, as plans were underway to create a "radiologic bomb"—using conventional explosives to scatter hazardous radioisotopes—discussions were also begun concerning the construction of an X-ray weapon for use in aerial combat, the idea being that a sudden burst of X-rays might be enough to kill or injure the crew of an enemy's aircraft. A 1944 report submitted to the Luftwaffe Research Institute at Gross Ostheim outlined plans for such a weapon, though it is not yet clear whether the idea ever got past the drawing board. Wartime urgencies were straining budgets for many such schemes, though air force chief Hermann Göring as late as January 1945 was still instructing his engineers to take seriously the idea of "nuclear methods of defense against enemy bombers."[74]

RADIUM AND URANIUM

"Radioactivity," a term coined by the Polish-born Marie Curie and her French husband, Pierre, was discovered at the end of the nineteenth century—less than a year after X-rays—in the course of efforts to explain the fluorescence of uranium ores. The discovery is a classic one in the annals of serendipity: Henri Becquerel in Paris had been exposing uranium salts to sunlight to explore the phenomenon of luminescence, when by chance he noted that uranium even when unexposed had the power to darken photographic plates. Within a couple of years, Madame Curie and her associates had isolated two new elements, polonium and radium, both of which exhibited *radioactivity* (a term she coined) with emissions thousands of times more powerful than those of uranium.

Hoping to have discovered a medical tool equal in significance to X-rays, physicians developed various forms of "radium therapy" that soon joined X-rays in the roster of fashionable medical treatments. Radium therapy was as popular in Germany as it was in the United States; a 1935 list of medical uses for "radium emanation" (radon gas) or radium salts included: radium baths, radioactive bandages, radium compresses and pads, radium insoles (footpads), radium bath tablets, radium eczema cremes (an ointment known as Thorium-X, for example), and radium needle implants. Inhalation therapies were designed to mimic the vapors of radioactive baths, and radioactive tonics were sold along with mesothorium-impregnated milk sugar and even radium-infused chocolate. Radium cures were provided to treat infections, rheumatism, and neuralgia, but also hormonal disorders such as premature aging, arteriosclerosis, hypertension, and diverse nervous disorders, real and imagined ("paralysis agitans," for instance).[75]

Opinions often differed concerning the optimal dose for such treatments, but by modern standards we are talking about extraordinary exposures. A Prof. Friedrich Gudzent of Berlin administered daily doses of up to 100,000 ME of radium (about 3,640 picocuries in the system of reckoning Americans use today) in his "drink cures," while the Viennese radiologist Leopold Freund advised up to 300,000 ME (more than 10,000 picocuries).* Radium compresses involved placing 2–12 micrograms of radium directly onto the area of skin to be treated, and the intramuscular or intravenous injections recommended by Dr. Gudzent were in the neighborhood of 1–5 micrograms of radium every three days for total dosages of up to 100 micrograms.[76] A fatal dose of ingested or injected radium was commonly believed to be in the range of 100 to 500 micrograms, though there was also evidence from the U.S. dial painters that some of the women showing a bodily contamination of only 1–2 micrograms were experiencing symptoms

---

* A curie is the quantity of radiation emitted by a gram of pure radium, and a picocurie is a trillionth of a curie. American environmental agencies today measure indoor radon in terms of "picocuries per liter" (pCi/l); one pCi/l means that there are about two radioactive disintegrations of radon 222 for each liter of air every minute. The unit most commonly used in Germany in the 1920s and 1930s was the "Mache-Einheit" (ME), a unit equal in present-day American terminology to 364 picocuries. The unit more commonly used today in international scientific literature is becquerels/m^3, where 1 becquerel corresponds to one decay event per second (1 pCi/l = 37 Bq/m^3). Picocuries and becquerels are both measures of decay events per unit time; the biological effect of a given dose, however, depends to a great extent on the specific isotopes to which one is exposed and the route of exposure (ingestion, inhalation, etc.).

of radiation poisoning. We now know, it should be pointed out, that fatal cancers can be produced by even tinier doses.

One reason medical professionals may have been slow to appreciate the hazards of radioactivity is that German spas were heavily invested in promoting the curative virtues of radiation. Therapeutic baths were a vital part of the upper-middle-class conception of healing in the 1920s and 1930s (Thomas Mann's *Magic Mountain* captures some of this ethos), and the discovery of "radioactive emanation" in the water of many of these spas led to a belief that radon must be the active ingredient. Millions of Germans traveled to the radioactive spas of Kreuznach, Gastein, and Oberschlema in the first half of the twentieth century, hoping to be revitalized by the experience. (Some of these are still open today, with just as much radon to inhale.)

Enthusiasm for spa cures continued in the Nazi era, urged on as part of the romantic push for natural forms of healing. In 1934, the German Society for Spa- and Climate Healing (Deutsche Gesellschaft für Bäder- und Klimaheilkunde) launched an academic journal, *Der Balneologe*, to boost the baths. Different approaches to water therapy were reviewed—the Finnish practice of throwing water on granite to produce radon in sauna steam, for example—along with ads for healing centers like the Radiumbad St. Joachimsthal, promising help for arteriosclerosis, rheumatism, and gout.[77] Several of Germany's most famous spas had extremely high levels of radioactivity—like Oberschlema, with a radioactivity of five million picocuries per liter.[78]

Today, when we try to understand why it took so long for radioactive hazards to be taken seriously, it is worth recalling that radium, along with its "emanation," was widely regarded as the health-giving ingredient in mountain springs and spas. Even some of the industry's sharpest critics were seduced by the radiant atom. In 1932, for example, Erich Marx, a Leipzig professor of radiophysics, published an essay on "the radium danger in Germany" in a Viennese daily, cautioning that radium and radon gas could kill. Marx was aware that radon and its daughter products were responsible for the bronchial tumors contracted by Joachimsthal miners, that radium mimicked calcium in the body, and that radiation's deadly effects could show up years after exposure. He warned that small children were being asked to drink or inhale tonics containing dangerous levels of radium, and that chocolate bars were being marketed with up to 0.064 micrograms of the radioactive element. He reviewed the famous case of Eben Byers, the Pittsburgh iron magnate who had died from his daily infusion of radium, and he called for a ban on chocolates and tonics containing radium salts. Even Marx, though, was convinced that as long as a tonic did not contain radium *salts* (radon gas was OK) and the doses were kept within reason (he did not specify a level), then radon inhalation and ingestion would "doubtless" have "a health-promoting effect."[79]

The most notorious early cases of radiation poisoning were those suffered by the American radium dial painters. The tragedy is well known: at least a hundred women died from radiation poisoning after "pointing" (swirling and licking) their radium paint brushes in their mouths in the course of producing luminous faces for instrument dials and novelty items made to "glow in the dark." The women died horribly and painfully, from bone and mouth cancers often classed as "venereal ulcers" and only later recognized as occupational cancers.[80] Luminous dial painting was an important military industry in Germany, too, and grew increasingly important when blackouts were imposed after the beginning of Allied bombing in 1941.[81] Fewer women seem to have been affected, however, apparently because Germany had much stricter occupational health and safety practices. (As in the United States, radium dial painting in Germany was almost exclusively a female occupation.) Injuries were not unknown—three workers at a Berlin compress factory complained of fatigue and nervous disorders after working in air with a radium content of about 13 ME—but German dial painters do seem to have suffered less than their American counterparts. The difference appears to have stemmed from the fact that German women did not "point" their brushes in their mouths.[82]

The U.S. radium dial painting scandal was important in certain symbolic respects: the victims were women, the diseases were dramatic and debilitating, and sometimes fatal, but the numbers involved were fairly small—probably only about a hundred deaths and several thousand injuries. In Germany, very few women are known to have died from radium dial painting. By far the largest occupational cancer hazard from radioactivity was that faced by *miners*, especially the uranium-cobalt-silver miners in and around the Saxon town of Schneeberg, near the Czechoslovakian border. The "Ore Mountains" (*Erzgebirge*) south of Dresden had long been mined for rare metals, and high rates of lung cancer had been discovered on the German side of the border, in Schneeberg, in the 1870s.[83] Lung cancers were discovered at Joachimsthal on the Czech side of the mountains in the 1920s,[84] by which time suspicions had begun to grow that the root cause of the malignancy was not a TB germ or arsenic or silica dust or molds from rotting mine shaft supports, but radiation.[85]

Radium emanation had been found in the air of the mines as early as 1905 by Viennese scientists; measurements conducted after the First World War showed that air in different mines of the region could vary from 1 to 50 "Mache-Einheiten" per liter— roughly 400 to 20,000 pCi/l in the units used in the United States today.[86] A detailed and insightful epidemiological study published in 1926—using workers at an Oberschlema dye factory as a control, plus a separate control group from the general population— showed that 60–75 percent of the uranium miners in the region were (still) dying from lung cancer, a very high rate for what, at that time, was still a rare disease in the general population.[87] Rostoski, Saupe, and Schmorl's three-year study prompted the German government to classify the *Schneeberger Krankheit* (uranium miners' lung cancer) as a compensable occupational illness. The hazard was clearly a real one—though not everyone at the time agreed that radiation was the primary cause.

In the 1920s, evidence began to accumulate that radium-derived alpha radiation was responsible for the *Schneeberger Krankheit*. Animal experiments were undertaken to test some of the alternative hypotheses—that the disease was caused by fungi on wooden mine posts, for example, or by arsenic—but the results were ambiguous. Mice were fed or forced to breathe various dusts from the mine under laboratory conditions,[88] but experimenters found it difficult to mimic the mine environment in the lab, and lung cancers were not easily induced in experimental animals under any circumstances.

Interest in the question of what exactly was causing the *Schneeberger Krankheit* was renewed in 1933, when Schneeberg's mines were reopened in anticipation of a Nazi-inspired economic recovery. (Most had been closed in 1928 for economic reasons; the need for war-critical metals such as radium and tungsten boosted interest in the operations). Boris Rajewsky, director of Frankfurt's Institute for the Physical Foundations of Medicine and later an important health and safety officer in Germany's atom bomb project,* showed that radiation in the mines was often on the order of 10,000 pCi/l—an extraordinary level.[89] Erich Neitzel of Berlin, working for the Reich Labor Ministry, found similar results and concluded that long-term work in air containing even very low levels of radon could be dangerous. Neitzel was already aware that the primary danger came not so much from the gas itself, but

---

* Rajewsky in February of 1943 was awarded a grant from the Army Weapons Office (Heereswaffenamt) to investigate "the biological effects of corpuscular radiation, including neutrons, with regard to the possibility of their use as a weapon." The weapon in question was a conventional explosive surrounded by highly radioactive nuclear waste intended primarily for use against American civilian populations. The bomb was originally intended to be delivered as the payload in the two-stage A9/10 intercontinental rocket (the "New Yorker"), a gargantuan missile planned for launch from silos in France. With the suspension of the A9/10 in October of 1942, efforts were concentrated on delivery by smaller rockets launched from submarines. The radionuclides used for the bomb had to be chemically separated from nuclear reactor waste products, a hazardous procedure for which thousands of forced laborers from concentration camps were conscripted. In September of 1943, the Army Weapons Office forced 15,000 inmates from Buchenwald and Natzweiler and 2,000 engineers to construct a huge subterranean factory at Niedersachswerfen in the Harz Mountains to assemble the radiologic bombs. Construction of the *SS-Mittelwerk*, as the new facility was known, was supervised by SS-Brigadeführer Hans Kammler, who had earlier supervised the construction of the Auschwitz satellite camp at Birkenau. V-2 rockets and V-4 bombs were both assembled in the facility, the largest underground factory in the world. Geoffrey Brooks in his history of the project notes that the radiation protection provided for the prisoners "is best left to the imagination"; see his *Hitler's Nuclear Weapons*, pp. 68 and 122–25.

rather from its "daughter products" (the offspring of radioactive decay), which tend to lodge in the lungs, where they continue to emit radiation.[90] Experiments were launched to determine how much radioactivity was present in the urine and exhaled air of miners, and how the radioactivity of the air varied with changing weather conditions.[91]

Experiments were also performed that finally produced—for the first time anywhere—lung cancers in animals raised in the mines. Julius Löwy had failed at this task as recently as 1936: the German-Jewish professor in Prague had earlier, in 1929, been the first to show that the disease faced by Joachimsthal miners was the same as the *Schneeberger Krankheit*;[92] in 1936, however, he reported that the rabbits and rats he had forced to breathe pitchblende dust had all died from the acute effects of radiation.[93] Arthur Brandt, an industrial physician working for the government in Dresden, was apparently the first to reproduce the cancer hazard under laboratory conditions. His results, published in 1938, showed that 25 percent of the mice raised for one year in the shafts evidenced tumors upon dissection.[94] This was the first conclusive animal experimental evidence that breathing air in the mines could cause lung cancer.

Radon by this time was generally regarded as the most likely cause of the *Schneeberger Krankheit*. The chief physician of the German Labor Front, Hermann Hebestreit, stated unequivocally in a 1939 review that "the lung cancer of the Joachimsthal uranium miners is traceable to exposure to radioactive materials."[95] Not everyone agreed: Franz Strnad in Prague in 1938, for example, stated that while radium emanation (radon) was the most likely cause of the *Schneeberger Krankheit*, the issue was "not yet finally decided."[96] The more common view, however, was that radon was in fact the primary cause. Germans were the first in the world to recognize—officially—that radon was the cause of the uranium miners' lung cancer; American health officials as late as the 1950s, by contrast, were still questioning the link. German uranium miners were obtaining compensation for occupational lung cancers by the end of the 1920s; Americans had to wait until the passage of the Radiation Exposure Compensation Act in 1991.[97]

What is also interesting, though, is how even inside Germany different professional communities came to very different views concerning the capacity of radiation to heal or to harm. Occupational health physicians recognized early on that radon was the most likely cause of miners' lung cancer, but spa health physicists—often working in the immediate proximity of the mines—tended to argue that the radioactive gas was more likely to heal the body than to harm it. Spa health physicists by 1939 had published evidence that even a millionth of a gram of radium lodged in the body could lead to death, but they usually maintained that the radon breathed in spas (e.g., from mineral springs) was entirely safe. Elaborate theories were put forward to explain how radon enlivened the body: a 1938 review of German radon therapy, for example, claimed that the radioactive gas "promotes oxidation" and "stimulates cells and tissues without injuring them very much." Radon therapy was described as "a special form of shock therapy," awakening and augmenting the body's own natural healing powers.[98]

Nazi ideology, of course, placed a higher value on certain people's health than on others, and this can be seen in correspondence concerning whom to employ in the mines. On November 19, 1938, SS Oberführer and Regierungspräsident Hans Krebs wrote to Himmler, asking him to install concentration camp prisoners in Joachimsthal to free "our poor Sudeten German miners" from work that was killing them in their forties. Himmler agreed on the condition that the prisoners be released after two to three years if they showed good conduct, though it is not yet clear whether such proposals were ever implemented.[99]

One thing we do know is that tens of thousands of political prisoners worked in the Joachimsthal mines after the war, producing 90,000 tons of uranium for the Soviet atomic arsenal and many thousands of deaths from lung cancer.[100] The Schneeberg mines were also exploited, generating an estimated 200,000 tons for the Soviet nuclear effort (sold cheap to the Russians as part of Germany's war reparations). These were enormous undertakings: the uranium mining operation in East Germany alone, for example (code-named *Wismut*—literally "bismuth" in both German and

Russian) in 1949 employed 80,000 men and women, many of whom had started work as forced laborers.[101] More than half a million people eventually worked for *Wismut* at one time or another, until the unification of Germany in 1989 closed most of the shafts.[102]

The Schneeberg area is now the target of Europe's largest environmental cleanup, an effort to bring to an end one of the world's most horrendous health and safety nightmares. In the early 1990s, the director of Germany's Federal Office of Radiation Protection forecast an eventual death toll among miners in the Schneeberg region in the neighborhood of 10,000 to 15,000 from radiation-induced lung cancer, and perhaps twice this many from silicosis.[103] (DDR health officials had already recognized 5,200 lung cancer deaths caused by radiation exposure prior to 1989.)[104] Radon is also high in the houses built on or near the abandoned tunnels riddling the region. German environmental authorities recommend no more than 250 Bq per cubic meter of indoor air, but houses have been found with four hundred times that level. As in certain parts of the United States, radon is common even in homes some distance from the mines—a consequence of the natural seepage from rocks and soils underlying foundations.[105]

Another interesting aspect of the Schneeberg uranium story is that the Americans who originally occupied the area were seemingly unaware of its military significance. American officials were divided over whether it would be possible to monopolize the postwar supply of uranium: General Leslie R. Groves in 1945 maintained that there was "no uranium in Russia," though James B. Conant and Vannevar Bush, administrators of the Manhattan Project, advised war secretary Henry L. Stimson as early as the fall of 1944 that it would not be hard for foreign nations to gain access to bomb-grade metal.[106] American officials seem to have overlooked the uranium in the region, perhaps because the abortive German atomic bomb project had neglected domestic sources in favor of Belgian Congo deposits.

The oversight is curious, given that fear of German control of the Joachimsthal mines had originally stimulated Albert Einstein to draft his famous letter to President Roosevelt about the possibility of a Nazi bomb. Compounding the oddity is the fact that J. Robert Oppenheimer, the man chosen to coordinate the Manhattan Project (and "father of the atomic bomb"), had actually written his senior thesis at the Ethical Culture School in New York on the mines at Joachimthal. Joachimsthal had monopolized the world's supply of radium prior to the First World War—and still had at least a century's supply left, according to a German cancer journal report of 1938[107]—making it strange indeed that U.S. authorities missed the atomic potential of the region. USSR officials were more astute: Soviet geologists were sent to Schneeberg to prospect for uranium in June of 1945, prior even to the end of the war in Asia. The Soviets did not assume control over the region until the end of that summer, when American armies retreated in exchange for a Soviet withdrawal from West Berlin. Recognition of the presence of uranium in the area may even have been a factor in the Soviet willingness to make the exchange. By January of 1946 the Soviets had completed their survey of the region, and by the summer of that year plans were in place to begin extracting uranium.[108] American military officials must have eventually regretted the oversight: in 1953, AEC chairman Gordon Dean wrote that the Joachimsthal mines alone "could support a sizeable atomic energy program."[109]

ARSENIC, CHROMIUM, QUARTZ, AND OTHER KINDS OF DUSTS

X-rays, radium, and uranium were not the only areas where German health leaders took early steps to combat an occupational hazard. German factory physicians had long been warning against the dangers of dust inhalation: by the end of the nineteenth century, for example, there were already concerns about sanding and inhaling lead-based paint, and awareness of silicosis—caused by inhalation of very fine particles of quartz—followed shortly thereafter. Labor activism was important in the new generation of concerns, but improved drilling, grinding, and cutting technologies were the root material cause of the problem, exposing workers to unprecedented levels of dust. Pneumatic drills and hammers, along with new electrically powered cutting and grinding tools of endless variety, raised much more dust than hand-powered tools, resulting in dust diseases (from asthma and TB to lung cancer) on a scale never seen before.

The most notorious early dust diseases had nothing to do with cancer. Acute toxic poisonings were the more immediate problem, given the absence of effective sanitary regulations and the willingness of many laborers to accept dangerous work. Cancer was only one of dozens of hazards that a nineteenth-century miner, grinder, or dye-mixer might face, and many did not live long enough to contract a malignancy.

Carcinogens were also obscured, however, by the long time lag—or "latency"—between exposure and the appearance of malignancy. Time delays of this sort had been observed in the nineteenth century, in the context of investigating chimney sweeps' cancer,[110] but it was not until the twentieth century that we find discussions of latency as a general feature of carcinogenesis. Rostoski, Saupe, and Schmorl in the 1920s recognized that miners in Schneeberg or Joachimsthal would generally work for ten or twenty years in the mines before coming down with lung cancer; they also noted that at least one of the victims had not worked underground for twenty-two years prior to being diagnosed.[111] Latencies were eventually recognized for many other kinds of cancer: Cecil W. Rowntree in England in 1922, for example, said that it could take up to seventeen years for cancer to develop after X-ray exposure. The conclusion drawn from this and other reports—from petroleum and chromate factories, for example—was that cancers generally do not appear until years or even decades after exposure.[112]

Chromium was one of the first metallic dusts to be designated a carcinogen, following the 1911 observation that chromate workers were falling ill and dying from lung cancer.[113] Chrome plating was becoming fashionable, and chromium salts and oxides were also beginning to be used in many popular dyes and paints. Injured workers began to be noticed toward the end of the nineteenth century, and by 1911 an entire book could be written about the perils of the industry.[114] A 1936 study showed that in the preceeding ten years, 40 percent of all workers in a Griesheimer chemical plant (where chromium sulfate and other industrial chemicals were produced) had developed lung cancer. The author predicted that "every important chromate factory in Germany will have lung cancers among its workers."[115]

Arsenic inhalation was a much older concern. In 1822 John A. Paris, a fellow of the Royal Society of London and a senior physician at Westminster Hospital, had reported skin cancers among Welsh and Cornish workers exposed to arsenic fumes in copper smelters and tin foundries. Animals were also said to have been affected—horses and cows in the region were seen crawling on their knees in pain from tumors.[116] People treated with potassium arsenite for psoriasis were found to have a higher-than-average risk of skin cancer in the 1870s, and communities where people drank arsenic-contaminated water were said to have above-average cancer rates.[117]

In the 1920s, concerns about poisoning arose when arsenic-based pesticides began to be sprayed onto vineyards to combat insect pests. Aerial spraying began shortly after the First World War, prompted not just by the wartime improvement of biplanes but also by growing recognition that some of the newer varieties of vines were especially vulnerable to pests. By 1929, Germany was producing 1,500 tons of arsenic, most of which was misted onto vineyards. German wine production grew by 60 percent from 1929 to 1938, the large part of which was attributed to the rising use of arsenic pesticides.[118] Poisonings were also increasingly common. The pesticide showed up in both wine and grape juice, but also in the dusts churned up when treated fields were plowed.[119]

Chronic arsenic poisoning had been recognized as an occupational disease prior even to the First World War; the affliction—especially among glass- and steelworkers—was one of the first occupational ailments requiring official notification, along with poisoning by lead, mercury, and phosphorus.[120] Arsenic poisoning was recognized as an occupational disease in Germany's Occupational Disease Ordinance (*Berufskrankheitenverordnung*) of 1925, along with eight other classes of poisonings warranting governmental compensation (lead, phosphorus, mercury, benzene, aromatic nitro compounds, carbon disulfide, X-rays and radioactive substances, and carcinogens such as paraffin, tar, anthracene, and pitch that primarily affect the skin).[121] Workers in the glass and steel industries were the best-known early sufferers from arsenic poisoning, but vineyard exposures were increasingly serious. Ernst W. Baader in 1929 called for the chemical industry to find a substitute for its use as a pesticide, and in 1937 argued that even in very low doses it could cause cancer (he also claimed that cancer was more common around factories releasing arsenic into the environment). Karl Reinhart in 1943 surveyed the situation, noting that by 1940 there were 589 verified cases of arsenic poisonings among vintners, including several cancers.[122] The problem began to soften somewhat in 1940, when insecticides such as pyrethrum and chrysanthol were introduced, replacing arsenic (nicotine sprays were also encouraged).[123] The Nazi party Chancellery banned the use of arsenic pesticides in February of 1942, allowing vintners to use up their stocks by June 30, 1942.[124] Vintners had earlier been barred from applying compounds containing lead. Arsenic pesticides were still allowed on nongrape crops such as strawberries and tomatoes, but strict precautions specified when and how workers might spray, what they were to wear, and so forth.[125]

German industrial hygienists generally recognized that while exposure to any dust was harmful, the worst in terms of the numbers of people affected was probably quartz or silica dust. Silicosis—the German is *Quarzstaublunge*, literally "quartz dust lung"—was regarded as the king of occupational lung disease, killing more, it was said (and perhaps rightly so) than all other dusts combined. Hundreds of scientific articles on the topic can be found in the German medical literature of the 1930s, describing everything from the maximally hazardous particle size to a possible cancer link.[126] Silicosis was a hazard wherever one inhaled quartz dust, but especially in iron foundry work (sand was used to make the molds for casting liquid pig iron), in work with quartz-based scouring powders (Comet Cleanser contains abrasive quartz), in porcelain or brick manufacture, in mining and sandblasting, and in other work involving exposure to sand or rock dust. The development of power-driven stone-cutting tools—the pneumatic hammer, for example, introduced around the time of the First World War—had dramatically increased exposure to rock dust, a fact well known to German factory physicians in the 1930s.[127]

Otto Schulz, medical director of Berlin's University Institute for Occupational Disease, pointed out in 1939 that one or two years of work in a dusty trade was often sufficient to bring on the disease, and that symptoms would typically not even begin until after exposures had ceased. Schulz drew attention to the "horrifying example" of Gauley Bridge, West Virginia, where hundreds of African Americans had died of acute silicosis following dust inhalation during the building of a Union Carbide tunnel. He also noted the economic toll exacted by the disease in Germany: from 1929 through the end of the 1930s, more than sixty million reichsmarks had been paid to silicotic workers or their relatives in accordance with Germany's occupational health and safety laws. Schulz called for a "solution to the dust problem" (*Lösung des Staubproblems*) involving regular checkups of workers and mandatory transfer of anyone showing early signs of the disease. Action was needed since "a great deal of valuable human material" (*Menschengut*) was being lost to the malady.[128]

Steps were taken early in the Nazi era to combat dust diseases in German industry. On April 4, 1934, a Dust Control Office (Staubbekämpfungsstelle) was established by the quarrymen's union (Steinbruchs-BG) to coordinate the struggle; the office explored new ways of constructing hoods and vacuum devices, new kinds of filters and ventilators, and new ways to service safety devices. In Thuringia, the office worked with the slate roofing industry to lower the dust involved in splitting slate and to reduce the dust inhaled by stonemasons and workmen handling cement, sand, and lime. Workers in many of these industries (sandblasters, for example) were required to undergo periodic medical exams for early signs of silicosis, though reservations were also expressed about how early such ailments could be diagnosed.[129] Much of the protective gear was still rather cumbersome (as it remains today, I might add), though improvements were made in the quality and comfort of masks. Synthetic abrasives were substituted for the more hazardous stone abrasives in the metal-cutting industry, and scuba-like breathing gear was introduced for high-risk industries, like sandblasting.[130] The office established a laboratory to test different kinds of masks; it also formed a special committee to explore innovations in mask design.[131] A journal devoted to research in the area of dust control technology was established in 1936 (*Staub: Reinhaltung der Luft*); it appeared until 1943 and was continued after the war by the Dust Research Institute of Dusseldorf. *Staub* was one of more than two dozen new health-related journals launched in the Nazi period.

Cancer was an occasional concern of the German industrial hygienists who worried about silicosis. A 1934 dissertation explored the coincidence of silicosis and lung cancer, the primary question being whether the quartz dust inhaled by Ruhr Valley coal miners could cause malignancies. Though the results of this particular study were negative (silicosis did not seem to predispose to lung cancer), the prescience of the interest is notable.[132] Research was also undertaken into the cancer-causing potential of sericite (a silky-green mica used in industry)[133] and the silicosis-producing potential of fiberglass.[134]

The question of whether silica exposure could cause cancer was never resolved in the Nazi era—and remains confused even today, more than half a century later. What was fairly clearly resolved, and earlier in Germany than anywhere else, was the deadly malignant force of asbestos.

THE FUNERAL DRESS OF KINGS (ASBESTOS)

One of the most remarkable aspects of dust research in this era was the recognition of a cancer hazard from asbestos. Asbestos is a magnesium silicate, but the dusts produced are long and fibrous—so much so that the mineral can actually be woven into fire-resistant fabrics. Charlemagne is said to have feasted on a tablecloth made from the substance, amazing guests by tossing the cloth after repast into the fire, from which it would later be withdrawn, unharmed. Medieval kings were cremated in a sealed shroud of asbestos—only the bones were left behind, clean and intact—earning for it the title of "magic mineral" and the "funeral dress of kings."

The same qualities that make it weavable, however, also make it deadly. The long tiny fibers are easily wafted into the air, inhaled, and trapped in the lungs, where they can remain for years, causing a slow and steady scarring known as *asbestosis*. The first modern medical description of the disease dates from England at the end of the nineteenth century, though asbestos was also worked in the ancient world and must have caused many deaths and infirmities.[135] Victims suffocate—or drown—from lung constriction and associated complications; the feeling is reportedly something akin to having an iron band slowly tightened around your chest.

Germany was never a major producer of raw asbestos, which may explain why asbestosis fatalities were not identified there until 1914, by which time English and American interest in the topic was already well underway. Germans tended to manufacture finished asbestos products, which is how workers there first began to contract the disease. Asbestos in these early years was commonly referred to as *Bergflachs*—literally "mountain flax"—and asbestosis soon became known as *Bergflachslunge* or "mountain flax lung,"[136] a rather rustic euphemism for such a devastating scourge.

The possibility of a cancer hazard was not suspected until the 1930s, by which time tens of thousands of workers—especially in the shipbuilding industry—were routinely handling the fiber. Naval officials were intrigued by its insulating and fire-resistant properties: asbestos was used, among other things, to insulate steam pipes and to seal and fireproof steam-engine boilers. Asbestos was used for brake shoes and clutch facings; it was also used to strengthen cement, to fireproof paints and textiles, and to render building materials fire-resistant (roofing and floor tiles, for example).

Recognition of a lung cancer danger came in 1938, when three German papers and an Austrian review provided strong evidence of a link.[137] An occasional association of asbestos and lung cancer had earlier been reported in both England and America,[138] but the German reports were the most comprehensive and convincing up to that time, and the most definite in their conclusions.[139] Franz Koelsch in his contribution noted that the twelve lung cancers thus far tied to asbestosis, while suggestive, did not absolutely prove the link; but others were not so reticent. Ludwig Teleky in Vienna reasoned that it was "extremely likely" that asbestosis was a predisposing factor for lung cancer.[140] The Hanover pathologist Martin Nordmann made the strongest case of the lot: lung cancer for him was an established hazard of asbestos workers, afflicting roughly 12 percent of those who suffer from asbestosis. Nordmann concluded that "a new occupational cancer" had arrived in Germany.[141]

By this time, German labor authorities had already taken steps to reduce the risk posed to workers handling the fiber—based on longer-standing knowledge of the scarring hazard. Asbestos was a major target of an "antidust campaign" launched in 1936.[142] New kinds of ventilators were introduced, and the dirtiest jobs were moved under hoods whence dust could be drawn away from the workplace. In 1937, a Subcommittee for Asbestosis was founded by the Labor Ministry in collaboration with the German Society for Labor Protection; headed by Ernst Baader, with members expert in mineralogy, dust technology, insurance engineering, clinical medicine, pathology, and physiology, the committee explored how the disease arose and how it might be prevented. Manufacturing sites were inspected, whereupon it was found that the highest exposures were in the early stages of production, when the mineral was pounded, shredded, and carded. The newly invented *Übermikroskop* (the Siemens company's electron microscope, with a magnifying power in the tens of thousands—see fig. 4.2) was used to address the question of whether asbestosis arose from chemical or mechanical irritation (extremely small fibers were found in lung tissues, suggesting a mechanical irritation).[143] Ventilation technologies were recommended, and workers in many factories were screened for the disease—usually by X-rays but sometimes also blood and urine tests. Gunther Lehmann's bizarre scheme of measuring nasal filtration capacity was evaluated to see whether this could be used to determine who was more or less susceptible to asbestos-related disease (the experts were not enthusiastic).[144]

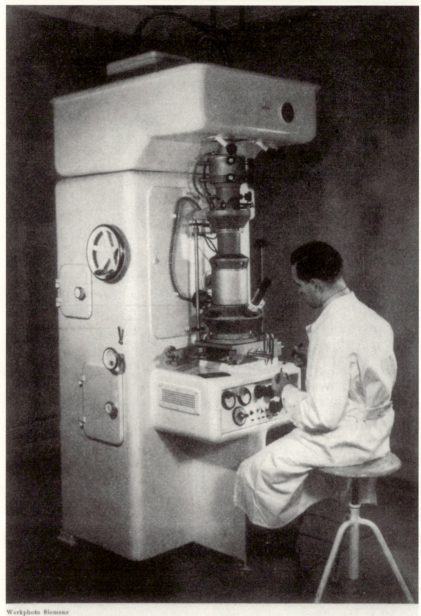

Werkphoto Siemens

Siemens-Übermikroskop für 4000- bis 40 000fache Vergrößerungen (vgl. S. 505).

FIG. 4.2. The Siemens company's electron microscope (*Übermikroskop*), with a magnifying power of 4,000 to 40,000, used to identify asbestos particles in lung tumors. Source: Reiter and Breger, *Deutsches Gold*, p. 476.

Recognition of a lung cancer hazard spurred occupational authorities to strengthen dust exposure standards. On August 1, 1940, the Baader subcommittee issued formal guidelines specifying acceptable levels of dust and techniques to be used in its reduction. The guidelines barred anyone under eighteen from working with asbestos and reaffirmed the cancer danger.[145] Research also continued into the mechanisms of carcinogenesis. A 1942 article by a student of Nordmann's, Alfred Welz, reported a lung cancer in a worker who had worked only four years with the fiber.[146] One year later, Hans-Wilfrid Wedler of Berlin published a paper showing that asbestos workers were prone to suffer from a rare form of cancer known as mesothelioma, a cancer of the tissues ("pleura") lining the outside of the lung.[147]

Germany by this time had become the world's undisputed leader in documenting the asbestos–lung cancer link. A 1939 textbook—Wedler's—was the first anywhere to state there was "not the slightest doubt" (*kaum ein Zweifel daran*) that asbestos in the lungs could cause cancer.[148] In 1941, Nordmann and his Hanover colleague, Adolf Sorge (a Nazi party member and SS officer), produced the first animal experimental evidence that asbestos could cause lung cancer (see fig. 4.3). Laboratory mice had been exposed to asbestos dust over a period of several weeks, and 20 percent of the surviving mice had developed tumors (a much higher percentage had developed precancerous growths).[149] A 1942 review praised the Hanover scholars' work, contrasting their affirmation of a hazard with the "reluctance" (*grosse Zurückhaltung*) of English and American scientists to admit a danger.[150] Nordmann himself noted that the head of Germany's Subcommittee for Asbestosis—Ernst Baader—was fully convinced of the reality of the cancer threat.[151]

In 1943, the Nazi government became the first to recognize asbestos-induced mesothelioma and lung cancer as compensable occupational diseases.[152] U.S. attorneys would later use this Nazi-era research to prove that knowledge of an asbestos-cancer link predated the time when Johns-Manville and other asbestos producers claimed they could first have become aware of the hazard.[153] German experts in occupational medicine—even in major industries

tem Chrysotilasbest gefüllt und durch eine motorbetriebene Turbine aufgewirbelt. Zwischen dem Asbestraum und dem Aufenthaltsraum

Abb. 1. Bestäubungskammer. In der kleinen Abteilung aufgewirbelter, gekrempelter Asbest, in der großen Abteilung in dichtem Staub die Versuchsmäuse.

der Mäuse befand sich eine Zwischenwand mit feinen Bohrungen, so daß während des Betriebes ein dichter Staub durch die Löcher und

FIG. 4.3. Martin Nordmann and Adolf Sorge, pathologists at the University of Hanover, used this device to show that inhaled asbestos dust could cause lung tumors in mice. The team also chided their English and American colleagues for failing to recognize a human asbestos cancer hazard. Both men were in the Nazi party; Sorge was an officer in the SS. Source: Martin Nordmann and Adolf Sorge, "Lungenkrebs durch Asbeststaub im Tierversuch," *Zeitschrift für Krebsforschung* 51 (1941): 170.

like I. G. Farben—had recognized the cancer hazard by the early 1940s;[154] popular health manuals also advertised the link.[155]

Why, then, did it take so long, outside Germany, for the lung cancer–asbestos link to be taken seriously?

What we have to reckon with is both the conservatism built into postwar epidemiology and the postwar political disregard for all things German, the *stigma* of Nazism. This latter point is fairly straightforward; as Philip Enterline suggests in his history of asbestos cancer: "German literature and German laws were not very popular in 1943,"[156] and for some time thereafter.

The epidemiologic point, however, is more subtle. To begin with, the science of epidemiology as developed in the 1950s required large numbers of "cases" (e.g., of lung cancers among people working with asbestos)—which were not always available to early asbestos researchers. Even after Nordmann's 1938 study, the sum total of *all* the world's known asbestos cancers was only six (Nordmann had added two new cases). Epidemiologists were not impressed. As late as 1956, American epidemiologists could claim there were "too few cases and too little epidemiologic data to establish a significant relationship" between lung cancer and asbestos; the prestigious *Journal of the American Medical Association* even in 1961 concluded there was still "no epidemiological evidence" of an association.[157] The difficulty was not just industrial obstinacy or epidemiologic myopia or distrust of German science (though all of these were involved); the difficulty was also in the new methods of obtaining scientific proof. The Nazi scholars who, two decades earlier, had claimed to have established the link relied not on epidemiology but on clinical and pathological insights. Clinicians examining patients and pathologists dissecting corpses had noticed asbestotics coming down with the disease, but also that lung cancers were most often found in those parts of the lungs where the inhaled fibers tended to concentrate (especially the lower lobes). Detailed study of individual cases was sufficient, for these early scholars, to generate reliable conclusions about causality.

Postwar epidemiologists and biostatisticians set little store by evidence of this sort. (Richard Doll even today ridicules Nordmann's claim to have "proven" the asbestos-cancer link by examining only two individual cases.)[158] The "higher" standard of proof required by the new field of epidemiology prejudiced scholars against the insights gained through clinical investigations, a loss Chris Sellers has characterized as "the vanishing clinician's eye."[159] The net effect in the field of cancer research was to slow recognition of the asbestos hazard: the consensus achieved in Germany in the early 1940s would not obtain in Britain or the United States until more than two decades later. Science and political stigma thus conspired—at least for a time—to confine the truth to shadows.

CHEMICAL INDUSTRY CANCERS

Chemical industry cancers are seemingly much less common than other kinds of cancer: over the course of the entire twentieth century, for example, there have been only about a thousand officially recognized cases of aniline dye bladder cancers in Germany—and aniline cancer is usually regarded as one of the more prominent occupational tumors. Numbers such as these are deceptive, however, since they include only cases recorded by factory physicians and registered with governmental health authorities. Even today, there is a great deal of debate over what proportion of cancers arise on the job, with estimates ranging from "negligible" to as many as a third of all cancers afflicting chemical industry employees.[160] However one plays the percentages game, the actual number of cancers is doubtless many times higher than has been recorded.[161]

Nazi medical interests in chemical industry cancers were often contradictory. Many health officials appear to have been genuinely worried about occupational health, but the rapid buildup of the arms industry and the single-minded focus on production eventually shifted attention away from cancer hazards. Efforts to eliminate illness turned into efforts to eliminate sick workers from the factory, from the hospital, and in certain cases from life itself. The war on disease turned into a war on the diseased. As one prominent Nazi doctor put it after the war, Nazi physicians wanted "to eliminate sickness by eliminating the sick."[162] I. G. Farben's Auschwitz plant put this into practice by never allowing more than 5 percent of its total workforce (all of whom were slave laborers) to be hospitalized at any given time. When the 5 percent figure was exceeded, camp physicians performed a selection, and the unfortunate selectees were sent to Birkenau and gassed.[163]

In this final section, I would like to look at one of the oldest and best-known occupational cancers: industrial bladder cancer. The malady was discovered in aniline dye workers in the 1890s by a Frankfurt surgeon—Ludwig Rehn—who had observed a disturbingly high incidence of the disease among his patients.[164] It is not surprising that Germans should have made the discovery, since German chemical factories up until the First World War were producing more than 80 percent of the world's aniline, aniline-derivatives, and aromatic amines—the crucial ingredients in synthetic dyes. Rehn had noticed three workers with the disease (in a factory with forty-five employees) some twenty years after the production of synthetic dyes had begun in earnest. Rehn himself did not draw out the point, but what soon became apparent was that cancers of this sort typically become visible ten or twenty years after the onset of exposure. Wilhelm Hueper eventually showed that bladder cancers were appearing in every nation with a synthetic dye industry, almost like clockwork.[165]

Germany's 1925 ordinance governing occupational disease (the *Berufskrankheitenverordnung*) required that protective measures be adopted.[166] I. G. Farben that year implemented a system by which workers were required to change both before and after work to avoid bringing contaminated clothing into their homes; new production processes were also introduced to minimize human contact with carcinogens (the so-called closed system of manufacturing). These and other measures led to claims that aniline bladder cancer was "a thing of the past," a premature boast with at best a political or public relations value.

As it turned out, German physicians actually continued to document bladder cancers throughout the 1930s. In 1938, Martin Staemmler, an influential Nazi doctor and friend of Reich Physicians' Führer Gerhard Wagner, pointed out that there were still dye factories in Germany in which a quarter of the workforce was falling ill from the disease—a risk roughly comparable to that faced by tar workers. This was in stark contrast to official records for that year, according to which there were only twelve new occupational cancers of all kinds for the entire nation.[167] Wilhelm Hueper in his 1942 *Occupational Tumors* cited Staemmler's estimate of five or six new cases of bladder cancer every year in Germany, a surprisingly high figure (in his view) for a country where the control measures were "not only the most thorough and extensive so far undertaken anywhere, but have been in operation over a longer period than in any other country."[168]

Nazi labor leaders were often ambivalent about what should be done to stop occupational cancers. German fascists wanted healthy workers, but they also wanted a peaceful and productive atmosphere on the shop floor. Factory health precautions might require expensive equipment redesign or time-consuming changes in the production process. Labor officials were reluctant to point to life-threatening industrial hazards—especially during the war, when factories were geared up for weapons production. Occupational health authorities focused less and less on cancer as the war dragged on: the 1944 volume of the journal *Arbeitsmedizin*, for example, discussed at great length how, when, and what workers should eat, but made no mention of cancer. A 1940 article in *Ziel und Weg*, the official journal of the National Socialist Physicians' League, proclaimed that there had "not been a single case" of occupational bladder cancer in Germany in fifteen years—contradicting Staemmler's more honest paper of only two years previously. This rosy proclamation by I. G. Farben's chief industrial physician was later shown even by the company's own cancer registry to be false; *Ziel und Weg*'s collaboration in this duplicity suggests that there may have been pressures not to air such dirty linens in public.[169]

When bladder cancer *was* discussed, it was often in the context of how to weed out workers judged particularly "vulnerable" to the disease. We have already seen how industrial hygienists such as Wilhelm Hergt prior even to 1933 seized on the idea that different racial or constitutional body types respond differently to carcinogenic exposures. In 1930 and 1932, the head physician of I. G. Farben's Institute for the Research and Treatment of Occupational Diseases argued that genealogical studies should be conducted to determine which among a pool of candidate workers were more likely to have "tumor predispositions." Identification of such persons would allow a "more appropriate selection" of workers for hazardous positions.[170] After 1933, with the new premium on genetic determinism, such proposals became more common. Ernst W. Baader, director of Berlin's Institute for Occupational Disease, in 1937 argued that bladder cancer developed only in workers "with a particular receptivity," though he was also well aware that tumors of this sort had been found in people contaminated by the clothing brought home by their fathers, husbands, or brothers.[171] Franz Koelsch, perhaps the most highly regarded occupational physician of the era, tried to identify certain "constitutional types" that would be more appropriate for work in the steel industry, others that would work well in the chemical industry, and so forth.[172] A great deal of effort went into the search for ways to identify resistant workers; *Selektionsmedizin* was said to have a bright future in German industrial medicine.

The idea of barring "cancer-sensitive" workers from jobs involving exposure to chemical hazards was eventually sidelined by the more radical prospect of using "enemies of the German state" to do the onerous work in the Reich. German labor took on an entirely different cast during the war, when hundreds of thousands of slave and foreign workers were forced to toil in German factories. Such people were excluded from the normal protections of German occupational health and safety, and we may reasonably assume that the cancers they contracted never made it onto the registries kept by public health officials.[173] The number of people involved was substantial: at I. G. Farben in Ludwigshafen alone, for example, an estimated 63,000 foreign workers, 10,000 concentration camp prisoners, and 10,000 prisoners of war were forced onto factory floors—usually to do the dirtiest jobs.[174] Thousands of prisoners worked at other facilities—the secret underground bomb factory near Nordhausen, for example, where concentration camp prisoners fashioned radioactive nuclear waste into radiological weapons.[175] Many of these men and women must have developed cancers, but records have simply not been kept. Cancer may have been the least of their concerns, since many succumbed to the regime's policy of "destruction through work" (*Vernichtung durch Arbeit*).[176]

Those who were not worked to death faced novel risks, both chronic and acute, owing to the extraordinary pace of German industrial production. The autarkic policy pushed by the government, compelling Germany to produce as many of its own raw materials as possible—synthetic rubber, liquefied coal, synthetic explosives, dyes, and drugs, and so forth—exposed countless workers to myriad hazards, as Nazi leaders were well aware. Reich Health Office President Hans Reiter in a 1939 speech pointed out that increased rayon production had led to increasing exposures to hydrogen sulfide, and that aircraft production was giving rise to skin injuries from metal splinters and lung injuries from spray paints. Skin irritations were on the rise from the use of artificial resins, and lead poisoning was becoming common from the use of tetraethyl lead in gasoline. Benzene injuries were being observed from rubber solvents, as were poisonings from new phosphorous-based pesticides.[177] It is difficult to gauge the cancer consequences of these twelve frenetic years of Nazi rule, but extra cancers there must have been—despite all the steps taken in the direction of industrial hygiene.

The Nazi struggle against occupational carcinogens must be understood in this context. German workers were to be protected, but only if this did not interfere with production schedules. Public health was a genuine concern (for the racial elite), but the exigencies of the war put cancer and other chronic diseases on the back burners of medical interest. War was a time for quick solutions, not the painstaking engineering needed for genuine prevention. Nazi leaders eventually decided simply to kill the mentally ill and physically handicapped, along with many epileptics, sick foreign workers, maladjusted adolescents, POWs, and sufferers from shell shock.[178] Severely injured soldiers returning from the eastern front may have been subjected to "euthanasia"; we even have hints that Hitler pondered the postwar confinement and sterilization of people suffering from chronic lung and heart disease.[179]

The social policies ultimately favored by the government equated value of life with ability to work. When policy-makers finally decided to kill the mentally ill and physically handicapped in German hospitals (200,000 men, women, and children eventually perished in the "euthanasia" program),[180] many of those patients capable of productive work were spared. The same philosophies that guided the transport of German schizophrenics and manic-depressives to the gas chambers were also expressed in other life-and-death decisions: concentration camp prisoners who could not work, for example, were routinely put to death.[181] The goal of occupational medicine likewise became a worker who would remain productive until retirement and then pass away shortly thereafter. As Hermann Hebestreit of the German Labor Front put the matter, the aim was to reduce the difference between the age of retirement and the age of death—ideally to zero.[182] Werner Bockhacker, chief of the DAF's health office, put forward pretty much the same idea—as did Hellmut Haubold, who characterized the elderly as people "no longer useful to the community."[183] In the idealized Nazi scheme of things, workers would work long and hard and then die—saving for the *Volksgemeinschaft* the financial burdens of the elderly and "unproductive" infirm.

5

The Nazi Diet

Your body belongs to the nation!
Your body belongs to the Führer!
You have the duty to be healthy!
Food is not a private matter!

Nazi slogans

FOOD was important for the Nazis. The healthy and powerful state required healthy and powerful bodies, and a proper diet was often taken to be the key to bodily strength. Nazi nutritionists mounted a frontal attack on Germans' excessive consumption of meat, sweets, and fat, and argued for a return to "more natural" foods such as cereals, fresh fruit, and vegetables. The emphasis upon bodily purity and natural healing was one source of the interest, but, as in the case of occupational medicine, questions of performance at work, at sport, and in the bedroom were also central—as was the quest for agricultural self-sufficiency. Nazi leaders wanted tough, lean, high-performing man-machines; a proper diet would reduce the incidence of ailments such as cancer and heart disease but would also increase labor productivity, maternal performance, and military muscularity. Moreover, it would aid in the regime's effort to free Germany from dependence on foreign food imports, a not-inconsequential aspect of the Nazi party's drive for economic independence.

It is not surprising that an improper diet was said to contribute to cancer at this time, since diet was popularly held to account for nearly every human malady.[1] Dietary theories of cancer were boosted by the fact that the digestive tract was the most commonly afflicted site of the body, in Germany as in many other countries prior to the explosive growth of smoking. Swiss and German statistics from the mid–nineteenth century suggested that between a third and half of all cancer deaths stemmed from stomach cancer,[2] and Dormanns's ambitious autopsy study of the early 1930s came up with similar figures.[3] Gastric malignancy was the leading cause of cancer death in the United States, too: a 1937 study of American physicians found that stomach and liver cancer together claimed more lives than any other kind of tumor, followed by cancers of the colon, breast, prostate, and so on down the list.[4]

No one really knows why stomach cancer was so common in the 1920s and 1930s—or even why incidence rates plummeted in the decades after the Second World War. In Germany today, age-adjusted death rates are less than a quarter of what they were in the early years of the century. The decline is a worldwide phenomenon—even in Japan, where gastric malignancy was, until recently, the number one cause of cancer death (lung cancer assumed first place in the 1990s, following the rapid increase in cigarette smoking). The decline of stomach cancer is almost certainly real, and not the product of better diagnostics or some other bias, since Germany by the 1920s led the world in autopsies and was thereby able to confirm the site of origin of many tumors.

One factor contributing to soaring stomach cancer rates must have been the dismal quality of food. Highly salted, often fermented, and not infrequently rotten, the meats, vegetables, and grains of the era were often tainted by molds, fungi, bacteria, and other potentially cancer-causing agents. People did eat fresh meat, but they also ate a lot of meat that had been salted, dried, or smoked. We know today that cancer-causing aflatoxins are common in the molds that grow on grains and many nuts; we also know that contamination from such substances was common in the early part of the century. (The stomach bacterium *Helicobacter pylori* has been shown to be a cause of gastric cancer—though little is known about how prevalence rates of infection may have changed over time.) We know that foods were often adulterated with spectacular colorants and preservatives, including vivid coal tar dyes, bright green copper sulfates (banned in 1887 but relegalized in 1928 so domestic vegetables could compete with French produce), and much else besides. (Licorice, for example, was often colored with lampblack soot derived from the burning of candles.) It is not hard to imagine that the liberal use of colorings and preservatives may have caused some of the stomach cancers of that era.

Here I want to look at Nazi views on food, but also at the fate of food itself—who ate what, why, and how much; what was promoted and what was reviled. Cancer, of course, was only one of several reasons Nazi food philosophers emphasized a healthy diet. Foods were often opposed or endorsed for complex symbolic reasons—whipped cream for its association with effete overindulgence,[5] for example, or whole-grain bread for its association with peasant culture (see fig. 5.1). Nazi ideologues didn't like the "false blonding" of butter, just as they disapproved of people altering the shape of their noses by cosmetic surgery or bleaching their hair to falsify racial ancestry. Dietary politics seeped into questions such as "What was the original human diet?" (meat or fruit?) and "How can we best achieve agricultural self-sufficiency?" (one answer: engineer new kinds of foods). Food is highly charged in any climate, and Germany in the 1930s–1940s was no exception.

It should not be forgotten, of course, that Germany's physician-führers were less concerned about the health of individuals than about the vigor of "the race," the so-called folk community (*Volksgemeinschaft*). Nazi food policies were supposed to prevent disease, but they were also supposed to elevate the fitness of Germans in other respects as well. Understanding this helps us grasp the Nazi fascination with performance-enhancing foods and drugs—such as caffeine and various synthetic "uppers." Research into such drugs culminates in the war years, when steps were taken to maximize human performance on both the military front and the factory floor. Efforts were also launched to engineer new dietary substitutes, especially for foods made scarce as a result of the war. All of these concerns—proximity to nature, work performance, and cheap ersatz foodstuffs—were at play in Nazi food reforms.

FIG. 5.1. Whole-grain bread, with the seal of approval of the NSDAP's Office of Public Health. German bakeries were required to produce whole-grain bread to strengthen the health of the German people. Source: Reiter and Breger, *Deutsches Gold*, p. 123.

As we shall see, some of these reforms were successful (the move to produce whole-grain bread and sweet ciders, for example), while others were not (notably the campaign to reduce alcohol consumption). Food quality in many instances deteriorated with the militarization of the economy, as shelf lives lengthened and synthetic substitutes flooded the market. Food habits changed in the Nazi era, but not always in directions favorable to health and well-being—especially for persons judged unfit or undeserving.

Resisting the Artificial Life

Nazi leaders paid a great deal of attention to what they ate and drank—and what the rest of the nation was supposed to be eating and drinking. If the health of the German state rested on the health of the German body, then the self-appointed guardians of the nation's health had to be careful about what was fed that body. What would make it healthy? What would corrupt it? Here as elsewhere in Nazi ideology, the liberal distinction between public and private spheres was abandoned. As one Hitler Youth health manual put it: "Nutrition is not a private matter!"[6] The body of the German citizen, after all, was supposed to be the material property of the German state. And since the state was identified with the Führer, it followed that your body belonged to the Führer—as was routinely announced on propaganda posters (*Dein Körper gehört dem Führer!*). The state thereby acquired a stake in the maintenance of the individual body—whether it was healthy or poisoned, exercised or abused, and so forth. Nazi philosophers and politicians contrasted this notion of "health as a duty" (officially embraced as a national slogan in 1939) with the purportedly "Marxist" notion of health as "the right to do whatever you want with your own body."[7]

One common theme of Nazi food rhetoric was the need to return to a more natural diet free of artificial colorings and preservatives. Foods were to be low in fat and high in fiber, while stimulants like coffee, alcohol, and tobacco were to be either avoided or used in moderation. Meat eating was to be minimized, and fresh foods were to be chosen over preserved foods in tins.

Erwin Liek had formulated many of these arguments in his 1932 and 1934 books on cancer (see chapter 1), and his was the lead followed by many Nazi food philosophers. Like his American contemporary, the insurance agent Frederick Hoffman, Liek maintained that cancer and other modern maladies were caused by improper eating. The human diet was becoming increasingly artificial—laced with preservatives, colorings, and other adulterations designed to achieve a superficial salability. Foods were being overcooked, which destroyed important vitamins; people were eating too much salt and protein and not enough vital minerals and hormones. The frantic pace of modern life was partly to blame, as more and more people preferred opening a can to foods prepared fresh. Equally lamentable was the "senseless swallowing of drugs" (*sinnlose Medikamentenschluckerei*) encouraged by doctors in the pocket of the pharmaceutical industry. Overmedication was a "pathology of therapy" caused by uncritical addiction to scientific medicine.[8]

Franz G. M. Wirz, a dermatologist and member of the Nazi party's Committee on Public Health, was one of many who followed Liek in criticizing the "unnatural directions" taken in the history of German eating. In a 1938 book, *Healthy and Secure Nutrition*, he noted that the German diet had taken a dramatic turn for the worse in the past century or so. Germans in the early nineteenth century had eaten 14 kilograms of meat and 250 kilograms of grain in any given year; by the mid-1930s, however, they were eating 56 kilos of meat and only 86 kilos of grain. This change from high-calorie "power foods" (*Betriebsstoffen*) to high-protein "structural foods" (*Aufbaustoffen*) had been accompanied by a dramatic increase in the consumption of fats and sugars. Per capita consumption of fat had increased by about a quarter from 1912 to 1936 (to 103 grams per day), and annual sugar consumption had soared from 4 to 24 kilograms per person over the past century or so.[9] The consequence was not just an increase in dental cavities ("fully unknown prior to 4,000 years ago") but also a wave of nervous ailments, infertility, stomach and digestive disorders (including tumors), and heart and vascular disease. Wirz complained that 17 percent of German military recruits were unfit for military duty in 1937, and that many of those were disqualified for dental problems—which could also lead to cancer, in his view. Lambasting the one-sided "materialistic" focus on calories in nutritional theory (*Kalorienlehre*), he argued that nutrition should never be left up to science alone.[10]

The dietary naturalism of this era was almost always tempered by the view that natural foods made economic sense. For Wirz, as for Liek and other food Nazis, proper nutrition was a matter not just of health but of economic efficiency. White bread, for example, was inferior to whole-grain bread on both counts: white bread was a "French revolutionary invention" and a bleached-out "chemical product" (Gerhard Wagner's derogation)[11]—but it was also more costly to produce. Lowering Germany's consumption of meat, sugar, and fat would result not just in health benefits but in financial savings: a reduction of meat consumption from 56 kilos per person per year to about 30–35 kilos, for example, would allow Germany to export meat, saving valuable hard currency. Germans would be both healthier and wealthier if they would stop bleaching their bread and canning their foods; Wirz also urged his countrymen to drink skim milk.[12] Much of this he couched in terms of a quest for "nutritional freedom" (*Nahrungsfreiheit*)[13]—the slogan often used in connection with the plan to eliminate German dependence on foreign imports.

Healthy food was supposed to make economic sense, but the reverse was not necessarily the case, and there were many even at the time who recognized that the rapid militarization of the German economy was threatening to degrade the German food supply, as we shall see in a moment.

Meat versus Vegetables

Dietary theories of cancer were most often accompanied by the argument that cancer was a disease caused not by particular germs or chemical agents but by some kind of general bodily disfunction.

Cancer was brought on by improper diet or stress—the theory being that anything which weakened the body as a whole would encourage cancer. Researchers' failure to find a "cancer germ"—the great hope of cancer theorists circa 1900—had given rise to suspicions that there was not in fact a single cause of cancer; Liek had made this point, and many physicians followed suit (Fritz Lickint and Friedrich Kortenhaus, for example). Cancer in this view—challenging Virchow's theory of cancer as the product of "local irritation"—was best understood as a constitutional disease, a "disease of the body as a whole" (*allgemeine Krankheit*), having multiple causes, including genetics, diet, stress, and much else besides.[14]

Those who subscribed to this "general dysfunction" theory tended to argue for a diet low in fat, sugar, and protein, and high in fruit and fiber.[15] This was the view presented by the German Hygiene Museum in its cancer exhibit; it was also the view of many of the homeopathy-oriented writers for *Hippokrates* magazine. Cancer was notorious—and much feared—for striking the well-fed and apparently healthy; perhaps a periodic fasting or other steps to limit what we eat could help prevent cancer. Hunger cures of diverse sorts were popular at this time—judging from the outpouring of books on the topic.

For those who upheld the dietary theory, excess consumption of meat was one of the most likely culprits. In the Nazi era, meatophobia was bolstered by the fact that several prominent leaders—notably Hitler and Himmler—were hostile to flesh eating, but worry about overzealous meat eating was also a popular theme of pre-Nazi organic literature. The *Lebensreform* movement of the Weimar era had urged moderation in this area; what was new in the Nazi period—or newly stressed—was the idea that "natural living" would augment military prowess.

A mid-1930s Hitler Youth manual, *Health through Proper Eating*, for example, includes an entire section under the rubric "Too Much Meat Can Make You Sick." The manual talks about the dangers of "empty calories" and champions soybeans as a wholesome (*vollwertig*) substitute for meat. High-fiber whole-grain bread is endorsed, with support in the form of the anticonstipation slogan "He who rests, rusts" (*Wer rastet, der rostet*). Young Nazi readers are urged that nutrition is "not a private matter" and that the children of the Reich have "a duty to be healthy"; eating right will make healthy citizens and soldiers.[16]

The question of whether meat was good or bad for you was not an easy one, however. Vegetarianism was already caught up in several different nets of political intrigue, complicated not just by Hitler's personal passions but by notions of sloth and gluttony, theories of personality (meat had been said to cause aggression), worries over the fate of the food supply (meat was a waste of agricultural resources), opposition to vivisection (see fig. 5.2), and much else as well.[17] Health questions mingled with all these other issues, slanting how people thought about both cancer causes and cancer cures.

An earlier generation, after all, had been taught that cancer might well be caused by consumption of *too many* fruits and vegetables. Tomatoes in the nineteenth century were often said to be a cause of tumors (the belief apparently based on their resemblance to fungoid growths),[18] as were fresh uncooked leafy greens like spinach or lettuce—often blamed for soaring German stomach cancer rates. This is odd from our point of view today, since we tend to believe that fresh fruits and vegetables are effective anticarcinogens—perhaps by virtue of (as Bruce Ames of Berkeley claims) the antioxidants contained therein. Stomach cancer is now more often said to have been the result of eating *too few* fresh fruits and vegetables, along with too many spoiled and/or highly salted and preserved foods.

Critics of the vegetables-as-carcinogens theory early in the century pointed out that one would expect countries where plant foods were a major part of the diet—like India—to have high stomach cancer rates, which was not in fact the case. Vegetarian peoples seemed to have very low cancer rates,[19] a view endorsed by Liek and one that grew in popularity in the Nazi era.[20]

Not everyone agreed, however. In 1942, the *Monatsschrift für Krebsbekämpfung* reported on the research of an Oslo physician, Arne Høgaard, claiming that the "pure race" Eskimos of eastern Greenland were entirely free of cancer, despite a diet consisting almost entirely of meat. The whale- and seal-hunting peoples near

FIG. 5.2. "Heil Göring!" The lab animals of Germany saluting Hermann Göring for his order barring vivisection. The Reichsmarschall in August of 1933 announced an end to the "unbearable torture and suffering in animal experiments" and threatened to commit to concentration camps "those who still think they can treat animals as inanimate property." Source: *Kladderadatsch*, September 3, 1933, with thanks to Phil Jenkins.

Angmagssalik still lived "a completely natural lifestyle" while consuming as much as 2.5 kilos of (low-fat) meat per day; the Europeanized Eskimos of western Greenland, by contrast, suffered cancer rates roughly comparable to those of Europe. The author concluded that the high protein, low-carbohydrate diet followed by the cancer-free Eskimos of eastern Greenland was similar in certain respects to the popular "cancer-fighting diet" promulgated by Johannes Kretz.[21]

Dissenting voices also came from scholars suggesting, oddly, that European butchers were relatively free of cancer, the prophylactic effect coming from the handling of meat. In 1935, a French physician had claimed that Parisian butchers had very low cancer rates; a Prague doctor by the name of Hans Truttwin in 1941 picked up on this, claimed that butchers "almost never get cancer," and proposed a survey to decide the question.[22] (In his own medical practice, Truttwin had treated cancer patients with bull testicle extracts, maintaining that the hormones contained therein possessed powerful antineoplastic potency.)[23] Victor Mertens, editor of the influential *Monatsschrift für Krebsbekämpfung*, countered by noting that there were already good statistics on the incidence of cancer by profession—that in England in the late nineteenth century, for example, while butchers had nowhere near the cancer rates of chimney sweeps, they were nonetheless still more likely to die of cancer than were fishermen, doctors, or farmers. Truttwin was simply wrong to have claimed, on the basis of a few French statistics, that butchers had "the fewest cancers of any profession." Mertens asked a doctoral student to research the topic and found that in Bavaria in 1935, 71 butchers had died of cancer (more than half from stomach tumors). There were 27,392 butchers in the state that year, implying a cancer death rate of 26 per 10,000, a higher figure even than was average for the population as a whole (16 per 10,000). Mertens concluded that the controversy should be "buried," since it was unsubstantiated in fact.[24]

Hermann Druckrey, a Himmler confidant and leading cancer experimentalist, claimed that vegetarians were neither more nor less vulnerable to cancer: "Meat eating and vegetarianism are both held up as either causes or cures for cancer, when evidence is lacking for either assertion. Statistical analyses have clearly shown that there is no connection in either case. Trappist monks, who eat a purely vegetarian diet, are neither more nor less likely to fall ill from cancer than other kinds of people."[25]

The *Fleischfrage* was larger, of course, than the question of what caused cancer. Carnivory has been equated with affluence for much of human history, and nineteenth-century dietary tracts tended to credit meat with everything from the rise of civilization to modern military ferocity. In the Nazi era, too, meat was often identified as the staple of all staples, the food without which there was none. Some of those who maintained a cancer link championed only an indirect causal chain: a 1941 Hitler Youth handbook thus claimed that people who ate a lot of meat were more likely to drink and to smoke.[26]

Meat issues spilled over even into questions of human origins: had the earliest humans eaten meat? Professor Paul Adloff of Königsberg in 1938 and again in 1940 repudiated the claim that vegetarianism was the original, and therefore more natural, human diet (Hitler, for example, believed this[27]—probably unbeknownst to Adloff). Writing in a leading dental journal, the Königsberg professor argued that the structure of the human teeth and jaw indicated an early adaptation to omnivory; there was little evidence for the view that early humans had been vegetarians. Adloff pointed out that the half-a-million-year-old human skeletons found in China ("Peking man," now classed as *Homo erectus*) had been found mixed with animal bones, suggesting a fleshy repast; he also speculated with the émigré anthropologist Franz Weidenreich that these early humans may have even practiced cannibalism. Adloff noted that very few apes were strict vegetarians, and reminded his readers that "the well-known gorilla, Bobby, in the Berlin Zoo, ate warm little wieners with gusto." Humans were omnivores from the point of view of anatomy; it was therefore wrong to suggest that vegetarianism was the more natural diet for *Homo sapiens*. There was in fact "no natural human diet."[28]

I have also drawn attention to the fact that economic considerations were vital for the meat detractors. Franz Wirz deplored the costly use of agricultural lands to grow grain to be fed to livestock, noting that it took about 90,000 calories of grain to produce 9,300 calories of pork. Göring in his Four Year Plan labeled as "traitors" farmers who fattened cattle on grains that could be used instead to make bread, and his claim was widely repeated. Wirz argued for a reduction in the acreage devoted to the cultivation of grains for livestock, and for an increase in land for growing fruits and vegetables.[29]

The campaign against meat also has to be seen, though, as part of the campaign against overindulgence. Meat was a luxury that, like whipped cream or bananas, had to be forgone as part of the sacrifice individual Germans made for the nation. A Viennese Nazi pamphlet cautioned against the gluttonous consumption of meat, cream, and fruit:

> There are people who have made their bellies their god, who in their greed want both goulash and a big helping of whipped cream before they feel they have had enough. But we industrious German racial comrades know what is at stake! We know that the serious and hardworking German does not live on whipped cream and bananas. This is not the time for gormandizers and hysterics who must have a new dainty every day.[30]

The *Deutsches Ärzteblatt*, the nation's leading medical journal, came close to branding overzealous consumerism as treason:

> The person who, in his greed for food, eats—or rather gobbles—more meat and fats than he needs for the maintenance of his health and working capacity, robs other racial comrades of these foods; he is a debauchee and a traitor to his land and his country. . . . Thus, for example, the Frenchman does not eat half as much butter as the German. Even in Paris it is forbidden to serve butter together with cheese, but in every German restaurant this is the accepted practice.[31]

Martin Gumpert, an émigré physician, cited these passages in a book published at the beginning of the war (*Heil Hunger!*) as evidence of the poverty of Nazi food policy. The campaign to dissuade Germans from eating so much meat and fat was callous, he maintained, given the food shortages caused by military stock-

TABLE 5.1
Gumpert's Data on Germany's
Changing Food Supply

	1928	1932	1936
Meat	100	96	91
Fats	100	104	96
Eggs	100	99	83
Potatoes	100	113	100

piling and the misguided goal of agricultural self-sufficiency. Gumpert offered as proof of the decline of Germany's food supply the chart reproduced here as table 5.1, standardized arbitrarily at 100 for the year 1928.[32] How strange for us today, though, to see this put forward as evidence of a dangerous trend, harmful to public health! Gumpert took the decline in meat and eggs as proof of a precipitous collapse of nutritional values, though we today might as easily take it as evidence of a successful shift from meat and fats to healthier foods. He was surely right to suggest that militarism and agricultural autarky were causes of the pullback from meat and fat, but his mockery of imperatives to reduce fats for health reasons—"health administration hyenas who proclaim to the public that butter is poison"[33]—sounds curiously out of synch with what we today know, and the Nazis thought they knew, about diet-health links.

Gumpert no doubt was correct in his overall assessment, though, that health was only one of several concerns when it came to food policy—the overarching one being the remilitarization of the Germany economy. Health was not the point when Rudolf Hess urged "guns instead of butter," which leads us to believe that health was not the primary reason meat and fat became scarce even for the privileged "healthy" elements of the German populace. And when the war started going badly, of course, Nazi leaders began to worry more about Germans' getting too little meat than about their getting too much: Goebbels, at least, had reached this point by February of 1942, cautioning that "no one will listen to well-reasoned arguments if butter and meat are taken away from him."[34]

THE FÜHRER'S FOOD

Complicating all of this, of course, was the fact that Hitler himself was a vegetarian, of sorts. This singular fact assumed striking proportions given the premium put on body and "lifestyle" politics by both Nazis and vegetarians; it has also become something of an embarrassment for non–meat eaters ever since (which I am not, I should confess). Hitler's vegetarianism crops up often in postwar discussions of food and animal rights, but also of antisemitism and much else as well. What were the Führer's eating habits, and what do they tell us about the Nazi movement?

Postwar Russian forensic experts examining body parts from a shallow grave outside Hitler's bunker confirmed that the skull in question—purportedly the Führer's—had the yellow color "typical of a vegetarian."[35] Hitler's vegetarianism was remarked on prior even to 1933, however, when the Führer-to-be's personal asceticism was held up as the model Nazi lifestyle. Foreigners eventually took note, recording also some apparent backsliding. Otto D. Tolischus in 1937 in the *New York Times* pointed out that the Führer was a vegetarian who "does not drink or smoke" but who also "occasionally relishes a slice of ham" along with delicacies such as caviar and chocolates.[36] Postwar observers have often—and understandably—used this to question whether Hitler was in fact a vegetarian.[37]

Food was clearly important to the Führer, though. He was intrigued by the possibility of a diet consisting entirely of uncooked fruits, grains, and vegetables, and often raised this topic with friends and subordinates. Shortly after taking office, for example, he arranged a meeting with an eighty-year-old woman from Bad Godesberg ("known up and down the Rhine as the *Seniorin* of vegetarianism, cold-water cures, and herbal healing") to discuss the benefits of a vegetarian diet. That same day, when his Gestapo chief tried to broach with him the need to simplify the party's complicated bureaucratic structure, Hitler responded that there were "far more important things than politics—reforming the human lifestyle, for example. What this old woman told me this morning is far more important than anything I can do in my life."[38]

Hitler later claimed that humans had once lived longer than they do today, the change coming not just from the shift to meat but also from the "sterilization" of food through cooking, resulting in "diseases of civilization" (*Kulturkrankheiten*). Cancer was such a disease: "and though we still don't know what causes cancer, it may be that whatever does becomes active only when the body is not properly nourished." Humans in his view had started eating meat only when Ice Age conditions forced them to; cooking had also arisen about this time. The Nazi push for raw fruits and vegetables had begun to reverse this trend, "revolutionizing" eating (*"Die Rohkost war eine Revolution!"*). Hitler doubted that fats derived from coal could ever be as good for you as olive oil; he also worried that the increasing consumption of whale oil was diminishing the population of whales. Germans in the future, he claimed, would be eating more margarines derived from the plant oils of the east.[39]

We have a pretty good idea of Hitler's daily regimen, faithfully recorded by the acolyte-scribes who hung on his every word. Hitler was indeed, for the most part, a vegetarian—though he did occasionally allow himself a dish of meat. Gestapo chief Rudolf Diels after the war wrote that Hitler would sometimes eat Bavarian liver dumplings (*Leberknödel*), but only when they were prepared by his photographer friend, Heinrich Hoffmann.[40] The *New York Times* mentioned ham and caviar, but Hitler was also said to have enjoyed squab—a pigeon-like game bird. Several reports attest to the disgust Hitler felt about flesh-eaters. In the 1920s, for example, on a romantic date, the future Führer scolded his female companion for having ordered *Wienerschnitzel*. Clearly bothered by his reaction, she asked if she had done something wrong, to which he replied: "No, go ahead and have it, but I don't understand why you want it. I didn't think you wanted to devour a corpse . . . the flesh of dead animals. Cadavers!" Hitler elsewhere referred to meat broth as "corpse tea."[41]

Joseph Goebbels explained his Führer's aversion as a consequence of his respect for "the animal element" in humankind:

> The Führer is deeply religious, though completely anti-Christian. He
> views Christianity as a symptom of decay. Rightly so. It is a branch of
> the Jewish race. . . . Both [Judaism and Christianity] have no point of
> contact to the animal element, and thus, in the end, they will be de-
> stroyed. The Führer is a convinced vegetarian, on principle. His argu-
> ments cannot be refuted on any serious basis. They are totally un-
> answerable.[42]

Unanswerable, perhaps, but Goebbels himself seems not to have
been moved, judging from the fact that he continued to eat meat
until he poisoned himself, his wife, and his five young children in
the final days of the war.

Hitler appears to have given up meat in 1931, though the reasons behind his decision (if reasons are to be expected in such matters) are not entirely clear. Several of his biographers point to the
influence of the nationalist antisemitic composer, Richard Wagner.
In an 1881 essay, Wagner had claimed that the human race had
become contaminated and impure through racial mixing and the
eating of animal flesh (the original human diet in his view, too,
was vegetarian); a new kind of socialism was needed to purify
Germany of these twin evils, calling upon "true and hearty fellow-
ship with the vegetarians, the protectors of animals, and the
friends of temperance" to save the German people from Jewish
aggression. Wagner claimed that abstaining from a fleshy diet
would allow a human moral redemption—possibly even for the
Jews.[43] Hitler seems to have taken at least part of the message to
heart: "I don't touch meat largely because of what Wagner says on
the subject."[44]

Hitler is said to have been unable to tolerate the idea of animals'
being killed for human consumption, but at least one author has
countered that this was an image deliberately crafted to popularize
the German leader as kind and gentle.[45] Animal-rights historians
Arnold Arluke and Boria Sax have noted that both claims may be
true; they also point to a report from the 1940s—by an American—

that Hitler gave up meat because of problems with digestion. Whatever his original motivation (the suggestion has also been made that the death of his niece somehow provoked his revulsion for meat),[46] the Nazi leader himself credited his dietary change with having greatly increased his health and stamina. In his meat-eating phase, he had sweated profusely during his long ranting speeches—losing four to seven pounds in the course of an evening—but once he gave up meat, he said, the sweating stopped. Later, in the 1940s, he characterized his wolfhound, Blondi, as a vegetarian—instructing visitors that the dog's grass-eating habits had helped her with her colic.[47] Vegetarianism was not the only idiosyncrasy in Hitler's diet: he had a lifelong sweet tooth and was known to have consumed as much as two pounds of chocolate in a day.[48] He also had a rather bizarre and lifelong fascination with crayfish, lobsters, and crabs, which some scholars have traced (spuriously, in my view) to the fact that the German word for such creatures (*Krebs*) is the same as that for cancer.[49]

It is often said that Hitler worried about getting cancer, though the evidence on this is somewhat sketchy. We know that he had the Dachau physician Gustav Freiherr von Pohl examine his Reichskanzlei (Chancellery) for "earth rays" (*Erdstrahlen*) by means of a dowsing rod of some sort in September of 1934.[50] ("Earth rays" were popularly said to cause cancer[51] and occasionally reappear in quack healing literature even today—see chapter 7.) We also know that Hitler suffered from stomach cramps, which he apparently interpreted as the early signs of cancer.[52] The suggestion has been made that his mother's death from cancer in 1907 may have added to his dread: Klara Hitler died from breast cancer while under the care of a Jewish physician, Eduard Bloch, prompting speculation that some of his antisemitism may have sprouted from this seed.[53]

Hitler was not the only "vegetarian" in the Nazi entourage. Himmler was big fan of both natural healing ("every doctor should be a nature doctor") and raw vegetables; he believed that "eastern peoples" had healthier bodies (and longer colons) in consequence of their vegetarian diets. Like Hitler, he too suffered from severe bouts of stomach pains and suspected—again like his Führer—that this might mean cancer (Himmler's own father died from stomach cancer). The SS supremo was convinced that a balanced diet was crucial for health maintenance; he rejected the single-minded focus on calories as the best measure of nutrition and emphasized instead the value of vitamins, minerals, fiber, and whole foods. He generally abstained from both alcohol and tobacco, allowing himself nonetheless an occasional cigar and glass of red wine. Obesity was anathema to him, and in August of 1940 he launched a campaign with *Sicherheitsdienst* chief Reinhard Heydrich to combat corpulence in the SS.[54] He urged his Waffen-SS men to be nonsmoking nondrinking vegetarians, though it is unclear how successful his proselytizing was. He did manage to have the SS take over most of Germany's mineral springs, and it was on his orders that many SS barracks and concentration camps planted herbal gardens (see below).[55] He longed for the time when all Germans would be vegetarians; only then would *Deutschland* return, per his fantasies of ancient Aryans, to its rightful place as dominator among nations.[56]

Himmler's food concerns were not unlike those of others in the Liekist, romantic axis of the Nazi party. He opposed the distribution of artificial honey to the Waffen SS and the adulteration of foods more generally: "The artificial is everywhere; everywhere food is adulterated, filled with ingredients that supposedly make it last longer, or look better, or pass as 'enriched,' or whatever else the industry's admen want us to believe." The root of the problem was that

> we are in the hands of the food companies, whose economic clout and advertising make it possible for them to prescribe what we can and cannot eat. City folk, living through the winter largely on canned food, are already at their mercy, but now they attack the countryside with their refined flour, sugar, and white bread. The war has interrupted these proceedings; after the war we shall take energetic steps to prevent the ruin of our people by the food industries.[57]

Asked how he would change the German diet, he gave as an example the state-mandated fixing of a certain minimal percentage of whole grains in bread. And how would he get people to eat such bread?

> we must influence them by propaganda to show the damage caused by refined foods. There's no lack of examples. The wrong diet always plays a decisive part in all the troubles of civilization, from the loss of teeth to chronic constipation and digestive ailments, not to mention bad nerves and defective circulation.[58]

Housewives and mothers were to be the targets of such propaganda, since theirs was the "gigantic responsibility" of preserving health with food. Himmler claimed to have learned the value of proper eating from his experience as a farmer, experience later confirmed by his reading of Max Bircher-Benner and Ragnar Berg, two of the leading natural food advocates of the era (Bircher-Benner is best known today as the inventor of Muesli). The SS Reichsführer was aware of the orthodox medical myopia in such matters ("Our medicines today are injections, our diet tinned food, and most of our doctors accept this without thinking"); he also knew that a full-scale campaign for healthy food—including propaganda films—would probably have to wait until after the war.[59] Hitler himself told Goebbels (in April 1942) that he would wait until after the war to tackle the issue of vegetarianism; he also confided that Nazism would never have triumphed in Germany if he had insisted on banning all consumption of meat.[60]

Rudolf Hess was another fussy eater. Like Himmler, Hitler's deputy and successor was fond of herbal remedies and homeopathy, and took great care in the foods he ate. He used to bring his own vegetarian food to meetings at the Chancellery, which he would then warm up for dinner. This annoyed Hitler, who complained to Hess, "I have an excellent dietician/cook here. If your doctor has prescribed something special for you, she could certainly prepare it. You cannot bring your own food in here." Hess countered that his food had to contain certain biodynamic ingredients, prompting Hitler to suggest that he (Hess) might prefer to eat at home. Hess was apparently less often invited to lunch with the Führer after that episode.[61]

Not all Nazi leaders were so fastidious. Goebbels was a careful dresser—his wardrobe contained more than a hundred different uniforms—but a gourmet he was not, as recalled by his biographer:

> Probably nowhere in Berlin-West was the food as scanty or bad as it was at the Goebbels' house. The minister simply didn't care about his food and continued to show a distinct partiality for his favorite dish, herring and boiled potatoes, which was frequently served to company. It became customary for his guests to eat their fill at a restaurant before showing up at his house, and during the war it was general knowledge that when one went to the Goebbelses' he got no more to eat than his allotted ration points permitted.[62]

Readers might wonder at this point what a discussion of the predilections of Hitler et al. is doing in a book on Nazi cancer combat. The answer, I would say, is that Hitler's habits and predilections—and even his body—assumed an unusual significance in a regime obsessed with health, bodily purity, and the potency of its all-powerful and image-conscious leader. Hitler was supposed to embody the ideal German, an understanding that, when taken literally, led to some rather obvious contradictions. (The most famous joke from the era asked: "What is the ideal German? Blond like Hitler, slim like Göring, masculine like Goebbels. . . . ") Hitler's body became the object of veneration and emulation—so much so that Red Army soldiers upon entering Berlin confronted legions of men sporting Hitler-style mustaches, several dozen of whom were interned on suspicion of being the German leader. Every German must have known that Hitler did not smoke or drink, a maxim often repeated in party literature. The oddities of the Führer's body led to predictable ridicule—the mustache designed, perhaps, to cover up a "Jewish nostrility," the genital deformity that led to countless sneers and Britain's most famous army song (sung to "Colonel Bogey's March": "Hitler has only got one ball; / Göring has two but very small; / Himmler is very sim'lar, / And Goebbels has no balls at all"). Hitler may have tired of the public scrutiny; a 1937 directive ordered that no further attention be drawn to his person or his habits. The commercial exploitation of his vegetarianism seems to have prompted the halt (the organic food industry was using the Führer-ly lifestyle to sell its products),[63] but the dictator may also have feared that the ridicule-to-veneration ratio would not remain low forever.

The Campaign against Alcohol

Alcoholic overindulgence was a frequent target of the Nazi push for a more "natural" way of living. As in the United States, the organized temperance movement dated from the nineteenth century: a German Antialcoholism Association had been founded in 1883, about which time a journal, *Auf der Wacht* (On guard), was launched to publicize the dangers of drink—and occasionally tobacco.[64] The movement was never as strong as its counterpart in the United States, where federally mandated Prohibition ruled from 1919 until 1933, but the German movement was by no means inconsequential. By the time Hitler seized power, the organization had 19 regional and 254 local associations, plus 16 women's groups. The Berlin women's branch alone had a thousand members. More than a hundred centers had been established to provide assistance to alcoholics, and efforts had been launched to keep young men from drinking.[65]

Support for temperance and/or abstinence came from across the political spectrum. In Austria, the leading abstinence organization was the Workers' Abstinence League (Arbeiter Abstinentenbund), a socialist body better organized even—or so some claimed—than the Austrian Social Democratic party itself. Alcoholic temperance was embraced by the nature-loving *Wandervogel* movement, by Catholic student fraternities, and by the Protestant churches. The financial deprivation of the immediate post–World War I period put a damper on certain kinds of social drinking (e.g., the ritualistic orgies of many student fraternities), and much of this same sense of austerity can be seen in the Nazi Students' League, founded in 1926. Hitler about this time forecast that students of the future would be judged not by their capacity for beer but by their capacity to remain sober.[66]

There were several common themes among those who opposed alcohol. Drinking was held to be a financial drain on the nation, a health hazard, and a source of endless corruption and vice. Alcohol was said to deaden the nerves and weaken the spirit. Drunkenness was judged a promoter of crime and delinquency, and at least one racial hygienist, Agnes Bluhm, made a career out of arguing that alcohol could cause genetic damage. Clear-cut distinctions were not always made between congenital and genetic injury, however, which led to confusion about the long-term implications of alcohol for genetic health. After 1933, the possibility of harm to the "German germ plasm" was used to justify the decision to sterilize "chronic alcoholics" in accordance with the Sterilization Law. Germans also spent a lot of time worrying about what today is known as "fetal alcohol syndrome," and the suggestion has been made that some of the offspring of the Jukes family of eugenics notoriety (defectives said to have passed down their taint through several generations) may have been victims of this syndrome.[67] It would be interesting to know whether the comparable German families ("Zero," "Victoria," and "Markus") were similarly afflicted—and whether, as in the American case, the post–World War II neglect of research in this era may have had something to do with its eugenics taint. (Historian Brian S. Katcher has pointed out that cirrhosis of the liver, cardiomyopathy, fetal injuries, and esophageal cancer were all well-known effects of alcohol at the turn of the century—and were later forgotten.)[68]

The idea that alcohol might be a cause of cancer dates back at least to the nineteenth century, when tumors began to figure in the list of harms flowing from the demon liquor. Stomach cancers were said to be caused by the hard ciders drunk in Normandy and the acidic wines imbibed in eastern Switzerland.[69] Karl B. Lehmann's influential 1919 textbook on occupational health and safety noted that bartenders, brewers, and others in "alcohol-related occupations" had high rates of cancer, especially oral and esophageal, the implication being that drink was the primary cause.[70] Work involving the sale of alcohol (especially bartending) became one of the two most cited occupational causes of cancer—the other being work with tar, paraffin, or oil.[71] The usual explanation, dating back to the nineteenth century, was that chronic alcohol consumption led to a general "stomach catarrh" which then progressed to cancer. There were some who doubted this theory (critics pointed out that cancer afflicted women as often as men, even though men drank much more),[72] but it persisted into the 1940s.[73]

One cannot understand the strength of Germany's antialcohol movement in the 1930s without appreciating the fact that many Nazi leaders were early advocates of abstinence or temperance. Erwin Liek had been a teetotaler prior to the First World War and never drank very much thereafter. Alcoholic overindulgence he blamed for a whole raft of diseases, cancer being just one of many.[74] Heinrich Himmler claimed that alcohol was the most treacherous poison humans ever faced, a greater cause of human failure than any other. (The SS chief had joined a fraternity as a student but successfully petitioned for exemption from the drinking bouts because of his sensitive stomach.)[75] Hitler himself attacked alcohol in a 1926 article in the *Völkischer Beobachter*, the official Nazi party newspaper, mourning "the valuable people—especially Germans—destroyed or rendered useless by alcohol, exceeding by an order of magnitude even the numbers of those lost on the field of battle." The NSDAP leader predicted that "a people managing successfully to rid itself of this poison" would likely come to dominate other parts of the world "unprepared to take that step."[76]

With so many Nazi leaders on the wagon, temperance advocates waxed confident that a Nazi future was a bright future. *Auf der Wacht*, the leading German antialcohol journal, in May of 1933 celebrated Hitler's rise to power in glowing terms: "We Germans stand at an important turning point: new men are shaping the destiny of our fatherland, new laws are being created, new measures put into place, new forces awakened. The struggle touches on everything that has been and is unclean."[77] Nazi leaders returned the favor: the fiftieth anniversary celebration of the founding of the Antialcoholism Association on October 22–25, 1933, was attended by many prominent politicos and racial hygienists—including Eugen Fischer and Fritz Lenz, interior minister Wilhelm Frick, and future Reich Health Führer Leonardo Conti. The Horst Wessel song was sung (the Nazi party anthem, essentially) and a radio address by Hitler ("Sports and the New Man") was pumped into the hall over loudspeakers. The *Gleichschaltung* of Germany's anti-alcohol organizations followed shortly thereafter: Jews were excluded and a new "Jew-free" organization was formed to unite the movement.[78]

Economic considerations were a mainstay of the Nazi distrust of alcohol. Nazi authorities complained as early as 1935 that Germans were spending three billion reichsmarks per year on alcohol,[79] enough to buy millions of Volkswagens or other useful commodities. At the forty-fourth annual meeting of the Antialcoholism Association that year, Dr. Werner Hüttig of the Office of Racial Policy argued for a stepped-up campaign against alcohol abuse in the Hitler Youth, in schools, and at work. Alcohol was cast as a threat to the "combat-readiness" of Germany's youth, and officials of the Hitler Youth equated the damage caused by drink to that caused by a brain tumor. Hitler Youth leaders pointed to the Führer's admonishment that the future of Germany belonged not to drinkers but to fighters.[80]

Plans to combat alcohol were put into place in the early months of 1933. The Nazi version of May Day—the "day of national work" in the new incarnation—was declared alcohol-free,[81] as were many other party-sponsored events and facilities, including the training quarters for Germany's Olympic athletes. A November 1, 1933, ordinance barred advertisements judged as violating the "political will of the German people"; the law explicitly prohibited ads for alcoholic products directed at youth or using nonadult imagery. A 1939 amendment barred any suggestion of "health-promoting" properties of brandy, cordials, or bitters; also barred was any hint of nutritional or hygienic virtues, or any suggestion that an alcoholic product might aid in digestion or stimulate the appetite (an exception was made for certain bitters containing soothing botanicals). Advertisers were no longer allowed to refer to alcohol as "liquid food," and in no case were terms implying medical endorsement to be permitted—terms like "stomach doctor" or "health inspector" (*Mageninspektor, Sanitätsrat, Blutlikör*, etc.). Stiff new penalties (fines and imprisonment) were decreed for anyone caught violating the bans—including editors or publishers printing such claims in their magazines or newspapers.[82]

Traffic accidents were another concern of Nazi *Anti-Alkoholiker*. Alcohol was recognized as a major cause of automobile accidents, a not insignificant matter in Germany of the mid-1930s, with more than a quarter of a million traffic accidents per annum resulting in more than ten thousand deaths. Accidents were much more common on Mondays than on Wednesdays, a consequence, in the eyes of some, of weekend binging. Official estimates were that more than two-thirds of the nation's traffic fatalities were the direct result of alcoholic intoxication.[83] The problem was taken seriously by Nazi leaders: Himmler in 1937 sent a letter to each of Germany's 1.7 million licensed drivers, cautioning against the dangers of drinking and driving.[84]

The campaign was extended to the workplace, when Robert Ley of the German Labor Front sought to replace on-the-job beer drinking with on-the-job tea drinking. In 1940, Ley launched a much-advertised "operation tea" (*Teeaktion*) to promote the consumption of nonalcoholic beverages at work: 120,000 kilograms of black tea were pressed into blocks and supplied to all factories where workers labored in temperatures in excess of twenty-eight degrees Celsius. (Alcohol was known to have particularly serious consequences in hot environments.) The project was apparently a success,[85] though it is perhaps not out of place to note that Ley himself was a notorious drunk and was reprimanded on at least one occasion for presenting a public speech while inebriated.

A more ambitious campaign was launched to increase the consumption of cider and fruit juices, along with alcohol-free malt beer, mineral water, and vegetable drinks. Labeling laws were an ongoing concern, and a great deal of effort went into deciding how much alcohol a beer could have and still call itself "alcohol-free." Energies also went into the creation of a new generation of beverages from liquefied vegetables—apparently something like tomato juice or V-8 juice today. The journal *Gärungslose Früchteverwertung* (Fruits without fermentation) described new methods of producing alcohol-free drinks, which Nazi magazines and public health journals vigorously promoted.

Fig. 5.3. "Mothers: Avoid alcohol and nicotine during pregnancy and while nursing. . . . Drink soft cider instead!" Graphic from Reiter and Breger, *Deutsches Gold*, p. 302.

Fig. 5.4. "Production of Soft Cider in the German Reich" from 1926 to 1937, in millions of liters. Fruit juices were encouraged as part of the campaign against alcohol. Source: Reiter and Breger, *Deutsches Gold*, p. 300.

Programs were also initiated to dissuade children from drinking. The 1933 ban on alcohol advertising directed at children was strengthened in 1936, at which time a certification system was also put into place to indicate whether certain drinks were suitable for children. Nonalcoholic fruit ciders, for example, had an official stamp of approval (*Jugendwert*) printed on their labels; Coca-Cola, by contrast, was declared unsuitable for children.[86] The state intervened in many other areas in similar fashion: films, for example, began to be officially rated as either "fit" or "unfit" for children to watch.

Despite propaganda and its pervasive twin, *Aufklärung*, these various efforts to solve the "drink question" (*Getränkefrage*) appear to have enjoyed at best a mixed success. On the one hand, production of fruit drinks did rise dramatically, from about sixteen million liters in 1930 to nearly five times that amount in 1937—during which time the prices of many fruit juices fell precipitously (see figs. 5.3 and 5.4). Reich Health Office president Hans Reiter declared sweet cider the official "people's drink" (*Volksgetränk*) in 1938,[87] and production continued to rise into the early war years.

Breweries caught the drift and began to move into the nonalcoholic beverage business. By 1936, a quarter of all mineral water in Germany was being manufactured and distributed by breweries. The outbreak of the war brought restrictions on where alcohol could be bought: a law passed on October 18, 1939, banned distribution of alcohol at taverns.

"Success" was also evident in the already-mentioned inclusion of alcoholics within the chilly embrace of sterilization legislation. Racial hygienists had long insisted that alcohol caused damage to the genetic material, but also that the propensity to drink was itself an inherited trait. As early as 1903, at the Ninth International Congress to Combat Alcoholism, in Bremen, the psychiatrist Ernst Rüdin had proposed the sterilization of "incurable alcoholics" to prevent the transmission of their afflicted seed. His proposal was roundly defeated,[88] but three decades later, on July 14, 1933, his dream came true with the passage of the Law for the Prevention of Genetically Diseased Offspring, allowing the forcible sterilization of chronic alcoholics and others deemed genetically inferior. Now director of the influential Kaiser Wilhelm Institute for Psychiatry in Munich, Rüdin was a major architect of the law, which eventually resulted in the *Unfruchtbarmachung* of some 350,000–400,000 German citizens. Compliance was facilitated by an Interior Ministry requirement that anyone being treated for alcohol abuse be reported to the Reich Health Office, where a registry of such persons was assembled.[89] Thousands of alcoholics were eventually sterilized; surveys conducted in the period 1934–1937 show that 5 or 6 percent of the men vasectomized in accordance with the law were targeted for their drinking habits. (Feeblemindedness was by far the largest category.) Women were slightly more likely than men to be sterilized, but alcoholism was less likely to be the reason.[90]

Considered as a whole, however, the antialcohol campaign seems to have done little to stem the tide of drinking in Nazi Germany. Some of the early declines in consumption, after all, were simply late effects of Germany's massive economic downturn. Beer consumption fell from 86 liters per person in 1929 to only 59 liters in 1936—roughly half what it had been in 1913. The same is true for hard liquor, which fell from 2.8 liters per person in 1913 to about half that figure in 1929 and only 0.6 liters in 1933, after which it slowly rose again to the levels of the late Weimar era.[91] The recession of the early 1930s slowed alcoholic consumption: six million men and women were out of work when Hitler took power, and alcohol had become an unaffordable luxury.

Alcohol consumption rose for the rest of the decade, as the economy recovered and, perhaps, as people sought refuge from Nazi terror. German purchases of hard liquor rose from about forty million liters in 1932 to more than twice this amount in 1938. Production of wine increased by nearly 80 percent in the first five years of Nazi rule, and the consumption of champagne increased by a factor of about five. Output also increased of alcohol made from inferior substitutes like cellulose and carbide, which by 1937 represented more than 20 percent of all hard liquor produced— apparently violating Germany's 1922 liquor monopoly law, which fixed an upper limit of 10 percent on such products. Martin Gumpert in 1940 concluded that Germans were poisoning themselves with alcohol on a scale comparable to the poisoning of the Chinese by opium: alcohol was "the Nazi opium for Germany."[92]

Why then did the Nazis consider alcohol a threat? And why did Nazi efforts to curb alcoholism and alcohol consumption fail?

For many at this time, again, the threat of alcohol was best understood in economic terms. Nazi leaders worried that alcohol was a drain on German finances and productivity—a serious concern given the drive to rationalize and militarize the economy. Prussian health minister Arthur Gütt in 1937 pointed out that Germans were spending a staggering 3.5 billion reichsmarks on alcohol and another 2.3 billion on tobacco every year: the total of 5.8 billion RM was 10 percent (!) of the entire German national income (*Volkseinkommen*).[93] Reich Health Führer Leonardo Conti voiced these same concerns a year later, by which time alcohol expenditures had grown by another billion RM.[94] Those figures continued to grow into the early war years, as German prosperity—and perhaps also psychological strain—prompted increased smoking and drinking. In many German cities, beer, wine, and harder drinks absorbed a sizable fraction of total disposable income: 5 percent in Lubeck, close to 7 percent in Berlin, and a whopping 13 percent in Munich.[95] A 1940 book by the nutritionist Hugo O. Kleine pointed out that Germans were spending more on alcohol than on any other "food product" (his quotation marks) with the exception of meat and bread.[96]

Nazi leaders also worried about the opportunity costs of using farmland crops for fermentation instead of food. In 1937, for example, the manufacture of high-octane alcohol ate up more than two million tons of potatoes, sixty thousand tons of grain, and nearly sixty million liters of fruit.[97] Nazi ideologues argued that agricultural resources could be put to far better uses, judging from the benefits Americans had reaped from Prohibition. A 1941 antialcohol treatise written by two SS officers claimed that the American ban had resulted not just in declines in mental illness, mortality, and days missed at work—but also in increased purchases of shoes, clothing, and foods like milk, coffee, and cheese. The authors quoted U.S. Steel magnate H. S. Dulaney's opinion that Prohibition ("one of the most remarkable chapters in the history of civilization") had enormously improved the lives of his 300,000 workers; Henry Ford is cited as stating that Prohibition had made possible the eight-hour day and the five-day week. The SS teetotalers blamed the repeal of Prohibition on the "unscrupulous propaganda of alcohol-capitalists" but also pointed to the hopeful fact that even after the collapse of the federal ban in 1933, many American states continued to bar the sale of alcohol (e.g., Alabama, Arkansas, Georgia, Idaho, Kansas, and Mississippi).[98]

Health, in short, was only one of several concerns behind the Nazi antialcohol campaign. Apart from cancer or the damage to labor power or even injury to the German "germ plasm," alcohol posed a symbolic threat to the Nazi state and body, as to culture and civilization generally. Racial subterfuge was sometimes invoked—as when Jewish manufacturers of alcoholic beverages were attacked as "liquor Jews"—but the more prominent theme was the equation of alcohol and degeneracy. The shiftless, out-of-work drunkard was the imagined polar opposite of the Nazi workaholic; the indolent, sedentary boozer violated the "man in motion" ethic of Nazism (see fig. 5.5). The loquacious exuberance

Zwei Männer – –
zwei Weltanschauungen

(„Der SA. Mann" 14. 5. 38)

FIG. 5.5. "Two Men—Two World Views." Germany's foremost antitobacco journal contrasts the sedentary boozer with the energetic "can-do" Nazi man in motion. Source: *Reine Luft* 21 (1939): 13.

prompted by drink may also have insulted the spartan sensibilities of the era. Hitler himself summarized these associations at the 1935 Nuremberg party congress:

> There were times—they now seem far away and almost incomprehensible—when the ideal German was the man who could handle his beer and hard liquor. Today, we no longer look to the guy who can handle his drink, but rather to the young man who can tough it out in rough weather, the hard young man. The point is not how much beer you can drink but how many blows you can take (*Schläge aushalten*), not how late you can stay out but how many miles you can march. We look no longer to the beer drinker as the ideal German, but rather to the men and women who are healthy, erect, and tough.[99]

Nazism was not unique in opposing drunkenness, of course, but it did tend to be rather intolerant of people defined as indolent or antisocial. Chronic alcoholism, especially if you were homeless or otherwise socially deviant, could get you into serious trouble. After 1939, homeless drunks branded anti- or asocial could easily end up in a euthanasia institution.[100] Prior even to the war, though, unsavvy alcoholism could land you in a concentration camp, especially if your political connections were weak or your inebriation interfered with your work.

Why did the campaign fail? The flip side of the economic argument, of course, is that alcohol was a cash cow for the state. In 1937 alone, the Reich treasury took in RM 840 million in alcohol taxes.[101] But alcohol was also a convenient way to drown sorrows. Many an evil deed must have been forgotten by perpetrators who drank themselves into a stupor (recall Gumpert's "opium" equation). Many concentration camp guards and euthanasia managers were notorious drunks, perhaps seeking alcoholic oblivion to quell their consciences. During the war, alcohol came to be used as both an enticement to encourage productivity and a bonus to those who carried out the "dirty work" of extermination. Members of the SS received special rations, but so did workers in less murderous trades.[102] On February 1, 1942, Joseph Goebbels ordered workers at high-performing factories to be given special rations of cigarettes and alcohol. He also barred the public sale of alcohol in Berlin, insisting that all available liquor be used instead "as a reward for outstanding performance in the factories." Two weeks later he ordered the diversion of 150,000 bottles of schnapps to soldiers on the northern front, confiding in his diary that "the Berliner will simply have to get along without."[103]

The different fates of alcohol and tobacco under the Nazis are revealing. Both were seen as harmful to health and as financial drains, but there were also important differences in how these two kinds of danger were viewed. Alcohol was the more obviously incapacitating intoxicant, and racial hygienists were far more ready to believe that alcohol might be a mutagen. (Alcohol today is known to cause *congenital* damage to the developing fetus, but there is no evidence of a *mutagenic* effect that might be passed via the germ-line into subsequent generations). The 1933 Sterilization Law allowed for the vasectomizing of alcoholics, though comparable steps were never taken against smokers. Drunks were confined to concentration camps as early as 1934, but, again, no such measures were ever taken against smokers (though tobacco withdrawal among female prisoners was studied). Smoking was regarded as a health threat, but strong punitive steps were only rarely taken against smokers as a group.

Nazi leaders were never in fact confident about how to proceed against alcohol. Beer had long been a staple of the German diet, and it was not at all obvious how to wean the German workingman. Temperance advocates took pains to argue that beer was not "a food"; the nutritionist Wolfgang Kitzing disputed the myth "propagated by the beer industry" that beer was simply "liquid bread."[104] America's repeal of Prohibition was a frequent topic of conversation, and German temperance advocates worried that their movement, too, might encounter a backlash. Nazi leaders often expressed concern about appearing overly "puritanical" when it came to alcohol or tobacco restrictions: a 1939 essay on the "health leadership of the German youth" pointed out that total bans—"like the Prohibition laws in America"—had done "more harm than good" in the struggle against alcohol.[105]

PERFORMANCE-ENHANCING FOODS AND DRUGS

Nazi racial theorists distinguished "negative" and "positive" eugenics: negative eugenics was designed to eliminate inferiors (by sterilization, for example), whereas "positive" eugenics was supposed to encourage the breeding of the "fit"—through financial rewards for healthy children, for example, and laws requiring scholars to be married. A similar distinction can be seen in Nazi food policy. I have already mentioned efforts to eliminate toxic contaminants and unwholesome adulterants, but there were also efforts to engineer foods with optimal nutritional value—"superfoods" that would optimize the functioning of the *Übermensch*.

Nature and "the organic" were therefore not the only themes of Nazi dietary interest. A complementary theme was performance (*Leistung*), the idea that normal corporeal capacity could be elevated through various means, including nutritional artifice. A great deal of attention was given to how different foods and drugs might increase stamina, concentration, or some other gauge of human physical or mental performance. Caffeine, for example, was studied to see whether human mental or physical efficiency could be enhanced without undue side effects; studies were also done to determine whether the caffeine added to soft drinks might be harmful to young people. Nervous folk were said not to be particularly tolerant; caffeine was also said to lead to hearing problems in certain people. A 1941 Hitler Youth handbook declared that for young people at least, caffeine was a poison "in every form and in every strength."[106] (Fritz Lickint declared coffee a carcinogen, but Hermann Druckrey challenged the idea, pointing out that Lickint's coffee beans had been roasted at an artificially high temperature, producing tars and carbonized chemicals that would not normally occur in the routine process of coffee making.[107] Decaffeinated coffee was widely available—and strictly regulated—by the end of the 1930s.)[108]

Extensive studies were also done on the stimulant Pervitin, one of the most popular "uppers" of the era.[109] Pervitin was discovered in 1938 by a chemist working at the Temmler Drug Company in

Berlin and was rapidly promoted by people convinced that the amphetamine—like caffeine or adrenaline—could increase mental performance. The new drug helped to stave off fatigue and was said to be able to reverse some of the effects of narcotics or alcohol. Pervitin was used to cheer up cancer patients prior to surgery,[110] and some even said it could awaken people from a coma. Pervitin became widely used in both psychiatry and psychotherapy, though in 1941, following reports of widespread abuse and chronic dependency, it was made available only by prescription. Experiments in psychiatric hospitals and concentration camps found that users could be kept awake for more than twenty-four hours, after which they fell into a disturbed sleep for up to twenty hours.[111] Enthusiasm for the drug diminished in the later years of the war, after it was found to present the risk of addiction and various unpleasant side effects. The drug clearly speeded certain tasks, but it could also hamper ability to concentrate,[112] and chronic use seemed to cause personality disorders similar to schizophrenia.[113] While it was clear that there was some value in occasional use (e.g., by pilots on long night-flights), routine use could lead to physical collapse.

Caffeine and Pervitin were not the only mind-altering drugs explored during the war. At Dachau, Nazi doctors fed prisoners mescaline to see whether it might be possible to manipulate their opinions. The general consensus, after thirty prisoners were treated with the drug, was that it was "impossible to impose one's will on another person as in hypnosis, even when the strongest dose of mescaline had been given."[114]

Military objectives were the primary interest in many such studies—as when Nazi scientists gave storm troopers testosterone to see if they could be made more aggressive—but the interest in such drugs also has to be understood as part of the crackdown on addiction. Addiction research becomes a major focus in the Nazi era, as does the larger question of how to combat illicit drugs. Nazi officials cracked down hard on cocaine, heroin, and other illegal narcotics: American drug enforcement officials in the mid-1930s praised German efforts in this area as among the best in the world. Illicit drugs were not the only problem, however, as the Reich

Health Office made clear in a 1939 report complaining that sleeping pills were being taken in extraordinarily high dosages—as many as forty per night for one popular brand (Phanodorm). Evidence began to grow that Germans were using sleeping pills to commit suicide, which obviously did not make the government sleep easy.[115]

Ordinary foods were also explored for their performance-enhancing power. A 1942 study found that a warm meal could "increase performance by 10 percent" among women doing night-shift work.[116] A 1941 investigation reported that workers exposed to extremes of heat were best served by foods high in carbohydrates.[117] Reduction of fatigue was a focus of many investigations of this sort: experiments done by Otto Ranke in 1940 and 1941, for example, showed that a high-protein diet could, under certain circumstances, stave off fatigue and increase capacity to work.[118]

One of the goals of such research was to determine how much protein the average adult man had to consume to maintain "full performance" (eighty grams per day, according to one study). Calorie intake was studied: Ranke, for example, showed that a diet of less than 2,000 calories per day could not be maintained without gradual weight loss, primarily owing to the loss of the body's fat reserves.[119] Attention also focused increasingly on finding out how little food a person needed to survive or work in different environments. A 1942 study explored the caloric needs of men and women of different ages and body size, recording how food needs varied with work pace and other variables. The author found that women, on average, needed only 90 percent of what men needed, but that children of both sexes needed almost the same as adult men. Professions involving standing or walking demanded an extra 10 percent, stressful occupations (foundry workers, carpenters, and camp workers [!], for example) even more, and trades requiring extreme physical exertion (smiths, riveters, construction workers) even more again.

Precise calculations of daily caloric needs were made for each of these groups in different types of conditions.[120] A 1939 study had found that students helping with the harvest burned an average of 3,610 calories per day, while farmworkers consumed about 5,700 calories. The highest consumption recorded was among mountain climbers and skiers: a 1944 analysis found that people involved in such activities could burn 9,000 or even 10,000 calories a day. Still other studies were done to investigate resistance to cold as a function of caloric intake. A series of studies begun in 1944 showed that resistance increased with protein consumption and decreased with fat intake. These last-mentioned studies were continued after the war with support from U.S. military authorities[121]—though there is often uncertainty concerning where the original experiments were carried out, whether concentration camp prisoners were used as subjects, for example (the published reports rarely say). More research needs to be done in this area—especially to find out whether such studies may have tied in somehow with the starvation of the handicapped in "euthanasia" institutions.

Efforts to rationalize German food can also be seen in the push to discover substitutes for foods made scarce by the war. Synthetic honey and margarine were already features of the First World War, as is clear from the first few pages of Erich Remarque's famous 1928 novel, *All Quiet on the Western Front*. In the Second World War, the list of synthetics was greatly expanded. Mineral oils were used in cooking, yeast was made from wood, and fish protein was encouraged in baking. Searches were launched to find new substitutes for coffee (malt coffee and a brew derived from oats), protein (soybeans were a hot item, earning them the label "Nazi beans"), and diverse fats and oils (hardened walnut oil, for example, used as a lard substitute). Experiments were performed to see whether nutrients could be extracted from fruit pits, and whether alfalfa could serve as a human food. Military, medical, and economic urgencies merged in many of these quests—as when articles began to appear on how to identify wild forest plants suitable for the brewing of herbal teas.[122] Children were encouraged to tell their parents to drink these "German teas," the rationale being that they were good for your health, good for the German economy, and good for the war effort (see figs. 5.6 and 5.7).[123]

Artificial fat was an object of special interest. Researchers at Otto Flössner's Reich Health Office laboratory in 1941 conducted both human and animal experiments on synthetic fat, though opinions

Fig. 5.6. "Apothecaries help you with their healing plants!" Support for natural herbs and medicines was strong in the Nazi era; the Dachau concentration camp became one of the world's leading producers of natural botanicals and spices. Source: *Der Stürmer* 14 (1936): Sondernummer 4.

ufn.: Reichsbildstelle der RJF, Berlin

Ieil- und Teekräutersammlung, ein Kriegseinsatz der Jugend im Dienste der Volksgesundheit.

FIG. 5.7. Children were encouraged to gather wild plants for "German teas"; health was part of the interest, but military planners also encouraged the practice as a way to cut down on medical costs. Source: Reiter and Breger, *Deutsches Gold*, p. 282.

differed on both the taste and the digestibility of the resulting substance.[124] Experiments were also performed to compare the food value of soybean oil, olive oil, coconut fat, and whale oil. (Germany in the 1930s had the world's largest commercial whaling fleet.) Investigators knew from nineteenth-century studies that about a third of the average German's caloric intake derived from fat; experiments were undertaken to determine how well the human body could tolerate higher or lower fractions. A series of unpublished studies conducted during the war found that 50–60 percent of one's calories could come from fat with "no reduction in bodily performance."[125]

Some of the proposals put forward to salvage the last gram of edible fat or protein from livestock were rather gruesome. In 1940, for example, the director of the Reich Health Office's Division of Nutritional Physiology proposed an effort to find new ways to exploit the forty million kilograms of cattle blood discarded every year in slaughterhouses. The Nazi nutritionist calculated that the wasted blood had an equivalent protein value of 100,000 head of cattle weighing five hundred kilograms each.[126] Many of the foods commonly eaten in Germany today trace to efforts to utilize every last scrap of food (think of blood sausage or poppy seed cakes made from crumbs)—but Germans of the 1930s and early 1940s seem to have taken these efforts to an extreme. (Recall, though, Upton Sinclair's critique of Chicago meat packers' using every part of the pig "except the squeal.") Ventures such as these must have given rise to the myth that the Nazis used human fat from Jews to make soap; many other personal effects were in fact "recycled"—gold from teeth, eyeglasses, prosthetic limbs, and even human hair—but fat, apparently, never was.[127]

Performance studies must be understood as part of the larger quest to rationalize resources. The Nazis were not the first to carry out such studies (the Royal Society of London's Food Committee had calculated caloric requirements for different occupations in the 1920s),[128] but Germans took this process further than anyone else—and with deadly consequences. Herbert Marcuse used to point out that reason in the small can buttress irrationality in the large; the rationalization of German food and work may have allowed certain short-term gains for some, but the militaristic inhumanity uniting these separate parts led down the road to genocide. Ian Kershaw reminds us that the road to Auschwitz was paved with indifference; technocratic myopia is always welcomed by the scheming dictator.

Foods for Fighting Cancer

The Nazi war on cancer was by and large a campaign waged with the goal of prevention, but novel treatments were also explored in many quarters. Orthodox treatments involved some form of surgery or radiation, but there were many other options. Heavy metals were a popular remedy, as were countless forms of chemother-apy, heliotherapy, protein therapy, vaccine therapy, viral therapy, hormone therapy, and therapies based on extracts of everything from mistletoe and hemlock to cobra venom, Chinese rhubarb, and formic acid.[129] Fischer-Wasels explored a therapy based on ura-nium salts, while a Dr. Flesch-Thebesius of Frankfurt tested a ther-apy based on injections of fruit juice.

Dietary therapeutics were enormously popular in Germany—more so here than anywhere else, according to observers at the time.[130] The most common view was that excessive nutrition fa-vored tumor growth while hunger inhibited it,[131] but countless other theories found expression. Thousands of popular books, pamphlets, and articles extolled the virtues or vices of particular foods or elements within foods—everything from aluminum to zinc. (As already noted, a widely debated fear of the late 1920s was that the use of aluminum pans and utensils was responsible for the upsurge of cancer.)[132] Dietary causes debated at this time included alcohol, carbohydrates, cholesterol, coffee, eggs, milk, po-tassium, pork fat, potatoes, protein, salt, sugar, tea, tomatoes, and even water; cancer was said to be caused by overeating, by consti-pation, by foods that were too salty or too hot or too spicy, by sharp or jagged teeth, by the inability to metabolize protein, or by putrefying poisons in the intestine. Tumors were supposed to be hindered by fruit, milk, periodic fasting, raw foods, diets low in meat or high in carbohydrates, and myriad other culinary varia-tions—no food or eating habit seems to have been spared from credit or blame at some point or another.

Cancer researchers spent a lot of time trying to sort out facts from fads in such matters. Selenium was tested as a cancer-fighting agent, as were bismuth, calcium, gold, iodine, magnesium, potas-sium, tellurium, and half a dozen other elements. The impact on tumor transplants was examined, as was the effectiveness of vari-ous substances in accelerating or retarding the growth of cancers caused by coal tar and other carcinogens.[133] Foods were tested for their capacity to starve or feed a tumor, to render it acid or alka-line; therapies were designed to slow the growth of tumors by rendering them oxygen-rich or oxygen-starved; therapies were devised to strengthen the body ravaged by cancer or to counteract the devastation caused by radiation or surgery. Therapeutics most often attached to one or another biochemical theory fashioned to make the whole seem plausible: cancer was said to be a "deficiency disease" or a "disease of excess"; cancers were alternately a product of local irritation, allergies, "chronic auto-intoxication," "asphyxial acidosis," or "local oxygen deficiency." Cancer was said to be a consequence of too little or too much of just about anything you might think of.[134]

Some of the more popular theories contradicted one another. Alfred Neumann recommended coffee while barring milk; Erwin Liek barred coffee and recommended milk. Ferdinand Blumenthal found that a restricted diet promoted tumor growth, while Wilhelm Caspari found the opposite to be true. Liek and others stressed raw vegetables, but Caspari "banned" spinach and tomatoes, cautioning against raw food as "purposeless and dangerous."[135] Fischer-Wasels limited carbohydrates, but Hans Auler allowed an abundance of bread, macaroni, corn, malt, and sugar, not to mention large quantities of raw meat and fat—especially butterfat.[136] Experimentation seemed to cloud the issue as often as it clarified, the problem being that laboratory results could vary precipitously according to the kinds of animals used or the conditions under which an agent was administered (for how long, in what combinations, etc.). Experiments also sometimes killed the patients, as one series of cold-water immersion studies found.* The "will to believe" must often have been strong, though the inherent difficulty of designing experiments to resolve such questions should not be underestimated.

* The *Monatsschrift für Krebsforschung* in 1942 reported on "whole body cooling" experiments by H. Eltrom of Copenhagen; Eltrom had placed eleven patients with late-stage cancers (*Malignomen*), all of whom had had undergone extensive radiotherapy, in very cold water for several hours. Six of the eleven died from cardiac arrest in the course of the experiment or shortly thereafter. One had been placed in water of 26.4° C for twenty-six hours, while also under the influence of narcotics. Germans reviewing the research concluded that while the treatment did help to reduce pain, "one could achieve better results with less dangerous methods"; see O. Kaum, "Referate," *Monatsschrift für Krebsforschung* 10 (1942): 223.

Vitamin therapies were among the more controversial. Vitamins had been discovered prior to the First World War, largely in consequence of exploring nutritional deficiency diseases like scurvy and pellagra in the British military. Germans were slow to accept the value of vitamins (Max Rubner's influential *Kalorienlehre*, popular around the time of the First World War, stressed only the human body's need to maintain a certain level of calories and ignored the value of fresh fruits and vegetables),[137] but by the 1930s the role of vitamins was widely appreciated. Vitamins were known to be unsaturated fats produced in the liver; fat- and water-soluble forms had been distinguished (A versus B, for example); and the primary vitamins A, B, C, D, and E were known to exist in different chemical subtypes (B_1–B_4, etc.). Vitamin C was known to protect against scurvy, vitamin D (from sunlight) against rickets,[138] and B_1 against beriberi. Sterility had been shown to be caused by a shortage of vitamin E (in 1927), and pellagra by a shortage of vitamin B_2 (in 1925). Fruit and vegetables were known to be good sources of vitamins,[139] but it was also becoming clear that vitamins were destroyed in the course of food processing and storage.[140] It was even known how much of a given vitamin was needed to reverse a specific ailment (only 0.01 mg of vitamin D per day to cure rickets, for instance).[141] Excitement over vitamins came to border on hype, as the first issue of the new Swiss journal *Zeitschrift für Vitaminforschung* (1932–) forecast a "future of medicine" lying "largely in dietetics."[142]

Cancer was an obvious candidate for vitamin cures: a host of other puzzling diseases had succumbed to dietary therapeutics—why not *Krebs*? Public health and medical journals of the 1930s are full of vitamin cancer therapies.[143] Hopes for a quick diet cure were dealt a blow, however, when it turned out that vitamin-rich foods seemed to promote tumor growth as often as they inhibited it. Wilhelm Caspari of Frankfurt's Institute for Experimental Therapy in 1933 reported that vitamin B and, to a lesser extent, vitamin A actually promoted tumor growth; the situation with vitamin C was not yet clear, while D seemed to have no effect one way or the other.[144] Caspari warned against giving cancer patients too much vitamin B or potassium; patients were cautioned against eating spinach, green cabbage, tomatoes, calves' liver, tongue, cocoa, legumes, almonds, chestnuts, vitamin B–rich soups, and tea (for its potassium). He recommended instead a calcium- and magnesium-rich diet, roughly comparable to what diabetics were supposed to follow.[145] Suspicion of vitamins as carcinogens was so high by 1933 that scholars at the Charité Hospital's Institute for Cancer Research in Berlin actually postulated that cancer mortality was high in June–July and October–November owing to the higher consumption of vitamins in those months. Like many others at this time, the authors recommended a low-vitamin diet for cancer patients.[146]

The problem with all such theories was that for every study seeming to indicate an effect, another failed to reproduce the result. Vitamins were obviously required for growth—but cancerous growths were not unlike any other kind of growth in this regard. Like hormones, vitamins were required for bodily metabolism whether cancerous or not. When Max Borst reviewed the state of cancer research in 1941, he noted that neither hormones nor vitamins could properly be regarded as carcinogens or anticarcinogens. Both were important for bodily function, but neither seemed to offer much hope as a cancer cure.[147]

The situation was similar to that of another popular craze designed to combat cancer: colonic cleansing. The Russian embryologist and yogurt enthusiast Elie Metchnikoff had popularized the idea early in the century, spurred by his observation that yogurt-eating Bulgarians had a surprisingly high percentage of centenarians.[148] The idea was that the human colon sometimes accumulates stagnating, putrefying, cancer-causing bacteria, which a proper dietary regimen can help to counteract. As it was developed in Germany in the 1920s and 1930s, the theory held that toxic coliform bacteria secreted poisons that could cause cancer and other digestive ailments; colonic cleansings were prescribed for stomach and colorectal cancer patients, along with medicinal enemas and more orthodox regimens of radiation and surgery.[149]

One of the most ardent advocates was a Prof. Alfred Nissle at the Bacteriologic Research Institute of Freiburg, who designed a special cancer diet to combat the *Dysbakterie* in the colon. In the late 1920s, Nissle marketed a dietary supplement known as "Mutaflor," a mistletoe leaf extract sold in various forms to redress purported imbalances in the bacterial "flora" of the colon. Mutaflor became very popular in Nazi era,[150] and not just for cancer but for chronic arthroses, skin and organ cancers (under the trade name "Plenosol"), and many other ailments.[151] Hitler was a devotee, allowing his feces to be routinely inspected for pathogenic bacteria, though the SS nutritionist Ernst Schenck after the war noted that whatever unhealthy germs may have been present in the Führer's stool must have perished beyond recognition after transport hundreds of kilometers back to the laboratories where it was scrutinized. Fecal inspection was popular in the Nazi era: there is at least one book devoted entirely to the structure and chemistry of human excrement.[152]

It is not possible even to mention all of the cancer diets proposed at this time; there are literally hundreds. The popularity of such therapies—often scoffed at by orthodox healers—must have derived in no small part from the desperation of cancer sufferers. The willingness to grasp at straws did not change when the Nazis took over; things are not so very different today.

Banning Butter Yellow

I mentioned earlier the Nazi-era distinction between "negative" and "positive" racial hygiene—the former designed to curb the reproduction of the "unfit," the latter to encourage the breeding of "superior" populations. There was also what was known as *preventive* racial hygiene, designed to protect the genetic material from harm. The goal of this third kind of *Rassenhygiene* was to safeguard the human genetic heritage by preventing exposure to hazardous genotoxins—substances like alcohol, radiation, and tobacco, but also other threats to genetic health stemming from a hazardous environment. The Nazi campaign against environmental carcinogens can be seen as part of this push for preventive racial hygiene.

One of the more interesting aspects of this campaign was the move to ban dimethylaminoazobenzene, a widely used coal tar

vereinigung der deutschen Gartenbauwirtschaft) agreed to reduce certain dyes in tomato products and marmalades, and to look into whether the "greening" of preserved vegetables could be eliminated (the trend was already to avoid copper colorings, since they tended to corrode food containers).[162] A trade association representing dairymen wanted to keep its colorings, though it, too, eventually agreed to reduce the dyes added to butter.[163] Reiter also wrote I. G. Farben—producer of almost all of Germany's food dyes—and asked the company to stop producing butter yellow;[164] archival evidence and postwar reports indicate that they complied.[165]

Reiter's goal by this point was to get at least half of all colorings removed from German foods, but it is unclear how close he came to achieving this. We do know that his office in 1940 and 1941 spent 48,000 RM investigating food colorings for possible cancer hazards, a fairly substantial sum;[166] we also know that he continued meeting with makers of bread, candy, cheese, marzipan, ice cream, and soft drinks to dissuade them from using colorings—and often got concessions.[167] He met with liquor producers and restaurant reps, and debated whether housewives should be allowed to purchase colorings for use at home. He even answered queries from the military, which had begun to worry that some of their synthetic spices and fragrances might be carcinogenic—especially artificial pepper (*Cinnamenylacrylsäurepiperidid*: don't ask me for a translation), but also artificial pimento, nutmeg, cinnamon, and cardamom. Reiter ordered that synthetic aromas be sold only in tiny packages, to discourage overuse; he also devised warning labels stating that suspect agents (e.g., artificial bitter almond) should not be used in undiluted form. He recommended that natural colorings like caramelized sugar or honey be used whenever possible, and asked the NSDAP's Public Health Office to help him replace synthetic dyes with plant-derived colors like carotene oil. It was important in this time of "total war," he said, for people to believe their food supply was safe.[168]

Reiter, though, was clearly disappointed by the pace of progress in the dye-ban campaign. Research efforts suffered a setback in June of 1943, when the animal laboratories of the Reich Health Office were destroyed in an Allied bombing raid.[169] In November of 1944, Reiter petitioned the Plenipotentiary for Total War Mobilization to ban all food dyes; German factories were still producing more than three hundred metric tons of food colorings every year—enough to fill an entire freight train—and Reiter argued that a ban would made military sense, given that the chemicals and labor freed up by such a ban could be used for more war-worthy pursuits. Reiter also knew, though, that the whole question of food dyes was receding in the face of deeper problems—like starvation—especially since many of the items in question (colored crab soup or tomato sauce, for example) were no longer available in any form—colored or not. Some Nazi leaders by this time had already taken matters into their own hands: the Reichsstatthalter for the Oberdonau region, for example, in December of 1941 had issued his own ban on butter yellow; Württemberg's interior minister defended such bans as helping to win the war.[170]

Protests against the use of dyes by influential German doctors continued throughout the war. Johannes Kretz in 1944 published a strong attack on German food dye policy, protesting the fact that little had been done to curb their use despite incontrovertible evidence of a cancer hazard. Kretz warned that since some people were especially sensitive, and that "even the tiniest" exposure could cause cancer, it was better to play it safe and ban the use of azo dyes in foods altogether.[171] Karl Heinrich Bauer that same year compared the continued use of butter yellow to a "mass human experiment":

> One often hears a food chemist or some other expert stating there is "no evidence of harm" from a given substance. Today, after thirty years of cancer research, we are dubious of such claims. Experiments can be performed to reveal or disprove a cancer hazard. Look at X-rays, or aniline dye, or scarlet red, or countless other carcinogens, and what you see is that all were assumed to be harmless until the human experiment we call "occupational cancer"—on a massive scale, and after a long period of latency—proved the reality of a cancer threat. . . . Heil Hitler![172]

Bauer's remarks show that influential German physicians were sensitive to the dangers of human experiments "on a massive scale" (*Massenexperimente*), but they also show that physicians were willing to protest the sale of carcinogens to the highest levels of the Nazi health apparatus—in this case to Paul Rostock, the right-hand man of Karl Brandt and a man who, after the war, faced charges of having helped to organize murderous human experiments in concentration camps.

What is most remarkable about this campaign against the false blonding of butter, again, is the fact that influential Nazi physicians saw themselves as duty-bound to eliminate life-threatening contaminants from German foods. The campaign against coal tar dyes is only one example: lead-lined toothpaste tubes were banned fifty years prior to a similar move in the United States, and in 1937, Reich Health Office president Hans Reiter banned the bleaching of flour. Efforts were made to improve water quality[173] and to curtail the use of artificial sweeteners such as saccharine (some said this was a carcinogen!).[174] By the 1940s, few nations were as conscious of, and willing to root out, hazards in the healthy citizen's food, air, and water.

IDEOLOGY AND REALITY

It is difficult to assess the overall impact of Nazi food reforms, difficult to separate boasts from facts, ideology from reality. There are biases that have to be reckoned with: Nazi-era scientific literature is not always to be trusted, since there was often a desire to highlight good news and suppress bad. Even the bad news cannot always be trusted, though, since apocalyptic prognoses were a regular feature of Nazi rhetoric before and after 1933—part of the ongoing Nazi "revolution." There is bias even in the accounts by émigrés like Martin Gumpert, who painted a dismal but probably exaggerated picture of declining health, rising hunger, and degraded intellectual life in the Thousand Year Reich prior even to 1940.[175]

One thing we must never forget, though, is that Nazi food reforms have a dark and sinister side, accompanied as they were by efforts to eliminate "useless eaters" from German society. Hitler at the start of the war declared that "the food supply does not allow for the incurably ill to be dragged through the war"[176]—the implication being that something would have to happen to make them stop eating. Prior even to the onset of "active euthanasia," patients at psychiatric hospitals had been placed on near-starvation diets: at the Eichberg asylum near Wiesbaden, for example, patients were living (and dying) primarily on root vegetables.[177] Food became a political lever, forcing some into starvation while keeping others alive and happy. Bavaria's "starvation diet decree" of November 1942 made this explicit, allowing patients capable of performing useful work to be given higher rations. No one knows exactly how many people were deliberately starved to death; the total number of those "euthanized" (a large portion by starvation) is close to 200,000.[178]

There is also evidence, though, that certain kinds of food deteriorated even for the large majority of ordinary Germans outside the camps or "euthanasia" institutions. Martin Gumpert in his 1940 *Heil Hunger!* pointed out that infant mortality in 1937 was 40 percent higher in Germany than in neighboring Holland. Many diseases were on the rise, among them rickets and dysentery, linked to malnutrition and contaminated food, respectively. Gumpert argued that the increase in such diseases stemmed from the stockpiling of food for use in the event of war; stockpiles would be sold just prior to spoilage, flooding markets with a lot of inferior food. His conclusion: Hitler's program of health restoration was "a crime against the health of 80 million people in the heart of Europe, a crime against the civilization of our world." He also predicted that the Nazi machine might continue for a time "to register high performance under pressure" but that "one day it will be nothing but a heap of scrap iron."[179]

Gumpert obviously could not comment on the impact of the war, but some of his predictions do appear to have come true. Food rationing started on August 28, 1939, only four days prior to the invasion of Poland.[180] The variety of foods was reduced (a single *Einheitsmargarine* replaced the three different grades of butter substitutes previously available, for example), and Jews were allowed only a fraction of the food given to non-Jews. Food rations even for "respectable" Germans were lowered several times in the course of the war. When rations were cut in March of 1942, a public opinion survey conducted by the Sicherheitsdienst (Heydrich's SS security service) found that no other announcement since the onset of war had delivered such a blow to public morale.[181]

We will probably never know what effect Nazi food and social policies may have had on German cancer rates. The British epidemiologist George Davey Smith has argued that Nazi healthy-eating campaigns "had no discernible long term impact" on German health and well-being; indeed, he suggests, the net effect may have been unfavorable, given the notorious *Fresswelle* ("wave of gluttony") that followed the war in the 1950s. Germans seem to have made up for the deprivations of war by feasting and fattening (and smoking) in subsequent decades. Germany today has roughly the same pattern of mortality seen in other overfed and over-smoked nations,[182] with some interesting exceptions that I will note in my concluding chapter.

We do know that postwar diabetes rates fell, as sugar was hard to come by; we also know that morbidity rates from several other illnesses fell. Cancer effects, though, are far more difficult to discern. Stomach cancer rates have declined everywhere in Europe and America, and probably have nothing to do with anything peculiar to what the Nazis did. Declining stomach cancer rates seem to be traceable to the increasing consumption of fresh fruits and vegetables, owing in no small part to improved transport networks—including better roads and highways but also the development of refrigerated trucks and trains.

The ascetic impulses of the 1930s and 1940s have not disappeared, but they no longer cling to the right-wing impulses we associate with murderous antisemitism—or at least not with the same force. Movements can be disengaged from their ideological support strings, however important those strings may be at any given time in history.

6

The Campaign against Tobacco

So many excellent men have been lost to tobacco poisoning.

Adolf Hitler, 1942

Die "Tabakdämmerung" hat begonnen.
(We are witnessing the beginning of the end of tobacco.)

Wolfgang Klarner, in his 1940 medical thesis

HISTORIANS of science tend to treat the 1950s as a kind of *Stunde
Null* (zero hour) of tobacco health research, especially when it
comes to the question of when a lung cancer hazard was first recognized.[1] In a recent review of Richard Kluger's *Ashes to Ashes*, for
example, Daniel J. Kevles remarked that the danger of smoking to
health "rested on little more than anecdotal evidence coupled with
moral censure until 1950, when studies appeared in the United
States and England that strongly incriminated cigarettes as a cause
of lung cancer."[2]

Was it, though, the Americans and British who first proved the
lung cancer link? The startling truth is that it was actually in Nazi
Germany that the link was originally established. German tobacco
epidemiology was, in fact, for a time, the most advanced in the
world, as were many other aspects of the antitobacco effort. Support for tobacco hazards research was strong among the Nazi medical elite; indeed, it was in Germany in the late 1930s that we first
find a broad medical recognition of both the addictive nature of
tobacco and the lung cancer hazard of smoking.

FIG. 6.1. The Nazi party barred smoking in many public spaces, including party offices and waiting rooms (*Diensträume*). Note the negroid
head on the cigar; Nazi antitobacco activists tried to characterize smoking
as the vice of degenerate Africans. Source: *Auf der Wacht* 58 (1941): 24.

That recognition was fostered, I shall argue, by a national political climate stressing the virtues of racial hygiene and bodily purity.
Tobacco in the Nazi view of the world was a genetic poison; a
cause of infertility, cancer, and heart attacks; a drain on national
resources and a threat to public health. The Nazi regime launched

FIG. 6.2. "You Have the Duty to Be Healthy!" Cover from the Hitler Youth manual, *Du hast die Pflicht, gesund zu sein!* vol. 1, *Nikotin und Alkohol*, ed. Reichsjugendführung (Berlin: n.p., n.d.), with thanks to Charles Rosenberg.

an ambitious antismoking campaign, involving extensive public health education, bans on certain forms of advertising, and restrictions on smoking in many public spaces (see figs. 6.1 and 6.2). The aggressive steps taken in this direction were consistent with the regime's larger emphasis on doctor-directed "health leadership"

(*Gesundheitsführung*), embracing both preventive health and the primacy of the public good over individual liberties—the so-called duty to be healthy (*Gesundheitspflicht*).

What may be most disturbing about the Nazi antitobacco campaign is the rather uncomfortable light it sheds on the relation between science and politics at this time. The story is not the familiar one of the suppression of science, or the unwilling conformity of science to political ideals; the relation between science and politics—at least in the aspect I shall be treating—was more symbiotic, more supportive. The Nazi war on tobacco shows that what most people would concede to be "good" science can be pursued in the name of antidemocratic ideals. It is therefore not enough to speak only of the suppression or even survival of science; we have to see how dictatorial ideals worked to inspire and guide the science and policies of the time.

Early Opposition

Antitobacco sentiments were nothing new to the twentieth century. German opposition to smoking, chewing, and snorting tobacco dates from early in the seventeenth century, when the yellow leaf was introduced into Germany by Dutch and English soldiers fighting in the Thirty Years War (1618–1648). The first recorded effort to grow tobacco in Germany, by an Alsatian farmer in Strassburg in 1620, met with resistance from the city council, apparently worried that tobacco growing would cut into the production of more worthy crops, like cereals. Cultivation was common in many parts of Germany by the end of the seventeenth century, though certain towns were not exactly tobacco-friendly.

In the late 1600s, smoking bans were enacted in Bavaria, Kursachsen, and certain parts of Austria. Smoking was banned in Berlin in 1723, in Königsberg in 1742, and in Stettin in 1744.[3] Penalties for violating such bans could be severe. In Lüneberg in 1691, for example, persons found smoking or "drinking" tobacco within the city walls could be put to death. Elsewhere, violation of tobacco laws could lead to fines (fifty gold gulden in Cologne, for example), arrest, beatings, banishment, conscription into forced labor, or the fire-branding of a mark on the offending individual.[4] Many such laws—though usually with lesser penalties—remained on the books in Germany until the "professors' revolution" of 1848, when most were lifted. (Nazi philosophers would later use this coincidence to argue that liberalism spurred the uptake of corrupting vices like alcohol and tobacco—and that absolute states had had a more reasonable approach to such matters.)

The rationale behind many of these bans is not always obvious today, though health was clearly only one of several concerns. The archbishop of Cologne in 1649, for example, complained that smoking corrupted the youth and caused fires. When Friedrich the Great of Prussia banned public smoking in 1764, the fear again was that smoking could pose a fire hazard. Goethe in 1806 sniffed at smoking as a companion of drunkenness, a corruption of the spirit, and a financial burden on the German nation, costing 25 million taler per year. The philosopher Arthur Schopenhauer derogated smoking as "a substitute for thought," and Immanuel Kant proclaimed tobacco a habit-forming nuisance that, like alcohol, was especially dangerous for children.[5]

The first German antitobacco organization was established in 1904 (the short-lived Deutsche Tabakgegnerverein zum Schutze für Nichtraucher); this was followed by a Bund Deutscher Tabakgegner based in the town of Trautenau, in Bohemia (1910), and similar associations in Hanover and Dresden, both founded in 1912. When Czechoslovakia was severed from Austria after the First World War, a Bund Deutscher Tabakgegner in der Tschechoslowakei was established in Prague (1920); that same year in Graz was founded a Bund Deutscher Tabakgegner in Deutschösterreich. The Bohemian organization published the first German-language antitobacco journal—Der Tabakgegner (1912–1932); Dresden's Bund Deutscher Tabakgegner gave rise to a second journal, the Deutsche Tabakgegner (1919–1935).[6] The Dresden organization proved to be the most durable of the three: Dresden was Germany's major center of tobacco manufacturing and home to the country's first cigarette factory—the Russian-owned firm Laferme, established in 1862 with six female rollers and one cutter. Dresden also had one of Germany's highest lung cancer rates—Chemnitz topped the list—and was home to the industry's most powerful critic, Fritz Lickint (1898–1960), whom we shall encounter in a moment.

One of the interesting things about these early antitobacco associations was their opposition to alcohol as well as tobacco. The situation was not unlike that in the United States, where "temperance" was intended to apply not just to alcohol but to other vices—idleness, gaming, and swearing, for example.[7] The founders of the Dresden-based Antitobacco League were almost without exception advocates of alcohol abstinence; the same was true of Hanover's association, whose very name betrayed the link (Alkohol- und Tabakgegnerverein = Association of Foes of Alcohol and Tobacco). American-style Prohibition was applauded by many racial hygienists, who feared the power of both smoke and drink to corrupt the German germ plasm. Germany's antialcohol campaign would remain important for the antitobacco movement of the Nazi era.[8]

MAKING THE CANCER CONNECTION

Coincident with the organization of broad-based antitobacco movements was the emergence of a strong, medically oriented critique of tobacco. The military physician E. Beck documented the ill-effects of tobacco during his service on the front in the First World War, and J. F. Lehmann's antisemitic *Münchener medizinische Wochenschrift* in 1921 published a call "To All German Doctors" to combat smoking as both a cause of harm to the body and a financial drain on the impoverished German nation.[9] Edgar Bejach in a 1927 medical thesis surveying German antismoking movements called for tobacco bans in trains, passenger ships, and public waiting rooms, and for Germany's health insurance agencies (the *Krankenkassen*) to publicize the hazards of the golden leaf.[10] Louis Lewin, a prolific professor of pharmacology at the University of Berlin, argued that smoking overstimulated women's reproductive organs, reducing their ability to bear healthy children. Women were asked to cultivate "a different flame: the fire that warms the hearth and home."[11] Robert Hof-stätter, the Viennese misogynist gynecologist, in his 1924 book *Die rauchende Frau* (The smoking woman) attributed dozens of fe-male maladies—including menstrual cramps, uterine atrophy, and ovarian dysfunction—to the action of the evil weed, and called for the conversion of tobacco fields into fruit and vegetable gardens.[12] Hysteria was sometimes traced to smoking, though for the famous Viennese surgeon Theodor Billroth smoking itself was a response to the nervousness brought on by the hectic pace of modern life.[13]

Many of these same themes were featured in Nazi antitobacco rhetoric. Tobacco was opposed by racial hygienists fearing the cor-ruption of the German germ plasm, by industrial hygienists fear-ing a reduction of work capacity, by nurses and midwives fearing harms for the "maternal organism." Tobacco was said to be "a cor-rupting force in a rotting civilization that has become lazy," a cause of impotence among men and frigidity among women.[14] The Nazi-era antitobacco rhetoric drew from an earlier generation's eugenic rhetoric, combining this with an ethic of bodily purity and performance at work.[15] Tobacco use was attacked as "epi-demic," as a "plague," as "dry drunkenness" and "lung masturba-tion"; tobacco and alcohol abuse were "diseases of civilization" and "relics of a liberal lifestyle."[16] Smoking was, in Reich Health Führer Leonardo Conti's words, a deadly "pharmacological mass experiment, the largest in world history."[17] The Jews were some-times blamed: Germany's Seventh-Day Adventist Church, for ex-ample, declared smoking an unhealthy vice propagated by Jews; the health-conscious sect denounced both alcohol and tobacco as "un-German" (*nicht artgemäss*).[18]

By the 1930s, the specter of cancer had also begun to figure in antitobacco rhetoric. Tobacco had been suggested as a cause of cancer as early as the eighteenth century: the English physician John Hill in 1761 had tied smoking to cancer of the nasal passages, and Samuel T. von Soemmerring in Germany three decades later identified pipe smoking as a cause of cancer of the lip.[19] (Thomas Harriot, the English naturalist who brought pipe smoking to En-gland from America, died of cancer of the lip in 1621; his is the first known cancer death thought to have been caused by smoking, though tobacco was not suspected at the time of his death.)[20] These early insights were confirmed in the 1850s, when a French physician by the name of Etienne-Frédéric Bouisson in Montpellier found that sixty-three of his sixty-eight patients with cancer of the mouth (*cancer des fumeurs*) were pipe smokers. (Extirpation of the afflicted organ was one of the most common operations at his hospital.)[21] The famous German pathologist Rudolf Virchow corroborated the connection in the 1860s, by which time the tobacco historian Friedrich Tiedemann had reported several cancers of the tongue brought on by smoking.[22]

Smoking remained a relative luxury throughout the nineteenth century, however, and the cancer contribution cannot have been substantial. As recently as the First World War, lung cancer was still a rarity in Germany as elsewhere in the world. A turn-of-the-century review put the entire number of cases known to medicine at only 140.[23] In 1912, when Isaac Adler produced the first book-length review of the anatomy and pathology of lung cancer, he felt he had to apologize for writing on such a rare and insignificant disease.[24] Medical professors when they did find a patient with the disease took special care to show it to their students, since they were not expected ever to see another case. Today, of course, it is the world's most common cause of cancer death, claiming more than 150,000 victims a year in the United States alone. China is soon going to have close to a million lung cancer deaths every year—thanks almost entirely, again, to cigarettes.

Smoking became more popular toward the end of the nineteenth century, in consequence of the development of mechanized cigarette rolling, tobacco advertising, and state promotion or monopoly—as in Austria or France—of cigarettes to generate tax revenues. Cigarettes were not even manufactured in Germany until the 1860s, and even then the factory girls of Dresden were able to produce only about 120 per hour.[25] *Zigaretten* (literally "little cigars") were said to be an appropriate indulgence for the faster pace of industrial society; cigarettes delivered a quick dose of nicotine to the blood, just as newly invented candy bars were delivering sugar, and prepackaged gun shells were speeding up reloading. Cigarettes were provided with rations to the soldiers of the First

World War (on both sides), facilitating the social acceptance of the habit in both Europe and America. German cigarette consumption rose from about eight billion cigarettes in 1910 to thirty billion only fifteen years later, culminating in eighty billion in 1942 (more on the meaning of this in a moment).[26] The introduction of milder types of tobacco and flue curing made it easier for smokers to inhale the burning fumes, encouraging a shift from pipes and cigars to cigarettes. The change was not a trivial one: indeed, as Henner Hess observes, we are talking about "a revolutionary development in the history of drug consumption, roughly comparable in significance to the invention of the hypodermic needle for opiate addiction."[27] By contrast with pipe smokers, cigarette smokers tended to draw the fumes more deeply into the lungs, delivering a much higher dose of tar, nicotine, and other noxious substances to their bronchial passageways.[28]

The cancer consequences were profound, as lung cancer rates grew by leaps and bounds. Dresden, Hamburg, and Berlin physicians were among the first to note the increase, around the turn of the century, followed by physicians in other German cities.[29] The dramatic growth of lung cancer in the 1920s and 1930s was not at first attributed to smoking: the influenza pandemic of 1918 was sometimes blamed, as were automobile exhausts, dust from newly tarred roads, diverse occupational exposures (including tars and chlorinated hydrocarbons), increasing exposure to X-rays, exposure to chemical warfare agents during the First World War, malnutrition in the aftermath of the war, or even the upsurge of racial mixing.[30] Some scholars doubted the reality of the increase—a 1930 article in the *Medizinische Klinik* argued that the widespread use of X-rays was simply allowing lung cancers to be diagnosed more often[31]—but the more common view by the middle of the Weimar era was that the disease was genuinely on the rise, for as yet unclear reasons.

Part of the difficulty, of course, was that many other things were on the rise which might plausibly be contributing causes of lung cancer. Automobility was growing faster even than lung cancer, which led some to suggest that engine exhausts might be the decisive factor—especially since many components of gasoline and several of its combustion products were proven carcinogens.[32] Roads were being paved at an accelerating pace: Gunther Lehmann of Dortmund pointed out in 1934 that German road tar production had increased from 3,000 tons in 1924 to 120,000 tons only five years later, a fortyfold increase. Dusts of all sorts were blamed, as people began to realize that the use of power tools in mining, metalwork, and other "dusty trades" was raising ever higher levels of irritating dust. Many of the other theories advanced in the 1920s and early 1930s—miscegenation, X-rays, etc.—could be lumped under the broader rubrics of industrialization or urbanization, making it hard to distinguish cause from effect.

In retrospect, it is surprising how long it took for tobacco to be implicated.[33] No one prior to the twentieth century seems to have imagined that smoking might cause lung cancer. One finds no such mention in articles dealing with the anatomy and pathology of the disease, nor in articles on the carcinogenic effects of tobacco. Smoking was widely recognized as a cause of cancer, but the focus was invariably restricted to malignancies of the lip, mouth, or tongue.[34] A French medical thesis of 1897 gives a splendid account of *cancers des fumeurs* afflicting the lips, tongue, jaw, pharynx, tonsils, and nasal passages, but does not even hint that the lungs might be harmed.[35] A German medical dissertation of 1898 documented a small cluster of lung cancers among Leipzig's tobacco workers, but even here the explanation given was that the cancers were being caused not by smoking but by the inhalation of tobacco dust.[36]

There are several reasons one can offer to explain why it took so long for smoking to be implicated as a cause of lung malignancies. The rarity of the disease must have been a factor: cancers of this sort were no doubt often confused with TB or some other unspecified lung disorder, but from what we today know about causality (80 to 90 percent of all cases are due to smoking), lung cancers really must have been quite unusual. Cigarettes were not popular until the end of the nineteenth century, and it was only then that tobacco smoke was mild enough to be inhaled. Lung cancer prior to this time was simply not a disease that attracted a lot of medical attention.

The oversight must also have something to do with the prestige of germ theories at this time. Turn-of-the-century European scholars were busily identifying microbes as the causes of heretofore mysterious diseases, displacing not just hoary humoral theories (tracing ill-health back to imbalances of blood, phlegm, or bile) but also materialist-environmental theories stressing the unhealthy effects of foul air and "miasmas." One also has to reckon with the style of etiological thinking. Under the influence of Virchow and Koch and others, the cause of a disease (most often an infecting microbe) came to be looked for in close temporal and physical proximity to the disease itself. The idea that the smoke you inhale today might give you cancer twenty years later was not yet something physicians were prepared to think about; the idea of a latent period between exposure and disease was not widely appreciated until the twentieth century, when occupational cancers forced the appreciation. The net effect was that far more attention was given to the anatomy and pathology of cancer than to its possible environmental causes. That would change when the explosive growth of lung cancer made it difficult to deny an external causal agent—like smoking.

FRITZ LICKINT: THE DOCTOR "MOST HATED BY THE TOBACCO INDUSTRY"

The Chemnitz (and later Dresden) physician Fritz Lickint in 1929 was one of the earliest to publish statistical evidence joining lung cancer and cigarettes.[37] He was not the first to suggest a link—Isaac Adler and others had already done this[38]—but his was the most thorough review up to that time, while also presenting new statistical information. His evidence was fairly simple, constituting what epidemiologists today call a "case-series" showing that lung cancer patients were particularly likely to be smokers. He also showed that in countries where women smoked as much as men, there was very little difference between male and female lung cancer rates. Lickint's article served as a springboard for

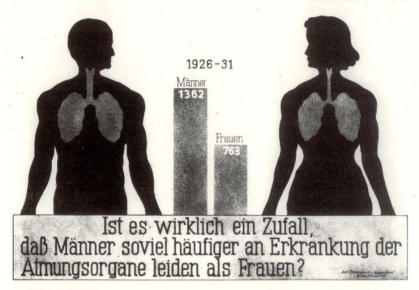

FIG. 6.3. "Is It Really Just by Chance That Men Suffer So Much More Often Than Women from Diseases of the Lungs?" This sexual asymmetry was an important early clue to the carcinogenic action of tobacco. Source: Fritz Lickint, *Tabakgenuss und Gesundheit* (Hanover: Bruno Wilkens, 1936).

many subsequent investigators: Victor Mertens, Angel Roffo, and T. Chikamatsu, for example, all of whom demonstrated the carcinogenic potency of tobacco tar while crediting Lickint's pioneering vision (see figs. 6.3 and 6.4).[39]

Lickint went on to become Germany's foremost exponent of the antismoking message, cautioning that tobacco had surpassed alcohol as a public health menace and that strong steps needed to be taken to counter the threat. In his monumental *Tabak und Organismus* (Tobacco and the organism), published in 1939, Lickint chronicled an extraordinary range of ills deriving from smoking, chewing, or snorting tobacco. The 1,100-page volume, produced in collaboration with the Reich Committee for the Struggle against Addictive Drugs and the German Antitobacco League, was advertised as *Das Standardwerk* and is arguably the most comprehensive scholarly indictment of tobacco ever published. Surveying eight thousand publications worldwide, the author blamed tobacco for cancers all along the *Rauchstrasse* ("smoke alley")—lips, tongue,

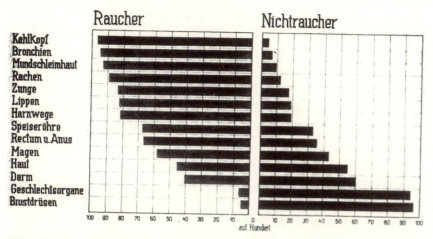

Raucher   Nichtraucher

Kehlkopf
Bronchien
Mundschleimhaut
Rachen
Zunge
Lippen
Harnwege
Speiseröhre
Rectum u. Anus
Magen
Haut
Darm
Geschlechtsorgane
Brustdrüsen

100 90 80 70 60 50 40 30 20 10 0 10 20 30 40 50 60 70 80 90 100
auf Hundert

Krebsverteilung auf Raucher u. Nichtraucher

FIG. 6.4. "Cancer's Distribution among Smokers and Nonsmokers." Angel H. Roffo assembled this chart to show that smokers (*Raucher*) were far more likely than nonsmokers (*Nichtraucher*) to suffer from cancer. The chart shows that 95 percent of all cancers of the larynx (*Kehlkopf*) occurred in smokers; cancers of the lung, mouth, throat, tongue, and bladder were also far more likely to strike smokers. Cancers of the breast (*Brustdrüsen*), by contrast, were far more common among nonsmokers (because the disease primarily afflicts women, and women did not smoke much). Source: *Reine Luft* 24 (1942): 17; also in Lickint, *Tabak und Organismus*, p. 919.

lining of the mouth, jaw, esophagus, windpipe, and lungs. Tobacco was an instigator not just of cancer but of arteriosclerosis, infant mortality, ulcers, halitosis, and dozens of other maladies.[40] Tobacco was a powerful drug: tobacco addiction he characterized as *Nikotinismus* (or, more properly, *Tabakismus*), and the people so afflicted as *Nikotinisten* (or *Tabakisten*).[41] He also compared tobacco addicts to morphine addicts and made a convincing argument that "passive smoking" (*Passivrauchen*—he seems to have coined the term) posed a serious threat to nonsmokers.[42] Lickint argued that thousands of cancer deaths could be prevented by curtailing tobacco use: 20 percent of all male fatal cancers began in the area he dubbed the "Rauchstrasse," leading him to speculate that tobacco might play a major role in as many as seven thousand male cancer deaths per year in Germany.[43]

Lickint by this time was heavily involved in Nazi tobacco politics, though he never joined the Nazi party. Prior to 1933, in fact, his sympathies were clearly with the Social Democrats—which caused him some grief when the political winds shifted. In 1940, he narrowly escaped political difficulties when Karl Astel, president of the University of Jena and director of Jena's Institute for Tobacco Hazards Research, checked into his political background and found that he had been a member of the Social Democratic party, the Association of Socialist Physicians (VSÄ), and the Liga für Menschenrecht, a human rights organization. Lickint had actually lost his medical license in 1934 for failing to indicate on his civil service form—required of all government employees to prove Aryan ancestry and political loyalty—that he had once been a member of the VSÄ. The court ruled that Lickint's membership in the VSÄ constituted membership in a communist association, though a later investigation decided that the Chemnitz branch to which Lickint had belonged had leaned more toward the SPD (social democrats) than the KPD (communists). Reich Health Leader Leonardo Conti came to his defense during the investigation, arguing that the minor infraction of 1934 paled by contrast with his groundbreaking tobacco work. Conti may have been influenced in this matter by the fact that his mother, Nanna Conti, was not just head of Germany's primary midwife association (the Reichsfachschaft der Deutschen Hebammen) but also a member of the governing board of the German Antitobacco League, the leading antitobacco association and the publisher of *Reine Luft*.[44] What the episode does show, though, is that an antitobacco stance could put you in good stead with Nazi authorities—provided, of course, that you were not of Jewish ancestry and were willing to admit to the error of your ways.

NAZI MEDICAL MORALISM

Lickint in 1939 was praised as the physician "most hated by the tobacco industry,"[45] but he was only one of many authors derogating tobacco at this time. Tobacco was said to hinder the military prowess of the German soldier; tobacco temperance was needed to preserve the soldier's "physical fitness and military readiness."[46] Luftwaffe physicians found that nicotine hampered a pilot's ability to function, and forensic physicians found that smoking contaminated the blood with carbon monoxide.[47] Smoking was said to cause automobile accidents, prompting criminal penalties for accidents caused by driving "under the influence" (of cigarettes!).[48] Rudolf Friedrich, a Viennese physician, reported that 80 percent of the men he had examined with ulcers were smokers, and blamed smoking for the skyrocketing incidence of stomach distress since the First World War.[49] Karl Westphal and Hans Weselmann argued that tobacco was the single most common cause of gastritis— but also that since gastritis had been linked to stomach cancer, tobacco was probably also a cause of gastric malignancies.[50] This was especially damning, given that stomach cancer was the leading cause of cancer death among European (and American) men in the 1920s.

German physicians were also aware that smoking was a major cause of heart disease (see figs. 6.5 and 6.6).[51] Nicotine abuse was often blamed for Germany's increased incidence of heart attacks; heart disease was sometimes said to be the single most serious illness brought on by smoking.[52] Late in the war, nicotine was suspected as a cause of the coronary heart failure suffered by German soldiers on the eastern front. Military physicians debated the point: a 1944 report by an army field pathologist found that the thirty-two young soldiers he had examined—all of whom had died from heart attacks at or near the front—had all been "enthusiastic smokers." The author cited the Freiburg pathologist Franz Büchner's view that cigarettes should be considered "a coronary poison of the first order"; he also recognized, though, that certain "spiritual changes" brought on by the war were likely to have contributed to the disease.[53]

Reproductive politics played a major role in Nazi-era opposition to smoking. Smoking women were said to be less marriageable, given that they age early and tend to lose their beauty.[54] Werner Hüttig of the NSDAP's Office of Racial Policy pointed out that nicotine had been found in the breast milk of smoking mothers, and

Verlag Reine Luft · Berlin=Charlottenburg 2, Schillerstr.9

ANGINA

TABAK-SUCHT

Die Schlange läßt „Schlange" stehen

FIG. 6.5. A devil-headed snake labeled "Angina" and "Tobacco Addiction" tempts its victims with cigarettes and cigars; the Nazi medical community by the end of the 1930s had recognized nicotine as both an addictive drug and a major cause of heart attacks. Source: *Reine Luft* 23 (1941): 145.

Jede Zigarette ist ein Schuß auf Dein Herz!

FIG. 6.6. "Every cigarette is a shot into your heart." Source: *Reine Luft* 23 (1941): 99.

Martin Staemmler, an influential Nazi physician, argued that tobacco use by pregnant women was responsible for the growing
incidence of stillbirth and miscarriage.[55] A 1943 article in Germany's leading gynecology journal reported that women who
smoked three or more cigarettes per day were almost ten times as
likely to be childless as women who did not smoke.[56] Agnes
Bluhm, Germany's most prominent female racial hygienist, argued
in a 1936 book that smoking could cause spontaneous abortions.
This was especially disturbing to Nazi authorities who placed a
premium on ensuring a high birthrate among healthy German
women.[57]

Smoking was also said to interfere with male sexual performance. A 1941 health manual published by the Hitler Youth told
how tobacco had been used by sailors to suppress their sexual de-
sires; the same text cited a nineteenth-century French proposal that
smoking should be encouraged in French schools to combat *Onanie*
(masturbation).[58] Tobacco was sometimes said to rob men of their
masculinity, but this does not seem to have implied a transformation into feminine delicacy. Sexual degeneracy was the more common image: tobacco was said to make women barren and men im-
potent. Women who smoked were often portrayed as sexually
loose, but smoking was also said to be a cause of frigidity.[59] The
problem for antismokers, of course, was that tobacco advocates
were, by far, the more cunning image makers (then as now, I might
add). Advertisers cultivated an image of smoking men as masculine and smoking women as feminine; tobacco was portrayed as a
sexual stimulant, while antismokers were depicted as sexually ambiguous (the males effeminate, the females prudes—see fig. 6.7).

For antitobacco activists, however, health was the primary issue.
The dangers of tobacco were magnified, in the Nazi view of things,
by the fact that tobacco was addictive. This was the view of Reich
Health Leader Leonardo Conti in 1939, and many shared his judgment.[60] Tobacco created an alien allegiance in an era when both
mind and body were supposed to belong to the Führer (fig. 6.8).
The charge was a serious one, given that addictions were often
seen as hereditary and hereditary ailments were said to be incurable.[61] The impression broadly shared was that while anyone
might become addicted, the genetically weak and degenerate were

Diese Anzeige wurde verboten!

Kleine Weisheit
aus dem
Raucherabteil

Wenn man den bloßen Theorien der Gesundheits-Aposteleln trauen dürfte, müßte man in den Raucher-Abteilen der Bahnen lauter zusammengebrochene Zwerge fahren sehen und in den Nichtraucher-Abteilen kraftstrotzende Riesen. Wie gut, daß der tägliche Augenschein uns eines Besseren belehrt.

Ist es nicht auch viel einleuchtender, daß der menschliche Organismus durch normale Mengen Alkohol oder Nikotin seine gesunde Widerstandskraft herausfordert und so viel weniger anfällig wird? Der richtige, gesunde, normale Mann kennt nur einen Maßstab für seinen Rauchgenuß: ob ihm seine Zigarette schmeckt oder nicht schmeckt. Und die Gold Dollar schmeckt ihm immer, denn diese herzhafte Zigarette wurde ja extra für richtige Männer geschaffen.

Gold Dollar

WELTMARKT - QUALITÄT

»richtig – für richtige Männer«

FIG. 6.7. *Auf der Wacht*, an antitobacco and antialcohol publication, derides a cigarette ad depicting smokers as manly and antismokers as prudes. The top caption reads: "This ad has been banned!" A commentary, not reproduced here, warns that such ads were "making a mockery" of the party's efforts to hold up Hitler as a model antismoker. The world's first anti-anti-antismoking image? Source: *Auf der Wacht* 54 (1937): 6.

far more vulnerable. Hence the charge that smoking was "especially popular among young psychopaths."[62]

It is not yet clear whether tobacco addicts were ever incarcerated for their addiction, but we do know that fate befell persons addicted to other substances. In 1941, Reich Health Leader Leonardo Conti ordered the establishment of an office to register addicts and combat addiction; similar registries were established to identify alcoholics, the homeless, and so forth.[63] Smokers may have been

FIG. 6.8. "You Don't Smoke It—It Smokes You! Signed, the Chain Smoker." Nazi authorities worried that nicotine created an alien allegiance when your body was supposed to belong to the state and the Führer. Source: *Reine Luft* 23 (1941): 90.

fearful of such moves, given the widespread conception of tobacco use as a "first stage" in the move toward abusing ever stronger substances—like morphine or cocaine.[64] Nazi Germany was famously rough on drug traffickers: a 1938 report by U.S. narcotics officials praised the Nazi regime for throwing a notorious Austrian drug trader into an internment camp "where he will undoubtedly remain for the rest of his life."[65]

FRANZ H. MÜLLER: THE FORGOTTEN FATHER OF EXPERIMENTAL EPIDEMIOLOGY

Documenting the lung cancer hazard of smoking was one of the most remarkable achievements of the Nazi era. Angel H. Roffo of Argentina (1882–1947), who published much of his work in

German cancer journals, had already shown by 1930 that tars derived from tobacco smoke could induce cancer in experimental animals; in subsequent experiments he found that certain tobacco tar distillates could produce tumors in as many as 94 percent of all animals exposed.[66] Roffo was important in shifting the emphasis away from nicotine and onto tar as the active agent of tumorigenesis; Lickint by 1935 could state that nicotine was "probably innocent" of carcinogenic potency and that benzpyrene was more likely the guilty party.[67]

Roffo's experiments were disputed by some—the English scientists Ernest Kennaway and R. D. Passey, for example, who claimed that he had burned his tobacco at temperatures too high to simulate actual smoking[68]—but the striking results prompted others to explore the hazard. Neumann Wender, a Viennese professor, in 1933 showed that tobacco smoke contained not just tar and nicotine but methyl alcohol and other toxins (see fig. 6.9); he also showed that the tar content of cigarette smoke increased when the woody stems of tobacco plants were used in the manufacturing process.[69] Enrico Ferrari of Trieste that same year pointed out that since tar had "excellent cancer-causing properties," it was not hard to imagine that the increasing use of these woody parts might be responsible for the upsurge in lung cancer. Ferrari claimed to have been long convinced ("without a doubt") that cigarettes were a major cause of the disease; he endorsed Wender's proposal for a ban on the use of woody stems as an illegal adulteration.[70] He also suggested that it was not by accident that Trieste had both the highest lung cancer rate and the highest smoking rate of any region in Italy.[71]

Lickint had pointed to the preponderance of smokers among lung cancer patients in 1929, and his was the lead most often followed when physicians began to nail down the link. Rudolf Fleckseder of Vienna in 1936, for example, reported a very high proportion of smokers among his lung cancer patients (48 of the 51 males were smokers; 35 were heavy smokers), and others noted the disproportion.[72] The stage was thereby set for the era's two most important statistical analyses: a 1939 paper by Franz Hermann Müller, a physician at Cologne's Bürgerhospital, and a 1943

Ein weit verbreiteter Irrtum!

Im Tabakrauch ist nicht
nur Nikotin enthalten!

Gifte
im
TABAKRAUCH

Wer die Tabakgefahren bekämpfen
will, muß die auf der vorstehenden
Seite verzeichnete Literatur lesen und
dem „Deutschen Bund zur Bekämpfung der Tabakgefahren"
beitreten!

Deutscher Bund zur Bekämpfung der Tabakgefahren e.V.
Berlin-Charlottenburg 2   ·   Schillerstraße 9

FIG. 6.9. This image is reproduced dozens of times in the back pages of *Reine Luft* in the late 1930s and early 1940s: it shows that tobacco smoke contains not just nicotine but carbon monoxide, ammonia, tar, and many other poisons. Most of these constituents had been identified in the nineteenth century. Top captions read: "A Widespread Misconception! Tobacco Smoke Contains Much More Than Nicotine!"

paper by two scholars—Eberhard Schairer and Erich Schöniger—
working at Jena's Institute for Tobacco Hazards Research. The papers are of historic interest, given that they provide the most sophisticated proofs up to that time that smoking was the major
cause of lung cancer. The 1943 paper is also noteworthy insofar as
it almost certainly would not have been written without the personal intervention of Hitler in the antitobacco effort. We begin
with Müller.

Franz H. Müller is one of the more enigmatic figures in the history of medicine. His 1939 medical dissertation[73] presents the
world's first controlled epidemiological study of the tobacco–lung
cancer relationship, but the paper is little known outside a narrow
circle of specialists. No one seems to have bothered to investigate
his biography: all we know is that he was born on April 8, 1914, in
Niederaula, near Cologne, as the seventh son of a railroad inspector, and this we know only from the short résumé attached to his
dissertation at the University of Cologne. According to local archi-
vists, his personnel records at the City Hospital of Cologne were
destroyed by Allied bombing. The only other records we have are
the captured German documents preserved at the Bundesarchiv in
Berlin and at College Park, Maryland (in the National Archives),
which indicate (as of 1939) that he was Catholic, single, "Arisch"
(Aryan), and a member of both the Nazi party and the Nazi motor
corps (NSKK).

We also know, though, that Müller's paper is an exquisite piece
of scholarship. Published in 1939 in Germany's leading cancer research journal, the paper begins by noting the dramatic upsurge in
lung cancers in the bodies autopsied at Cologne University's pathology institute. The point is made that though lung cancer was
extremely rare in the nineteenth century, it had now become the
second largest cause of cancer death, accounting for nearly a quarter of all cancer mortality in the Reich. (Stomach cancer still held
first place, with about 59 percent). Müller mentions the usual list
of causes—road dust and road tar, automobile exhaust, trauma,
TB, influenza, X-rays, and industrial pollutants—but argues that
"the significance of tobacco smoke has been pushed more and
more into the foreground."[74] German tobacco use had grown by a

factor of five from 1907 to 1935, exposing lung tissues to unprecedented levels of carcinogenic tar. Roffo and Lickint had shown
that smokers could inhale up to four kilograms of tar over a period
of ten years—to which Müller added that the tar content of cigarettes had actually risen in recent years, a phenomenon which he
blamed—following Wender and Ferrari—on the increasing use of
tobacco stems in cigarette manufacture. He worried also about the
economic burden of smoking, trotting out the widely publicized
fact that 10 percent of the entire national income was going to cigarettes and alcohol.

Müller's most important contribution, however, was his statistical investigation, prompted by his observation that the lung cancer
patients in his care were often heavy smokers and that men were
far more likely than women to contract the disease (his own Cologne data showed a sex ratio of six to one; a Lickint review of
twenty-five publications gave a figure of five to one).[75] His analysis
was what we today would call a survey-based retrospective case-
control study, meaning that he compared, through questionnaires
and medical histories, the smoking behavior of lung cancer patients with that of a healthy "control group" of comparable age.
The survey was sent to the relatives of the deceased (lung cancer
kills rather quickly) and included the following questions:

1. Was the deceased, Herr _____ a smoker? If so, what was his
   daily consumption of cigars, cigarettes, or pipe tobacco? (Please be
   numerically precise in your answer!)
2. Did the deceased smoke at some point in his life and then stop? Until
   when did he smoke? If he did smoke, what was his daily consumption of cigars, cigarettes, or pipe tobacco. (Please be precise!)
3. Did the deceased ever cut down on his smoking? How high was his
   daily use of tobacco products, before and after he cut back? (Please be
   precise!)
4. Can you say whether the deceased was ever exposed to polluted air
   for any length of time, either at work or off the job? Did this unclean
   air contain smoke, soot, dust, tar, fumes, motor exhaust, coal dust or
   metallic dust, industrial chemicals, cigarette smoke, or similar substances?[76]

Müller does not say how many questionnaires were sent out, but we are told that 96 "cases" were eventually obtained—86 males and 10 females. All had died of lung cancer, as confirmed at autopsy by Cologne's university pathology institute or one of six other hospitals in the region. Additional information was gathered from the patients' medical records, and in some cases from their place of work. The 86 male "cases" (*Krankheitsfälle*) were divided into five classes: "extremely heavy smoker," "very heavy smoker," "heavy smoker," "moderate smoker," or "nonsmoker." The same was done for a group of 86 healthy "controls" (*gesunden Männern*) of the same age as the cases.[77]

The results were stunning. The lung cancer victims were more than six times as likely to be "extremely heavy smokers"—defined as daily consumers of 10–15 cigars, more than 35 cigarettes, or more than 50 grams of pipe tobacco. The healthy group, by contrast, had a much higher proportion of nonsmokers: 16 percent, compared with only 3.5 percent for the lung cancer group. The 86 lung cancer patients smoked a total of 2,900 grams of tobacco per day, while the 86 healthy men smoked only 1,250 grams. Müller concluded not just that tobacco was "an important cause" of lung cancer, but that *"the extraordinary rise in tobacco use"* was *"the single most important cause of the rising incidence of lung cancer"* in recent decades (emphasis in original).[78] This is an extraordinary claim—the strongest ever issued up to that time, stronger even than any of the claims made by British or American scientists until the 1960s. Richard Doll and A. Bradford Hill's oft-cited paper of 1950, for example, concluded only that cigarette smoking was "a factor, and an important factor, in the production of carcinoma of the lung."[79] Wynder and Graham's famous paper from the same year characterized tobacco only as a "possible etiologic factor" in the increase of the disease.[80]

Müller's article is notable in several other respects. For one thing, there is no obvious Nazi ideology or rhetoric in the piece. There is one brief hint that "the genetically vulnerable" should be advised not to smoke, but race is never mentioned and there are no other remarks that would lead one to identify the article as a "Nazi" piece of scholarship. The brief bibliography (twenty-seven sources) refers the reader to the work of at least three Jewish scientists (Max Askanazy, Walther Berblinger, and Marx Lipschitz), each of whom is also cited approvingly in the text. This is not as unusual as one might imagine: Jewish scientists from the Weimar period were often cited in Nazi-era medical literature, despite occasional pressures to put an end to the practice.

Also interesting is his discussion of possible causes of lung cancer other than tobacco. Müller was well aware that tobacco was unlikely to be the sole cause, given that a third of his "cases" were either moderate smokers or nonsmokers. He disagreed with the Englishman W. Blair Bell and other "lead therapy" advocates who claimed that the heavy metal showed promise as a cancer treatment (the theory was that lead selectively destroyed cancer cells); Müller's inclination was rather to follow Carly Seyfarth's view that exposed workers—printers, metalworkers, plumbers, painters, and typesetters, for example—actually faced an *increased* risk of contracting the disease. In his own sample of eighty-six men with lung cancer, seventeen showed a history of exposure to lead dust, from which he concluded that inhalation of this heavy metal must be considered a "promoting factor" in the development of cancer. Other factors were no doubt involved, as was suggested by the work history of his cases, which included a forty-eight-year-old locksmith exposed to soot, smoke, and coal dust; a twenty-six-year-old housewife who for two years had worked in a cigarette factory, inhaling tobacco dust; three women who had worked during the First World War in a munitions factory, exposing themselves to nitrates, phosphorous, mercury, chromium, picric acid, and other noxious substances; a forty-eight-year-old dye worker known to have inhaled aniline vapors; and several workers exposed to chromium in one form or another. All smoked only moderately or not at all, leading him to believe that occupational exposures may have played a role in their becoming ill.[81]

It is not yet clear what became of Müller, author of the world's first case-control epidemiologic study in the field of tobacco. There is no trace of the man after the war, and it is quite possible that he died on the front, prior even to his thirtieth birthday. We need to know more about how and why this obscure young physician—

the Galois of tobacco science*—came to pioneer the field of tobacco epidemiology, only to vanish into obscurity.

We do know that his pathbreaking article was sometimes cited in the 1950s, when Ernst Wynder and Evarts Graham in the United States, along with Richard Doll and A. Bradford Hill in England, confirmed the lung cancer–tobacco link.[82] The U.S. surgeon general's report of 1964 cited Müller's paper, along with Schairer and Schöniger's, to which we shall turn in a moment. What is not often recognized, however, is that leading German physicians by the 1940s—more than a decade earlier than their English and American counterparts—were convinced that smoking was both addictive and the major cause of lung cancer.[83] Fritz Lickint concluded in 1935 in Germany's leading medical weekly that there was "no longer any doubt" that tobacco played a significant role in the rise of bronchial cancer.[84] Max de Crinis, one of the era's most influential psychiatrists (and a notorious architect of the murderous "euthanasia operation"), in 1941 stated that the question of whether tobacco was behind the explosive rise in lung cancer "can now be answered in the affirmative."[85] That consensus[86] died with the Nazi regime and would be rekindled only after the war under the leadership of Anglo-American scientists.

MOVING INTO ACTION

Armed with the requisite scientific expertise and political power, Nazi authorities moved to limit smoking through a combination of propaganda, public relations, and official decrees.[87] The Ministry of Science and Education ordered elementary schools to discuss the dangers of tobacco, and the Reich Health Office (the "Roland" of Reich health leadership, in Reiter's boast) published pamphlets warning young people not to smoke. Public lectures sponsored by the Reich Health Office—on maternal health or vaccination, for example—were declared "smoke-free," and the Reichsstand des

---

* Evariste Galois was the nineteenth-century French mathematician who pioneered the field of group theory, only to die in a duel at the age of twenty (in 1832).

Deutschen Handwerks, the now-Nazified craft guild, advised its members against smoking while at work.[88] A Bureau against the Hazards of Alcohol and Tobacco was established in June of 1939 from the remnants of Germany's leading antialcohol association; a Bureau for the Struggle against Addictive Drugs (Reichsstelle für Rauschgiftbekämpfung) performed similar work against morphine, sleeping pills, Coca-Cola, Pervitin (the prescription stimulant), and occasionally tobacco. Fifteen thousand people attended a March 5–7, 1939, congress in Frankfurt on the hazards of tobacco and alcohol, at which Reich Health Office president Hans Reiter and other Nazi luminaries—including Leonardo Conti, Robert Ley, and Ferdinand Sauerbruch (standing in for Gerhard Wagner)—attacked both vices as reproductive poisons and drains on the German economy.[89]

Throughout this period, magazines like *Die Genussgifte* (Poisons of taste or habit),* *Auf der Wacht* (On guard), and *Reine Luft* (Pure air) published a regular drumbeat against this "insidious poison," along with articles charting the unhealthful effects of alcohol, teenage dancing, cocaine, and other vices. More than a dozen books denounced the "smoking slavery" or "cultural degeneration" feared from the growth of tobacco use.[90] Tobacco was branded "the enemy of world peace," and there was even talk of "tobacco terror" and "tobacco capitalism."[91] Karl Astel of Jena proclaimed tobacco "an enemy of the people" (*Volksfeind*), and at least one medical thesis—on tobacco addiction—characterized cigarettes as "coffin nails."[92] Hitler himself in 1941 denounced tobacco as "one of man's most dangerous poisons."[93] Antismoking activists repeatedly reminded readers that Hitler neither smoked nor drank hard

---

* The German term *Genussmittel* is notoriously difficult to translate. David Jacobson has rendered it "articles of pleasure," especially those which "are eaten, drunk, or inhaled to create pleasures of the senses, as opposed to those foods and beverages consumed as necessities." Included are all spices and condiments, but also stimulants, intoxicants, and narcotics such as tobacco, coffee, tea, alcohol and opium. "The word *Genussmittel* therefore also implies that these substances are luxuries for sybaritic enjoyment, means for creating epicurean delights and, by extension, a state of sensual bliss." See the translator's note in Wolfgang Schivelbusch, *Tastes of Paradise: A Social History of Spices, Stimulants, and Intoxicants* (New York: Pantheon Books, 1992), p. xiii.

FIG. 6.10. "Our Führer Adolf Hitler drinks no alcohol and does not
smoke. . . . His performance at work is incredible." From *Auf der Wacht* 54
(1937): 18.

liquor (see fig. 6.10); attention was also drawn to the fact that neither Mussolini nor Franco were smokers. Max Schmeling, Germany's nonsmoking world-heavyweight boxing champion, was also held up for emulation—at least until 1938, when the African-American Joe Louis knocked him out in the first round of their championship bout, much to the embarrassment of Nazi leaders.

In the late 1930s and early 1940s, antitobacco activists called for increased tobacco taxes, advertising bans, and bans on unsupervised vending machines and tobacco sales to youth and to women in their child-bearing years. Activists called for bans on smoking while driving, for an end to smoking in the workplace, and for the establishment of tobacco counseling centers.[94] The Hitler Youth and the League of German Girls published antismoking propaganda,[95] and the Reich Health Publishing House printed manuals describing simple experiments teenagers could perform to demonstrate the hazards of alcohol and tobacco.[96] Counseling centers were established where the "tobacco ill" (*Tabakkranke*) could seek help—dozens of such centers had been set up by the end of the 1930s.[97] Tobacco-free restaurants and sanitoria were also opened, often with financial support from the German Antitobacco League.[98]

Another response was to initiate research into the production of nicotine-free cigarettes. Nicotine had been recognized as the active ingredient in tobacco since early in the nineteenth century, and by the 1890s techniques were available to lower or remove entirely the offending/delighting substance.[99] The Reich Institute for Tobacco Research in Forchheim, near Karlsruhe, launched a series of studies to eliminate nicotine from cigarettes through novel breeding techniques and chemical treatment of the harvested plants, and by 1940 fully 5 percent of the entire German harvest, or roughly 3,000,000 kilos, was "nicotine-free tobacco."[100] (Yes, there were tobacco farmers in Germany—60,000 in the mid-1930s—producing about a third of the tobacco used in the German tobacco trade.)[101]

High-nicotine tobacco plants were also bred at this time, primarily to obtain the pure nicotine commonly used as a pesticide. Russian tobacco refuse had been a major source of raw nicotine, and when supplies became difficult to obtain after the mid-1930s—owing to the souring of German-Russian relations—the substance was obtained from high-nicotine tobacco plants bred expressly for this purpose by the Reich Institute for Tobacco Research (Reichsanstalt für Tabakforschung—an industry group).[102] Anyone who doubts that tobacco companies have "manipulated" the nicotine content of cigarettes need only consult German tobacco literature, where we have countless examples of such manipulation.

The proliferation of "low-nicotine" and "nicotine-free" tobacco products—often with varying levels of the intoxicant—led to efforts to regulate advertisements and to standardize nicotine contents. The Ordinance on Low-Nicotine and Nicotine-Free Tobacco of May 12, 1939, for example, required "low-nicotine" tobacco to contain less than 0.8 percent of the alkaloid, and nicotine-free cigarettes no more than 0.1 percent.[103] Antitobacco activists by this time were fond of pointing out that nicotine was only one of many harmful elements of tobacco, and that low-nicotine products might actually cause smokers to increase their smoking to maintain a comfortable level of nicotine intake.[104]

Research was also launched to investigate the psychology and psychopharmacology of smoking. A 1940 medical thesis explored why blind people seldom smoked, and why soldiers found smoking more pleasurable in the daylight than at night.[105] A 1937 article explored the "psychopathology" of smoking, including a purported connection between smoking and pyromania.[106] Antitobacco journals routinely blamed fires, thefts, and even murders on the criminal perversions caused by smoking (the 1936 murder of the Viennese philosopher Moritz Schlick by a deranged smoking student, for example).[107] Dozens of preparations were available to assist people in quitting smoking, ranging from a silver nitrate mouthwash—1 part in 10,000 was said to cause tobacco to have an unpleasant taste—to a substance known as "transpulmin," injected into the bloodstream to produce a similar effect (it was said to bond with the terpenes and other aromatic compounds in tobacco, producing a disagreeable sensation). Trade name compounds such as "Analeptol" and "Nicotilon" were offered, as were tobacco substitutes such as chewing gums, ginger preparations, atropine, and menthol cigarettes. Hypnotism was popular, as were various forms of psychological counseling.

Legal sanctions began to be put into place in 1938. The Luftwaffe banned smoking on its properties that year, and the post office did likewise. Smoking was barred in many workplaces, government offices, hospitals, and rest homes,[108] and midwives were ordered not to smoke while on duty.[109] "No-smoking" cars were established on all German trains, with a fine of two reichsmarks to be levied upon violators.[110] The NSDAP announced a ban on smoking in its offices on April 29, 1939, and within a year SS chief Heinrich Himmler had announced a smoking ban for all on-duty uniformed police and SS officers.[111] (The secret police were presumably still allowed to smoke while working under cover.) The *Journal of the American Medical Association* that year reported Hermann Göring's decree barring soldiers from smoking on the streets, on marches, and on brief off-duty periods.[112] Sixty of Germany's largest cities banned smoking on streetcars in 1941, and smoking was banned in air-raid shelters—though there is evidence that some reserved separate rooms for smokers.[113] During the war, tobacco rationing coupons were denied to pregnant women (and to all women below the age of twenty-five or over fifty-five), while restaurants and cafés were barred from selling cigarettes to female customers— though some of these regulations were relaxed over time.[114] In July of 1943, a law was passed making it illegal for anyone under the age of eighteen to smoke in public.[115] Smoking was banned on all German city trains and buses in the spring of 1944; Hitler personally ordered the measure to protect the health of the young women serving as ticket takers.[116]

Some of these wartime bans, it should be noted, were designed primarily to prevent fires. That was clearly the case with the May 23, 1940, ban on smoking in fire-endangered factories, but it was also true for the May 18, 1940, police ordinance against smoking near open grain storage bins.[117] Fire-sensitive workplaces were required by law to have "no-smoking" areas clearly marked, though violations were apparently so common that Heinrich Himmler ordered "police prophylactic measures" against anyone found smoking in a restricted area.[118] Punishment for violators could be severe: in the summer of 1942, a man was sentenced to death for having caused a fatal and costly fire in a spray-paint facility designated as a "no-smoking" area. The sentence had already been carried out by the time *Die Tabakfrage* (successor to *Reine Luft*) could celebrate the case.[119]

Health was clearly the predominant concern, however, in the restrictions placed on tobacco advertising. The term *Damen-Zigarette* (ladies' cigarette) was banned, as was the use of sexual or female-centered imagery to advertise tobacco products. Ads implying that smoking possessed "hygienic values" were barred, as were images depicting smokers as athletes or sports fans or otherwise engaged in "manly" pursuits. Advertisers were no longer allowed to show smokers behind the wheel of a car and were explicitly barred from ridiculing antismokers, as they once had done quite unabashedly (see again fig. 6.7, also fig. 6.11).[120] The restrictions, formalized on December 17, 1941, and signed by Advertising Council president Heinrich Hunke, are interesting enough to warrant reproduction in full:

1. The Content of Tobacco Advertising

   Tobacco advertisements should be reserved and tasteful in both images and text. They must not run counter to efforts to maintain and promote public health (*Volksgesundheit*), and must not violate the following principles:

   a. Smoking may not be portrayed as health-promoting or as harmless.

   b. Images that create the impression that smoking is a sign of masculinity are barred, as are images depicting men engaged in activities attractive to youthful males (athletes or pilots, for example).

   c. Advocates of tobacco abstinence or temperance must not be mocked.

   d. Tobacco advertising cannot be directed at women, and may not involve women in any manner.

   e. Tobacco advertising may not be directed at sportsmen or automobile drivers, and may not depict such activities.

   f. Attention may not be drawn to the low nicotine content of a tobacco product, if accompanied by a suggestion that the smoker may thereby safely increase his tobacco use.

Fɪɢ. 6.11. Ads banned in the Nazi era. Laws passed during the Nazi era barred the use of athletic or sexual imagery in tobacco ads; here, *Reine Luft* presents a collage of the kinds of ads barred under the advertising law. Source: *Reine Luft* 21 (1939): 15.

2. Limits on Advertising Methods

   Advertising for tobacco products may not be conducted:

   a. In films.
   b. Using billboards or posters, especially on gables but also along railway lines, in rural areas, at sports fields and racetracks.
   c. On posters in post offices.
   d. On billboards in or on public or private transportation, at bus stops or similar facilities.
   e. On posters (*Bogenanschläge*) on walls, fences, at sports arenas or racetracks, or by removable tags on commercial products or adhesive posters on storefronts and doors of shops.
   f. By loudspeaker (on top of cars, for example).
   g. By mail.
   h. By ads in the text sections of journals and newspapers.[121]

Tobacco ads did continue to be published, however, even in Nazi magazines. Austrian tobacco ads occasionally featured a prominent swastika—an outcome of the fact that the Austrian industry was a state-run monopoly. The weekly storm-trooper periodical *Die SA* published full-page ads for Reemtsma cigarettes in nearly every issue in 1940 and 1941—an ironic development, given the brownshirts' rabid attacks on the company a decade earlier. (Some patriots protested the fact that cigarette ads were taking up 25 percent of all German advertising space—when even the parents of fallen soldiers were being asked to keep obituaries as brief as possible.)[122] Tobacco ads in the war years often featured rustic farm or village scenes in Bulgaria, Turkey, Greece, or Macedonia— where much of Germany's raw tobacco originated. The peaceful, romantic landscapes contrast sharply with the images of war perfusing the magazine.

KARL ASTEL'S INSTITUTE FOR TOBACCO HAZARDS RESEARCH

Antitobacco activism culminated in the seventh and eighth years of Nazi rule, encouraged by the success of the early military campaigns and the recognition that rationing might provide a palatable excuse for a broader effort to curb tobacco consumption. Wolfgang Klarner began his 1940 Erlangen medical thesis by proclaiming that Germans were witnessing "the beginning of the end" of tobacco,[123] amid rumors that tobacco was slated to "disappear entirely from the Reich" once the war was over.[124] Hitler in April of 1941 issued a strongly worded order barring any increase in the acreage devoted to tobacco farming;[125] Nazi party leaders by this time had already begun to pressure tobacco manufacturers to convert their factories to nontobacco ends,* the initiative apparently coming from Gauleiter Fritz Sauckel's office in Thuringia but also from the NSDAP's Economic Policy Commission.[126]

It was in this climate of mounting antitobacco sentiment that scholars launched the single most important antitobacco institution of the Nazi era, the Institute for Tobacco Hazards Research (Wissenschaftliches Institut zur Erforschung der Tabakgefahren), established at the University of Jena in the spring of 1941 by a grant of 100,000 RM from Hitler's Reichskanzlei.[127] The institute was advertised as the first such institute anywhere in the world, and the boast is probably not without merit. Fritz Lickint applauded the founding of the institute in a letter to its director:

> Now, finally, it will be possible to establish an effective bulwark against the efforts of the heretofore omnipotent "tobacco interests" to monopo-

* On February 28, 1939, Philipp F. Reemtsma, Germany's all-powerful tobacco mogul, wrote to Bernhard Köhler, head of the NSDAP's Economic Policy Commission, protesting Köhler's call for tobacco factory owners "over the course of time to convert their manufacturing centers, that is to liquidate their factories." Reemtsma in his ten-page letter comes off as nonchalant, noting that his personal fortunes extend far beyond tobacco, but he also counters that cigarettes are the mildest form of tobacco with the lowest nicotine content, and that if German tobacco manufacturers were to cease production, then the important tobacco markets of the Orient—notably Bulgaria, Greece, and Turkey—would come to be dominated by London companies. He comes close to labeling Nazi propagandists "fanatics," but he also cautions that the prohibition of one form of *Genussmittel* would likely lead to its replacement by another. Appealing to the homeopathic medical practices institutionalized in the Rudolf-Hess-Krankenhaus, he argues that a substance functioning as a poison at one dose might well be beneficial at another; he also states that tobacco companies were working "full steam" to lower the nicotine content of cigarettes. See Philipp F. Reemtsma to Bernhard Köhler, February 28, 1939, R43/745b, BAP.

lize tobacco science. It will now be possible to counter the broad impression, created with the help of the industry's research institutes in Vienna and Forchheim, that they alone have the right to speak the truth about tobacco, and to shape or even dominate public opinion concerning matters of tobacco.[128]

The April 5–6, 1941, conference celebrating the opening of the institute, comprising two days of lectures, featured many of Germany's foremost antitobacco activists. Gauleiter Fritz Sauckel proclaimed that the struggle against tobacco was necessary to keep the German working man healthy and strong; Reich Health Leader Leonardo Conti pointed out that tobacco was an addictive drug, weakening the ability of leaders to serve their nation. Karl Astel, the SS doctor who founded and directed the institute, denounced the health and financial costs of smoking, but also the "ethic of apathy" fostered by the habit. Hans Reiter of the Reich Health Office emphasized the harms to female fertility and called for research into the possible connection between tobacco and stomach cancer. The chief of Germany's National Accounting Office outlined the economic costs of smoking—approaching four billion reichsmarks per annum—while the deputy director of the Bureau against the Hazards of Alcohol and Tobacco (Reichsstelle gegen die Alkohol- und Tabakgefahren) attacked the tobacco industry for popularizing deceptive terms like "tobacco enjoyment" (*Tabakgenuss*) and "tobacco abuse" (*Tabakmissbrauch*).[129]

Johann von Leers, editor of the journal *Nordische Welt* and a rabid antisemite, added a "comical" tone to the meeting, accusing "Jewish capitalism" of having helped to spread the tobacco habit in Europe. Leers described how Jews had brought the first tobacco to Germany and still controlled the tobacco industry of Amsterdam, the main port of entry for *nicotiana* into Europe. The French Revolution had spurred the uptake of tobacco (*Der liberale Revoluzzer rauchte*), as had the ambient salon culture. Leers's talk was one of only two to mention a link to "the Jewish question"; his was also the only speech characterized by the *Deutsches Ärzteblatt* as "humorous"—the amusement apparently lying in his ridicule of Jews.[130]

The conference featured other high-profile representatives of German medicine and academe. Otto Schmidt, director of the Forensic Medical Institute of Danzig's Medical Academy, described the toxic effects of carbon monoxide, and Fritz Lickint trotted out his by-now-familiar tally of hazards. The director of Dortmund's Institute for Labor Physiology (a Prof. Dr. Otto Graf) argued that tobacco should be entirely banned in the workplace, owing to the dangers of "passive smoking." Germany's leading medical journals reported at length on the conference, and Hitler sent a telegram wishing those assembled "best of luck in your work to free humanity from one of its most dangerous poisons" (see figs. 6.12–6.14). There may never have been a more august assemblage of antitobacco activists, anywhere in the world.

Jena by this time was a center of antitobacco activism[131]—mainly through the labors of Karl Astel, director of the new institute and president, since the summer of 1939, of the University of Jena. Astel was head of Thuringia's Office of Racial Affairs and a notorious antisemite and racial hygienist (he had joined the Nazi party and the SS in July of 1930); he was also an energetic advocate of "euthanasia" who toured local hospitals to encourage physicians to kill their psychiatric patients. (Astel was so vocal in his support for murdering the mentally ill that at one point he had to be reminded that the operation was supposed to be kept secret.)[132] Astel helped organize the dismissal of Jews from university posts and later helped organize deportations to the death camps.

Astel was also a militant antismoker and teetotaler who once characterized opposition to tobacco as a "national socialist duty."[133] On May 1, 1941, he banned smoking in all buildings and classrooms of the University of Jena, and the following spring, as head of Thuringia's Public Health Office, he announced a smoking ban in all regional schools and health offices. Tobacco in his view had to be fought "cigar by cigar, cigarette by cigarette, and pack by pack"—hence his notoriety for snatching cigarettes from the mouths of students who dared to violate his Jena University tobacco ban.[134] Tobacco abstinence was understandably a condition of employment at his Institute for Tobacco Hazards Research: the proposal for the institute—authored by Gauleiter Sauckel—noted

FIG. 6.12. Cover page from *Reine Luft* (May/June 1941), the leading anti-tobacco journal in the Nazi era. The platform, labeled "tobacco addiction," displays a devil-headed tobacco snake ensnaring smokers, a takeoff on the classical sculpture *Laocoön and His Children* (now in the Vatican). The cursive caption below asks "Suffer or Struggle? *We* Struggle!" above a photograph of the April 5–6, 1941, meeting in Weimar celebrating the founding of Jena's Institute for Tobacco Hazards Research.

Reine Luft

Zugleich Fortsetzung der „Tabakfreien Kultur", ehem. Organ des Österreichischen Tabakgegnerbundes (Wien und des Bundes deutscher Tabakgegner im Sudetenland
Amtliches Organ der Reichsstelle gegen die Alkohol- und Tabakgefahren
Amtliches Organ des I. Wissenschaftlichen Institutes zur Erforschung der Tabakgefahren an der Universität Jena

Herausgeber: Deutscher Bund zur Bekämpfung der Tabakgefahren e.V
Angegliedert der Reichsstelle gegen die Alkohol- und Tabakgefahren
Sitz Berlin-Charlottenburg 2 · Schillerstraße 9

Verlag: „Reine Luft", Berlin-Charlottenburg 2, Schillerstraße 9 – Verantwortlicher Hauptschriftleiter i. N. (auch für Anzeigen) Ernst Lindig, Berlin-Charlottenburg 2 – Erscheinungsweise: Jährlich 6 Doppelhefte RM. 3.–, Doppelheft 50 Pfg. – Auflage: 15 000 – Postzeitungsamt Berlin. – Postscheckkonto: Berlin NW 7, Nr. 13267

| 23. Jahrgang | Berlin, Mai/Juni 1941 | Folge 3 |

FIG. 6.13. Title page from *Reine Luft* 23 (1941): 81, reproducing Hitler's April 5, 1941, telegram congratulating dignitaries assembled in Weimar for the First Scientific Conference on Tobacco Hazards Research and the opening of Jena's Institute for Tobacco Hazards Research. The Führer conveys his "best wishes for your work to free humanity from one of its most dangerous poisons."

FIG. 6.14. Karl Astel, president of Jena University and director of Jena's Institute for Tobacco Hazards Research. Astel barred smoking on the Jena University campus and became known for snatching cigarettes from the mouths of campus smokers. A virulent antisemite and euthanasia advocate, Astel committed suicide in April of 1945. Source: Bundesarchiv Berlin.

that this was "as important as Aryan ancestry"; freedom from tobacco addiction was said to be necessary to guarantee the "independence" and "impartiality" of the science produced.[135]

Astel's antitobacco institute promoted both medically informed
propaganda and politically informed scientific work. One of the
more ambitious activities was the making of an antitobacco film,
Genussmittel Tabak, directed by Prague medical professor Emil von
Skramlik and produced in cooperation with Bavaria Film. It is not
yet clear whether the film was ever completed (I have been unable
to locate a copy), but production consumed tens of thousands of
reichsmarks from the institute budget and received a stamp of approval from the Propaganda Ministry (Goebbels's diary entry for
June 24, 1941, notes his approval of the "propaganda film against
tobacco abuse").[136] On November 4, 1942, Skramlik persuaded Dr.
Hellmuth Unger, author and inspiration for the notorious euthanasia film *Ich klage an* to work on the project—yet another bond
between Nazi criminality and the campaign against tobacco.[137]

The scientific work of the institute embraced several areas. The
radiologist Wolf Dietrich von Keiser investigated the influence of
nicotine on the stomach, and the pathologist Eberhard Schairer
compared the damage caused by nicotine to that caused by rheumatism. The institute funded the work of Günther Just, director of
Greifswald's Institute for Human Genetics and Eugenics, and Karl
Thums, director of Prague's Institute for Genetics and Racial Hygiene.[138] Cancer was a prominent focus, as illustrated by Horst
Wüstner's 1941 medical thesis confirming the increased incidence
of lung cancer and its likely connection to the growth of smoking.
Analyzing pathological reports from 20,000 autopsies performed
by the university between 1910 and 1939, Wüstner concluded that
the number of lung cancers had increased by more than a factor of
ten (from 8 to 88), even though the number of cancers as a whole
had not even doubled (from 363 to 734). Lung cancers accounted
for only about 2 percent of all cancer deaths in the earlier period,
but autopsies for the years 1935 to 1939 revealed a much higher
fraction, about 12 percent.[139]

The most intriguing work of Astel's institute, however, was the
astonishingly sophisticated 1943 publication by Eberhard Schairer

and Erich Schöniger—the most convincing early demonstration of the central role of smoking in the development of lung cancer.[140] We do not know much about Schöniger, the younger of the two men, but we do know a bit about Schairer. Eberhard Schairer (1907–) was deputy director of Jena's Institute of Pathology and a *habilitierter* professor of medicine with a long bibliography in fields like tumor transplant research and pediatric blood biochemistry. Schairer was Schöniger's *Doktorvater* (doctoral thesis adviser) and apparently the one to have suggested the topic in the first place— judging from the acknowledgments at the end of Schöniger's thesis. Schairer applied to join the Nazi party in 1937 and had already entered several other Nazi organizations (he was a *Sturmarzt* for the SA, for example) prior to joining the Jena medical faculty in 1938. He seems to have fallen from favor toward the end of the war and was sent to the Russian front. The historical record is not entirely clear on this point, but his son says that he refused to exonerate a prominent Nazi driver who killed a man in a traffic accident. He also says that his father deliberately halted a series of animal experiments he was working on—exploring whether saccharine could cause liver cancer—fearing that a negative result (no evidence of cancer) might tempt the government to reduce sugar rations and increase production of artificial sweeteners. As of 1997 he was still alive, but not granting requests for interviews.[141]

All we know about Erich Schöniger is what we find on the résumé printed, as was customary, at the end of his 1944 medical thesis. He was born in 1917 in Bad Schwartau near Lübeck and volunteered for military duty in the summer of 1937. Two years later, in the spring of 1939, he began studying medicine at Jena. He reentered the military in 1940 to serve in the campaign against France, after which he returned to finish his medical studies at Jena. There is no record of his having ever joined the Nazi party. His 1944 thesis (*Lungenkrebs und Tabakverbrauch*) has the same title as his 1943 paper with Schairer, though the text is different and there is more historical background. I have not been able to find out how or when he died: he may have died during the war, but he could conceivably still be alive today.

Schairer and Schöniger's paper is remarkable for its subtlety, surpassing even Müller's study of four years previously. The authors concede several different sources of possible bias and develop ways to get around that bias. They begin by noting that lung cancers were increasingly common among the cancers revealed at autopsy and that men were far more likely than women to contract the disease (six times more often, by their count). They reject several of the customary nontobacco explanations of the increase—automotive exhausts, for example—by noting that rural as well as urban lung cancer rates were on the rise and that operators of motorized equipment did not have high rates of the disease. They then draw attention to the fact that a heavy smoker could easily inhale several kilograms of tar over a lifetime, a frightening figure given Roffo's discovery of benzpyrene in cigarette smoke and his demonstration that animals painted with tobacco tars develop high rates of cancer.

The most original aspect of Schairer and Schöniger's study is their analysis of how lung cancer rates correlate with smoking behavior. Following closely the method pioneered by Müller, the authors sent questionnaires to the relatives of 195 lung cancer victims, inquiring into the smoking habits of the deceased. Going beyond Müller, however, they sent an additional 555 questionnaires to the families of patients who had died from other kinds of cancer—320 stomach, 108 colon, 60 prostate, 35 esophagus, and 32 tongue—the presumption being that smokers would be more likely to develop certain kinds of cancer than others. Questionnaires were also sent to 700 male residents of Jena aged 53–54, the average age at death of the lung cancer victims, to determine smoking habits among a population seemingly free of cancer.[142]

The results were clear: among the 109 lung cancer cases for which usable data were obtained, only 3 were nonsmokers, a far lower proportion than among the population as a whole (about 3 percent, versus 16 percent for the noncancer controls). The smokers were not necessarily "cancer prone," because when other kinds of cancer were looked at—stomach, for example—smokers were found to be no more likely to develop cancer than nonsmokers.

Their conclusion: smoking was very likely a cause of lung cancer, but much less likely a cause of other kinds of cancer. The results were declared to be of the "highest" statistical significance, though the authors did not attempt to quantify that significance (as they certainly could have, using the chi-square statistical techniques already available at that time). A 1994 reevaluation of Schairer and Schöniger's study showed that the probability of the results' having come about by chance was less than one in ten million.[143]

Schairer and Schöniger's study provided the most conclusive epidemiological evidence up to that time, anywhere in the world, that smoking posed a major lung cancer hazard. The paper is also notable for its discussion of possible biasing factors. Attention was drawn to the fact that in both this study and Müller's there was a surprisingly high fraction of nonsmokers among the men (15–16 percent—compared with Lickint's estimate of 5 to 10 percent for the general population)—which the authors suggested might be due to a reluctance of smokers to respond to the survey. The authors speculated that the sample they investigated—with an average age of 54—may have included more nonsmokers than one would have found in a younger population; they also entertained the alternative hypothesis that smokers may not have been "entirely candid" in their responses. The low response rate of the 700 noncancer controls (only 270 men responded in a satisfactory manner) might have something to do with "war conditions," they suggested, but they also noted that one would not have expected such a bias to yield a difference between the reported smoking behavior of lung and stomach cancer sufferers—which was, after all, the major finding of the study. By contrast with the lung cancer cases, stomach cancer victims were no more likely than the general population to have smoked.[144]

Schairer and Schöniger's paper was not the last tobacco research of the Reich (a 1944 study showed that lung cancer was now the number one cause of cancer death among soldiers—a result not inconsistent, in this military man's view, with a tobacco etiology),[145] but the more interesting fact is the fate of the paper after the war. Müller's prewar paper is occasionally cited, but Schairer and Schöniger's is little known.[146] A 1953 German bibliography on the smoking-cancer link does not even mention Schairer and Schöniger's paper; nor does an otherwise admirable 1990 historical review of lung cancer–tobacco epidemiology.[147] The 1964 U.S. surgeon general's report, *Smoking and Health*, cites both articles,[148] but the equally famous report by Britain's Royal College of Physicians—issued in 1962—cites neither Müller nor the Jena paper.[149] There is nothing to suggest that either paper was ever widely read. Sir Richard Doll, the man most often credited with documenting the link, told me in February of 1997 that he had never seen the Schöniger and Schairer piece.[150] (I sent him a copy.) Science can be a forgetful enterprise.

Gesundheit über Alles

How are we to understand the Nazi-era campaign against tobacco? The emphasis on preventive medicine was one source, but pressure also came from the insurance bureaucracy, whose administrators worried that tobaccogenic illnesses could lead to financial drains on the health insurance system. (Life insurers by this time had already begun to consider nicotine addiction a statistically significant cause of death.)[151] Cancer treatments cost the Reich an estimated fifteen million marks in 1933, and Nazi authorities worried that this would only grow with the aging of the population.[152] Pressures also came from industrial hygienists worried about a tobacco-instigated loss of German manpower. By the end of the 1930s, people missing more than four weeks of work due to "cigarette stomach" (especially gastritis or ulcers) were required to report to a hospital for examination; repeat offenders—people who failed to quit smoking and kept missing work—could be remanded to a nicotine-withdrawal clinic.[153] A 1942 essay argued that cancer should be fought more aggressively because it was killing Germans in the prime of their working years. The author noted that three-quarters of the people succumbing to cancer were skilled or professional workers (*Facharbeiter*), whereas children, pensioners, and invalids made up only 24 percent. He also endorsed the idea that people wanting to get married should consult genetic counselors to ensure that individuals from two separate cancerous families did not marry.[154]

There is also, as already hinted, an important gender aspect. Women and girls were much more strongly dissuaded from smoking than were men and boys. The Nazi antitobacco campaign was rooted in a presumption of the sanctity and delicacy of the female body; hence the ubiquitous slogan "Die deutsche Frau raucht nicht!" (The German woman does not smoke!).[155] Part of this emphasis derived from the notion that the primary duty of females was to bear and care for children; there was also the idea that the female body was more fragile than the masculine body and therefore more in need of protection. Lickint was typical in his insistence that women were "much more sensitive" to tobacco smoke than men, being rather "like children in this respect," with easily excitable nervous systems. He worried that women's child-rearing duties might be impaired by tobacco abuse; he also worried that nicotine might damage the German germ plasm (though he does not mention a possible impact on sperm).[156]

A great deal of research at this time focused on the vulnerability of the female organism to tobacco smoke and tobacco habits. One remarkable medical thesis at the University of Jena looked at how female prisoners coped with tobacco withdrawal while incarcerated (women were not allowed to smoke in prison); the subtext of the study was not just that "bad women" smoked, but also that women were more easily addicted and more easily damaged.[157] Women's groups joined in the struggle: the Reich Mothers' Service (Reichsmütterdienst) launched an antismoking and antialcohol initiative in the summer of 1942, though the effort was supposed to be "low-key" lest it incite "unrest among the population."[158]

Gender images blurred with other associations, including stereotypes of race and class. Smoking becomes associated not just with sexual depravity and licentiousness, but with communism and Judaism. Jewish and communist women were said to be especially likely to smoke, and to foist their filthy habit on others. Racial hygiene journals depicted decadent women with cigarettes dangling from their mouths. Smoking was associated with jazz, with swing dancing, with rebellion, with Africa, with degenerate

blacks, Jews, and Gypsies (see figs. 6.15–6.17), with many of the
other fears that inspired the Nazi retreat into a paranoid, xenophobic fortress of purity, cleanliness, and muscular macho health
fanaticism.

It is therefore an oversimplification to say that the antitobacco
movement can be traced either to the personal fanaticism of Hitler
or to the effort to stanch the flow of precious hard currency out of
the country.[159] Hitler was clearly disgusted by the tobacco habit:
Eva Braun he would not allow to smoke in his presence, and Martin Bormann was similarly barred. The Führer was never particularly happy about the fact that Hermann Göring continued to puff
away in public, and at one point early in the war he chided his
Reichsmarschall about being commemorated in a statue with a
cigar in his mouth. Hitler encouraged his close associates not to
smoke and is known to have rewarded those who did manage to
quit with a gold pocket watch.[160]

We also know that the Führer at one point characterized tobacco
as "the wrath of the Red Man against the White Man, vengeance
for having been given hard liquor." Hitler seems to have regretted
having allowed his soldiers to smoke: on March 2, 1942, he noted
that "it was a mistake, traceable to the army leadership at the time,
to have started giving our soldiers daily rations of tobacco at the
beginning of the war." He added that it was "not correct to say that
a soldier cannot live without smoking," and vowed to put an end
to military tobacco rations once peace was achieved. Hitler himself
had smoked some twenty-five to forty cigarettes per day in his Viennese youth, until he realized how much money he was wasting,
whereupon he "tossed his cigarettes into the Danube and never
reached for them again." He also claimed—strange as this sounds
today—that Germany might never have achieved its present glory
if he had continued to smoke: "perhaps it was to this, then [that is,
his giving up smoking], that we owe the salvation of the German
people."[161] Of course, one could also counter, paraphrasing Freud,
that sometimes giving up smoking is just giving up smoking.

Hitler's personal aversion was only one of several factors in the
Nazi war on tobacco. The more important concern, repeated over
and over again in public health literature, was the productive and

Wahrheit

Tabak=Gebrauch
ein Hemmnis
für Bevölkerungs= und Raſſepolitik

Tabakanbau
Tabakeinfuhr
Tabakverarbeitung

schädigen die
Volkswirtschaft

Tabakgebrauch

vermindert die
Arbeitskraft

Tabakgebrauch

setzt die
Wehrkraft herab

Tabakgebrauch

schaltet die Hem=
mungen des Ner=
vensystems aus

Tabak
Alkohol
Spielen
Wetten
Kaschemmenmilieu

gehören zusam=
men

Tabakgebrauch

läßt frühzeitig
altern und macht
häßlich

Zwei Rassen

Kurz nach der Rückkehr der Ostmark ins Reich wurde bekanntlich eine Verfügung erlassen, nach der in Zukunft alle arbeitsfähigen Zigeuner zu Straßenbauten herangezogen werden, und zwar streng getrennt von den üb.igen Arbeitern. Mit dieser Maßnahme ist der erste Schritt zur Beseitigung einer Landplage getan worden, die in der Systemzeit großmütig geduldet, sich förmlich zu einer Gefahr auszuwachsen drohte.

Falsches Mitleid und Gedankenlosigkeit haben sich früher damit abgefunden, daß die Zigeuner ein zweifelhaftes, an keine Ordnung und sittliches Gesetz gebundenes Leben führten und zum Inbegriff der Verwahrlosung überhaupt wurden. Erst die verantwortungsbewußte Staatsführung des Dritten Reiches hat kurz und schonungslos eingegriffen. Sie gewährt den Zigeunern zwar das Gastrecht, schützt sich aber vor jeglicher Berührung und Ansteckung, aus der klaren Erkenntnis, daß hier zwei wesensfremde Rassen und zwei Welten einander gegenüberstehen. (Aus einer Zeitschrift des Gaues Ostmark)

Volksgenossen, denkt an Eure biologische Wehrpflicht!

FIG. 6.15. "The Truth about Tobacco Use: Tobacco Is an Obstacle to Racial Policy." At the height of Germany's antitobacco fever, smoking was equated with racial and sexual degeneracy. Side captions warn that tobacco hurts the economy, labor power, and military preparedness; smoking also encourages theft and "makes you ugly." The text below the picture ("Two Races") describes the forced labor of Gypsies following the "return of Austria to the Reich," a first step in the assault on the "Gypsy plague." Source: *Reine Luft* 21 (1939): back pages of nos. 1/2.

FIG. 6.16. Graphic from *Reine Luft* equating smoking and drinking with capitalists, Jews, Indians, Africans, degenerate intellectuals, and loose women. Source: *Reine Luft* 23 (1941): 121.

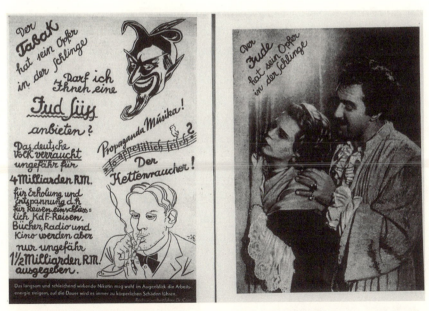

FIG. 6.17. "Tobacco has its victims by the neck; the Jew has his victims by the neck." At the peak of Nazi antitobacco fervor, cigarettes were equated with Jews; both were *Volksfeinde*. Here, cigarettes are equated with "Jud Süss," the villain of the period's most notorious antisemitic film. Source: *Reine Luft* 23 (1941): 10–11.

reproductive performance of the German Volk (see figs. 6.18–6.20). Tobacco, like alcohol, was said to be sapping the strength of the German people—at work, at school, in sports, in the bedroom and the birthing clinic, and on the field of battle (experiments conducted by the German military in the late 1930s found that smoking impaired a soldier's marksmanship and reduced his ability to march for long distances).[162] What we find is a merger of the earlier moral critique with an increasingly medical critique. The moral element is not lost but is in fact strengthened through the incorporation of the Nazi-era rhetoric of bodily purity, racial hygiene, performance at work, and the "duty to be healthy." *Gesundheit über Alles* is one of the hallmarks of Nazi ideology.

This leads us to the larger question of why Germany had such a powerful antitobacco movement, given that in the 1920s it was the United States—not Germany—which possessed the world's most powerful organized opposition to alcohol and tobacco. A clue is to be found in John C. Burnham's discussion of American attitudes toward tobacco at this time. Burnham's argument is that, in the United States, the moralistic certainties that had led to alcohol prohibition and tobacco temperance in the 1920s were under attack by the 1930s. Several of the "diseases" crusaded against at the height of Prohibition (masturbation, for example) turned out to be pseudodiseases, and it was easy to believe that the same might turn out to be true for tobacco. Where, after all, was the evidence that smoking caused impotence or led to crime? The public grew weary of such imaginative scaremongering, and the burden of proof shifted from the defenders of tobacco to its accusers. The net effect was to stymie the medical critique: critics of smoking were easily tarred as advocates of the same kind of puritanical prudery that had brought us Prohibition and cautions against dancing, coffee drinking, card playing, and many forms of sexual expression. American physicians rarely criticized tobacco in the 1930s or 1940s, and those who did object to tobacco use—at medical meetings, for example, where the smoke was often so thick that physicians were unable to see the slides—were easily and often dismissed as prudes or even cranks.[163]

FIG. 6.18. A rain of "Tobacco Capital" is ruining German health, labor power, purchasing power, and racial goals. Source: *Reine Luft* 23 (1941): 117.

FIG. 6.19. Antismoking activists lamented the economic costs of smoking, complaining that the equivalent in value of "two million Volkswagens" went up in smoke every year. From *Reine Luft* 23 (1939): 103.

Fig. 6.20. Think of all the things you could buy, if you didn't smoke! I don't know who was buying kayaks in Germany in 1941, but that is the implication of this image. Source: *Reine Luft* 23 (1941): 171.

Burnham does not discuss Germany, but what is interesting is how the situation there was inverted. In Germany, the tobacco and alcohol temperance movements of the 1920s were actually strengthened by the rise of national socialism. Nazi rule was welcomed by antialcohol and antitobacco forces, and even in the United States, at least one antialcohol journal applauded the election of Hitler.[164] Germany therefore experienced nothing comparable to the sea change experienced in America when Prohibition was repealed in 1933 (at least not until the 1950s—see below). German physicians rarely felt that by criticizing tobacco they were caving in to an outdated puritanical zeal; in Germany under Hitler, temperance or abstinence in matters of habit was more in fashion than ever—at least at the level of public propaganda.

Germans never experienced prohibition and never suffered the backlash against tobacco moralism felt by American physicians. German doctors in the 1930s were therefore much more likely than their counterparts in the United States to endorse the claims of antitobacco activists. The health effects of smoking were more aggressively studied, more broadly condemned. Germans found it easier to castigate tobacco, having never suffered the moral excesses of Prohibition. The burden of proof was not so much on those affirming a danger; there was little risk of appearing puritanical or "moralistic" by attacking tobacco. Indeed, many of the same moralistic tones we associate with American Prohibition can be found in Nazi-era rhetoric. Thus in 1941 we hear Germany's leading public health journal arguing that tobacco causes not just diarrhea and diminished sexual performance but also criminal sexual deviance. The author of this essay suggested that "most of the men condemned for violating Paragraph 175 [barring homosexuality] were heavy cigarette smokers," and called for further research into links between smoking and sexual deviance.[165] Other physicians linked smoking to gambling, prostitution, alcoholic overindulgence, and other depravities of the antisocial *Untermensch*.[166]

If we expand our field of view for a moment, we can in fact see a kind of backlash—it just occurs two decades later in Germany than in America. After the war, Germany loses its position as home to the world's most aggressive antitobacco science and policy. Hitler, of course, was dead, and many of his antitobacco underlings either had lost their jobs or were otherwise silenced. Karl Astel, head of the Institute for Tobacco Hazards Research, committed suicide in his Jena University office on the night of April 3–4, 1945. The death of this SS officer and war criminal was a major blow to antitobacco activism. So was the death of Reich Health Führer Leonardo Conti, who hanged himself with his shirt on October 6, 1945, in an Allied prison awaiting prosecution for his role in the "euthanasia operation" and other crimes against humanity. Hans Reiter, the Reich Health Office president who once characterized nicotine as "the greatest enemy of the people's health" and "the number one drag on the German economy,"[167] was interned in an American prison camp for two years, after which he worked as a physician in a Kassel clinic, never again returning to public service. Gauleiter Fritz Sauckel, the guiding light behind Thuringia's antismoking campaign and the man who actually drafted the grant application for Astel's antitobacco institute in Jena, was executed on October 1, 1946. The Nuremberg Tribunal had found him guilty of war crimes and crimes against humanity, after reviewing his role as chief of Germany's system of forced labor.[168] It is hardly surprising that much of the wind was taken out of the sails of Germany's antitobacco movement.

Some tobacco research did continue: Fritz Lickint continued to write on tobacco topics, as professor of public health at Dresden's Technische Hochschule and as an adviser to the German Hygiene Museum. Ernst Wynder in the United States had shown that Seventh-Day Adventists—who were supposed neither to smoke nor to drink—died of lung cancer far less often than did Americans as a whole; Lickint performed a similar study, showing that among 3,626 German Adventist deaths there was not a single case of lung cancer. A 1968 West German review of health and smoking praised Lickint as "one of the first people in the world to have drawn attention to the role of cigarettes in the genesis of lung cancer,"[169] but the more interesting fact is that Lickint's antitobacco work was taken much more seriously in the twelve years of Hitler's rule than in the postwar climate of a divided Germany.

Even today, the German antitobacco movement has not surpassed the activism and seriousness of the climax years of 1939–1941. Tobacco health research is muted, and it is not hard to imagine that memories of the earlier generation's activism must have helped to perpetuate the silence. Popular memory of Nazi tobacco temperance may well have handicapped the postwar German antitobacco movement, though this would have to be explored as a topic in its own right. It does seems to have shaped how we regard the history of the science involved: the myth that English and American scientists were first to show that smoking causes lung cancer (Richard Doll was knighted for his work in this area) was a convenient one—both for scholars in the victorious nations and for Germans trying to forget the immediate past. The hoary specter of fascism is perhaps healthier than we are willing to admit.

REEMTSMA'S FORBIDDEN FRUIT

I do not want to exaggerate Nazi success in combating tobacco. Tobacco consumption grew dramatically during the first six or seven years of Nazi rule (see table 6.1 and figs. 6.21 and 6.22), a consequence of the post-1933 economic boom but also evidence that whatever propaganda may have been launched seems to have had—at least in these early years—little or no effect on habits.

TABLE 6.1
Cigarette Consumption, per Capita per Year

Year	Germany	U.S.	Year	Germany	U.S.
1930	490	1,485	1950	460	3,552
1935	510	1,564	1955	866	3,597
1940	1,022	1,976	1960	1,280	4,171
1944	743	3,039	1963	1,523	4,345

Sources: "Rauchen: Wie Gut," *Der Spiegel*, January 22, 1964, p. 61; Economic Research Service, U.S. Dept. of Agriculture. American figures are per capita for persons 18 and over.

Deutschlands Zigarettenverbrauch

Zahlen, die zu denken geben

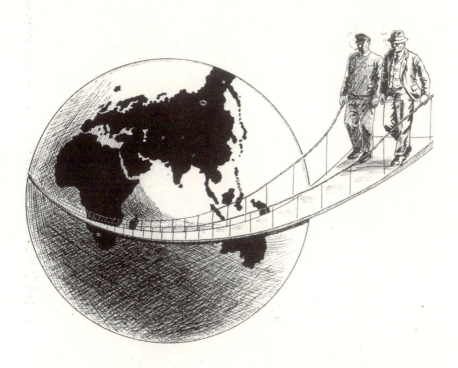

Legte man die 74,8 Milliarden Zigaretten nebeneinander, so ergäben si
ein Band von 564 000 km Länge und würden
15 mal um den Äquator reichen. Man könnte auch
einen Fußpfad von 93 cm Breite rund um die Erde damit belegen. -
Die im Rechnungsjahr 1940/41 verrauchten 10 Milliarden Zigarren
würden für ein Geländer zu beiden Seiten ausreichen.

FIG. 6.21. "Germany's Cigarette Consumption: Numbers That Make You Think." Caption below reads: "If you placed the 74.8 billion cigarettes [smoked by Germans in fiscal year 1940/41] end to end, this would extend for 564,000 kilometers and circle the earth fifteen times. Alternatively, you could build a footpath 93 cm wide all the way around the earth. The ten billion cigars smoked in 1940/41 would be enough to make a railing on both sides." From: *Reine Luft* 23 (1941): 191.

Deutschlands Zigarettenverbrauch

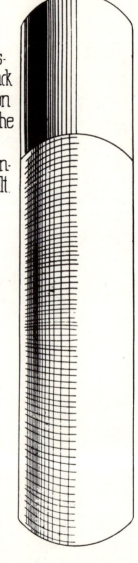

Die 74,8 Milliarden des Rechnungs-
jahres 1940/41 würden, zu 10 Stück
verpackt, einen gewaltigen Block von
100 qm Grundfläche und 436 m Höhe
ausmachen.
Unser Bild zeigt diesen Zigaretten-
turm neben den Kölner Dom gestellt.

FIG. 6.22. In 1940/41, Germans smoked 75 billion cigarettes, or enough to form a cylindrical column of tobacco 436 meters high with a base of 100 square meters, dwarfing the Cathedral of Cologne by comparison. Source: *Reine Luft* 24 (1942): 70.

(Tobacco consumption actually grew more rapidly in Germany than in France: both nations consumed roughly 570 cigarettes per capita in 1932; by 1939 Germans were smoking 900 cigarettes per year while the French were smoking only 670.)[170] The argument has been put forward that smoking itself may have functioned as a kind of passive "resistance": young people smoked or listened to jazz or went to clandestine "swing" dance parties as a kind of cultural opposition to Nazi macho puritanism.[171] It is difficult to say how ordinary citizens responded to the rhetoric and policies of the time, though we do have evidence that Nazi officials worried about appearing overly ascetic or "puritanical."[172] Robert Ley, chief of the German Labor Front, tried at one point to distinguish between "indulgence" (*Genuss*) and "joy" (*Freude*)—the former bad, the latter good—but it is not really clear whether anyone grasped the gravity of the distinction. Nazi antitobacco activists were aware of the American backlash against Prohibition and clearly had this in mind when they cautioned against a total ban on cigarettes. As one activist articulated the predicament, "forbidden fruit is tempting" (*verbotene Frucht reizt*).[173]

There is also evidence that some Nazi officials worried about public opposition to the antitobacco campaign, especially during the war. Propaganda chief Joseph Goebbels was basically in favor, but he also recognized a difficulty in that several Nazi luminaries—notably Reichsmarschall Göring, hardly the paragon of asceticism—continued to smoke in public. (Goebbels himself had been a heavy smoker since the 1920s, and though he tried to confine his habit to his home, some film clips from the era show him trying to hide his cigarette as the camera pans in his direction. He did finally manage to give up smoking in June of 1944, but the attempt on Hitler's life shortly thereafter drove him back to tobacco.)[174] Goebbels worried that the campaign might not be practical in wartime, and that its failure would reflect badly on the agencies involved.[175] On June 18, 1941, he ordered all tobacco propaganda to be cleared through his office.[176] Others worried about the impact of shortages on civilian morale. Reich economics minister Walther Funk complained that miners and armaments workers were not getting enough tobacco; he also cautioned that tobacco workers were being stigmatized as persons "outside the *Volksgemeinschaft*" and "on a par with Jews"—dangerous charges in 1941.[177] Funk wrote to the party leadership for a ruling on the question in May of that year,[178] but Hitler allowed the campaign to continue. The health consequences of smoking outweighed economic concerns, he argued, and tobacco workers should probably be employed in more "war-important" pursuits.[179]

We do have reason to believe, however, that Nazi tobacco bans were not always effectively enforced. A 1940 medical dissertation complained that smokers sometimes indulged their habit in train cars reserved for nonsmokers, and that conductors occasionally had to be called to get the affronting transgressors to cease. Smoking bans in hospitals were sometimes violated, even by physicians, a practice recognized as compromising the counsel given to patients not to smoke.[180] As the war dragged on, in fact, the antitobacco campaign lost much of its steam. Wartime urgencies led a military physician in 1944 to write that "only a fanatic" would withhold a drink or a smoke from a soldier trying to calm his nerves after the horrors of battle.[181] The surgeon Ferdinand Sauerbruch, an occasional contributor to antitobacco literature, argued that it was "wrong to regulate, slavishly, the life of every individual" by tobacco bans and the like.[182] Complaints about the inadequacy of tobacco rations began to grow, and in 1943 Heydrich's Security Service (SD) produced a secret report detailing the nature and extent of public grumblings.[183] When agricultural authorities again raised the question of increasing tobacco yields in the spring of 1944—mainly to satisfy military demands—Hitler acquiesced and said that cultivation could rise again to 1941 levels.[184]

Economic factors were important in the early failure to curb German smoking. The economic recovery in the first six years of Nazi rule boosted the average German's purchasing power, and tobacco companies took advantage of the boom to promote their products. German antitobacco activists were aware of this and frequently complained that their own efforts were no match for the powerful "American-style" ad campaigns waged by the industry—

campaigns redolent of (in Hans Reiter's words) "the tasteless methods of the era of Jewish domination."[185]

One also has to reckon with the fact that, in Germany as elsewhere, tobacco provided an important source of revenue for the national treasury. In 1937/38, German national income from tobacco taxes and tariffs was in excess of a billion reichsmarks—a not inconsiderable sum for a government striving both to modernize and to militarize the nation's economy.[186] By 1941, as a result of new taxes and the annexation of Austria, Germans were paying about twice this amount. According to Germany's National Accounting Office, tobacco taxes by this time constituted about a twelfth (!) of the government's entire income.[187] Hundreds of thousands of Germans were said to owe their livelihood, directly or indirectly, to tobacco—an argument that was also easily reversed by those who pointed to Germany's need for an additional three million men in its labor force—some of whom could presumably be supplied from the tobacco trade.[188]

Of course, German tobacco companies were not entirely passive in such matters. German cigarette manufacturers early on recognized the direction of the nation's political drift and by 1933 were casting themselves as eager supporters of the regime. One place this can be seen is in the elaborate cigarette card albums published by tobacco companies. American companies had begun to package card-like photos with cigarettes in the previous century, and by the First World War Germans had begun to follow suit. There were many different series, from "The German Army" and "The 1936 Olympics" to the more upscale "Paintings of the Gothic and Early Renaissance."[189] The albums—now collectors' items—sold for as little as fifty pfennigs, and tempted smokers with the prospect of completing their collections. Cigarette albums were often very patriotic and sentimental, as when the Waldorf-Astoria Company lamented the passing of the time (Germany's *grosse Vergangenheit*) when German naval forces projected "power over countries and oceans." The Kosmos company's 1933 album glorified the first eight months of Nazi rule and bragged on its title page of having been a "purely German enterprise [i.e., *judenfrei*] since 1886."[190]

Not all cigarette companies were enthusiastic about the rise of German fascism. Indeed, for a time prior to 1933, Germany's largest manufacturer—the firm controlled by Philipp F. Reemtsma in Hamburg—waged a quiet miniwar with the regime; the story is an interesting one, so permit me to digress for a moment.

The rise of the Reemtsma Cigarette Company (Reemtsma Zigarettenfabrik GmbH) is one of the most stunning success stories in the history of German business. The firm had played only a minor role in the trade prior to the First World War and even as late as 1921 produced only 360 million cigarettes per year, or about 1.5 percent of the German market. Capitalizing on the runaway inflation and financial ruin of the early 1920s, however, the company expanded rapidly, primarily by purchasing the working stock of fiscally stressed companies. By the end of the twenties, the firm was producing nearly 20 percent of the cigarettes smoked in Germany. And after negotiating financial agreements with several other companies (notably Neuerburg), the conglomerate came to control roughly three-quarters of all German tobacco manufacturing. Its share remained over 70 percent in 1939, when the company took over the six largest Czechoslovakian tobacco companies. In the twelve years of Nazi rule, the Reemtsma empire produced some 400 billion cigarettes[191]—enough, by my calculation, to cause some 200,000 deaths from lung cancer and perhaps twice this many from heart disease.

Reemtsma came under attack in the late 1920s for antitrust violations and unethical business practices. These attacks continued in the early 1930s, spurred partly by the fact that Ernst Röhm's *Sturmabteilung*—more commonly known in English as the "brownshirts" or "storm troopers" or "SA"—had begun to manufacture its own brand of cigarette to raise much-needed cash (see fig. 6.23). In many parts of Germany, proceeds from sales of so-called Storm cigarettes, manufactured by Trommler in Dresden, accounted for a sizable fraction of the SA's total income.[192] At least one other political party tried to cash in on the scheme: the SPD shortly before the Nazi seizure of power introduced its own *Freiheits-Zigarette* (freedom cigarette), though the venture did not last long.[193]

Reemtsma was also vulnerable, however, because one member of his governing board, David Schnur, was Jewish. In 1931 or 1932, SA officials accused the firm of producing "Jewish cigarettes" (*Juden-Zigarette*), prompting Philipp F. Reemtsma's refusal to purchase advertising space in Nazi newspapers and magazines. The tobacco magnate met with Hitler to iron out their differences—the exact date is uncertain, but it was before 1933—who ordered his party press to stop its attacks. Party officials were relieved to recover the advertising revenues, though isolated attacks on the firm continued for some time thereafter. Germany's first Gestapo chief, Rudolf Diels, recalled these events after the war:

> The Hamburg industrialist Reemtsma was among the "monopoly-capitalist" hyenas Justice Minister [Franz Gürtner] wanted to neutralize. Reemtsma's empire was charged with corruption and perjury; the SA became involved by virtue of the fact that the cigarette manufacturer Trommler was supported by the SA. SA men were supposed to smoke only Trommler ["Storm"] cigarettes. Retailers of Reemtsma brands were beaten, their display windows smashed. The Berlin SA could not stop Reemtsma by themselves, so they appealed to the police to assist them in this regard. In August [of 1933] a meeting was arranged between Reemtsma and Göring. After professing his honor as an officer, the wheeler-dealer Göring made it clear he had no desire to kill the hen that laid the golden eggs. He proposed a truce—actually a deal—and Reemtsma accepted. Göring needed sponsors for his art addiction, for the Berlin Opera, and for his project to breed bison and elk.[194]

The story as it is most often told has Reemtsma providing the Reichsmarschall with three million marks and (later) an additional sum of nine million marks. Göring after the war testified under oath at Nuremberg that the total amount turned over to the "Adolf Hitler Fund" was RM 7.276 million.[195]

The SA apparently stopped the manufacture of "Storm cigarettes" shortly after 1933; the decapitation of the SA in the 1934 "night of long knives" may have put an end to the practice, or Trommler may have been bought up by Reemstma or dissolved as part of the agreement made with Hitler. We need more historical work to answer this question.

FIG. 6.23. Ads for Trommler's "Storm Cigarettes," manufactured in Dresden to generate income for the Nazi party's Stormtroopers (Schutz-abteilung, or SA). The SA stopped manufacturing cigarettes in 1934. From *Der Stürmer*, January 1932 and December 1933, with thanks to Claudia Koonz.

Jederzeit nur...

Trommler Zigaretten

STURM-ZIGARETTEN-FABRIK

TROMMLER

$3\frac{1}{3}$

Geschmacksvollkommen!

The Industry's Counterattack

German tobacco manufacturing continued relatively unobstructed throughout the 1930s. Hitler never moved on his early suggestion to transform the trade into a state monopoly—the Reemtsma conglomerate was a de facto monopoly by the 1930s, which may have made nationalization seem unnecessary. Tobacco industry trade journals were allowed to continue publishing, and in fact a new journal, *Der Tabak*, was founded in 1937 to publish articles of interest to growers, rollers, and other tobacco tradesmen. One year later, in Bremen, an International Association for Scientific Tobacco Research was founded, with *Der Tabak* as its official organ.[196] That journal cleaved off another organ, the *Chronica Nicotiana*, in 1940, to review events of significance to the industry—everything from news in the field of nicotine chemistry to updates on tobacco taxes. A book series (*Monographiae Nicotianae*) was also launched, publishing claims by psychobiologists (for example) that total tobacco "abstinence," like excessive tobacco "abuse," was to be regarded as a psychopathic "perversion."[197]

Chronica Nicotiana gives us a sense of how the industry fared at the height of the antitobacco fervor. The journal reported on the hygiene of tobacco workers, and whether tobacco dust could adhere to bacteria in the air. A doctoral thesis was cited to show that women working in tobacco factories suffer no ill-effects from contact with nicotine, and a pharmacology text was cited to argue that the nicotine in smoking mothers' milk could not harm the breastfed infant. The journal conceded that people with ulcers probably should not smoke, but it also cautioned that sex hormones might have something to do with the malady.[198] (A Berlin physician by the name of Margarete Focken had claimed that hormones were more important than smoking in the genesis of ulcers; Focken injected female hormones into at least two dozen men suffering from ulcers, and though it is unclear whether other physicians emulated the practice, the tobacco industry encouraged explorations in this area.)[199] The journal again identified "extreme opponents" of tobacco as "fanatic psychopaths"[200] and cautioned against the "statistical games" played by those who claimed that smoking shortens one's life.

The German tobacco industry's response to criticism will sound familiar to anyone who has followed the past fifty years or so of American tobacco politics; the basic strategy is to claim the "high ground" of sober science for pro-tobacco forces.[201] What is interesting about the German debate, however, is the strength of the response from German health authorities—who were not exactly pleased with the industry's foray into medical research—as the following episode will demonstrate.

Helmuth Aschenbrenner, head of the International Association for Scientific Tobacco Research, in the summer of 1941 announced the formation of a health research commission—the *Tabacologia medicinalis*, based in Budapest—to explore the health effects of tobacco.[202] German health authorities were told that the association had planned to explore health issues from its founding, but it is hard to imagine that the recent spate of antitobacco propaganda was not weighing on the minds of the founders. The widely publicized March 1939 antitobacco congress in Frankfurt had been followed by new rounds of rhetoric from *Reine Luft*, and Müller's epidemiology had turned out pretty solid proof of a lung cancer hazard.[203] Tobacco sales were doing fine, but the industry seemed to be losing the PR battle with antitobacco forces—especially after the founding of Astel's institute. In September of 1941, Goebbels's ministry added insult to injury when it barred the association from creating a "Lavoisier Foundation" (to award prizes for tobacco research) on the grounds that this would pander to French propaganda interests.[204] (Best known for discovering that breathing is a form of combustion, Antoine Lavoisier also headed France's tobacco monopoly prior to losing his head in the French Revolution.)

Aschenbrenner claimed that the *Tabacologia medicinalis* was established in the normal course of an industry's legitimate concerns for industrial hygiene, but Nazi health authorities were not impressed. Reich Health Führer Leonardo Conti read about the formation of the commission in the *Tabakzeitung* and immediately launched an investigation, demanding that Aschenbrenner give him the names of all participating German physicians. He also asked that all work of the commission be halted, including preparations for future meetings.[205] Aschenbrenner politely refused, offering instead to consider any recommendations Conti might have of qualified physicians to join the commission. Aschenbrenner recognized that the tobacco question was "a very dear one" for the Reich Health Führer (*sehr am Herzen liegt*), and urged him to collaborate with the commission rather than opposing it.[206]

Conti, though, had already made clear his antitobacco sentiments in many speeches and publications; he had also already barred the commission's parent association from advertising the International Tobacco Congress (scheduled for September 25–30 in Bremen but aborted after the outbreak of war) in German medical journals.[207] In August or September of 1941, Conti forced one of the guiding lights of the commission, a Dr. Johannes Bresler of Kreuzburg ("the Nestor of medical tobacco research," in Aschenbrenner's estimation) to withdraw from the Hygiene Division, prompting Aschenbrenner to accuse the Reich Health Führer of threatening the "basic freedom of research" (*Grundsatz der freien Forschung*).[208] Conti met with Philipp F. Reemtsma in December of 1941 and warned that he would hold the tobacco magnate personally responsible if Aschenbrenner's group did not cease all medical research.[209] It is not yet clear whether Reemtsma cut his financial support (he did attempt to distance himself from the association), but we do know that by 1941 the association was hurting. The cancellation of the International Tobacco Congress had deprived it of most of its income, and the outbreak of war had further dried up donations from countries no longer friendly to Germany.[210]

The tobacco health war of the Nazi era ended up as a battle between the (pro-tobacco) Economics Ministry and the (antitobacco) Ministry of Interior represented by Conti's powerful office. The issue was brought before Goebbels's ministry, where Conti's side was taken and the argument was made that since health research was properly the realm of Conti's office, Aschenbrenner's medical commission was "a clear attack on the rights of the Reich Health Führer." The error (Goebbels said) was with the Economics Ministry for having failed to consult with the Interior Ministry earlier in the process.

Aschenbrenner had strong friends in high places, however, and was not so easily silenced. When Franz Wirz, a Conti ally, protested to Aschenbrenner that tobacco industry scientists were not qualified to conduct medical research, Aschenbrenner responded that the chemists and biologists associated with the industry—like Adolf Wenusch—were more familiar with the medical aspects of tobacco than anyone. Aschenbrenner mocked Wirz in his capacity of organizing the rose-hips harvest in Bulgaria and said that if the Germans were to give up the commission, it would simply go over to the Italian-run Internationale Zentralstelle für Tabak, based in Rome—and Germany would lose influence. Wirz said this was unlikely given that no one would knowingly cross Germany, now the superpower of Europe.

It is one measure of the power of German tobacco that someone like Aschenbrenner could stave off the repressive hand of Leonardo Conti, the most powerful man in German medicine and one of the most potent figures in all of Nazi Germany. What is also remarkable, however, is how the struggles of these years foreshadowed similar struggles in Britain and the United States in the 1950s. In both cases, evidence of a tobacco hazard was demonstrated by respected physicians; in both cases, the tobacco industry moved to counter the research as "unscientific." The attention of top-ranking governmental health officials was attracted in both cases, and in both cases the industry responded with a campaign to defame antitobacco forces as "antiscientific fanatics."

The comparison is not a perfect one, however, on several counts. For one thing, there is the fact that many of Germany's leading antitobacco activists were also war criminals. At the same time he was taking steps to curtail medical research by tobacco propagandists, Leonardo Conti was actively organizing Germany's "euthanasia operation"—the sole purpose of which was to murder some 200,000 physically and mentally handicapped people. Astel campaigned against tobacco, while also traveling to psychiatric hospitals urging doctors to murder their patients. Hitler himself funded Astel's antitobacco institute in March of 1941—only two months after his henchmen had met at Wannsee to plan the Final Solution.

There is another interesting difference between the two cases: whereas health officials in Germany defeated the tobacco industry's plans (the *Tabacologia medicinalis* never got off the ground), in the United States and in England it was tobacco authorities who emerged victorious (the Council for Tobacco Research has funded hundreds of millions of dollars' worth of medical research since the 1950s).[211] Could American tobacco companies have learned a lesson or two from their German counterparts about how to survive in the face of hostile political forces?*

TOBACCO'S COLLAPSE

German tobacco consumption did not begin to decline until 1942, the turning point also in Germany's fortunes of war. (Consumption peaked that year at eighty billion cigarettes, which included cigarettes purchased not just in the "Old Reich" but also in Germany's newly acquired territories in Austria and Czechoslovakia.)[212] Wartime priorities brought tobacco rationing and emergency restrictions—on tobacco sales to pregnant women, for example—and bombing raids began to cut into finished supplies (e.g., in Cologne). Hitler's 1941 cap on the acreage devoted to tobacco stymied the industry's efforts to make up for these losses. By February 1944, German tobacco farmers were growing three thousand hectares less than in 1941, and raw tobacco imports had measurably declined.[213] The quality of the tobacco suffered, giving

---

* After the war, Helmuth Aschenbrenner continued on as secretary general of the International Association for Scientific Tobacco Research. In the March 1964 issue of the London journal *World Tobacco*, the Bremen tobacco apologist is cited suggesting that "before reports on smoking and health are taken seriously [the reference is to the 1964 U.S. surgeon general's report], those making the reports should have psychiatric certification that they are not suffering from pyrophobia (fear of fire)." Aschenbrenner is taken to have proven that "tobacco antagonism often springs from a morbid (and often unconscious) pyrophobia—a phenomenon whose many manifestations include suppressed fear of the 'big fire' or atom bomb." See "International Perspective on Smoking and Health," *World Tobacco*, March 1964, pp. 19–20. We need a good history of Germany's postwar tobacco science, tracing both the apologetics and the amnesia.

rise to at least one smoker's likening of the available pipe tobacco to "a poor grade of mattress filling." After Rommel's occupation of Cyrenaica in northern Libya, a rumor circulated that the main ingredient of the once-popular brand "Johnnies" was now camel dung, brought home as booty from the African campaign.[214]

Availability was one reason tobacco use fell, but direct efforts were also undertaken to lower tobacco use among soldiers. On June 20, 1940, Hitler ordered tobacco rations to be distributed to the military "in a manner that would dissuade" soldiers from smoking.[215] Cigarette rations were limited to six per man per day, with special nontobacco rations available for nonsmokers (chocolates or extra food, for example). Extra cigarettes were sometimes available for purchase (up to fifty per man per month), but these were often unavailable—as during times of rapid advance or retreat. Tobacco rations were entirely denied to women accompanying the Wehrmacht. New wartime taxes made the habit somewhat less affordable: a November 3, 1941, ordinance increased the cigarette tax to 80–95 percent of the base retail value— nearly twice what Germans would pay in the first two decades after the war.[216]

The net effect of these and other events—the primary one, of course, being the increasing shortages caused by the war—was to lower military tobacco consumption during the final years of the Reich. A 1944 survey of 1,000 servicemen found that while the proportion of soldiers smoking had increased since the start of the war, the total consumption of tobacco had actually decreased—by just over 14 percent. More men were smoking (101 of those surveyed had taken up the habit, while only 7 had given it up), but the average soldier was now smoking about a quarter less tobacco than in the immediate prewar period (23.42 percent less, according to the overly precise survey). The number of very heavy smokers (30+ cigarettes per day) was down dramatically—from 4.4 percent to only 0.3 percent—and similar declines were recorded for moderately heavy smokers. This same survey maintained that smoking among Russian prisoners of war had increased by 24 percent[217]—a rather bizarre statistic, given that most were in the process of being shot or starved to death.

ZIGARETTEN IM VORMARSCH

Jahresverbrauch an Tabakwaren
in Deutschland
(pro Einwohner)

Zigaretten 498 550 743 1022 465 866 1280 1523

Jahr 1930 35 40 44 50 55 60 63
geschätzt

FIG. 6.24. German cigarette consumption declined by about half from 1940 to 1950, primarily as a result of wartime deprivations. Source: *Der Spiegel*, January 22, 1964, p. 61.

Postwar poverty further cut consumption. According to official statistics, German tobacco use did not reach prewar levels again until the mid-1950s. The collapse is dramatic: German consumption dropped by half from 1940 to 1950; American consumption in this same period nearly doubled (see fig. 6.24 and, again, table 6.1).

It is important to recognize, of course, the possible sources of bias in such figures. In both the German and the American case, the numbers indicated are domestic sales recorded for taxation purposes (both therefore exclude production for export). In the German case, there are several reasons official records may have underestimated actual tobacco use in the immediate postwar period. For one thing, official statistics could not take into account the flourishing black-market trade in foreign tobacco. American cigarettes were highly prized in the postwar period. American brands ("Amis") were commonly used as currency, and elderly Germans today recall a single American cigarette's selling for as much as five or even seven marks (versus several pfennigs for German brands). Tobacco smuggling was rampant: in 1949, an estimated 400 million American cigarettes found their way into Germany every month. As late as 1954 two billion Swiss cigarettes—a quarter of that country's production—were estimated to have been smuggled into Germany and Italy.[218]

Smuggling was fostered by the fact that German cigarette manufacturing had sunk to only about 10 percent of prewar levels, mainly owing to the industry's inability to secure raw tobacco from outside Germany.[219] Shortages remained so severe that American authorities decided to ship tobacco, free of charge, into Germany as part of the Marshall Plan. Twenty-four thousand tons were shipped in 1948, followed by another sixty-nine thousand tons in 1949. The net cost to the U.S. government was on the order of seventy million dollars; the benefit, at least for American tobacco firms, was a gradual shift in German tobacco tastes from the traditionally favored black tobacco to the milder, blond-Virginia blend (the latter was also purportedly more popular among women). American tobacco companies were understandably pleased with the arrangement.[220]

Two other factors can be mentioned, both of which indicate that tobacco consumption may have been higher than is recorded in official figures. The first is that, by contrast with later years, cigarettes in the immediate postwar period were often smoked down to the very end. Discarded cigarette butts were gathered and smoked, and one has to conclude that the amount of tar, nicotine, and ash inhaled per cigarette produced or smuggled was significantly higher than in less desperate years (cigarette butts contain disproportionately high concentrations of harmful substances). Such factors can be important in calculating the cancer consequences of the tobacco habit. In the 1950s, for example, Richard Doll and others figured that American smokers had a significantly lower cancer risk per cigarette smoked, in consequence of the fact that U.S. smokers were less likely to smoke down to the very end. Americans smoked 1,285 cigarettes per person in 1930, producing some 19 lung cancers per 100,000 males in 1950. In Holland, by contrast, 470 cigarettes per person had yielded a whopping 24 lung cancers per 100,000 males.[221] Asuming a twenty-year time lag between exposure and cancer, that cigarettes were the only cause of lung cancer, that only males smoked, and that the statistics capture real phenomena (all of which are rough approximations), this would mean that a cigarette smoked in America was less than half as likely to give you cancer as a cigarette smoked in Holland. The numbers suggest that it took about seven million cigarettes to make a lung cancer in America, and only about two million in Holland. The figures for Germany are about the same as those for Holland.[222]

The second factor that should be mentioned is that many Germans grew their own tobacco for home use or trade. The Reich Institute for Tobacco Research in Forchheim—Germany's foremost pro-tobacco industry research organization before and after the war—actually promoted backyard tobacco cultivation in the 1940s: a 1944 book published by the institute's director provided detailed instruction for how to grow and cure your own.[223] Home cultivation continued after the war, and popular memory records many a soldier returning home from the East to transform gardens being used to grow vegetables into tobacco plots. It is difficult to say how much home cultivation, the black-market trade, and the gathering and smoking of discarded butts added to overall cigarette consumption; we may be talking about a 10 or even a 20 percent increase over official figures.

It is unlikely, however, that even all of these factors combined made up for the shortages imposed by the collapse of the German tobacco trade. Recall again that German domestic tobacco production in the immediate postwar period was only a tiny fraction of prewar production. Recall also that much of the home-grown variety was eventually sold to tobacco companies (and therefore counted in official statistics), that postwar rations were only about a fifth of the early wartime rations, and that women, even after the war, continued to receive half rations.[224] Recall finally that, at one hundred marks or more per pack and in a time of extreme poverty, American brands were more often traded than smoked. Taking such things into account, we have to conclude that the decline in tobacco consumption was real. We also have to conclude, as we shall see in a moment, that the decline must have had cancer consequences.

7

The Monstrous and the Prosaic

We are living in an enlightened age.

Adolf Radermacher, German cancer researcher, 1942

The fully enlightened earth radiates disaster triumphant.

Max Horkheimer and Theodor Adorno, German-Jewish
émigré philosophers, 1944

THE STORY of cancer research and policy under the Nazis has tended to elude the attention of historians for various reasons, the most important being, perhaps, that it may not seem to be in anyone's interest to dredge up such things. The subject appears to fall into an "ideological gap": as with indoor domestic radon prior to the 1980s,[1] there are not strong predilections driving attention to the topic. Historical memory is selective in any event, and we seem to prefer to focus on the barbarism of the era, a move that allows us to neatly cordon off a sanctimonious "us" from a fallen "them."

The episode is intriguing, however, for the light it sheds on the experience of science and public health under the "extreme" conditions of a health-conscious dictatorship. The story is not simply one of the suppression of science or its unwilling conformity to political chicanery: public health initiatives were launched in the name of national socialism; Nazi ideals informed the practice and popularization of science, guiding it, motivating it, and reorienting it in ways we are only beginning to appreciate. The Nazi war on cancer shows that what many of us would consider "good" science can be pursued in the name of antidemocratic ideals. Public health initiatives were pursued not just *in spite of* fascism, but also *in consequence of* fascism. It is therefore not enough to speak simply of the suppression or even the survival of science; one has to see how dictatorial ideals worked to inspire and guide the science of the time.

In these final pages, I would like to broaden this inquiry to encompass some of the legacies of Nazi-era cancer research, including the question of whether the cancer policies of the time might have had an impact on postwar cancer rates. I want to complicate how we think about quackery (not all Nazi doctors were quacks!), but I also want to draw attention to Posen's mysterious Reich Institute for Cancer Research, which seems to have served as a laboratory for biowarfare research, exploited after the war by Allied authorities. I will also say something about how we should interpret the Nazi war on cancer—and what it tells us about the nature of fascism.

I should caution, though, that my endpoint is not a very cheerful one. There is an eerie familiarity in Nazi cancer research that does not sit very well with how we customarily regard the winds that generated the Holocaust.

THE SCIENCE QUESTION UNDER FASCISM

Most people when they think about Nazi medicine think about the crimes for which the period is notorious. Nazi doctors sterilized some 350,000 Germans, murdered 200,000 mentally or physically handicapped people, and killed at least a thousand concentration camp inmates in the course of medical experiments designed to advance the cause of German military medicine. Nazi doctors collaborated in the exploitation of slave labor, and in the wholesale extermination of European Jews and Gypsies.

Nazi medical horrors are familiar, but it is also important that we recognize the political diversity and tensions of the era. We are accustomed to thinking of Nazi political culture as "totalitarian," but historians have also begun to appreciate the "polycratic" nature of Nazi governance. There were competing factions with different agendas, and the policies undertaken were generally the result of struggles among different groups—the SS, the Interior Ministry, the powerful offices of Goebbels and Göring, not to mention Hitler's own predilections.

In science and medicine, too, it is wrong to speak of a coherent Nazi cancer research or policy. Rudolf Hess and his fellow romantics pushed for organic food and spiritual union, while Hans Auler and other champions of orthodoxy pushed for belt-tightening and technical finesse. Hitler eschewed meat, though some Nazi philosophers boosted pork as the sine qua non of Nordic life.[2] Antitobacco activists had to fight against industry apologists, of course, but also against the medical myopia that either disregarded statistics or focused exclusively on curing cancer rather than preventing it. Radiotherapists pushed X-rays and radium therapy, while racial hygienists pushed for strict controls on genetic hazards. Organicists stressed the importance of exercise and fresh vegetables, while military planners were busy stockpiling thousands of tons of food in tins. Nazi science was not a monolith; there was rarely a simple translation between ideology and policy.

Conflicting agendas are clear, for example, in the contrary hazard histories of X-rays and radium. Radiation was known to be a cause of both cancer and genetic mutations prior even to the 1930s, and by the middle of the Nazi era one begins to encounter the view that there is no "threshold" dose below which radiation is completely safe. Racial hygienists were notoriously afraid of genetic damage, championing stringent rules to protect "healthy Germans" against exposure to radiation and to prevent the carriers of damaged genes from reproducing. Nazi fears of radiation, however, were more than matched by the (equally Nazi) push to root out illnesses (and sometimes individuals) perceived as threats to public health. The campaign to implement mass screening led to an enormous upsurge in X-ray exposures—riding roughshod over the cautions voiced by eugenicists. The people doing the exposing were not the same as those issuing the warnings—though the interesting difference is not between Nazis and anti-Nazis, but rather between different kinds of Nazis, with different sorts of training and different conceptions of health. The SS radiologist Hans Hol-felder, who spearheaded an ambitious drive to X-ray hundreds of thousands of Germans, was trying to identify illness so steps could be taken to treat or isolate afflicted individuals; Eugen Fischer's concern in warning against overexposure was the longer-term "ge-netic health of the race." Both were solid Nazis, but the two had very different conceptions of how to preserve the health of the fa-vored race.

Similar complexities are visible in the case of radium. Radium was known since the 1920s to be a cause of cancers and fetal mal-formations, and warnings against breathing the emanating gases emerged within a few years of their discovery. People found it dif-ficult to believe, however, that inhaling the vapors from a clean mountain spring could make you sick. Complacency was fostered by the fact that some of the most serious harms came only months or even years after exposure, but also by the fact that radium showed early promise as a therapy. Radium became a mark of in-ternational medical prestige, as nations competed to accumulate the precious element, often said to be "the rarest and most costly metal on the planet"[3] (radium cost thousands of dollars per gram in the 1930s). New disciplines sprang up to explore the curative powers of the rays (e.g., radiology), leaving questions of potential hazards largely up to amateurs or ad hoc committees. Knowledge of potential benefits was privileged over knowledge of potential harms, the end result being that far more physicians came to see radium as a cure for cancer than as a cause of cancer.

Nazi ideology was not obviously relevant in many of these machinations. Radium research and therapy had an inertia that cannot be understood as a response of scientific actors to external political authority; there were ideologies other than Nazism suf-fusing the practice of medicine at the height of Nazi power.

What these examples suggest is that there was no one single "community of science" or medicine under the supposedly totali-tarian conditions of Hitler's fascism—even after the exclusion of the Jews and the banishment of communists. What they also show, though, is that relations between "science" and "society" are more complex than is commonly imagined. Even in the microcosm of

Nazi cancer research we find very different ways that science can express politics, and vice versa. Scientists were boosting fascism, while fascists were boosting science. Fascists were arguing over what kinds of science should be supported, and scientists were arguing over what kinds of fascism should be supported. The boundary between science and politics was not (and can never be) a fast or formal one.

I should reassure the reader that I have no desire to efface the brute and simple facts—the complicity in crime or the sinister stupidities of Nazi ideology; I am also aware that complexity and nuance are sometimes the historian's cheap shot, an easy retreat from clear-line moral judgment. What I would maintain, however, is that we too often construct a scarecrow image of Nazi doctors—of monstrous and sadistic demons hell-bent on genocide and murderous experimentation. There were, of course, such men, but there were also fertile, creative faces of fascism, as perverse as this may sound.

COMPLICATING QUACKERY

To repeat, most people when they think about Nazi medicine think about the more bizarre, cruel, or murderous parts: Mengele's injection of dyes into eyes to see if they could be changed from brown to blue, or the horrific high-pressure, freezing, and transplant experiments exposed at Nuremberg.[4] This is consistent with a larger view of science which holds that inquiries driven by ideologies are invariably corrupted in some fundamental sense. This conception of ideology as distortion (or worse) ignores the fact that passions are often involved in the pushing of science in one direction rather than another—for better or for worse. With such a puritanical conception of science, it becomes too easy for us to dismiss a body of widely held medical knowledge or practice as "quackery."

Cancer in the 1930s was a mysterious disease—as it still is today to a great extent. The failure of orthodox physicians to come up with a cure or even a satisfactory set of palliatives made it easy for countless quacks and charlatans to sell their wares, and even for

orthodox physicians to try out therapies that today sound somewhat flaky: Fritz Lickint X-rayed the spleens of cancer patients to
stimulate the production of "cancer-fighting hormones";[5] Karl
Heinrich Bauer treated cancer patients with benzpyrene, the theory being that if something possessed the power to cause cancer,
it could perhaps also cure it.[6]

After publishing his first cancer book in 1932, Erwin Liek received more than three hundred letters from people claiming to
have discovered a cure for cancer: most claimed to have been ignored by moneygrubbing doctors, some declared themselves willing to divulge their secret for a very high price, several magnani-
mously declared themselves "ready to share the Nobel Prize" with
the Danzig surgeon. Germans were not alone in their desperate
enthusiasm: in 1931, a New York City Cancer Commission had announced a prize for anyone offering an effective remedy; some
3,500 entries were submitted, though none, according to Liek's account, was judged promising enough to warrant a follow-up.[7]

Nazi leaders were ambivalent about many of these "alternative," organic, or otherwise heterodox theories and therapies. On
the one hand, there was a decided willingness to open up medical
therapeutics, consistent with the ambient critique of myopic medical orthodoxy. The Reich Anticancer Committee in 1934, for example, set up a subcommittee to evaluate folk cancer remedies and
eventually tested more than a hundred different kinds of cures. On
the other hand, there was worry that charlatans would profit from
untested methods, distracting attention from proven therapies
while robbing sufferers of their hard-earned cash. Tensions of this
sort persisted throughout the Nazi period, as they do to a certain
extent even today. Doctors in the Nazi era were not unlike doctors
of other times and places in wanting to establish standards to rou-
tinize practice and protect the public. The crackdown on quackery[8]
was part of this process.

We often hear that Nazi medicine was quack medicine,[9] but
what I find interesting is how the question of quackery becomes
confused—in the eyes of some postwar observers—with the question of resistance. Quackery has been celebrated as a form of resistance, but then so has orthodoxy. Neither oversimplification holds

much water, as can be seen in postwar readings of the von Brehmer affair.

Wilhelm von Brehmer was one of the more controversial figures to become the target of Nazi antiquackery. Brehmer was an "organic" physician who maintained that cancer was an infectious disease caused by a microorganism (the "cancer bacterium"), that cancer cells could be detected by an "alkaline shift" in the blood, and that tumors could be successfully treated by blood transfusions and a chemotherapeutic agent consisting of mercuric cyanide and extracts from Chinese rhubarb. Academic cancer specialists were understandably skeptical: the contagion theory of cancer had been on the wane since the turn of the century, and Brehmer's bid to revive it—with support from Gauleiter Julius Streicher and others in the "Paracelsian wing" of the party—was widely regarded as false or even fraudulent. The issue came to a head in 1936, when a struggle arose over whether Brehmer was to be included in the German delegation sent to the International Congress of Pathology in Brussels. Brehmer wanted to present his findings at the congress, but Max Borst, the Munich pathologist who headed the delegation (he was also head of the Reich Anticancer Committee), opposed his inclusion on the grounds that it would embarrass German scientific medicine. Borst and others on the delegation resolved to boycott the meeting unless Brehmer were excluded; Borst also took the rather bold step of requesting a judgment from Hitler on the matter (he actually wrote a lecture explaining the controversy to the Führer).[10] Hitler ordered an inquiry at the Nuremberg party congress of 1936; Leonardo Conti headed the commission and, after an investigation, rejected Brehmer's theory.[11] Brehmer was barred from attending the Brussels meeting and lost much of his influence from that time.

What is interesting about the Brehmer story is how differently it has been told by people with differing politico-medical agendas. Among advocates of alternative cancer therapeutics, for example, the incident has been turned into a tale of maverick, unorthodox science versus closed-minded Nazi obstinacy. David Hess in his book *Can Bacteria Cause Cancer?*, for example, states that Brehmer's blood microbe theory after the war "remained unpopular, particularly among the former Nazi doctors who continued to practice and influence German medicine."[12] The implication is that Nazi dogmatists opposed the radical novelty of Brehmer's theory (which Hess clearly finds persuasive), an interpretation which ignores the fact that Brehmer had allies of the most despicable sort—like Julius Streicher, publisher of *Der Stürmer* and one of the most rabid antisemites the world has ever known (Streicher helped Brehmer establish his "Tumor Research Institute" at the Theresien Hospital in Nuremberg in 1935 where he was also head of the "Paracelsus Institute").[13]

There are also those, though, who take the suppression of Brehmer as evidence of the courage some doctors showed in standing up to Nazi ideology. Wolfgang Weyers in his recent *Death of Medicine in Nazi Germany*, for example, takes Brehmer's suppression as a sign of how "opposition to the Nazis was not only possible, but at times could be successful"[14]—ignoring the fact that Brehmer's opponents were generally as Nazi as his supporters, and that Brehmer saw himself as a victim of Nazi terror.[15] Borst, it is true, was not a member of the Nazi party, but he did preside over the *Gleichschaltung* of Germany's Anticancer Committee[16] and cannot be regarded as an opponent of Nazism. Hermann Druckrey was an ardent Nazi and an active opponent of von Brehmer (and a very good scientist, I should add). It should also not be forgotten that it was Leonardo Conti, the SS officer and future Reich Health Führer, who ultimately silenced Brehmer to save the science of the Reich from embarrassment. Brehmer was the victim of neither Nazi stodginess nor anti-Nazi orthodoxy; both accounts come up short.

What the story really shows is that health officials—in Germany, as elsewhere—often found it difficult, then as now, to sort out cancer fads from cancer facts. The confusion also illustrates the importance of distinguishing *Germans* from *Nazis*: Brehmer encountered opposition from German doctors—some of whom were Nazis (Druckrey and Conti) and others who were not (Borst). The same can be said for his supporters. It might be comforting to believe that good science tends to travel with good politics (however one defines either term), but that is unfortunately wishful thinking.

Another lesson of the Brehmer affair is that support from Nazi ideologues was not always enough to guarantee the survival of a theory or a therapy. That is also clear in the curious case of "earth rays"—a popular theory according to which diverse human ills were supposed to derive from exposure to invisible, underground "rays" or "currents" (*Erdstrahlen*) purportedly flowing through the earth. Devotees throughout Germany earned sizable fees for "dowsing" a piece of ground—to determine its suitability as a building site, for example—and installing "shields" of one sort or another to protect against the purported rays. The idea was already a hoary one in occult literature (it shares a certain kinship with geomancy), but its popularity must also have piggybacked on evidence emerging at this time that radon, X-rays, and even cosmic rays could cause cancer. In March of 1934, Baden's Anticancer Committee had supported a survey to test the theory; the prestigious homeopathic journal *Hippokrates* was publishing open-minded investigations into the question as late as 1937.[17]

Campaigns against quackery are as old as medicine itself, but the Nazi-era push for uniformity and "standards" does seem to have given courts a freer hand to quash unproven therapies. In 1937, the Reich Ministry of Justice declared there was no foundation for the view that "earth rays" (*Erdstrahlen*) could affect health, and no evidence even that such rays existed.[18] In 1939, a man was convicted of selling thousands of "earth-ray shields" to protect against cancer and other maladies caused by the rays. The designer, a master mason from Potsdam, was asked to demonstrate his dowsing technique in court and, after failing the test, was declared a "dangerous chronic criminal" and sentenced to three years in prison.[19]

What is interesting about this "earth ray" business is that dowsing was suppressed despite its popularity among a number of high-ranking Nazi leaders. Hitler had had his Reichskanzlei dowsed in 1934, and several others in his entourage took similar precautions. Hess was probably the oddest of the lot: he was known to have suspended powerful magnets above his bed to draw out "negative magnetic forces" from his body—which bothered more down-to-earth Nazis like Joseph Goebbels, who used

Hess's May 1941 flight to England as an excuse to begin a clamp-down on occult medicine (see again chapter 2). Within days of Hess's flight, the propaganda minister wrote in his diary: "Anti-cancer film checked [the reference is to Auler's *Jeder Achte*]. Sharp attack on quackery. Now that that crazy Hess is gone, we can set this ball rolling."[20] Two months later, on July 16, naturopathic healers were barred from using "occult methods" (e.g., dowsing rods, "pendula," or shields against earth rays) to diagnose or treat diseases. Chiropractors were also barred from treating cancer.[21] Natural healers were still allowed to treat cancer using "recognized practices" like homeopathy, natural herbs, and physical therapy (massage); they could also use "magnetism" and "bio-chemistry" in combination with these. Some local medical societies took a harsher view, condemning all treatment of cancer by non-physicians.[22]

How should we understand the Nazi campaign against quackery? The most commonly expressed concern was that people would squander their money or their health on useless remedies, but the campaign must also be understood as a move by medical professionals to consolidate their monopoly over the healing arts. (Danzig's famous Cancer Law, for example, barred anyone except physicians from treating cancer patients.) The suppression of quacks was part of a larger quest for standards, a primary goal of which was to maximize medical efficacy. Quack medicine was (by definition) ineffective medicine, and ineffective medicine was regarded as a drag on German economic and fighting power.

What we cannot say, though, is that the medicine and medical research moved by "Nazi ideology" at this time was invariably "quack" or "bogus"—by the standards of the time or even by today's standards (since there is obvious disagreement even today over what is genuine and what is fraudulent in many spheres). That is the irony—and the complexity—of Nazi medicine: Nazi-inspired research was often idiotic, but not always.

Let me close this section with one last irony: the Nazi campaign to establish "truth in advertising." Nazi officials strengthened Weimar-era advertising laws, passing new measures designed to curb exaggerated claims for the potency of drugs or medical procedures. Drug companies were barred from displaying letters of thanks from satisfied customers and from making unsubstantiated claims of efficacy. Ads for cancer drugs were allowed to be published only in medical journals, and ads construed as raising public fears (of cancer, for example) were banned altogether.[23] Auler was one of those calling for limits on what could be said about cancer: "The time is past when every physician and non-physician can publicly express his opinion about the nature of cancerous growths."[24] The campaign extended beyond cancer, as when Reich Health Leader Conti in 1939 stated that the regime would no longer tolerate "exaggerated advertising for infant formulas" which diminished a mother's "will to nurse" (*Stillwillen*).[25] The head of the government's Advertising Council boasted that the ads produced since the Nazi revolution were "far more honest" than ads published prior to that time; six years of Nazi rule had finally produced a genuine "truth in advertising."[26] The Nazis were obviously somewhat selective in their deceptions.

BIOWARFARE RESEARCH IN DISGUISE

It is important not to exaggerate the success of the Nazi war on cancer. Nazi militarism cut short many of the long-term hopes of the regime, including several of the most promising cancer initiatives. Anticancer efforts slowed dramatically as the war dragged on: in the face of mounting casualties on both fronts and the demand for breakneck production at home, more immediate priorities came to the fore. Hans Auler in 1943 complained that plans to conduct mass screening for cervical and uterine cancer had had to be scrapped,[27] and many other programs suffered. This is not hard to understand: nations offering up hundreds of thousands of men to be killed on the front are not likely to spend a lot of time thinking about how to prevent cancer at home. The same was true in other nations; in the United States, for example, Wilhelm Hueper's *Occupational Tumors and Allied Diseases*, the most comprehensive analysis of occupational cancer of the century, was essentially ignored when it appeared in the spring of 1942, only a few weeks after the declaration of war against Japan.[28]

This is not to say, however, that there were not important research initiatives undertaken during the five and a half years Germany was at war. The *Zeitschrift für Krebsforschung* and *Monatsschrift für Krebsbekämpfung* continued publishing through the end of 1944, as did several other journals reporting on cancer topics. Tobacco hazards research continued, as did experiments on food dyes, asbestos, hormones, and viral and radiation carcinogenesis. Efforts were even launched to find out whether the trauma and deprivation caused by the war might result in cancers. The *Monatsschrift für Unfallheilkunde* reviewed the medicolegal aspects of tumors caused by accidents, and whether gunshots could cause cancer. Such pursuits continued late into the war (e.g., explorations of whether frostbite or scarring or gas warfare could cause cancer).[29]

Some of what passed for "cancer research," though, was not what it seemed to be on the surface. Ute Deichmann in her *Biologists under Hitler* has shown that participation in "cancer research" was successfully used to evade the draft, especially after the outbreak of war. Adolf Butenandt, winner of the 1939 Nobel Prize for his work on sex hormones, employed three DFG-supported scientists, all of whom obtained military deferments for their work. Then as now, it seems, the attachment of the label "cancer research" gave basic biology an aura of utility and respectability—and in Germany in the early 1940s could actually save your life. Richard Kuhn, head of Heidelberg's Kaiser Wilhelm Institute for Medical Research, in 1942 argued that the Göttingen cancer chemist Hans Lettré should be exempted from uniformed service on the grounds that his work had military potential: "In the U.S. this problem [of chemical carcinogenesis] is being actively researched, and the suggestion has been made that cancer-causing substances may be deployed in the war"[30]—as biowarfare agents, in other words. Suggestions such as this may help explain why some of Germany's leading cancer researchers tried to marry cancer research and biowarfare work, as we shall see in a moment.

Several of the projects proposed in the final months of the war border on the comical. In late February or early March of 1945, for example, when the Russians were already chopping into German territory, Himmler wrote SS Reichsarzt Ernst Grawitz, asking him to investigate why there were "no people with cancer" in Germany's concentration camps:[31]

> It would be interesting to determine exactly what these people [concentration camp prisoners] are dying of. The mortality in the camps is, as you know, no higher, on average, than outside the camps. [And since so few are dying from cancer] it makes no sense to test new cancer therapies on these prisoners. But there is another question that can be asked from a somewhat different angle: How many people are suffering from cancer in the German population as a whole? What percent of the population finds itself at the beginning or some other stage of cancer? If you were to apply this proposition to our prisoners, many of whom are foreigners, you could calculate how many cancer patients you would expect among our 700,000 prisoners [This figure seems to include prisoners outside the concentration camps, and possibly POWs—RP]. I am therefore assigning you the task of exploring why the prisoners are not getting cancer. I think that in this way we can do an even greater service to science.[32]

It is hard to say which is the most bizarre aspect of this proposal: the idea that cancer was absent in the camps, that the prisoners were healthy ("robust"), that Grawitz would still have the wherewithal to conduct such studies, or that whatever results might be obtained would have meaning for the population as a whole. Himmler by this time must have been living in a kind of fantasy world—the would-be cancer sage was spending the last weeks of his life exterminating Jews as fast as was humanly possible; he also apparently hoped to have one last go at *Volksfeind Krebs*.

Himmler's cancer follies might be dismissed as the musings of a murderous tyrant, but there was another cancer project of the war years that was far more substantial—with major support from the German Research Council and the Kaiser Wilhelm Gesellschaft—yet remains somewhat enigmatic even today. The Reich Institute for Cancer Research (Reichsinstitut für Krebsforschung) was established in the fall of 1942 in Nesselstedt, near Posen (Poznán), about two hundred kilometers east of Berlin in "what used to be Poland." The institute is remarkable for the timing of its establishment (in the middle of the war, when one would imagine cancer research a low priority) and its placement (deep in conquered Poland). Most curious of all is how generously it was funded: from July 1943 through December 1944, the institute received a total of 1.5 million reichsmarks, an enormous expenditure at a time when most other scientific projects were being curtailed. Why the funding on such a scale?

Plans for the establishment of a Reich Institute for Cancer Research began in the early 1940s, primarily through the efforts of Rudolf Mentzel, president of the German Research Council, and Kurt Blome, deputy Reich Health Leader and Plenipotentiary for Cancer Research and one of the most powerful men in German medicine.[33] Cancer journals from the early 1930s had lamented the absence of a single, Reich-wide institute to coordinate German cancer research, and though some had argued forcefully for a decentralized campaign,[34] the example of centralized institutes in other nations was too tempting to ignore. Italy had the Milan Institute for Cancer Research, and the United States had had its National Cancer Institute since 1937. England's Imperial Cancer Research Fund was already four decades old,[35] and other countries had comparable institutes. Germany, while a leader in cancer research, had no central research institution; the Reich Institute was designed to fill this gap.

Hopes were high for the institute when construction began in the fall of 1942. Hitler was at the height of his power, with much of Europe under his heel. Expectations were still that the Russians would fold in fairly short order: the capture of the German Sixth Army at Stalingrad, the turning point in the war, did not take place until January of 1943. The Institute for Cancer Research was launched with great media fanfare: Hermann Göring visited the site while it was under construction, and Heinrich Himmler made several inspections. The institute boasted separate divisions for gynecology and physiology and a sizable "tumor farm" to raise animals for use in experiments. Hopes were also high for its neighbor

ORGANIC MONUMENTALISM

A lot has been written about whether Hitler was "modern" or "antimodern"—which has always struck me as a rather fruitless debate, given the ambiguity of the terms. Does modernity mean technical finesse? Secular or rationalized institutions? Gender and/or racial equalities? A certain aesthetic style or attitude toward urbanization? Things that are sort of recent?

Nazism should not, of course, be regarded as totally foreign to the "modern" world we live in, something alien and otherworldly, but there is also a "back to nature" aspect of its ideology, expressed (for example) in the push for natural foods and "rural values" and much else that smacks of an imagined Teutonic yesteryear. There is a twisted mix of enlightenment and romance in this view of the world: many in the Hitler camp were opposed to cities, to "the artificial," and to several central trends in twentieth-century physics (notably quantum mechanics and relativity theory), but there is also a kind of retread classical/technical monumentalism that we must appreciate. A stadium designed to seat half a million people—the largest in the world—lies unfinished and rotting in Nuremberg, a testament to the Führer's passion for monumental spectacle. Grandiose plans for intercontinental ballistic missiles, rocket-powered bombs and planes, and high-speed freeways are all reflections of this monumentalist vision, as are the era's ambitious cancer registries and mass screening programs.

Monumentalism also pervades the Nazi organic impulse. The largest swastika in the world today, for example, is a grove of conifers planted in a farmer's field near Berlin in the form of a huge, one-hundred-meter *Hakenkreuz*. More than sixty years after planting, the design emerges every autumn, as the surrounding deciduous trees change colors. It is visible only from the air.

Another interesting example of this organic gigantism can be seen in the Nazi era's promotion of herbal remedies. From 1934 to 1937, the amount of land devoted to herbs and healing plants (*Gewürz- und Heilkräuter*) increased by more than a factor of ten—from 820 hectares to 3,896 hectares (a hectare is about two and a half acres). Cultivation was especially strong in the forests of Thuringia and north-central Germany, but every part of the country was involved.[42] Popular magazines celebrated the importance of natural foods and drugs, and professional apothecaries took steps to evaluate the efficacy of medicinal herbs. Schoolchildren were urged to gather local herbs, and military men even took an interest. Naturopathic medicine aroused so much excitement that academics felt obliged to warn against the potential hazards of gathering such plants. (Natural botanicals often contain strong chemicals, and prolonged exposure—from contact with the skin through gathering or processing—could and did result in poisonings.)[43]

In the late 1930s, SS botanists under Himmler's direction established extensive herbal gardens at Dachau to grow spices and botanicals for experimental purposes and for distribution to the SS and Wehrmacht. Germany's first concentration camp eventually boasted the largest medico-botanical research station in the world, with a thousand prisoners cultivating, drying, and packaging herbal medicines and spices from two hundred tediously tilled acres on the "Dachauer Moor."[44] According to Auschwitz commandant Rudolf Höss, the *plantage* produced almost all of the army's seasonings for the duration of the war. The operation was a profitable one, earning hundreds of thousands of marks for the SS every year—so profitable, in fact, that it was continued for several years after 1945 as a local cooperative, employing hundreds of former KZ prisoners.[45]

I am a historian of science by profession, and if there is one thing members of my clan like to stress, it is that scientific ideas do not flourish in a vacuum. Ideas often have a "value-slope" (Iain Boal's felicitous phrase), are pushed or pulled by social forces in odd and intricate ways that reveal an often torn or permeable membrane between science and society. In the Nazi era, one expects to find intellectual efforts tied somehow to larger nationalist, xenophobic, and racio-purist currents. I have already mentioned many examples, but there are, of course, many others. In the Nazi conception of landscape architecture, for example, native indigenous plants were to be favored over exotic species. Trees in the Reich were supposed to be tall and unyielding, not bent or "degenerate" like the contorted hazelnut or beech. The Nazi garden was similar in certain respects to the "wild garden" favored by fin de siècle English landscape gardeners such as William Robinson—though the stress on eliminating the exotic set the German movement somewhat apart. A new discipline of plant sociology—a kind of agroeugenics—was invoked to incorporate Nazi ideals into garden architecture,[46] and plans were made to harmonize natural landscapes with military/political goals (e.g., by planting hedgerows north-to-south in occupied territories of the east to slow potential tank attacks of the future).

At the risk of straying further still from cancer, let me mention one last example of the Nazi era's paternalist, Nordic supremacist organicism, expressed in Walther Schoenichen's 1942 book on nature conservation. Schoenichen's book is a remarkable defense of environmental ethics, conservation, and ecological restoration (*restituierender Naturschutz*); it also contains a review of world genocide and of steps taken to protect indigenous cultures. The book presents an elaborate plan for the "conservation of native peoples in their native habitats," conceived as part of a larger design to save the world's vanishing flora and fauna.[47] Schoenichen conceded that the disappearance of "primitive human races" was often a necessary part of the struggle for existence, but he also rejected the two dominant paths carved out by followers of the "liberalistic worldview"—the "extermination model" of the Americans and the Australians, and the "assimilation theory" of the French. Nazi native policy rejected both of these models, favoring instead "the development of indigenous peoples according to their own racial heritage." In Schoenichen's view, at least, such a policy would include bans on intermarriage, to preserve racial integrity; on tourist travel into or out of native reservations (reservations "were not zoos"); on colonial settlements; and on the importation of alcohol and cotton (to prevent the *Verkitschung* of indigenous cultures). These and other policies were to ensure that the native highlanders of New Guinea, for example, would avoid the twin "liberalistic" fates of extermination or assimilation. Movement within reservations was to be tightly controlled—the "dwarf Papuans," for example, were to be allowed to travel only as far as the capital of Ambon. Travel further than this—to Java or even Europe—would only harm the natives: "all too soon they would burn their wings on so much light."[48]

Schoenichen's "enlightened" confinement model of native/nature preservation is typical of a great deal of Nazi environmental/anthropological thought: racialist exclusions are mingled with organic prescriptions for things (or peoples) to remain in their proper place, macromanaged by superstates with superior reach and designs to make the world a purportedly better place. Nazi cancer policy can also be understood in these terms: registries, routine exams, and the sanitary body and workplace were all supposed to strengthen the German Volk as they beautified the world.

Did Nazi Policy Prevent Some Cancers?

The Nazis envisioned a manipulation of organic life unprecedented in the modern world, but it is difficult to say whether Nazi cancer policy—or any other nation's cancer policy, for that matter—had any noticeable effect on cancer rates. The question is immediately mired in complexity: the agonies and upheavals of the age must have affected long-term health, quite apart from the physical and mental savageries on battlefields and in death camps, but it is difficult to say how and to what degree.

Medical historians are well aware, of course, that wars can have dramatic and often unexpected consequences for human health. The Dutch famine of 1944–1945 is a particularly striking case: the famine was the result of a Nazi transport embargo launched in response to a Dutch strike organized in anticipation of a British liberation; even though the famine lasted only six months—until May 7, 1945—it exacted a terrible toll on the population. Babies born during that period were often small or premature, and showed an increased incidence of birth defects, including mental retardation.[49] There are many similar examples from other parts of the world: there is evidence that the Persian Gulf War of 1991, for example, resulted in the deaths of a million Iraqis—most very young and elderly—mainly from lack of medicine and maladies caused by poor-quality drinking water.

There are also well-known cases, however, where aspects of human health actually *improved* as a result of wartime privations. We know from the First World War, for example, that while rickets and other vitamin deficiency diseases rose in many European nations (from the low consumption of fresh fruits and vegetables), diabetes rates actually plunged from the unavailability of refined sugar. Many similar effects were observed after the Second World War—low rates of arteriosclerosis, for example, caused by the low consumption of meat and fat.[50]

What can we say about long-term cancer consequences in the German case? One interesting fact is that, over the period 1950–1990, German women appear to have experienced one of the most dramatic declines in cancer rates of any First World population. Female age-adjusted cancer mortality rates dropped by about 12 percent from 1952 to 1990—while many other populations of the world continued to show increases.[51] Since cancer rates today are generally expressions of exposures twenty or thirty years previously, it is not inconceivable that Nazi social policies—combined with the low-fat diet of the war and the postwar poverty—may have played a role in these declining rates.

When I began work on this book, I imagined that Nazi policies toward women—financial support for female athletics and for childbearing, for example, along with incentives for women to nurse their own children—might have played a role in the decline of female cancer rates. It now appears, however, that this was not the case—or at least not to any substantial degree. I say this because German breast cancer rates, precisely the rates that, according to what we now believe, should have declined in response to the above-mentioned policies, do not in fact show a decline in the postwar period. From 1952 to 1990, the West German age-adjusted breast cancer mortality rate showed a growth of more than 40 percent, from 16 per 100,000 to 23 per 100,000.

How then do we explain the fact that the overall cancer rate for men has grown in the postwar period, while that for women has

TABLE 7.1
West German and U.S. Lung Cancer Mortality,
per 100,000 Inhabitants[a]

	West Germany		United States	
	1952	*1990*	*1952*	*1990*
Men	22	49	25	75
Women	4	8	5	32

Sources: Deutsches Krebsforschungszentrum (Nikolaus Becker); American Cancer Society.
[a]All figures are age-adjusted.

declined? The crucial point seems to be that, apart from sex-
specific cancers (breast and cervical cancer, for example, or testicu-
lar and prostate cancer), the most important cancer from which
males and females suffer dramatically different rates is lung cancer. The difference is substantial. In 1952, the annual lung cancer
death rate among German women was only 4 per 100,000; that
same year, however, the rate for German men was 22 per 100,000.
By 1990 the rate for women had climbed to 8 per 100,000, while
the rate for men had increased to a whopping 49 per 100,000 (see
table 7.1). In Germany today, more men die from lung cancer than
from any other kind of cancer. Among women, by contrast, lung
cancer is still in third place, behind breast and colon cancer. The
difference in lung cancer mortality between the sexes is so great
that if this particular difference were somehow to vanish, most of
the difference in overall cancer mortality between men and women
would also disappear.

How can we explain the difference in the lung cancer mortality
between German men and women? One could plausibly argue
that German men were far more likely to be exposed to dangerous
chemicals in the workplace, but such an argument cannot help us
explain why American women's lung cancer rates have grown so
much higher than German women's rates.[52] There is, in fact, a better explanation. I would suggest that the most important factors
behind the relatively slow rise of female lung cancer rates by comparison with male rates in Germany and female rates in the United
States, are: (1) Nazi *paternalism*, which discouraged, often with police force, women from smoking; and (2) Nazi *militarism*, which

forced large numbers of males into a situation where smoking was not just tolerated but de facto encouraged (recall that the proportion of men smoking increased, while the average cigarette consumption decreased).[53] The Nazis failed to stop the growth of overall tobacco consumption, which culminated in 1942, but they did manage to channel most of that growth away from women. What did cut tobacco use—and dramatically—was the poverty and rationing of the war years and immediate postwar period.

One can never know how many women's lives may have been saved by the campaign against tobacco and the 1945 collapse of the tobacco industry. Even so, it is still perhaps worth noting that far more women would have died of lung cancer had German rates continued to grow as rapidly as they did in the United States. American women's lung cancer rates increased by more than a factor of six between 1952 and 1990 (see again table 7.1). German women's rates, by contrast, only doubled. Had the German rate increased as rapidly as the American rate, about twenty thousand more women would have died than actually did die. One could plausibly argue that whatever prevented German women from taking up the habit as rapidly as American women, eventually prevented the lung cancer deaths of some twenty thousand German women.

Playing the Nazi Card

Nazism remains a powerful symbol, and it is hardly surprising that it has been exploited for a circus of philosophical and commercial ends. Nazism is the moral low point of many of the "slippery slopes" that bioethicists worry about, the dangerous potential end of everything from euthanasia to abusive experimentation. It is difficult to overestimate the impact of Nazism on medical ethics, race relations, and much else as well; but I would also maintain that the "implications" of Nazi medicine are not as obvious as some would like us to believe. There is no immediate or unproblematic comparison, for example, between the Nazi extermination of the handicapped and current efforts to allow people to choose the manner and timing of their death (through "living wills," for example). Bioethical discussions are full of facile identifications of Nazism with everything from abortion and rationalized medicine to doctor-assisted suicide. I would tend to agree with Michael Burleigh that "the Nazi analogy is pretty marginal to contemporary discussions about euthanasia"; I would also agree with Arthur Caplan that comparisons invoking Nazi medicine must be drawn with care lest we mischaracterize contemporary policies or diminish the genuine extremity of the Nazi experience.[54]

Bioethicists are not the only ones eager to draw out "lessons" from the Holocaust, however. Pro-tobacco advocates have begun to play the Nazi card, with talk of "NicoNazis" and "tobacco fascism." In 1997, when antitobacco activists in Winthrop, Massachusetts, tried to ban all sale of tobacco within the city limits, an offended tobacco merchant suggested that the Board of Health was "taking up where Hitler left off."[55] A Toronto newspaper has accused antitobacco activists of being "NicoNazis" and "health fascists."[56] The most stunningly offensive case I know of came in the summer of 1995, when Philip Morris of Europe ran ads in many European magazines seeking to identify smokers with ghettoized Jews and antismokers with Nazis. The ads showed a map of Amsterdam with an area near the traditional Jewish quarter cordoned off and labeled "Smoking Section." The headline asked, "Where will they draw the line?"—implying that society's efforts to restrict smoking are comparable to Nazi efforts to isolate Jews (see fig. 7.1). We are likely to see more efforts to play the Nazi card, as anti-antitobacco campaigns move into higher gear.

Is Nazi Cancer Research Tainted?

A great deal of ink has been spilled over the question of what is to be done about "tainted" Nazi data—the most common conundrum being whether it is proper for contemporary researchers to "use" scientific information generated under suspect circumstances. The debate is often raised amid a number of misconceptions—as if "the Nazi data" were something singular and well

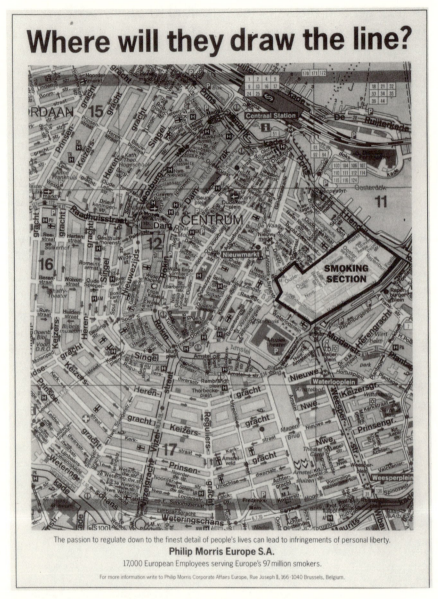

Where will they draw the line?

The passion to regulate down to the finest detail of people's lives can lead to infringements of personal liberty.

Philip Morris Europe S.A.

17,000 European Employees serving Europe's 97 million smokers.

For more information write to Philip Morris Corporate Affairs Europe, Rue Joseph II, 166-1040 Brussels, Belgium.

FIG. 7.1. "Where will they draw the line?" Philip Morris identifies smokers with Jews, and antismokers with Nazis. The company does not point out that the German tobacco establishment eagerly embraced the Nazi cause, nor that tobacco companies fought the antitobacco movement tooth and nail, then as now. Source: *Newsweek* (European edition), June 25, 1995, n.p.

defined, as if hidden gems of wisdom lie waiting, unexplored, in the archives of concentration camps. There is also the titillation value: in an era of fashionable interest in cover-ups and conspiracies, the imagination flies to the idea that people in high places have been sitting on great and potent secrets of one sort or another, barred perhaps from bringing them to light by military secrecy or some other lofty and powerful taboo.

Much of the discussion has been carried out with this tone, the idea being that unexploited "Nazi data" may harbor cures or treatments that could save lives. Use of "Nazi data" is therefore defended, according to this logic, as a kind of atonement: the argument is that people may not have died in vain if some medical use may be found for the tainted data.[57]

The truth, I think, is rather less sensational. For one thing, it is not as if Americans were not interested from the beginning in Nazi scientific talent. Nazi science and technology became the object of American military attention prior even to the end of the war, when the Office of Strategic Services and other agencies began assembling files on Nazi science, art, and culture.[58] Spy missions were launched to find out how far along the Germans had come in their project to build an atom bomb,[59] and German work on biological weapons began to come under scrutiny. After the war, the U.S. government set up the FIAT commission (with help from the French and the British) to summarize and review the achievements of German scientists and engineers; the result was a veritable encyclopedia of German wartime science—some fifty volumes altogether—on topics ranging from biophysics to viral diseases of man.[60] One cannot question whether "Nazi data" should be used without recognizing that it *has* been used, from day one, by Allied military authorities.

There are admittedly cases, however, where the ethical question remains a real one. The most notorious example in recent years has been what to do about the *Pernkopf Atlas*, a widely used anatomical text that may have used victims of Nazi terror as subjects for its anatomical illustrations.[61] The atlas is sometimes regarded as the greatest of its kind ever created, "the standard by which all other illustrated anatomical works are measured."[62] Surgeons consult it prior to surgery, and even computer-generated atlases reference the volume, much admired for its precision and realism.

The volume first aroused suspicion in the mid-1980s, when an American medical illustrator noticed that early editions contained hidden swastikas and the double lightning-bolt symbol of the SS (e.g., in the signature of an illustrator by the name of Karl Entresser). Suspicions then arose that the cadavers used as models may have been harvested from the Nazi campaign against Jews and Gypsies, or from the "euthanasia operation"[63] (the heads of several of the cadavers are closely shaved, concentration camp–style, and at least one of the models was circumcised). Suspicions also derived from the fact that Prof. Dr. Eduard Pernkopf himself had been an ardent and influential Nazi, having joined the Austrian branch of the party, secretly, in 1933. Following Austria's "return to the Reich" on March 15, 1938, he was appointed dean of the University of Vienna medical faculty, whereupon he ordered the dismissal of 153 of the university's 197 professors, including everyone of Jewish extraction or communist conviction. As a reward, Pernkopf was named president of the university in 1943. And though he was imprisoned for three years after the war (he was never convicted of a crime), he still managed to publish the third and final volume of his magnum opus in 1952.

What should be done if it turns out that the cadavers used for the Pernkopf atlas were victims of Nazi terror? Should the book be suppressed? Withdrawn from library shelves? Dedicated to the memory of the victims? What difference does it make if the persons portrayed were Jews, or euthanasia victims, or anti-Nazi patriots, or common criminals? The volume has been routinely used by physicians since the 1950s, with apparently little knowledge of its origins (the 1990 English translation received glowing reviews in both the *Journal of the American Medical Association* and the *New England Journal of Medicine*—with no reference to the politics of its author or the questionable origins of his cadavers).[64] That is the dilemma: what to do with a text that has (potentially) immoral origins yet might still be of medical value.

The University of Vienna has launched a historical inquiry into the case; as of this writing, its report is expected to be available by the end of 1998. (A great deal of prodding by medical historians and Holocaust-memorial activists was needed to launch the investigation.)[65] The American company that now owns the copyright—Waverly, Inc.—has required that every volume sold in Germany carry a disclaimer stating that the author's Nazism and antisemitism "cast a shadow" on the book, but others have called for stronger measures. At least one medical library (at the National Eye Institute in Bethesda) has inserted into the front of each volume a notice describing Pernkopf's political background and the questionable origins of his specimens (a similar notice was put into the computerized card catalog), while other medical librarians have "expunged" the book from their collections. A New Jersey physician summed up the outrage of many physicians in a 1996 letter to *JAMA*:

> The Nazis, Nazi physicians, and their era represented a horrible, unprecedented evil, repugnant to all humanity and medical tradition. The extraordinary aberration of Nazism transcends the usual concerns regarding perceived responsibilities to retain or disseminate science (and arguably also art, literature, and music). Many historians and ethicists concur that the Nazi medical legacy should be expunged from our legitimate professional heritage and literature, preserved symbolically to remind us that Pernkopf and his ilk were outside the bounds of human decency.[66]

How tainted must a work be, though, to deserve such treatment? Is membership in the Nazi party or SS sufficient to warrant banishment from the pantheon of cited scholars? That, of course, would rule out much of the cancer work I have discussed, plus a sizable chunk of postwar German science (much of the field of human genetics, for example), since a good deal of it was produced by former Nazi sympathizers. And what about other kinds of crimes? If a philosopher commits an act of murder, should this be noted in the copies of library volumes? (Louis Althusser, the prominent French communist philosopher, murdered his wife and then committed suicide—but no steps have been taken to deface his works, so far as I am aware.) What about scholars who worked on the atom bomb, or once owned slaves, or committed other reprehensible acts (if these are considered reprehensible)? And how far does the stain extend? To people who cite the tainted the work? To the funders of such work?

Such questions are by no means limited to medicine. Similar quandaries confront the reflective reader of Martin Heidegger, the Nazi rector of the University of Freiburg, who celebrated the "inner truth and greatness of Nazism" while purifying that university of Jews;[67] or Paul de Man, the literary theorist who authored pro-Nazi Belgian tracts prior to becoming the dean of American deconstructionists. But what about the anarchic Paul Feyerabend, who spent 1943 and 1944 as an officer of the German army on the eastern front but recalls that period in his autobiography as a kind of fog,[68] or Karl H. Bauer, who enjoyed postwar success as chief of Germany's National Cancer Institute, despite having enthusiastically supported the Nazi Sterilization Law? The question is easier asked than answered, once we broaden the inquiry: does Plato's defense of slavery blacken the elegance of his ethics and aesthetics? Is Jefferson the statesman diminished by Jefferson the slave-owner?

In the Pernkopf case, most commentators agree that it was wrong to have ignored the origins of the victims, and that steps must be taken to find out who they were. The forgetfulness we find with regard to Nazi-era cancer research raises different issues, but is also similar in certain respects. The Nazi war on cancer has been ignored because we do not seem to be comfortable with the idea that people with rotten ethical ideals could have been "ahead of their time" in the spheres of medicine and public health. The more comfortable image seems to be a sweeping chiaroscuro: if Nazism is the absolute embodiment of evil, we need not look at the disturbing links to what came before or after. We need not dwell on Hitler's vegetarianism, or campaigns to ban food dyes, or struggles against tobacco, radiation, and asbestos that were at least partly inspired by Nazi ideology.

Nazi medicine is rightfully remembered for its murderous legacy—but that is only part of the story and, if taken for the whole, distorts our understanding. Not because the crimes have been exaggerated—that would be difficult—but rather because there is a danger of our failing to understand the origins and appeal of German fascism. We have to understand the fertility of fascism and not just its cruelty. Nazism has to be seen as more than a demonic caricature, a straw man fabricated to efface the links to other times and places. It is not very pleasant to think about American doctors debating the gassing of their mental patients,[69] or the fact that Josef Mengele has a paper listed in the *Index Medicus*,[70] or that Nazi doctors looked to America to defend their policies of racial sterilization, racial segregation, and abusive experimentation. We need to challenge the comfortable notion that Nazi Germany was unique and defies comparison. The threads stretch before 1933 and after 1945, east into the communist block and Asia, and west into the rest of Europe and the Americas.

THE FLIP SIDE OF FASCISM

By focusing on Nazi efforts in the area of public health, my goal has not been to fabricate banalities (that "good can come from evil," for example), or to rescue the honor of this era. My point is not to deflect attention from well-documented atrocities, or to "put Hitler behind us," as James Watson has urged (to get the biotechnology ball rolling in the Federal Republic of Germany).[71] My intention is not to argue that today's antitobacco efforts have fascist roots, or that public health measures are in principle totalitarian—as some libertarians seem to want us to believe.[72]

My point is rather to show that the Nazification of German science and medicine was more complex than is commonly imagined. The history of science under Nazism is a history of both forcible sterilization and herbal medicine, of both genocidal "selection" and bans on public smoking. We do not want to forget Mengele's crimes, but we should also not forget that Dachau prisoners were forced to produce organic honey and that the SS cornered the European market in mineral water. Both elements—the monstrous and the prosaic—are key.

I do not believe, per Horkheimer and Adorno, that there is an inherently authoritarian tendency in modern science or an "indefatigable self-destructiveness" of enlightenment;[73] such pessimism ignores the diversity of ends for which science can be practiced, not to mention the power of *scientia* to act in opposition, in resistance, in restoration.

What I do believe, though, is that we need to better understand how the routine practice of science can so easily coexist with the routine exercise of cruelty. The history of Nazi cancer suggests that not everything the Nazis did can be regarded as stifling public health, and in some instances Nazi policies actually promoted it— at least for a time, and for certain segments of the population. The exclusive focus on the more horrific aspects of Nazi scientific practice makes it easy to relegate the events of this era to the monstrous or otherworldly, but there is more to the story than "medicine gone mad." The Nazi campaign against tobacco and the "whole-grain bread operation" are, in some sense, as fascist as the yellow stars and the death camps. Appreciating these complexities may open our eyes to new kinds of continuities binding the past to the present; it may also allow us better to see how fascism triumphed in the first place.

NOTES

PROLOGUE

1. Joseph Goebbels, *Die Tagebücher von Joseph Goebbels: Sämtliche Fragmente*, ed. Elke Fröhlich, pt. 1, vol. 4, *Aufzeichnungen 1924–1941* (Munich: K. G. Saur, 1987), pp. 710–11.

2. William E. Seidelman, "Animal Experiments in Nazi Germany," *Lancet* 1 (1986): 1214.

3. Herbert Mehrtens, "Irresponsible Purity: The Political and Moral Structure of Mathematical Sciences in the National Socialist State," in *Science, Technology and National Socialism*, ed. Monika Renneberg and Mark Walker (Cambridge: Cambridge University Press, 1994), pp. 324–38.

4. Billy F. Price, *Adolf Hitler: The Unknown Artist* (Houston: Billy F. Price, 1984).

5. Omer Bartov, "An Idiot's Tale: Memories and Histories of the Holocaust," *Journal of Modern History* 67 (1995): 55–82. I would not challenge Daniel J. Goldhagen's claim that antisemitism was central to the Holocaust (what else?), but I would challenge his dismissal of other antecedents—the bureaucratization of the killing process, for example, and the linkage of Jews with other "lives unworthy of living"; see his *Hitler's Willing Executioners: Ordinary Germans and the Holocaust* (New York: Knopf, 1996).

6. Such arguments are becoming fashionable: see, for example, William A. Rusher, "The Health Fascists Are Blowing Smoke," *Kerrville Daily Times*, January 4, 1996.

CHAPTER 1
HUEPER'S SECRET

1. Hueper gave as a reference his brother, Heinz, a Nazi party functionary (*Ortsgruppenleiter*) in Bochum who had joined the NSDAP in the fall of 1932. Hueper's brother was an early member of the Nazi Teachers' League (no. 21,327) and listed his religion on the NSDAP party form as "nat.-soz." See Heinz Hueper's party file in the Bundesarchiv Berlin (BDC) and W. C. Hueper to Bernhard Rust, Geheimes Staatsarchiv, Preussischer Kulturbesitz, Berlin-Dahlem, Rep. 76 Va Sekt.1 Tit. IV, no. 5, vol. 27, p. 19. Robert Rössle, director of Berlin's Pathologisches Institut, evaluated Hueper's letter (which also contained a list of publications and a two-page biography), noting that since "pathology in America was not the same as in Germany," it was difficult to say

whether Hueper would be appropriate for a German academic post. Hueper in his view was not yet senior enough for a professorship (*Berufung*), as he was "not a major figure [*Grosse*] in the field"; Rössle also noted that it would not be fair to Germany's many junior professors to appoint a man who had not "remained true to Germany in its difficult time" (Rössle to Ministerialrat Schnöring, November 13, 1933, in ibid.). My thanks to Michael Hubenstorf for drawing these files to my attention.

2. See my *Cancer Wars: How Politics Shapes What We Know and Don't Know about Cancer* (New York: Basic Books, 1995), pp. 36–53; also Christopher Sellers, "Discovering Environmental Cancer: Wilhelm Hueper, Post–World War II Epidemiology, and the Vanishing Clinician's Eye," *American Journal of Public Health* 87 (1997): 1824–35.

3. For recent overviews, see Ernst Klee, *Auschwitz, die NS-Medizin und ihre Opfer* (Frankfurt: S. Fischer, 1997); Christoph Meinel and Peter Voswinckel, eds., *Medizin, Naturwissenschaft, Technik und Nationalsozialismus: Kontinuitäten und Diskontinuitäten* (Stuttgart: Geschichte der Naturwissenschaften, 1994); also Renneberg and Walker, *Science, Technology and National Socialism*.

4. Michael H. Kater, *Doctors under Hitler* (Chapel Hill: University of North Carolina Press, 1989); Ute Deichmann, *Biologen unter Hitler: Vertreibung, Karrieren, Forschung* (Frankfurt: Campus, 1992).

5. Robert N. Proctor, "From *Anthropologie* to *Rassenkunde*: Concepts of Race in German Physical Anthropology," in *Bones, Bodies, Behavior: Essays on Biological Anthropology*, ed. George W. Stocking, Jr. (Madison: University of Wisconsin Press, 1988), pp. 138–79.

6. Paul Weindling, *Health, Race and German Politics between National Unification and Nazism 1870–1945* (Cambridge: Cambridge University Press, 1989); Christian Pross and Götz Aly, eds., *Der Wert des Menschen: Medizin in Deutschland 1918–1945* (Berlin: Edition Hentrich, 1989); Götz Aly and Karl Heinz Roth, *Die restlose Erfassung: Volkszählen, Identifizieren, Aussondern im Nationalsozialismus* (Berlin: Rotbuch, 1984); also my *Racial Hygiene: Medicine under the Nazis* (Cambridge: Harvard University Press, 1988).

7. Jeffrey Herf, *Reactionary Modernism: Technology, Culture, and Politics in Weimar and the Third Reich* (Cambridge: Cambridge University Press, 1984); compare also Zygmunt Bauman, *Modernity and the Holocaust* (New York: Oxford University Press, 1989), and Mario Biagioli, "Science, Modernity, and the 'Final Solution,'" in *Probing the Limits of Representation: Nazism and the "Final Solution"*, ed. Saul Friedlander (Cambridge: Harvard University Press, 1992), pp. 185–205.

8. *Trials of War Criminals before the Nuernberg Military Tribunals*, vol. 7 (Washington, D.C.: U.S. Government Printing Office, 1953), p. 27.

9. John Gimbel in his *Science, Technology, and Reparations: Exploitation and Plunder in Postwar Germany* (Stanford: Stanford University Press, 1990) includes the following in his list of innovations of the Nazi era: cold-steel extrusion, aerial infrared photography, new kinds of optical glass, power circuitbreakers, die-casting equipment, wind tunnels, acetylene chemistry, new textiles and textile machinery, new forest products and ceramics, X-ray tubes, tape recorders, heavy presses, diesel motors, high-tension cables, radio con-

densers, insecticides, color film processing, precision grinding machines, and "a unique chocolate-wrapping machine" (p. 22).

10. Office of Military Government for Germany, Field Information Agency Technical *FIAT Review of German Science, 1939–1946, Complete List of Review Titles* (Wiesbaden: Klemm, 1947); Gimbel, *Science, Technology, and Reparations*.

11. Kristie Macrakis, *Surviving the Swastika: Scientific Research in Nazi Germany* (New York: Oxford University Press, 1993), pp. 110–11.

12. A minor exception is Gustav Wagner and Andrea Mauerberger's institutional hagiography: *Krebsforschung in Deutschland* (Berlin: Springer, 1989); compare also Evelyn H. Salazar, *Krebsforschung und Krebsbekämpfung in Berlin bis zum Jahre 1945* (Berlin: Med. diss., 1986); Ronald Woitke, *Zur Entwicklung der Krebserfassung, -behandlung und -fürsorge im "Dritten Reich"* (Leipzig: Med. diss., 1993); and Achim Thom, "Zur Entwicklung, staatlichen Förderung und Wirksamkeit der ausseruniversitären Krebsforschungszentren in Deutschland zwischen 1900 und 1945" (unpub. MS). Ute Deichmann has a brief discussion of cancer research in her *Biologen unter Hitler*, pp. 126–29. The most comprehensive bibliography of cancer research in the Nazi and immediate post-Nazi period is Ernst Rückert and Heinz Kleeberg, *25 Jahre Krebsforschung im deutschsprachigen Schrifttum: Eine Auswahl von Buch- und Zeitschriftenliteratur aus den Jahren 1931–1955* (Berlin: Volk und Gesundheit, 1961); the most extensive bibliography of pre-twentieth-century literature, with many flaws, is Robert Behla, *Die Carcinomlitteratur. Eine Zusammenstellung der in- und ausländischen Krebsschriften bis 1900* (Berlin: R. Schoetz, 1901).

13. See, for example, Gerhard Baader and Ulrich Schultz, eds., *Medizin und Nationalsozialismus: Tabuisierte Vergangenheit—Ungebrochene Tradition?* 2d ed. (Berlin: Verlagsgesellschaft Gesundheit, 1983); Johanna Bleker and Norbert Jachertz, eds., *Medizin im Dritten Reich* (Cologne: Deutscher Ärzte-Verlag, 1989); Gisela Bock, *Zwangssterilisation im Nationalsozialismus: Studien zur Rassenpolitik und Frauenpolitik* (Opladen: Westdeutscher Verlag, 1986); Fridolf Kudlien, ed., *Ärzte im Nationalsozialismus* (Cologne: Kiepenheuer & Witsch, 1985); Achim Thom and Genadij I. Caregorodcev, eds., *Medizin unterm Hakenkreuz* (Berlin: Volk und Gesundheit, 1989); also my *Racial Hygiene* and Robert Jay Lifton's *The Nazi Doctors* (New York: Basic Books, 1986).

14. Ludwig Rehn, "Blasengeschwülste bei Fuchsin-Arbeitern," *Archiv für klinische Chirurgie* 50 (1895): 588–600.

15. E. Pfeil, "Lungentumoren als Berufserkrankung in Chromatbetrieben," *Deutsche medizinische Wochenschrift* 61 (1935): 1197–1200.

16. Paul G. Unna is usually credited as the first to associate skin cancer with sunlight; see his *Die Histopathologie der Hautkrankheiten* (Berlin: A. Hirschwald, 1894).

17. Albert Frieben, "Cancroid des rechten Handrückens," *Deutsche medicinische Wochenschrift* 28 (1902): 335; Kurt Ziegler, *Experimentelle und klinische Untersuchungen über die Histogenese der myeloiden Leukämie* (Jena: G. Fischer, 1906); Heinrich W. Schmidt, "Radioaktivitätsmessungen in St. Joachimsthal," *Physikalische Zeitschrift* 8 (1907): 1–5; Ekkehard Schmid, "Messungen des Radium-Emanationsgehaltes von Kellerluft," *Mitteilung aus dem physikalischen Institut der Universität Graz* 82 (1932): 233–42. Austrians were the first to report a high

rate of leukemia among radiologists; see Nikolaus von Jagič et al., "Blutbefunde bei Röntgenologen," *Berliner klinische Wochenschrift* 48 (1911): 1220–22.

18. Richard von Volkmann, surgeon-in-chief of the German army during the war of 1870–1871, in 1875 described scrotal cancers in men engaged in the manufacture of paraffin from lignite; see his *Beiträge zur Chirurgie* (Leipzig: Breitkopf und Härtel, 1875), pp. 370–72. Germans pioneered the study of benzene-induced leukemia: see Carl G. Santesson, "Chronische Vergiftungen mit Steinkohlentheerbenzin: Vier Todesfälle," *Archiv für Hygiene und Bakteriologie* 31 (1897): 336–76; also Martha Schmidtmann, "Experimentelle Untersuchungen über die Wirkung kleiner Benzin- und Benzolmengen auf Atmungsorgane und Gesamtorganismus," *Klinische Wochenschrift* 9 (1930): 2106–8.

19. Johannes Müller, *Über den feinen Bau und die Formen der krankhaften Geschwülste* (Berlin: Reimer, 1838); Rudolf L. Virchow, *Die krankhaften Geschwülste*, 3 vols. (Berlin: Hirschwald, 1863–1867).

20. Arthur Hanau, "Erfolgreiche experimentelle Übertragung von Carcinom," *Fortschritte der Medizin* 7 (1876): 321–39.

21. Kurt Rostoski, Erich Saupe and Georg Schmorl, "Die Bergkrankheit der Erzbergleute in Schneeberg in Sachsen," *Zeitschrift für Krebsforschung* 23 (1926): 360–84, where note is taken of the fact that Schneeberg's uranium miners could develop cancer ten to eighteen years after leaving the mines; also Otto Teutschlaender's discussion of the "Latenzstadium der Krebsentstehung" in "Die Berufskrebse (mit besonderer Berücksichtigung der in Deutschland vorkommenden)," *Zeitschrift für Krebsforschung* 32 (1930): 614–27.

22. Jens Paulsen, "Konstitution und Krebs," *Zeitschrift für Krebsforschung* 21 (1924): 126–28.

23. Karl Heinrich Bauer, "Krebs und Vererbung," *Münchener medizinische Wochenschrift* 87 (1940): 474–80; Peter Karlson, *Adolf Butenandt: Biochemiker, Hormonforschung, Wissenschaftspolitiker* (Stuttgart: Wissenschaftliche Verlagsgesellschaft, 1990), pp. 126–32 and 184–86.

24. Charles Steffen, "Max Borst (1869–1946)," *American Journal of Dermatopathology* 7 (1985): 25–27.

25. Rudolf Roosen, *Die Isaminblautherapie der bösartigen Geschwülste* (Leipzig: Kabitzsch, 1930).

26. Theodor Blühbaum, Karl Frik, and Helmut Kalkbrenner, "Eine neue Anwendungsart der Kolloide in der Röntgendiagnostik," *Fortschritte auf dem Gebiete der Röntgenstrahlen* 37 (1928): 18–29.

27. Otto Jüngling, "Polyposis intestini," *Beiträge zur klinischen Chirurgie* 143 (1928): 476–83; Theodor H. Boveri, *Zur Frage der Entstehung maligner Tumoren* (Jena: G. Fischer, 1914), pp. 25, 41.

28. George Meyer, "Verhandlungen der Internationalen Konferenz für Krebsforschung vom 25.–27. September 1906 zu Heidelberg und Frankfurt a. Main," *Zeitschrift für Krebsforschung* 5 (1907): vii–xxxvi.

29. The *Zeitschrift für Krebsforschung* began publishing in 1904. The first general cancer journal was the *Revue des maladies cancereuses*, published in France from 1896 through 1901; the Japanese journal *Gann* was established in 1907, and Italy's *Tumori* in 1911. Germany's *Zeitschrift* published regularly until 1944; publication resumed shortly after the war, and in 1971 the journal

changed its name to *Zeitschrift für Krebsforschung und klinische Onkologie*. It was discontinued in 1978.

30. Leopold Schönbauer and Erna Ueberreiter, "Erlaubt das vorliegende statistische Material ein Urteil über eine Zunahme der Krebskrankheit?" *Wiener medizinische Wochenschrift* 100 (1950): 556. The first internally lit endoscope (using a gas flame) was developed by Antoine Jean Desormeaux in France in 1865; an electrical version was produced by Josef Leiter in Vienna in 1879 (ibid.). The Nazi era sees the development of the world's first multiviewer colposcope (*Polykolposkop*), allowing several investigators to peer into the uterus at the same time; see Helmut Kraatz, "Farbfiltervorschaltung zur leichteren Erlernung der Kolposkopie," *Zentralblatt für Gynäkologie* 63 (1939): 2307 ff.

31. Katsusaburo Yamagiwa and Koichi Ichikawa, "Experimentelle Studie über die Pathogenese der Epithelialgeschwülste," *Mitteilungen aus der medizinischen Fakultät der kaiserlichen Universität zu Tokyo* 15 (1916): 295–344.

32. "It is of course possible that the [seventeen women Schönherr observed with lung cancer] had often sat in the company of cigar smokers and had thereby been forced to breathe substantial quantities of cigar smoke"; see Ernst Schönherr, "Beitrag zur Statistik und Klinik der Lungentumoren," *Zeitschrift für Krebsforschung* 27 (1928): 443.

33. "Mitteilungen," *Monatsschrift für Krebsbekämpfung* 9 (1941): 23. In 1939 alone there were 180 German medical doctoral dissertations written on cancer topics; cancer was the subject of 3.5 percent of the 5,232 medical theses completed that year (ibid.).

34. Michael Hubenstorf, "Ende einer Tradition und Fortsetzung als Provinz. Die medizinischen Fakultäten der Universitäten Berlin und Wien 1925–1950," in Meinel and Voswinckel, *Medizin*, pp. 33–53.

35. Wilhelm C. Hueper in his *Occupational Tumors and Allied Diseases* (Springfield, Ill.: Charles C. Thomas, 1942) noted that aniline dye cancers had generally been identified ten to twenty years after the introduction of dye production into a particular country (pp. 470–71). The Mannheim pathologist Otto Teutschlaender constructed a remarkably similar argument in his "Arbeit und Geschwulstbildung," *Monatsschrift für Krebsbekämpfung* 1 (1933): 106.

36. Hermann Holthusen and K. Englmann, "Die Gefahr des Röntgenkarzinoms als Folge der Strahlenbehandlung," *Strahlentherapie* 42 (1931): 514–31.

37. G. H. Gehrmann, "The Carcinogenetic Agent—Chemistry and Industrial Aspects," *Journal of Urology* 31 (1934): 136; compare also Wolfgang Hien, *Chemische Industrie und Krebs* (Bremerhaven: Wirtschaftsverlag, 1994), pp. 252–71.

38. Ferdinand Blumenthal, "Zum 25-jährigen Bestehen des Deutschen Zentralkomitees," *Zeitschrift für Krebsforschung* 22 (1925): 97–107. The Zentralkomitee was originally called the Comité für Krebssammelforschung, renamed in 1906 the Zentralkomitee für Krebsforschung. Honorary members of the original Comité included Rudolf Virchow, Robert Koch, and, from London, Lord Joseph Lister. Germany's first cancer research institutes were established in 1903 (at Berlin's famous Charité hospital) and 1904 (at Heidelberg, on the initiative of the surgeon Vinzenz Czerny). Similar institutions had already been established in London, Moscow, and Buffalo. Britain established its own

Central Committee for Cancer Research in 1900, the same year London's Middlesex Cancer Research Laboratories were established.

39. Blumenthal, "Zum 25-jährigen Bestehen," pp. 97–107. The surgeon Theodor Billroth (1829–1894) claimed to be seeing higher cancer rates in his clinical practice in Austria; his fears were confirmed by Robert Behla in "Über vermehrtes und endemisches Vorkommen des Krebses," *Centralblatt für Bacteriologie* 24 (1898): 780 ff., and by F. Reiche (for Hamburg) in his "Zur Verbreitung des Carcinoms," *Münchener medizinische Wochenschrift* 47 (1900): 1337–39.

40. Fritz Lickint, *Die Krebsfrage im Lichte der modernen Forschung* (Berlin: F. A. Herbig, 1935), p. 5. Lickint's characterization of cancer as Germany's number one cause of death involved a statistical sleight of hand: he distinguished two types of heart attack, allowing cancer rates to appear higher than either type separately. Cancer in the 1930s was more commonly—and accurately—described as Germany's second leading cause of death. In 1892, 126,000 Germans died of tuberculosis; this had fallen to 48,000 by 1932. The numbers for cancer in these two years, by contrast, were 28,000 and 87,000.

41. "Mitteilungen," *Monatsschrift für Krebsbekämpfung* 9 (1941): 158.

42. See my *Racial Hygiene*, pp. 21–22 and 227–50.

43. Georg Boehncke, "Tabak und Volksgesundheit," *Öffentlicher Gesundheitsdienst* 1 (1935): 625.

44. Responding to critiques of his 1932 book on cancer, Liek compared his own plight to that of other much-maligned scientific greats, including Paracelsus, Vesalius, Lister, Pasteur, and Freud. According to Liek, the Viennese psychoanalyst was shamefully "laughed out of court" when he presented his pioneering ideas to the Viennese Medical Society. See Erwin Liek, *Der Kampf gegen den Krebs* (Munich: Lehmann, 1934), p. 13.

45. Erwin Liek, "Versuche am Menschen" (1928), in his *Gedanken eines Arztes* (Dresden: Carl Reissner Verlag, 1937).

46. On Liek's life and work, see Wolfgang Schmid, *Die Bedeutung Erwin Lieks für das Selbstverständnis der Medizin in Weimarer Republik und Nationalsozialismus* (Erlangen-Nuremberg: Med. diss., 1989); Michael Kater, "Die Medizin im nationalsozialistischen Deutschland und Erwin Liek," *Geschichte und Gesellschaft* 16 (1990): 440–63; Heinz-Peter Schmiedebach, "Der wahre Arzt und das Wunder der Heilkunde: Erwin Lieks ärztlich-heilkundliche Ganzheitsideen," in *Der ganze Mensch und die Medizin* (Berlin: Argument-Sonderband, 1989), pp. 33–53; and Michael Jehs, *Erwin Liek: Weltanschauung und standespolitische Einstellung im Spiegel seiner Schriften* (Frankfurt: Mabuse, 1994).

47. Werner Zabel, "Erwin Liek zum Gedächtnis," *Hippokrates* 6 (1935): 188; Kater, *Doctors under Hitler*, p. 227. According to Liek's close friend Alfred Brauchle, Wagner asked Liek to head the Rudolf Hess Hospital in Dresden, but Liek was forced to decline for health reasons; see Brauchle's *Naturheilkunde in Lebensbildern* (Leipzig: Philipp Reclam, 1937), p. 397.

48. Erwin Liek, *Die Welt des Arztes: Aus 30 Jahren Praxis* (Munich: Lehmann, 1933), pp. 239–41.

49. Weindling, *Health*, pp. 169–70; Michael A. Grodin, "Historical Origins of the Nuremberg Code," in *The Nazi Doctors and the Nuremberg Code: Human*

Rights in Human Experimentation, ed. George J. Annas and Michael A. Grodin (New York: Oxford University Press, 1992), pp. 127–28.

50. The Lehmann Verlag, the most important publisher of racial theory and racial hygiene during the Nazi period, was disbanded after World War II as a Nazi-affiliated press. The firm's medical and military books were distributed to the Springer and Berg publishing houses, and the racial books went to the Hamburg-based Deutsche Gesellschaft für biologische Anthropologie, an organization with strong neo-Nazi ties. Scandalously, all official German medical bookstores still today bear the Lehmann name. For the early history of the house, see Hermann Wilhelm, *Dichter, Denker, Fememörder: Rechtsradikalismus und Antisemitismus in München von der Jahrhundertwende bis 1921* (Berlin: Transit, 1989), pp. 118–27.

51. Liek, *Welt des Arztes*, pp. 239–44; Jehs, *Erwin Liek*, pp. 36–38.

52. Frederick L. Hoffman, America's premier cancer preventionist of the era (and a dyed-in-the-wool racist), praised Liek as "an outstanding contributor to medical literature" and "a very earnest and competent authority"; see his *Cancer and Diet* (Baltimore: Williams & Wilkins, 1937), pp. 92, 105. Liek was a talented writer, priding himself on his clarity and his avoidance of the jargon (*Kauderwelsch*) of his academic colleagues. He was a member of the governing board of the Deutsche Sprachverein, an organization devoted to preserving the German language. Liek's gift was conceded even by critics such as Fischer-Wasels, who labeled him a "seductive stylist," and Georg Wolff, who said his cancer book read "almost like a novel" (Liek, *Der Kampf*, pp. 14–15).

53. Erwin Liek, *Krebsverbreitung, Krebsbekämpfung, Krebsverhütung* (Munich: Lehmann, 1932).

54. See Frederick L. Hoffman, *The Mortality from Cancer throughout the World* (Newark: Prudential Press, 1915); Vilhjalmur Stefansson, *Cancer: Disease of Civilization?* (New York: Hill and Wang, 1960); also my *Cancer Wars*, pp. 16–34.

55. Liek, *Der Kampf*, p. 24.

56. Ibid., pp. 25–27.

57. Georg Ernst Konjetzny, "Chronische Gastritis und Magenkrebs," *Monatsschrift für Krebsbekämpfung* 2 (1934): 76–78. Opinions on Liek's 1932 book ranged, as noted in his 1934 preface, from *Meisterwerk* to *Mist* (masterpiece to horseshit). Fischer-Wasels of Frankfurt claimed that it contained "not a single new fact"; a reviewer in the *Ärztliche Wegweiser* stated that it brought forth "nothing new." The natural lifestyle advocate Max Oskar Bircher-Benner, by contrast, praised the book as revealing "the only way to combat cancer"; see Liek, *Der Kampf*, pp. 9–10.

58. Liek, *Der Kampf*, pp. 11–12.

59. *Nürnberger Zeitung*, no. 266 (1935): 5. Streicher said that *Krankheitsverhütung* was more important than *Krankheitsbekämpfung*.

60. "Die Aufgabe," *Monatsschrift für Krebsbekämpfung* 1 (1933): 2. Hermann Druckrey claimed that "Die beste Therapie ist die *Prophylaxe*" in his "Ergebnisse der experimentellen Krebstherapie," *Zeitschrift für Krebsforschung* 47 (1938): 124. The *Monatsschrift für Krebsbekämpfung* was subtitled *Verhütung, Erkennung und Behandlung bösartiger Geschwülste*, which makes it the world's first cancer journal to include the word "prevention" in its title.

61. Herbert Assmann, "Über Nikotinschäden," *Die Genussgifte* 36 (1940): 39.

62. See Robert Pois, *National Socialism and the Religion of Nature* (New York: St. Martin's Press, 1986); Gert Groening and Joachim Wolschke-Bulmahn, "Some Notes on the Mania for Native Plants in Germany," *Landscape Journal* 11 (1992): 116–26; also my *Racial Hygiene*, pp. 223–50.

63. Ernst G. Schenck, *Patient Hitler: Eine medizinische Biographie* (Dusseldorf: Droste, 1989), p. 32.

64. D. Bauer, "So lebt der Düce," *Auf der Wacht* 54 (1937): 19–20. German propaganda also portrayed Churchill as an excessive drinker.

65. Georg Bonne, "Nachbehandlung nach Krebsoperation," *Hippokrates* 9 (1938): 612–13.

66. Karl Kötschau, "Über Umweltschädigungen," *Hippokrates* 9 (1938): 1282–83.

67. Gustav Riedlin, "Das Kochsalz als Kulturgift," *Fortschritte der Medizin* 53 (1935): 543–44; compare also Hugo O. Kleine, *Ernährungsschäden als Krankheitsursachen: Versuch einer Darstellung der gesundheitsschädlichen Folgen zivilisationsbedingter Fehlernährung* (Stuttgart: Hippokrates, 1940).

68. Roland Blaich, "Nazi Race Hygiene and the Adventists," *Spectrum* 25 (September 1996): 14.

69. Felix Grüneisen, "Krebsbekämpfung im nationalsozialistischen Staat," *Deutsche medizinische Wochenschrift* 59 (1933): 1498. In a bizarre case of strawmanning, Grüneisen accused "Bolshevist-materialists" of claiming that cancer should not be fought, since it was a "natural" consequence of growing old and a "natural regulator" of the human population (p. 1499).

70. Anton Missriegler, "Die Krebsangst," *Hippokrates* 9 (1938): 469–71.

71. Hans Hinselmann, "14 Jahre Kolposkopie. Ein Rückblick und Ausblick," *Hippokrates* 9 (1938): 661–67; compare also the historical introduction in Hanskurt Bauer, *Farbatlas der Kolposkopie*, 4th ed. (Stuttgart: Schattauer, 1993). Hinselmann developed the colposcope in 1924. He joined the Nazi party on May 1, 1933, and three years later was awarded Germany's first Dozentur (lectureship) for colposcopy and early uterine cancer diagnosis. The American Society for Colposcopy, publisher of *The Colposcopist*, was founded in 1963.

72. Georg Winter, "Die erste Krebsbekämpfung, ihre Erfolge und Lehren," *Monatsschrift für Krebsbekämpfung* 1 (1933): 3–10.

73. There were some seventy Krebsberatungsstellen in Germany in 1941. Counseling centers were also established in the occupied East; see, for example, "Krebsberatungsstelle Litzmannstadt," *Monatsschrift für Krebsbekämpfung* 11 (1943): 72. Not every counseling center was heavily patronized: the center in Lodz, for example, recorded only two hundred visitors in 1941 (ibid.).

74. Rudolf Ramm, "Systematische Krebsbekämpfung," *Die Gesundheitsführung*, November 1942, pp. 268–69. *Jeder Achte*, also known as *Ein Film gegen die Volkskrankheit: Krebs*, was produced by Walter Ruttmann in 1941 with scientific advice from Hans Auler. There are at least two Weimar-era cancer films: *Die Krebskrankheit* (1925), produced by Julius Mayr, Paul P. Gotthardt, and Carl Moncorps; and *Krebs* (1930), an eighteen-minute silent film produced and distributed by the Deutsches Hygiene-Museum in Dresden. The best analysis of

Nazi medical films is Ulf Schmidt, *Medical Research Films, Perpetrators, and Victims in National Socialist Germany, 1933–1945* (Oxford: D.Phil. diss., 1997).

75. Rachel Carson, *Silent Spring* (Boston: Houghton-Mifflin, 1962), pp. 219–44.

76. Felix von Mikulicz-Radecki, "Vorsichtsuntersuchungen im Rahmen der Bestrebungen um die Krebsfrüherfassung," *Monatsschrift für Krebsbekämpfung* 9 (1942): 84–88.

77. Georg Winter, "Die Früherfassung des Krebses in der Zukunft," *Monatsschrift für Krebsbekämpfung* 10 (1942): 1–5.

78. Robert Hofstätter, "Über die Notwendigkeit der periodischen Gesunden-Untersuchung und der allgemeinen Meldepflicht zur Bekämpfung der Krebskrankheit bei der Frau," *Wiener medizinische Wochenschrift* 89 (1939): 931–34. The calculations were actually those of Carl H. Lasch.

79. Hofstätter file, BDC.

80. Walter Niderehe, "Bericht über die Vorträge betr. Krebsbekämpfung auf dem 3. internat. Kongress f.d. ärztl. Fortbildungswesen in Berlin," Aug. 24, 1937, p. 4, E 1496, Thüringisches Hauptstaatsarchiv, Weimar (hereafter THW).

81. Ibid., p. 8. Felix von Mikulicz-Radecki upheld this view.

82. Hermann Langbein, *Menschen in Auschwitz* (Vienna: Europaverlag, 1972), pp. 427–28. I would like to thank Scott Lentz for drawing this material to my attention.

83. Lifton, *Nazi Doctors*, p. 391.

CHAPTER 2
THE *GLEICHSCHALTUNG* OF GERMAN CANCER RESEARCH

1. Three of the cancer researchers fired from the Charité—Ferdinand Blumenthal, Eduard Jacobs, and H. Rosenberg—obtained professional positions, at least for a time, in Belgrade; see Michael Hubenstorf and Peter Th. Walther, "Politische Bedingungen und allgemeine Veränderungen des Berliner Wissenschaftsbetriebes," in *Exodus von Wissenschaften aus Berlin: Fragestellung, Ergebnisse, Desiderate*, ed. Wolfram Fischer et al. (Berlin: Walter de Gruyter, 1994), pp. 34–35.

2. Blumenthal was fired on September 24, 1933; his replacement, Hans Auler, with whom Blumenthal had long worked, was named deputy director of the Charité's Cancer Institute. (Ferdinand Sauerbruch was named director in 1935; see Wagner and Mauerberger, *Krebsforschung*, pp. 13–14.) Blumenthal (1870–1941) had been chief physician at the Charité's Fürsorgestelle für Krebskranke und Krebsverdächtige in 1906; he later explored the heritability of cancer and the role of trauma. In 1931 he predicted that if Germany and England each were to build one less Dreadnought and invest the resulting RM 40 million in forty cancer institutes for each country, "we would not only see the cancer question solved but would also see the number of cancer victims reduced by half." See his "Zum 25-jährigen Bestehen," p. 543. Blumenthal fled to Czechoslovakia in 1933, then to Vienna and then Belgrade after the annexation of Austria. From Belgrade he traveled first to Tirana, Albania, and finally

to the city of Reval in Lithuania, where he was captured and interned by the Russians. He was deported to the USSR in 1941, where he died under unclear circumstances.

3. Heinrich Cramer, "Das allgemeine Institut gegen die Geschwulstkrankheiten im Rudolf Virchow-Krankenhaus, Berlin," *Zeitschrift für das gesamte Krankenhauswesen* 32 (1936): 492–94. The new institute was strong on radiation and experimental hormonal therapies; its biological division cooperated closely with the I. G. Farben conglomerate to produce new chemotherapies (ibid., p. 494).

4. Salazar, *Krebsforschung*, p. 83. Many other Jewish cancer researchers were forced from Germany or, after 1938, from Austria. Gustav Bucky (1880–?), a radiologist who had emigrated to the United States in 1923, returned to Germany in the late 1920s, whereupon he was named director of the Radiology Department at the Rudolf Virchow Hospital in Berlin (from 1930 to 1933). He returned to the U.S. in 1933, where he worked at the Albert Einstein College of Medicine in New York. Ludwig Teleky was forced to leave Vienna; see Heinrich Buess, "Der Wiener Sozialmediziner Ludwig Teleky (1872–1957) und seine 'History of factory and mine hygiene,'" *Wiener medizinische Wochenschrift* 131 (1981): 479–83. There seem to have been relatively few Jews in official antialcohol or antitobacco groups, though more research needs to be done in this area. On the history of medical emigration from Nazi Germany, see Fischer et al., *Exodus*, pp. 34–35, 343–591, and 615–30.

5. Eckhart Henning, "Otto Warburg," in *Berlinische Lebensbilder*, vol. 1, *Naturwissenschaften*, ed. Wilhelm Treue and Gerhard Hildebrandt (Berlin: Colloquium, 1987), pp. 299–315.

6. See, for example, David Nachmansohn, *German-Jewish Pioneers in Science, 1900–1933* (New York: Springer, 1979), p. 254.

7. Macrakis, *Surviving the Swastika*, pp. 63–64.

8. "Mitteilungen des Deutschen Reichsausschusses für Krebsbekämpfung," *Zeitschrift für Krebsforschung* 41 (1935): 522–38.

9. "Vorwort zur neuen Folge," *Zeitschrift für Krebsforschung* 40 (1934): 1–2. The journal stressed that, henceforth, the journal must try to better represent the "diversity" (*Vielseitigkeit*) of views concerning how to research and treat cancer.

10. "Die Aufgabe," p. 1.

11. The organizational structure of the Reichsausschuss für Krebsbekämpfung is detailed in Gerhard Krug, *Die Organisation des Kampfes gegen den Krebs in wissenschaftlicher und sozialer Hinsicht* (Marburg: Med. diss., 1938), pp. 18–30.

12. Planning for the Deutsches Hygiene-Museum exhibit "Kampf dem Krebs" began in 1930; the exhibit opened in February of 1931 and was expanded during the Nazi period, eventually traveling to hundreds of cities all over the Reich. As late as August 1944 the exhibit was still on display at Lauenburg and Stolp ("Ausstellungsverzeichnis 1903–1994," Deutsches Hygiene-Museum Archive; personal communication, Marianne Schneider). The exhibit catalog is Bruno Gebhard, *Kampf dem Krebs* (Dresden: Deutscher Verlag für Volkswohlfahrt, 1931 and 1933).

13. "Vorwort zur neuen Folge," p. 1. Hitler was generally dismissive of "science for its own sake": in a conversation of March 27, 1942, the Führer remarked, "We don't know anything about the origins of a lousy fistula; the simplest and most widespread disease is not even researched! But the magnificent netherworld of heaven and hell and all other nonsense are thoroughly explored"; see Henry Picker, *Hitlers Tischgespräche im Führerhauptquartier, 1941–42* (Bonn: Athenäum, 1951), p. 354.

14. William E. Seidelman, "Mengele Medicus: Medicine's Nazi Heritage," *Milbank Quarterly* 66 (1988): 221–39.

15. Wagner and Mauerberger, *Krebsforschung*, pp. 14–15. The forms used for these registries are reprinted in the "Mitteilungen des Deutschen Reichsausschusses," pp. 525–38. Results from these registries were not made public, apparently for fear of an unfavorable public response. The city of Nuremberg had established a cancer registry in the summer of 1933; see the *Nürnberger Zeitung* 172 (1935): 5. For a review of the Nuremberg program, see Maximilian Meyer, "Schicksal der Krebskranken," *Reichs-Gesundheitsblatt* 15 (1940): 177–93.

16. Adolf Radermacher, *Krebssterblichkeit und -bekämpfung in der Hansestadt Köln von 1932–1940* (Med. diss.: Cologne, 1942), pp. 11–12.

17. Connecticut's famous Tumor Registry was established about this same time—in 1937—see J. T. Flannery and D. T. Janerich, "The Connecticut Tumor Registry: Yesterday, Today and Tomorrow," *Connecticut Medicine* 49 (1985): 709–12.

18. "Mitteilungen des Deutschen Reichsausschusses," p. 525.

19. Ernst Dormanns, "Die vergleichende geographisch-pathologische Reichs-Carcinomstatistik 1925–1933," *Referate des II. Internationalen Kongresses für Krebsforschung und Krebsbekämpfung* 1 (1936): 460–79. Zurich was probably the autopsy capital of the world, with about a third of all bodies being autopsied in the early decades of the twentieth century. See Hans R. Schinz and Adolf Zuppinger, *Siebzehn Jahre Strahlentherapie der Krebse: Zürcher Erfahrungen 1919–1935* (Leipzig: Georg Thieme, 1937), p. 1. Dormanns joined the Nazi party on May 1, 1937; he also served in the party's Amt für Volksgesundheit beginning in 1941 (BDC).

20. Walter Niderehe, "Bericht über die Vorträge betr. Krebsbekämpfung auf dem 3. internat. Kongress f.d. ärztl. Fortbildungswesen in Berlin," Aug. 24, 1937, E 1496, THW; compare also n. 40 in chap. 1.

21. Ramm, "Systematische Krebsbekämpfung," p. 266.

22. Otto Bokelmann, "Die Rolle der Propaganda im Kampfe gegen den Krebs," *Zentralblatt für Gynäkologie* 64 (1940): 770–77.

23. Ostpreussischer Landesausschuss and NSDAP Amt für Volksgesundheit, "Abschrift! Durchführung von sogenannten Reihenuntersuchungen," July 12, 1937; Mikulicz-Radecki to Gesundheitsamt Weimar, November 9, 1937, E 1496, THW. Thuringia's plan was similar in many respects, emphasizing a collaboration with the NS Frauenschaft, an exclusive focus on cancer of the breast and uterus/cervix, the cost-free provision of regular screenings for women over thirty, establishment of cancer counseling centers, and so forth. The Reichsarbeitsgemeinschaft für Schadenverhütung helped Thuringia's

Health Office put on a play entitled *Zu spät* (Too late) featuring cancer prevention propaganda; see Fritze and Morchutt, "Abschrift," July 13, 1937, E 1496, THW.

24. "Mitteilungen des Deutschen Reichsausschusses," pp. 524–25; and especially the "Niederschrift über die Mitgliederversammlung des Reichsausschusses für Krebsbekämpfung am 1.Dezember 1933," E 1498, THW, which contains a long discussion of preparations for the law. Hans Reiter of the Reich Health Office was the main advocate of a Cancer Law; the Hamburg radiologist Hermann Holthusen championed the view that the law should regulate radiation to protect "das Keimgut des ganzen Volkes" (ibid., p. 4). German gynecologists unanimously endorsed a nationwide *Krebsgesetz* ("Lex Lönne") at their annual meeting in Munich in 1933, the stress being on a campaign to encourage early detection. See Friedrich Lönne, "Wirksame Krebsbekämpfung," in *Neuere Ergebnisse auf dem Gebiete der Krebskrankheiten*, ed. Curt Adam and Hans Auler (Leipzig: S. Hirzel, 1937), p. 205. Berlin medical and insurance authorities in 1933 had sought to implement a comprehensive cancer *Meldepflicht* for the city (mandatory registration), but it is not clear how far this was put into practice; see the *Vertrauensarzt* 1 (1933): 48.

25. "Verordnung zur Bekämpfung bösartiger Geschwulstkrankheiten," *Monatsschrift für Krebsbekämpfung* 7 (1939): 202–4.

26. Friedrich Kortenhaus, "Krebs," in *Deutsches Gold: Gesundes Leben—Frohes Schaffen*, ed. Hans Reiter and Johannes Breger (Munich: Carl Röhrig, 1942), p. 440. Hans Fuchs was the guiding light of Danzig's Cancer Law.

27. Denmark's cancer registry is discussed in Johannes Clemmesen, *Statistical Studies in the Aetiology of Malignant Neoplasms*, vol. 1 (Copenhagen: Munksgaard, 1965), pp. 35–59; for the earlier history of registries, see Carl H. Lasch, "Krebskrankenstatistik: Beginn und Aussicht," *Zeitschrift für Krebsforschung* 50 (1940): 245–98.

28. "Berichte," *Öffentlicher Gesundheitsdienst* 7 (1941): 333.

29. Meyer, "Schicksal," p. 178. The Verordnung zum Reichsbürgergesetz of July 7, 1938, barred Jews from the practice of medicine effective September 30, 1938; see the *Reichsgesetzblatt* 1 (1938): 969.

30. On computers and the Holocaust, see David Luebke and Sybil Milton, "Locating the Victim: An Overview of Census Taking, Tabulation Technology, and Persecution in Nazi Germany," *IEEE Annals of the History of Computing* 16 (1994): 25–39.

31. A good example is Angela von Elling and Michael Wunder, eds., *Krebsregister: Erfassung als Politik* (Hamburg: Konkret Literatur, 1986); compare also Hien's critique of industry registries in his *Chemische Industrie*, pp. 250–52.

32. Joseph Goebbels, *The Goebbels Diaries: 1942–1943*, ed. Louis P. Lochner (Garden City, N.Y.: Doubleday, 1948), p. 93.

33. Goebbels's diary entry for March 11, 1942, records the propaganda minister's taking "energetic measures to stop the discussion about the 'Yellow Peril'" (ibid., pp. 120–21).

34. Joseph Wulf, *Aus dem Lexikon der Mörder: "Sonderbehandlung" und verwandte Worte in nationalsozialistischen Dokumenten* (Gütersloh: S. Mohn, 1963).

35. On homosexuals, see Goebbels, *Diaries*, p. 102. On June 15, 1941, the

propaganda minister labeled the Auswärtiges Amt "ein Staat im Staate. Oder besser noch: ein wachsendes Krebsgeschwür"; see his *Tagebücher*, p. 692. On June 22, 1941, Goebbels characterized communism as a "Krebsgeschwür" that "muss ausgebrannt werden" (tumor that must be burned out—see ibid., p. 710).

36. American Eugenics Society, *A Eugenics Catechism* (New Haven: The Society, 1935).

37. Richard Doll, personal communication, August 3, 1997. SS Oberführer Holfelder was killed in combat near Budapest on December 14, 1944; it would be interesting to know if his slides have been preserved in Frankfurt University's archives.

38. "The idea of the social parasite, as exemplified in the Jew amongst our people, can also be seen, symbolically, in the human body in many cases. The alien germ living in the body whose prosperity depends upon a conflict with a particular organ, a disharmony in the body, a disease—is this not the same role played by the Jew in the body of the people?" See Wolfgang E. Kitzing, *Erziehung zur Gesundheit* (Berlin: Reichsgesundheitsverlag, 1941), p. 41.

39. Examples of the Nazi medical bureaucracy's implementation of "clear and simple speech" and its campaign against foreign words ("Fremdwörter sind Fremdkörper") can be found in Ernst Schliack, *Die Amtssprache* (Berlin: Langewort, 1941); compare also C.R.H. Rabl, "Sprachreinigung," *Deutsches Ärzteblatt* 63 (1933): 117 ff. For examples of "Germanized technical expressions" in genetics, see "Verdeutschte Fachausdrücke in der Vererbungslehre," *Volk und Rasse* 11 (1936): 100–102. Martin Staemmler's *Rassenpflege im völkischen Staat* was sometimes taken as exemplary in its avoidance of foreign words; see Otto Rabes, "Eins tut not," *Volk und Rasse* 9 (1934): 54–55. For an overview and critique of Nazi speech more generally, see Carl F. Graumann, "Die Sprache der NS-Propaganda und ihre Wirkung," in *Von der Heilkunde zur Massentötung: Medizin im Nationalsozialismus*, ed. Gerrit Hohendorf and Achim Magull-Seltenreich (Heidelberg: Wunderhorn, 1990), pp. 185–202.

40. Fischer-Wasels in 1906 showed that the aminoazo dye scarlet red could cause cancer when injected into rabbit ears; see his "Die experimentelle Erzeugung atypischer Epithelwucherungen und die Entstehung bösartiger Geschwülste," *Münchener medizinische Wochenschrift* 53 (1906): 2041–47.

41. Bernhard Fischer-Wasels, "Die Bedeutung der besonderen Allgemeindisposition des Körpers für die Entstehung der Krebskrankheit," *Strahlentherapie* 50 (1934): 7, 28.

42. Teutschlaender, "Arbeit und Geschwulstbildung," p. 75. Rudolf Ramm in 1942 characterized cancer cells as "parasites in the marrow of the people's power" (*Parasiten am Mark der Volkskraft*); see his "Systematische Krebsbekämpfung," p. 269.

43. Hans Auler, *Der Krebs und seine Bekämpfung* (Berlin: Reichsdruckerei, 1937), p. 5; compare Curt Thomalla's reference to cancer as a *Revolution im Zellstaat* and to malignant cells as *bösartige revolutionäre Zellen* in his *Gesund sein—Gesund bleiben* (Berlin: F. W. Peters, 1936), p. 352; also the radiologist Albert Kukowka's characterization of carcinogenesis as a *revolutionäre krebsige Umwandlung der Zelle*. The references, interestingly, are to the French *révolution*

and not to the German *Umwälzung*. Friedrich Kortenhaus argued that cancer was the product of "degenerate" (*entartete*) hormones; see his "Krebs," p. 427. Cancer is elsewhere described as the result of a "bastard marriage" between two cells; see Fritz Niedermayer, *Was ist nun eigentlich Krebs?* (Vienna: Deuticke, 1941).

44. Max Borst in 1941 equated cancer with rebellion: "Bei der Infektion ist— kurz gesagt—Krieg, bei den bösartigen Geschwülsten aber Revolution oder Anarchie. Dort Kampf des Organismus gegen äussere Feinde, die Bakterien, hier Kampf der Körperzellen gegeneinander—Bruderkampf"; see his *Streiflichter über das Krebsproblem* (Munich: Lehmann, 1941), p. 26. Military metaphors are common: a 1939 report on the experimental production of sarcomas through the use of radium needles describes the *stürmisch* development of the malignancies after irradiation; see Hans Hellner, "Experimentelle Knochensarkome und ihre Beziehungen zu allgemeinen Geschwulstproblemen," *Bruns' Beiträge zur klinische Chirurgie* 168 (1938): 547.

45. Wilhelm Frick, *Bevölkerungs- und Rassenpolitik*, speech of June 28, 1933 (Langensalza: Beyer & Söhne, 1933), p. 15; compare Paula von Groote Siber, *Die Frauenfrage und ihre Lösung durch den Nationalsozialismus* (Berlin: Kallmeyer, 1933).

46. Franz G. M. Wirz of the Reichsvollkornbrotausschuss in 1940 proposed a "final solution to the whole-grain bread question"; see his *Vom Brot: Wissen und Erkenntnisse*, 3d ed. (Stuttgart: Hippokrates, 1940), p. 7; also my *Racial Hygiene*, pp. 235–37.

47. Wolfgang Klarner, *Vom Rauchen: Eine Sucht und ihre Bekämpfung* (Nuremberg: Rudolf Kern, 1940), p. 48.

48. Adolf Gaschler, "Zentrale Krebsbekämpfung, eine neue Aufgabe für die Sozialversicherung," *Vertrauensarzt und Krankenkasse* 9 (September 1941): 10. There are many other examples of "problem-solving" rhetoric at this time— e.g., of the "drink question," the "question of making potable water from seawater," and so forth. Adolf Wenusch called for an "endgültige und einzig richtige Lösung des Entnikotinisierungsproblems" in his *Der Tabakrauch: Seine Entstehung, Beschaffenheit und Zusammensetzung* (Bremen: Arthur Geist, 1939), p. 72; Goebbels called for the establishment of brothels as a "final solution" to "the problem of sexual activities of the numerous foreign workers now in Germany" in early 1942 (see his *Diaries*, p. 48). Schroeder in June 1944 wrote to Himmler asking for permission to conduct experiments on humans to achieve a "final solution" to the problem of how to make seawater drinkable; see *Trials of War Criminals*, 1:46.

49. D. Roeck, "Krebsbekämpfung!" *Monatsschrift für Krebsbekämpfung* 7 (1940): 32.

50. *Aufklärungsarbeit* was what the Bavarian Landesverband zur Erforschung und Bekämpfung der Krebskrankheit said it was doing when it showed films on how to prevent cancer; see "Mitteilungen," *Monatsschrift für Krebsbekämpfung* 7 (1940): 47 and 189.

51. These various examples of *Aufklärungsrhetorik* are culled from "Berichte," *Öffentlicher Gesundheitsdienst* 7 (1941): 333; Klarner, *Vom Rauchen*, p. 45;

and "Mitteilungen," *Monatsschrift für Krebsbekämpfung* 7 (1940): 166, 189, 238–39, 324.

52. Bock, *Zwangssterilisation*, p. 269.

53. Goebbels, *Tagebücher*, p. 121.

54. See, for example, Friedrich Lönne, "Früherfassung des weiblichen Genitalkarzinoms durch Aufklärungspropaganda," *Öffentlicher Gesundheitsdienst* 9A (1943): 58 ff.

55. Max Horkheimer and Theodor Adorno seem not to have noticed the popularity of the term *Aufklärung* during the Nazi era; or at least they never commented upon it. They did identify an affinity between fascism and "the" Enlightenment, drawing attention to the rationalizing character shared by both movements. Fascism for Horkheimer and Adorno was in many ways the culmination of the Enlightenment, just as for Georg Lukács, fascism was the culmination of capitalism. Horkheimer and Adorno claimed that while Enlightenment moral theory tended toward propaganda and sentimentality, German fascism raised "the cult of strength to a world-historical doctrine" and by its "iron discipline" saved "its subject peoples the trouble of moral feelings." See their *Dialectic of Enlightenment* (New York: Herder and Herder, 1972), pp. 85, 100–101, 86.

56. Karl-Heinz Brackmann and Renate Birkenhauer, *NS-Deutsch: "Selbstverständliche" Begriffe und Schlagwörter aus der Zeit des Nationalsozialismus* (Darmstadt: Straelener Manuskripte, 1988), p. 27. The Nazis wanted a selectively transparent society—hence the 1938 ban on attic storage, to prevent people from hiding things.

57. Karl H. Zinck, "Entstehungsbedingungen des Krebses und die Frage seiner Erblichkeit," *Öffentlicher Gesundheitsdienst* 7 (1942): 497.

58. Ibid., pp. 497–507.

59. The *Gleichschaltung* of German cancer research and combat continued into the war years: in 1942, for example, Conti ordered the unification (*Vereinheitlichung*) of the German cancer campaign, subordinating the Reichsarbeitsgemeinschaft für Krebsbekämpfung (originally headed by Gottfried Frey) to the Reichsausschuss für Krebsbekämpfung, now under the direct control of Conti. Max Borst of Munich was president of the new organization; Rudolf Ramm became Borst's deputy vice president, and Hans Auler was responsible for cancer research and statistics. Conti's order concerning the "Vereinheitlichung der Organisationen zur Krebsbekämpfung" is reported in the *Monatsschrift für Krebsbekämpfung* 10 (1942): 155–56; also "Mitteilungen," in the same issue, p. 169.

60. Erwin Liek cites and responds to these and other criticisms in his 1934 book, *Der Kampf gegen den Krebs*.

61. For evidence, see Karl Richter, "Die Krebskrankheiten arzneilich heilbar," *Fortschritte der Medizin* 53 (1935): 249; for objections, see Bernhard Fischer-Wasels, "Bekämpfung der Krebskrankheit durch Erbpflege," *Deutsches Ärzteblatt* 64 (1934): 92–95.

62. The Viennese physician Sigismund Peller held this view; see his "Die säkulare Krebskurve," *Zeitschrift für Krebsforschung* 40 (1934): 465–509; also his

"Zu- oder abnehmende Krebsbedrohung im Lichte der Statistik und neuer Beobachtungen," *Zeitschrift für Krebsforschung* 45 (1937): 437–48. Peller held the curious view that cancer in one part of the body could actually prevent cancer in another: he therefore advised sun exposure, believing that the cancers thereby produced would be more curable than other kinds of cancer. See his *Not in My Time: The Story of a Doctor* (New York: Philosophical Library, 1979), p. 98.

63. Schönbauer and Ueberreiter, "Erlaubt," p. 556.

64. Ernst Dormanns in 1933 noted that most leading German statisticians (Robert Rössle, Karl von Wolff, Karl Freudenberg, Sigismund Peller, and Friedrich Prinzing, for example) believed that the increase observed in cancer rates was purely the result of aging and improved diagnostics; see his "Beitrag zur Frage der Zunahme der Krebskrankheit," *Zeitschrift für Krebsforschung* 39 (1933): 40–53. Dormanns also cautioned, however, against the conceit implicit in the notion that growing cancer mortality was always evidence of ever-improving diagnostic capabilities; earlier generations of physicians were not, he insisted, as incompetent as such a thesis implied (ibid., pp. 40–41). Dormanns used autopsy data to show that as many as one in five cancers was still being misdiagnosed, and that the fraction of misdiagnoses for the period 1901–1911 was about the same as for 1922–1931 (p. 42). This was evidence, for him as for many others, that cancer mortality rates were actually higher than officially reported; it was also evidence that improving diagnostics could not be responsible for all of the observed increase in cancer mortality. Physicians in the 1930s seemed to be just as likely to misdiagnose a particular kind of cancer as their counterparts in the decade prior to the First World War.

After the war, Karl Freudenberg at Berlin's Freie Universität ridiculed the suggestion (put forward "by quacks") that cancer rates were on the rise; see his "Die scheinbare Zunahme der Krebssterblichkeit," *Archiv für Hygiene und Bakteriologie* 136 (1952): 129–38. Neither tobacco nor lung cancer, interestingly, was mentioned in Freudenberg's article.

65. Hellmut Haubold, "Statistik und volksbiologische Bedeutung des Krebses," in Adam and Auler, *Neuere Ergebnisse*, pp. 144–49.

66. Hellmut Haubold, *Krebs und Krebsbekämpfung in Frankreich* (Leipzig: J. A. Barth, 1936), p. 248.

67. See my *Cancer Wars*, pp. 54–74. Juraj Körbler in 1973 argued that modern foods were actually more natural—preservatives notwithstanding—than the foods of earlier decades; see his *Geschichte der Krebskrankheit: Schicksale der Kranken, der Ärzte und der Forscher* (Vienna: Ranner, 1973), p. 187.

68. The Swiss radiologists Hans R. Schinz and Adolf Zuppinger in 1937 presented statistical evidence that age-adjusted cancer death rates were not in fact increasing in Zurich; cancer was becoming more common for no other reason than that people were living to loftier ages. See their *Siebzehn Jahre Strahlentherapie*, pp. 2–16. The authors did point out, however, that while certain cancers were on the decline (stomach and uterine), others were becoming more common (e.g., breast and lung); see pp. 11 and 15.

69. The medical faculty at the German University of Prague was such a bastion of pro-Nazi sentiment that the entire faculty was arrested (by Czech po-

lice) when German troops began their invasion of the Sudetenland in the spring of 1938. Three years earlier, Czech authorities had banned Germany's most widely read medical weekly—J. F. Lehmann's *Münchener medizinische Wochenschrift*—as a subversive publication; see my *Racial Hygiene*, pp. 169 and 275–76.

70. Hans Schwarz, "Nimmt die Krebssterblichkeit zu?" *Zeitschrift für Krebsforschung* 42 (1935): 426–31; Fischer-Wasels, "Bekämpfung der Krebskrankheit."

71. Pfeil, "Lungentumoren," pp. 1198–99.

72. Fritz Lenz, "Zur Erneuerung der Ethik," *Deutschlands Erneuerung* 1 (1917): 42–43. Lenz's essay was republished in 1933 as *Die Rasse als Wertprinzip* (Munich: Lehmann, 1933).

73. Leonardo Conti, ed., *Sauna: Ein Weg zur Volksgesundheit* (Berlin: Reichsgesundheitsverlag, 1942), p. 3; compare Hans Hoske's "Im Kampf gegen die Zivilisationsschäden" in the same volume.

74. Albert Wolff, "Zur Krebsfrage: Erwin Liek zum Gedächtnis," *Hippokrates* 8 (1937): 63–65.

75. Detlef Bothe, *Neue Deutsche Heilkunde: 1933–1945* (Berlin: Matthiesen, 1991), p. 290.

76. Goebbels, *Tagebücher*, pp. 651–52, 706.

77. Ibid., p. 688.

78. *Trials of War Criminals*, 1:656, 668. Gebhardt testified that Himmler "always attempted to discover old-fashioned popular remedies" (p. 669). The homeopathic agents used in the Dachau experiments are described on p. 658. Ten fatalities were recorded in these experiments (p. 659).

CHAPTER 3
GENETIC AND RACIAL THEORIES

1. See my *Racial Hygiene*, pp. 55 ff.

2. Friedrich Hoffmann, *Opera Omnia physico-medica* (Geneva, 1761), 3:446.

3. See my *Cancer Wars*, pp. 218–22.

4. The first study of twins with cancer is apparently Tito Spannocchi's "Contributo alla ereditarietà dei fibromi dell' utero," *Archivio italiano di Ginecologia* 2 (1899): 251–54. Heinrich Kranz reviewed efforts to use twin studies to resolve the nature-nurture question for cancer in his "Tumoren bei Zwillingen," *Zeitschrift für induktive Abstammungs- und Vererbungslehre* 62 (1932): 173–81; compare also J. J. Versluys, "Zwillingspathologischer Beitrag zur Ätiologie der Tumoren," *Zeitschrift für Krebsforschung* 41 (1935): 239–59.

5. Juraj Körbler, "Zur Frage der Vererbung und der Kontagiosität bei Krebs," *Zeitschrift für Krebsforschung* 47 (1938): 86.

6. Fritz Lenz, *Menschliche Erblichkeitslehre* (Munich: Lehmann, 1921), pp. 258–62. A 1944 article in the *Zeitschrift für Krebsforschung* identified Charles Otis Whitman, Fritz Lenz, and Karl H. Bauer as the earliest pioneers of the somatic mutation hypothesis, followed later by Frederik G. Gade of Norway, (Hans?) Schwarz, and Hans R. Schinz; see Ulrich Henschke, "Über Geschwulsttheorien und die Möglichkeit der Entstehung der Geschwulstzelle

durch Spontanmutation," *Zeitschrift für Krebsforschung* 54 (1944): 12–14. Henschke noted the resistance in the medical community to the idea that only mutagens (*mutationsauslösende Faktoren*) could cause cancer, and that all carcinogens—e.g., X-rays, radium, ultraviolet irradiation—caused mutations (p. 15). Henschke correctly perceived that cancer was not weeded out in the course of evolutionary history, since it tended to affect only persons past the age of reproduction. He also noted, though, that evolution was possible only through mutation, so cancer was in this sense the unfortunate consequence (*Opfer*) of the possibility of evolution (p. 23).

7. Karl Heinrich Bauer and Felix von Mikulicz-Radecki, *Die Praxis der Sterilisierungsoperationen* (Leipzig: J. A. Barth, 1936). American occupation authorities in 1945 named Bauer Rektor of the University of Heidelberg. On the 1968 accusations of Nazi collaboration, see Christian Pross, "Nazi Doctors, German Medicine, and Historical Truth," in Annas and Grodin, *Nazi Doctors*, pp. 41 and 49 n. 31.

8. Karl Heinrich Bauer, *Mutationstheorie der Geschwulst-Entstehung* (Berlin: Springer, 1928).

9. Otmar Freiherr von Verschuer, *Leitfaden der Rassenhygiene* (Leipzig: Georg Thieme, 1941), p. 158. Albert Dietrich of Tübingen also followed Bauer in asserting that all mutagens are carcinogens: "Alle positiv mutationserzeugenden, strahlenden Energien sind aber zugleich krebserzeugend (K. H. Bauer)"; see his "Der Stand der Krebsforschung," in *Krebsbehandlung und Krebsbekämpfung*, ed. Landesausschuss für Krebsbekämpfung in Bremen (Berlin: Urban & Schwarzenberg, 1938), p. 15.

10. Max Schüller, "Gibt es eine Prädisposition für Krebs und worin besteht sie?" *Archiv für Rassen- und Gesellschaftsbiologie* 1 (1904): 831. Schüller himself regarded the differences as not yet proven to be racial in origins.

11. Germany's most important racial hygiene journal in 1904 reported the commonly held belief that "the white race is particularly predisposed to cancer" and that "some colored races, some of the Negro populations of Africa, for example, are entirely free of cancer and immune to it" (ibid., p. 825). Schüller maintained that recent immigrants to a country were more likely to contract cancer than persons native to that country (p. 826), a view consistent with germ theories popular at the time.

12. Ukrainian women were apparently more than four times as likely to die of genital cancer as were Jewish women living in the Ukraine; Ukrainian Jews were also only half as likely to die of breast cancer. See Arkadii M. Merkow, "Zur vergleichenden Charakteristik der Krebsaffektion der wesentlichsten nationalen und sozialen Gruppen der Stadtbevölkerung der Ukraine," *Zeitschrift für Krebsforschung* 34 (1931): 285–98.

13. Gerhard Wagner, "Unser Reichsärzteführer Spricht," *Ziel und Weg* 5 (1935): 432–33; Theobald Lang, "Die Belastung des Judentums mit Geistig-Auffälligen," *Nationalsozialistische Monatshefte* 3 (1932): 23–30; Walter Gross, "Die Familie," *Informationsdienst*, no. 58 (September 20, 1938). For a provocative critique and review, especially of pre-Nazi literature, see Sander L. Gilman, *The Jew's Body* (London: Routledge, 1992).

14. Sander L. Gilman, *Freud, Race, and Gender* (Princeton: Princeton University Press, 1993), p. 172.

15. Wagner, "Unser Reichsärzteführer spricht," *Ziel und Weg* 5 (1935): 432; compare Walter Schottky, ed., *Rasse und Krankheit* (Munich: Lehmann, 1936), and Wilhelm Hildebrandt, *Rassenmischung und Krankheit: Ein Versuch* (Stuttgart: Hippokrates, 1935).

16. The best review of bias in cancer reporting is probably still Clemmesen's *Statistical Studies*, pp. 1–34.

17. Hoffman, *Mortality from Cancer*, pp. 15–16, 129. Not everyone regarded blacks as less susceptible: a professor of physiology and medical jurisprudence in the Medical College of South Carolina at Charleston in 1892 wrote: "If we look again to the accepted etiology of carcinoma of the womb we should undoubtedly consider the colored people as specially liable to it. When we remember the unbridled licentiousness of this people, their profligacy, the attendant traumatisms about the cervix in women who have borne many children, we surely find conditions that, to say the least, could scarcely be supposed to render the black race exempt." See Middleton Michel, "Carcinoma Uteri in the Negro," *Medical News* 11 (1892): 402.

18. Alfredo Niceforo, "Cancer in Relation to Race in Europe," in *Report of the International Conference on Cancer* (Bristol: J. Wright & Sons, 1928), p. 502; Eugene Pittard, "Can We Ignore the Race Problem in Connection with Cancer?" in the same volume, pp. 503–7.

19. Hermann Stahr, "Vom Lungenkrebs," *Monatsschrift für Krebsbekämpfung* 5 (1938): 212.

20. Arthur Purdy Stout, "Tumors of the Neuromyo-Arterial Glomus," *American Journal of Cancer* 24 (1935): 255–72.

21. Gilman, *Freud*, pp. 170–73. Adolf Theilhaber was one of the first to show that uterine cancer was relatively rare among Jewish women; see his "Zur Lehre von der Entstehung der Uterustumoren," *Münchener medizinische Wochenschrift* 56 (1909): 1272–73. Adolf's son, Felix, the zionist author of the Jewish *Untergangstheorie* who also studied uterine cancer, fled Germany in 1935. The best review of cancer among European Jews prior to the Nazi period is probably Sigismund Peller, "Über Krebssterblichkeit der Juden," *Zeitschrift für Krebsforschung* 34 (1931): 128–47. Peller was a Viennese Jew who left for Palestine with his wife in 1934; see his *Not in My Time*.

22. Lenz, *Menschliche Erblichkeitslehre*, pp. 264 ff.

23. Sigmund Rascher, "Denkschrift," May 1, 1939, BDC; Wolfgang Benz, "Dr. med. Sigmund Rascher: Eine Karriere," *Dachauer Hefte* 4 (1988): 193–94. The meeting described in Rascher's memorandum took place on April 24, 1939. In addition to the rat plan, Himmler apparently wanted Rascher to find out whether cancer rates in the remote villages of Memel, in eastern Prussia, were lower than elsewhere. Himmler was also interested in whether chemical fertilizers could cause cancer, especially whether the fertilizers commonly used on grass could be tied to cancers among cows. Rascher was supposed to contact local veterinary surgeons, Nazi farm leaders, and church leaders to determine local cancer rates; he was also supposed to investigate how much

artificial fertilizer was being used on agricultural lands. Himmler also wanted to examine the blood of persons confined to concentration camps, to see whether a blood test could be developed that would signal cancer's early onset (ibid.).

24. Otmar Freiherr von Verschuer, *Erbpathologie, Ein Lehrbuch für Äzte und Medizinstudierende* (Munich: Lehmann, 1937), pp. 86, 103, 159, 182, 137.

25. Karl Heinrich Bauer, "Fortschritte der experimentellen Krebsforschung," *Archiv für klinische Chirurgie* 189 (1937): 123–84; compare also his "Krebs und Vererbung," p. 479. The Berlin pathologist Robert Rössle concluded that cancer was only rarely heritable, though Wolfgang Denk in Vienna in 1939 argued from twin and genealogical evidence that heredity must account for "a minimum of 20 percent" of all cancers; see his "Zur Frage der Erblichkeit des Carcinoms," *Zeitschrift für Krebsforschung* 49 (1939): 241.

26. Bauer, "Krebs und Vererbung," pp. 475–79.

27. Arthur Hintze, "Kultur und Krebs," *Jahreskurse für ärztliche Fortbildung* 7 (1939): 67–71. Hintze was named head of radiology at the Rudolf Virchow Hospital's newly created Allgemeines Institut gegen die Geschwulstkrankheiten in 1935. He was aware that lifestyle factors could impact occupational cancers—the custom of daily bathing, for example, to which he attributed the low Japanese incidence of occupational cancers caused by oil, tar, or soot; he was also aware that anecdotal impressions of cancer incidence could be misleading if a certain class of people—Muslim women, for example—would not allow themselves to be examined by Western physicians.

28. Ibid., p. 73.

29. Verschuer, *Leitfaden*, pp. 159–61.

30. Martin Staemmler and Edeltraut Bieneck, "Statistische Untersuchungen über die Todesursachen der deutschen und jüdischen Bevölkerung von Breslau," *Münchener medizinische Wochenschrift* 87 (1940): 447–50. The *British Medical Journal* pointed out that Staemmler and Bieneck had failed to discuss the role of state violence in producing these statistics; see "German Medicine, Race, and Religion," *British Medical Journal*, August 17, 1940, p. 230.

31. Hintze, "Kultur und Krebs," pp. 75–76.

32. A review of *Konstitutionslehre* can be found in Gerhard Koch, *Die Gesellschaft für Konstitutionsforschung: Anfang und Ende 1942–1965* (Erlangen: Palm und Enke, 1985).

33. Hans Weselmann, "Über die Nicotingastritis," *Die Genussgifte* 36 (1940): 23.

34. Robert Hofstätter, *Die rauchende Frau: Eine klinische, psychologische und soziale Studie* (Vienna: Hölder-Pichler-Tempsky, 1924), p. 71.

35. Friedrich Voltz, "Pigmentbildung und Strahlenbehandlung," *Radiologische Rundschau* 1 (1933): 96.

36. Friedrich Voltz, "Biologische Probleme in der Röntgenstrahlentherapie," *Strahlentherapie* 47 (1933): 137–43.

37. Robert Ritter, "Rothaarigkeit als rassenhygienisches Problem," *Volk und Rasse* 10 (1935): 385–90.

38. Hien, *Chemische Industrie*, p. 219.

39. George Reid, "Weltanschauung, Haltung, Genussgifte," *Die Genussgifte* 35 (1939): 66–67.

40. Klarner, *Vom Rauchen*, pp. 18–19. The body-type categorization mentioned here traces back to the psychiatrist Ernst Kretschmer.

41. "Erkennung und Bekämpfung der Tabakgefahren," *Deutsches Ärzteblatt* 71 (1941): 185.

42. Kleine, *Ernährungsschäden als Krankheitsursachen*, pp. 62–63.

43. The official commentary on the law specified that sufferers from retinoblastoma should be sterilized; see Arthur Gütt, Ernst Rüdin, and Falk Ruttke, *Kommentar zum Gesetz zur Verhütung Erbkranken Nachwuchses* (Munich: Lehmann, 1934).

44. August Wagenmann, ed., *Bericht über die einundfünfzigste Zusammenkunft der Deutschen Ophthalmologischen Gesellschaft in Heidelberg 1936* (Munich: Bergmann, 1936), pp. 91–102; compare also Karl A. Reiser's critique of Clausen's views in "Bemerkungen zur Erblichkeitsfrage beim Glioma retinae," *Klinische Monatsblätter für Augenheilkunde* 99 (1937): 350–55.

45. Fischer-Wasels, "Die Bedeutung der besonderen Allgemeindisposition," p. 26; compare Kurt Blome's similar views in "Krebsforschung und Krebsbekämpfung," *Ziel und Weg* 10 (1940): 412.

46. Fischer-Wasels, "Bekämpfung der Krebskrankheit," pp. 92–95. The gynecologist Wilhelm Lahm prior even to 1933 argued that marital counselors should use cancer registry data to counter the pairing of persons genetically predisposed to cancer; see his "Die ärztliche Fortbildung auf dem Gebiet der Krebsbekämpfung," *Strahlentherapie* 37 (1930): 397–401; also the similar views expressed in W. Helmreich, "Erblichkeit, Rassenhygiene und Bevölkerungspolitik," *Münchener medizinische Wochenschrift* 83 (1936): 484.

47. Hien, *Chemische Industrie*, pp. 219 and 271–304.

48. Gunther Lehmann, "Die Bedeutung des Staubbindungsvermögens der Nase für die Entstehung der Lungensilicose," *Arbeitsphysiologie* 8 (1934): 218–50; also his "Untersuchungen an Staubmasken," *Arbeitsphysiologie* 9 (1936): 182–205. Rostoski, Saupe, and Schmorl in 1926 had urged Schneeberg's miners to breathe through their noses to lower their risk of developing lung cancer (by trapping carcinogenic particulates); the authors had also advised workers "not to be shy" about having their nasal passages surgically enlarged to enable better nasal ventilation ("Die Bergkrankheit," p. 375).

49. Lehmann's efforts were part of an attempted "Lösung des Staubproblems"; see Otto Schulz, "Gesundheitliche Schäden durch gewerblichen Staub," *Die Gasmaske* 11 (1939): 57–66.

50. Hans Waniek, "Die Verhütung der Staublungenkrankheiten, insbesondere der Silikose," *Klinische Wochenschrift* 23 (1944): 288–89.

51. H. Hamperl, U. Henschke, and R. Schulze, "Vergleich der Hautreaktionen beim Bestrahlungserythem und bei der direkten Pigmentierung," *Archiv für pathologische Anatomie und Physiologie* 304 (1939): 21.

52. Hueper, *Occupational Tumors*, p. 765.

53. Wilhelm C. Hueper, "Causal and Preventive Aspects of Environmental Cancer," *Minnesota Medicine*, January 1956, pp. 10–11.

54. Cited in Krug, *Die Organisation des Kampfes*, p. 21. A November 1941 article in the *Berliner Börsenzeitung* predicted that the sheer "idealism" of the Third Reich would result in a lowering of German cancer rates; see "Nationalsozialismus schützt vor Krebs," *Internationales Ärztliches Bulletin* 2 (1935): 17–18.

55. Auler met with Goebbels on February 15, 1941; the propaganda minister called his work "truly wonderful." Education minister Bernhard Rust awarded him an additional 7,000 RM; see Goebbels's *Tagebücher*, p. 504. It is not yet clear what this money was used for. It may have gone to defray some of the costs of the antiquackery film Auler was helping to make (*Jeder Achte*); this is plausible, since support of this sort was one of the primary tasks of Goebbels's ministry.

56. On genotoxic contraceptives, see Karl E. Fecht, "Über die Keimschädigung durch chemische Schwangerschaftsverhütungsmittel," *Volk und Rasse* 10 (1935): 215–17.

CHAPTER 4
OCCUPATIONAL CARCINOGENESIS

1. Two of the best early reviews are Ludwig Teleky, "Der berufliche Lungenkrebs," *Acta Unio Internationalis Contra Cancrum* 3 (1938): 253–73, and Wilhelm Hueper's *Occupational Tumors*. The best history of German occupational cancer is Wolfgang Hien's *Chemische Industrie*. For the history of German occupational health and safety more generally, see Franz Koelsch, *Beiträge zur Geschichte der Arbeitsmedizin* (Munich: Bayerischer Landesärztekammer, 1967); also Alfons Labisch, "Social History of Occupational Medicine and of Factory Health Service in the Federal Republic of Germany," and Dietrich Milles, "From Workers' Diseases to Occupational Diseases: The Impact of Experts' Concepts on Workers' Attitudes," both in *The Social History of Occupational Health*, ed. Paul Weindling (London: Croom Helm, 1985), pp. 32–51 and 55–77.

2. Karl-Heinz Karbe, "Das nationalsozialistische Betriebsarztsystem während des Zweiten Weltkrieges—ein Instrument arbeitsmedizinischer Praxis," in *Medizin für den Staat—Medizin für den Krieg: Aspekte zwischen 1914 und 1945*, ed. Rolf Winau and Heinz Müller-Dietz (Husum: Matthiesen, 1994).

3. Heinz von Pein, "Über die Ursachen der chronischen Arsenvergiftung der Weinbauern," *Medizinische Klinik* 37 (1941): 293–95.

4. For overviews, see Hueper's *Occupational Tumors*; Martin Staemmler, "Beruf und Krebs," *Münchener medizinische Wochenschrift* 85 (1938): 121–25; Otto Teutschlaender, "Die Berufskrebse mit besonderer Berücksichtigung ihrer Verhütung und der Unfallgesetzgebung," *Medizinische Welt* 11 (1937): 1267–72; and Franz Koelsch, "Krebs und Beruf," *Monatsschrift für Krebsbekämpfung* 5 (1937): 7–12.

5. Fischer-Wasels, "Bekämpfung der Krebskrankheit," p. 94. Officially, there were only about twelve occupational cancers registered with German health authorities every year—mostly tar cancers, bladder cancers of dye workers, lung cancers among chromium workers, and X-ray skin cancers. The true number, however, as even Nazi health authorities recognized, must have been many times higher (Staemmler, "Beruf und Krebs," p. 122).

6. P.E.R., "Arbeit als sittliche Pflicht," *Volksgesundheit* 1 (1936): 239; see also pp. 267–271.

7. Abteilung Volksgesundheit, "Der öffentliche Gesundheitsdienst im Deutschen Reiche 1937," *Öffentlicher Gesundheitsdienst* 4 (1938): 161–86.

8. Hans Reiter, "Genussgifte und Leistung," *Reichs-Gesundheitsblatt* 14 (1939): 187.

9. Gine Elsner, "Die Entwicklung von Arbeitsmedizin und Arbeitsschutzpolitik nach 1933," in *Arbeitsschutz und Umweltgeschichte*, ed. Hamburger Stiftung (Cologne: Volksblatt, 1990), p. 90.

10. Martin Gumpert, *Heil Hunger! Health under Hitler* (New York: Alliance Book Corp., 1940), pp. 12–13 and 23. In his diary on May 12, 1941, Joseph Goebbels mentioned a recent mining accident in Neurode, south of Breslau in Upper Silesia, near the Czech border, that suffocated 189 miners (*Tagebücher*, p. 636).

11. For a sampling, see Ernst W. Baader, "Kohlenoxyd-Basedow," *Archiv für Gewerbepathologie und Gewerbehygiene* 7 (1936): 227–34; Willy Matthes, "Zur Staubbeseitigung in der Textilindustrie," *Zentralblatt für Gewerbehygiene*, N.F. 15 (1938): 200–201; Ludwig Teissl, "Strahlenschutz in gewerblichen Radiumbetrieben," *Zentralblatt für Gewerbehygiene* N.F., 15 (1938): 89–91.

12. Walther Liese, "'Gute Luft' als raumhygienische Forderung in Arbeitsräumen," *Gesundheitsingenieur* 60 (1937): 374–80.

13. Articles on occupational safety and health also appeared in journals like *Bauwelt*, the *Rundschau Technischer Arbeit*, and *Die Chemische Industrie*. The *Monatsschrift für Krebsbekämpfung* and the *Zeitschrift für Krebsforschung* often discussed occupational cancers, as did the two major journals devoted to radiation therapy: *Strahlentherapie* and *Radiologische Rundschau: Röntgen, Radium, Licht*. Journals such as *Feuerpolizei*, the *Zeitschrift des Vereins Deutscher Ingenieure*, and *Die Pressluftindustrie* treated health and safety topics in specific professions, and further coverage can be found in public health journals such as *Öffentlicher Gesundheitsdienst*. There were also two major series devoted to occupational health: the *Schriften aus dem Gesamtgebiet der Gewerbehygiene* and *Arbeitsmedizin: Abhandlungen über Berufskrankheiten und deren Verhütung*, published before and after the war by J. A. Barth of Leipzig.

14. Dietrich Milles, "Tendenzen und Konsequenzen. Arbeit und Krankheit under dem Einfluss nationalsozialistischer Sozialpolitik," in *Berufsarbeit und Krankheit*, ed. Dietrich Milles and Rainer Müller (Frankfurt: Campus, 1985), pp. 124–25.

15. Karl Heinz Roth, "Public Health—Nazi Style: Gesundheitspolitische Kontroversen in der NS-Diktatur (1935–1944)," *1999* 2 (1995): 2.

16. On high-performance medicine, see Sepp Graessner, *Leistungsmedizin während des Nationalsozialismus* (Hamburg: Med. diss., 1990).

17. Gumpert, *Heil Hunger!*, pp. 23–28.

18. Cäcilie Hennes, *Arbeitsschäden der Frau durch Fabrikarbeit* (Freiburg: Med. diss., 1941).

19. *Trials of War Criminals*, 8:1173.

20. *Reichsarbeitsblatt* 1 (1944): 22.

21. Peter W. Becker, "Fritz Sauckel: Plenipotentiary for the Mobilisation of Labour," in *The Nazi Elite,* ed. Ronald Smelser and Rainer Zitelmann (New York: New York University Press, 1993), pp. 194–201.

22. "Glashüttenverordnung," *Reichs-Gesundheitsblatt* 14 (1939): 72 ff.; Gumpert, *Heil Hunger!,* pp. 29–30.

23. Gumpert, *Heil Hunger!,* p. 30.

24. Ernst W. Baader obtained his medical degree in 1918 and in 1924 founded Germany's first occupational disease division at the University of Berlin, reorganized in 1934 as the Universitätsinstitut für Berufskrankheiten. Baader joined the Nazi party on May 1, 1933; he was also a member of the Hitler Youth, the NS-Dozentenbund, the Nazi Physicians' League, and the Kolonialbund (BDC).

25. Elsner, "Die Entwicklung von Arbeitsmedizin," p. 90.

26. Schinz and Zuppinger, *Siebzehn Jahre Strahlentherapie,* p. 318.

27. Cecil W. Rowntree, "Contribution to the Study of X-Ray Carcinoma and the Conditions Which Precede Its Onset," *Archives of the Middlesex Hospital* 13 (1908): 182–205; Otto Hesse, *Symptomologie, Pathogenese und Therapie des Röntgenkarzinoms* (Leipzig: J. A. Barth, 1911).

28. Heinrich Depenthal, "Doppelseitiges Mammakarzinom (Röntgenkarzinom)," *Münchener medizinische Wochenschrift* 66 (1919): 354–55; Ernst Bumm, "Über Röntgenkarzinome bei der Frau," *Zeitschrift für Geburtshilfe und Gynäkologie* 86 (1923): 445–53; Max Lüdin, "Chondrosarkom der Kaninchentibia nach experimenteller Röntgenbestrahlung," *Schweizerische medizinische Wochenschrift* 60 (1930): 162. Lüdin was actually a Swiss radiologist working at the University of Basel.

29. See, for example, Bruno Bloch, "Die experimentelle Erzeugung von Roentgen-Carcinomen beim Kaninschen, nebst allgemeinen Bemerkungen über die Genese der experimentellen Carcinome," *Schweizerische medizinische Wochenschrift* 54 (1924): 857–65; Andries R. Jonkhoff, "Röntgencarcinom bei Mäusen," *Zeitschrift für Krebsforschung* 26 (1928): 32–41. Jonkhoff was Dutch. For the history of radiation carcinogenesis, see Jacob Furth and Egon Lorenz, "Carcinogenesis by Ionizing Radiations," in *Radiation Biology,* vol. 1, *High Energy Radiation,* ed. Alexander Hollaender (New York: McGraw-Hill, 1954), pp. 1145–1201; Antoine Lacassagne, *Les cancers produits par les rayonnements électromagnétiques* (Paris: Hermann & Cie, 1945); and Juraj Körbler, *Strahlen: Heilmittel und Gefahr, Eine Geschichte der Strahlen in der Medizin* (Vienna: Ranner, 1977).

30. Walter Kikuth, "Über Lungencarcinom," *Archiv für pathologische Anatomie und Physiologie* 255 (1925): 115.

31. Staemmler, "Beruf und Krebs," p. 123.

32. See, for example, Lothar Loeffler, "Röntgenschädigungen der männlichen Keimzelle und Nachkommenschaft: Ergebnisse einer Rundfrage bei Röntgenärzten und -technikern," *Strahlentherapie* 34 (1929): 735–66; Heinrich Martius, "Keimschädigung durch Röntgenstrahlen," *Strahlentherapie* 41 (1931): 47–66; Kötschau, "Über Umweltschädigungen," p. 1289.

33. Heinrich Albers-Schönberg, "Ueber eine bisher unbekannte Wirkung der Röntgenstrahlen auf den Organismus der Tiere," *Münchener medizinische Wochenschrift* 50 (1903): 1859–60.

34. Otto Friedrich, "Histologische Untersuchung eines intrauterin mit Röntgenstrahlen bestrahlten menschlichen Fötus," *Zeitschrift für Röntgenkunde und Radiumforschung* 12 (1910): 404–12. C. R. Bardeen at the University of Wisconsin about this time showed that toads whose sperm had been irradiated evidenced congenital defects; see his "Abnormal Development of Toad Ova Fertilized by Spermatozoa Exposed to Roentgen Rays," *Journal of Experimental Zoology* 4 (1907): 1–44.

35. Lenz, *Menschliche Erblichkeitslehre*, p. 258.

36. Eugene Apert and Yves Kermorgant, "L'enfant des rayons X," *Presse médicale* 31 (1923): 1010; R. Pauly, G. Cantorné, and J. Bentégeat, "Un microcéphale, 'enfant des rayons X': Etude clinique et anatomo-pathologique," *Journal de médecine de Bordeaux* 118 (1941): 537–51.

37. W. A. Newman Dorland and Maximilian J. Hubeny, *The X-Ray in Embryology and Obstetrics* (Saint Paul: Bruce, 1926), pp. 26, 312–13.

38. Lenz, *Menschliche Erblichkeitslehre*, p. 264. Lenz pointed out that radiologists, X-ray technicians, and chemists died more often than average from cancer (p. 260).

39. Eugen Fischer, "Strahlenbehandlung und Nachkommenschaft," *Deutsche medizinische Wochenschrift* 55 (1929): 89–91; also his "Erbschädigung beim Menschen," *Das kommende Geschlecht* 5 (1930): 1–19.

40. The Russian émigré geneticist Nikolaj Timoféeff-Ressovsky in 1935 showed that a single quantum of light could kill a cell—which cancer researchers recognized as having implications for carcinogenesis; see N. Timoféeff-Ressovsky, Karl G. Zimmer, and Max Delbrück, "Über die Natur der Genmutation und der Genstruktur," *Nachrichten der Gesellschaft der Wissenschaften Göttingen, Fachgruppe VI*, N.F., 1 (1935): 189–241; Robert Bierich, "Über den Einfluss genetischer Faktoren auf Entstehung und Ausbildung der Krebsanlage," *Zeitschrift für Krebsforschung* 48 (1938): 87–91.

41. Julius Zappert, "Über röntgenogene fötale Mikrozephalie," *Archiv für Kinderheilkunde* 80 (1927): 34–50; Paul Feldweg, "Ein ungewöhnlicher Fall von Fruchtschädigung durch Röntgenstrahlen," *Strahlentherapie* 26 (1927): 799–801.

42. Körbler, *Strahlen*, p. 85.

43. Fischer, "Erbschädigung."

44. Hans Luxenburger, "Temporäre Strahlenamenorrhoe und menschliche Erbforschung," *Strahlentherapie* 45 (1932): 685–88.

45. Hermann Holthusen, "Erfahrungen über die Verträglichkeitsgrenze für Röntgenstrahlen und deren Nutzanwendung zur Verhütung von Schäden," *Strahlentherapie* 57 (1936): 255.

46. Karl Kaestle, "Zwecke und Ziele der Bayerischen Gesellschaft für Röntgenologie and Radiologie," *Radiologische Rundschau* 1 (1933): 28–29.

47. "Zur Frage der Keimschädigung durch Röntgenstrahlen," *Radiologische Rundschau* 1 (1933): 56–58 and 97.

48. See my *Racial Hygiene*, pp. 251–81.

49. Julian Marcuse, "Geschlecht gegen Rasse," *Sozialistischer Arzt*, February/March 1932, pp. 54–55; see also his "Nationalsozialistische Rassenexperimente," *Sozialistischer Arzt*, April/May 1932, pp. 76–78. The pro-Nazi Sudeten-

deutsche Partei in 1936 proposed a law for the protection of uranium miners in Joachimsthal (*Gesetz zum Schutz der Bergarbeiter in Joachimsthal*); the Czech government shortly thereafter implemented new ventilation requirements, wet drilling, new dust recovery systems, use of protective masks, shift changes, and better vacation privileges. Radioactivity in the mines reportedly declined to an average of 2 ME (see the explanatory note on p. 94n); see also "Mitteilungen," *Monatsschrift für Krebsbekämpfung* 5 (1938): 325.

50. *Deutsches Ärzteblatt* 63 (1933): 182.

51. Hans Holfelder, "Einsatz und Tätigkeit der Röntgenreihenbildnertruppe der SS in Mecklenburg," *Zeitschrift für Tuberkulose* 83 (1939): 257–64.

52. "Die Berufskrankheiten im Jahre 1935," *Arbeitsschutz* 3 (1936): 258; compare also Alfred Brinkmann, *Reihenuntersuchung in einem Sprengstoffwerk* (Münster: Med. diss., 1941). On the apparatus used in these mass screenings, see Robert Janker, "Die Röntgenreihenuntersuchung in Betrieben," *Arbeitsschutz* 3 (1942): 319–21. On the campaign to screen tubercular Poles, see Franz Puntigam, "Ein Jahr Röntgenuntersuchung polnischer Arbeitskräfte," *Öffentlicher Gesundheitsdienst* 9 (1943): nos. 19/20.

53. Hermann Braeuning, "Die Röntgen-Reihenuntersuchung," *Röntgenpraxis* 11 (1939): 391 ff.

54. Holfelder, "Einsatz und Tätigkeit," pp. 258–61. Holfelder published an atlas analyzing nearly a million X-rays taken in the course of this operation; see his *Atlas des Röntgenreihenbildes des Brustraumes auf Grund der Auswertung von über 900000 Röntgenreihenschirmbildern* (Leipzig: Georg Thieme, 1939), coauthored with Friedrich Berner.

55. Heinrich Zeiss, "Forschung, Lehre und zivile Krankenversorgung im 4. Kriegsjahr" (1943), BDC.

56. On silicosis, see Rudolf Hoffmann, "Statistische Ergebnisse aus Reihenuntersuchungen auf Silikose in zwei schlesischen Betrieben," *Archiv für Gewerbepathologie* 10 (1940): 378–83; on tuberculosis, see Hans Stoffels, "Durchführung und Ergebnis von Nachuntersuchungen auf Grund der Röntgen-Reihendurchleuchtung nach Prof. Holfelder," *Öffentlicher Gesundheitsdienst* 6 (1941): 637–40; on asbestosis, see Ehrhardt, "Der heutige Stand der Asbestosebekämpfung," *Arbeitsschutz* 3 (1940): 193.

57. Janker, "Röntgenreihenuntersuchung," p. 321.

58. Susanne Hahn, "Ethische Grundlagen der faschistischen Medizin, dargestellt am Beispiel der Tuberkulosebekämpfung," in *Medizin im Nationalsozialismus*, ed. Achim Thom and Horst Spaar (Oberlungwitz: VEB Kongress- und Werbedruck, 1983), pp. 133–47; also K. Kelting, *Das Tuberkuloseproblem im Nationalsozialismus* (Kiel: Med. diss., 1974); and Götz Aly, "Tuberkulose und 'Euthanasie,'" in *Menschenverachtung und Opportunismus: Zur Medizin im Dritten Reich*, ed. Jürgen Pfeiffer (Tübingen: Attempto, 1992), pp. 131–46. The plan was never carried out.

59. *Trials of War Criminals*, 1:721.

60. Ibid., p. 720.

61. Ibid., p. 702.

62. *Reichsgesetzblatt* 1 (1936): 119.

63. Franz Schwanitz, "Mutationen und ihre Bedeutung," *Volk und Rasse* 10 (1935): 353.

64. Heinrich Martius and Friedrich Kröning, "Zur Frage der Erbgutschädigung durch Röntgen- und Radiumstrahlen," *Medizinische Welt* 12 (1938): 947–50.

65. Gerhard Schubert and Artur Pickhan, *Erbschädigungen* (Leipzig: Georg Thieme, 1938), p. 136.

66. *Reichsgesetzblatt* 1 (1941): 88 ff.; "Unfallverhütungsvorschriften für Anwendung von Röntgenstrahlen," *Arbeitsschutz* 3 (1940): 238–40. Richard Glocker and E. Kaupp in Stuttgart in 1925 adopted the American A. Mutscheller's X-ray "tolerance dose" recommendations, noting that the radiation (*Streustrahlung*) received by German operators standing 1¾ meters from the device was several times higher than this; see their "Über den Strahlenschutz und die Toleranzdosis," *Strahlentherapie* 20 (1925): 144–52. The U.S. Advisory Committee on X-Ray and Radium Protection adopted a tolerance dose of 0.2 R/day in 1931 and 0.1 R/day in 1936; the International X-Ray and Radium Protection Commission in 1934 and 1937 proposed daily limits of 0.2 R. See Körbler, *Strahlen*, p. 96. Even during the war, German industrial physicians were instructed not to allow employees working with X-rays or radium to exceed exposure limits; see "Kleine Mitteilungen," *Vertrauensarzt* 9 (1941): 176.

67. Heinrich W. Ernst, *Über die Unfallverhütungsvorschriften für nichtmedizinische Röntgenbetriebe* (Leipzig: Georg Thieme, 1942). A special pamphlet was prepared to explain the hazards of X-rays to nonmedical workers; see "Merkblatt für Röntgenarbeiter," *Arbeitsschutz* 3 (1942): 363–64.

68. See, for example, Berthold and Trost, "Messungen zu den Strahlenschutzregeln für technische Röntgenanlagen," *Arbeitsschutz* 3 (1942): 274–75. More research needs to be done on how German radiation standards and enforcement at this time compared with, say, those of France or the United States or the Soviet Union.

69. "Röntgenverordnungen," *Arbeitsschutz* 3 (1942): 206.

70. Carl Kruchen, "Spätschädigungen durch Röntgenstrahlen," *Strahlentherapie* 60 (1937): 466–75; Wilhelm Weitz, "Über einen von Anfang an beobachteten Fall von myeloischer Leukämie bei einer Röntgenlaborantin," *Klinische Wochenschrift* 17 (1938): 1579–80; K(arl?) Kindler, "Beitrag zur Frage der Entstehung des Röntgenkrebses in inneren Organen," *Zeitschrift für Krebsforschung* 54 (1944): 153–69.

71. Körbler, *Strahlen*, pp. 75–76.

72. Susan E. Lederer, *Subjected to Science: Human Experimentation in America before the Second World War* (Baltimore: Johns Hopkins University Press, 1995).

73. Warren Weaver in 1937 noted J. Lawrence's characterization of the 1937 Chicago Congress of Radiologists as a "congress of cripples"; see Weaver's dairy entry for October 29, 1937, Rockefeller Foundation Archives 4263–64.

74. Geoffrey Brooks, *Hitler's Nuclear Weapons: The Development and Attempted Deployment of Radiological Armaments by Nazi Germany* (London: Cooper, 1992), pp. 74–75.

75. Erich Neitzel, "Berufsschädigungen durch radioaktive Substanzen," *Arbeitsmedizin* 1 (1935): 13. Paul Lazarus in his *Handbuch der gesamten Strahlenheilkunde II* (Munich: Bergmann, 1931) ridiculed radium compresses as a useless swindle, but as late as 1940 Vienna's Institut für Radiumtherapie was recommending radon inhalation for various ailments; see V. Karg, "Künstliche Radiumemanationstherapie für den praktischen Arzt," *Wiener medizinische Wochenschrift* 90 (1940): 97 ff. and 119 ff.

76. Neitzel, "Berufsschädigungen," p. 14.

77. "Die finnische Badestube," *Der Balneologe* 8 (1941): 113–14. Germany, with its twelve officially recognized *Radiumkurorte*, was hailed about this time as *"the* land of radium baths"; see Boris Rajewsky, "Balneologische Forschung," *Der Balneologe* 9 (1942): 221.

78. Erich Wollmann, "Natürliche und künstliche Radiumwässer," *Der Balneologe* 6 (1939): 386–89. The so-called Salzufler Bestimmung of 1932 had specified minimal levels of radioactivity producing a "medical effect" for radon inhalation (3 nanocuries per liter), bathing (30 nanocuries per liter), and drinking (300 nanocuries per liter); see Erich Wollmann, "Die Technik der Einatmung radonhaltiger Luft," *Der Balneologe* 5 (1938): 60–66.

79. Erich Marx, "Die Radiumgefahr in Deutschland," *Neue Freie Presse*, September 25, 1932, p. 25, and September 27, 1932, p. 9; compare also the dismissive response of Albert Fernau, a Viennese professor of medical physics and radium chemistry, who argued that it was wrong to draw too close a comparison with the Joachimsthal miners, since the lung cancers prevalent there must have been caused by rock dust as well as radium exposure; see his "Die Radiumgefahr in Deutschland," *Neue Freie Presse*, October 4, 1932, p. 9. Fernau also took comfort from the argument of Stefan Meyer, head of Vienna's Institut für Radiumforschung, that most of the radon inhaled during emanation therapy was quickly expelled from the lungs.

80. The best history of the U.S. radium dial painters is Claudia Clark's *Radium Girls: Women and Industrial Health Reform, 1910–1935* (Chapel Hill: University of North Carolina Press, 1997).

81. P. Rössing, "Über eine ungewöhnliche Form der Radiumvergiftung in der Leuchtfarbenindustrie," *Archiv für Gewerbepathologie und Gewerbehygiene* 11 (1942): 395–401.

82. There are other examples of poisoning connected with the chemical isolation of radium: in Joachimsthal in 1928, for example, apart from the miners there were also sixty workers involved in extracting and purifying radium, at least five of whom contracted lung cancer. Three had been miners, but two had never worked underground. A 1935 review of radiation health and safety concluded that the cases "could be attributed only to radiation" (Neitzel, "Berufsschädigungen," p. 29).

83. Friedrich H. Härting and Walter Hesse, "Der Lungenkrebs, die Bergkrankheit in den Schneeberger Gruben," *Vierteljahrsschrift für gerichtliche Medizin* 30 (1879): 300, and 31 (1879): 109–112, 325. Härting and Hesse's paper is one of the classics of epidemiology, tracing the lung cancer epidemic to changing work practices (e.g., the increase in piecework), changing technologies

(e.g., the use of dynamite), and changing patterns of ore in the earth (depletion of strongly irritating ores, which had formerly caused extra-high exposures); see ibid., pp. 319–21.

84. Julius Löwy, "Über die Joachimstaler Bergkrankheit; vorläufige Mitteilung," *Medizinische Klinik* 25 (1929): 141–42. Löwy here describes the first two cases of lung cancer diagnosed among Joachimsthal miners—one discovered at autopsy at Prague's Pathologisches Institut in 1926, the second in 1928 at Wilhelm Nonnenbruch's clinic at the same university. Herman Sikl in 1930 reported lung cancers in eight of ten Joachimsthal miners autopsied; see his "Über den Lungenkrebs der Bergleute in Joachimstal (Tschechoslowakei)," *Zeitschrift für Krebsforschung* 32 (1930): 609–13.

85. Neitzel, "Berufsschädigungen," p. 19; also Hueper, *Occupational Tumors*, pp. 435–56. The first to publish a radiation etiology for the Schneeberger disease was Margarete Uhlig; see her "Über den Schneeberger Lungenkrebs," *Archiv für pathologische Anatomie und Physiologie* 230 (1921): 76–98. Erich Marx in 1932 stated unequivocally that Joachimsthal's high lung cancer rate was traceable to "radon and its daughter products" (*Radon und seine Zerfallsprodukte*); see his "Radiumgefahr," p. 25.

86. Paul Ludewig and Eduard Lorenser, "Untersuchung der Grubenluft in den Schneeberger Gruben auf den Gehalt an Radiumemanation," *Zeitschrift für Physik* 22 (1924): 178–85. Heinrich Mache and Stefan Meyer in 1905 were apparently the first to detect "radium emanation" in the mines of Joachimsthal; see Werner Schüttmann, "Aus den Anfängen der Radontherapie," *Zeitschrift für die gesamte innere Medizin* 41 (1986): 451–56. Carl Schiffner, M. Weidig, and R. Friedrich in 1908 reported up to 2,050 ME/l in water issuing from the mines around Joachimsthal; see their *Radioaktive Wässer in Sachsen, I-IV* (Freiberg: Craz & Gerlach, 1908–1912), p. 63. There was no suggestion of a possible danger; the primary concern was whether such waters were radioactive enough to be put to "medical uses" (p. 119). A postwar review prepared for U.S. military authorities noted that the maximum value ever recorded in the air of a German mine was 150 ME; see Gerhard Kahlau and A. Schraub, "Krebserzeugung durch Strahlung, insbesondere Schneeberger Lungenkrebs," in *Biophysics: Part I*, ed. Boris Rajewsky and Michael Schön (Wiesbaden: Office of Military Government, 1948), p. 134.

87. Rostoski, Saupe, and Schmorl, "Die Bergkrankheit," pp. 360–84. There were about 700 miners active in the Schneeberg region during peak production in the 1880s; by 1921 this had fallen to 149 (p. 363). This number fell to 54 in 1926, and the mines were closed shortly thereafter.

88. Neitzel, "Berufsschädigungen," p. 20. The arsenic experiment in question was performed by Schmittmann, "Experimentelle Untersuchungen über die Wirkung des Schneeberger Staubes auf das Bronchial-Epithel," *Zeitschrift für Krebsforschung* 32 (1930): 677 ff. Rostoski et al. in 1926 had proposed that animals be reared in the mines to see whether "radium emanation" (radon) alone was sufficient to cause the disease; see their "Die Bergkrankheit," p. 374. Teutschlaender in 1931 exposed mice, axolotls, and carp to radon, assuming this to be the cause of the *Schneeberger Krankheit*, but he was not able to

generate tumors; see "Niederschrift über die Sitzung des Wissenschaftlichen Ausschusses beim Reichsausschuss für Krebsbekämpfung," April 13, 1935, THW 1493, p. 27.

89. Arthur Brandt, "Bericht über die im Schneeberger Gebiet auf Veranlassung des Reichsausschusses für Krebsbekämpfung durchgeführten Untersuchungen," *Zeitschrift für Krebsforschung* 47 (1938): 108–11. Rajewsky continued animal experiments on radiogenic cancer into 1945; see his article with A. Schraub and G. Kahlau, "Experimentelle Geschwulsterzeugung durch Einatmung von Radiumemanation," *Naturwissenschaften* 31 (1943): 170–71. In 1942/43, Rajewsky's institute erected a three-million-volt X-ray apparatus for cancer therapy, the largest in the world at this time; see Hans Danzer, "Boris Rajewsky zum 60. Geburtstag," *Strahlentherapie* 94 (1954): 3–11.

90. Neitzel, "Berufsschädigungen," pp. 15–21. Neitzel in 1937 showed that one Schneeberg mine regarded as particularly dangerous contained some 35–44 ME, and that on Mondays, after ventilating fans had been off for the weekend, radiation could rise to 111 ME. See his "Bericht über die in den Monaten Oktober–November 1936 im Schneeberg-Neustädter Erzbergbau ausgeführten Untersuchungen zur Frage der Lungenschädigung der Bergarbeiter," *Arbeitsschutz* 3 (1937): 70–72. Boris Rajewski in 1935 began a project to determine the "tolerance dose" for radium stored in the human body; his 1936 *Toleranzmenge* was used as late as 1950 by the London-based International Congress of Radiologists. The value in question was apparently 3 to 30 ME, an extraordinarily high figure that seems to have considered radium poisoning but not cancer effects—see Kahlau and Schraub, "Krebserzeugung," p. 134.

91. Kahlau and Schraub, "Krebserzeugung," pp. 132–66.

92. Löwy, "Über die Joachimstaler Bergkrankheit."

93. Julius Löwy, "Die Wirkung der Joachimsthaler Pechblende im Tierversuch," *Medizinische Klinik* (Prague edition), no. 18 (1936): 619–20.

94. Neitzel, "Berufsschädigungen," p. 17; Brandt, "Bericht," pp. 108–9; and the more extensive report in Hans Rudolph Döhnert, "Experimentelle Untersuchungen zur Frage des Schneeberger Lungenkrebses," *Zeitschrift für Krebsforschung* 47 (1938): 209–39. Döhnert joined the Nazi party in May of 1933 (BDC).

95. Hermann Hebestreit, *Schutz und Erhaltung der Arbeitskraft* (Berlin: Otto Elsner, 1939), p. 204. Compare the similar assertions in Bauer, "Krebs und Vererbung," p. 475; and in Erwin A. Uehlinger and Otto Schürch, "Über experimentelle Erzeugung von Sarkomen mit Radium und Mesothorium," *Deutsche Zeitschrift für Chirurgie* 251 (1939): 12–33. Rajewsky about this time measured the radiation in homes of miners who had contracted cancer; see Brandt, "Bericht."

96. Franz Strnad, "Der Lungenkrebs," *Monatsschrift für Krebsbekämpfung* 6 (1938): 309–10.

97. See my *Cancer Wars*, pp. 186–92.

98. Wilhelm Engelmann, "The Present Position of Radium Emanation Therapy in Germany," *British Journal for Physical Medicine*, n.s., 1 (1938): 229–30 and 244.

99. Hans Krebs to Heinrich Himmler, November 19, 1938, and Himmler to

Krebs, December 15, 1938, T-175 #87, folder 193, Captured German Documents, National Archives.

100. See my *Cancer Wars*, pp. 192–95.

101. Wolfgang Zank, *Wirtschaft und Arbeit in Ostdeutschland 1945–1949* (Munich: R. Oldenbourg, 1987), pp. 65–66.

102. Forschungsinstitut der Friedrich-Ebert-Stiftung, *Wismut und die Folgen des Uranbergbaus* (Bonn: Friedrich-Ebert-Stiftung, 1992), p. 15.

103. Patricia Kahn, "A Grisly Archive of Key Cancer Data," *Science* 259 (1993): 448–51; "The Legacy of Schneeberg," *Nuclear Engineering*, February 1991, p. 7; Reimar Paul, *Das Wismut Erbe* (Göttingen: Die Werkstatt, 1991).

104. Forschungsinstitut, *Wismut und die Folgen*, pp. 15–16.

105. Ibid., p. 13. A 1991 survey by Bavaria's environmental ministry found that about half of all homes in the Oberpfälzischen town of Neunburg have radon concentrations in excess of 415 Bq/m^3(= 11 pCi/l) in the winter; see Max Daunderer, *Gifte im Alltag: Wo sie vorkommen, Wie sie krank machen, Wie man sich vor ihnen schützt* (Munich: Beck, 1995), p. 137.

106. Jonathan E. Helmreich, *Gathering Rare Ores: The Diplomacy of Uranium Acquisition, 1943–1954* (Princeton: Princeton University Press, 1986), p. 248.

107. "Mitteilungen," *Monatsschrift für Krebsbekämpfung* 5 (1938): 324.

108. Norman M. Naimark, *The Russians in Germany: A History of the Soviet Zone of Occupation* (Cambridge: Harvard University Press, 1995). The Soviet director of *Wismut*, Major General Andrei Mal'tsev, had earlier organized the construction of the Moscow subway and, by forced labor, a massive, secret tunnel under the Amur River in Soviet Asia. See Nikolai Grishin, "The Saxony Uranium Mining Operation ('Vismut')," in *Soviet Economic Policy in Postwar Germany*, ed. Robert Slusser (New York: Research Program on the U.S.S.R., 1953), pp. 127–52.

109. Helmreich, *Gathering Rare Ores*, p. 248.

110. See my *Cancer Wars*, p. 27.

111. Rostoski, Saupe, and Schmorl, "Die Bergkrankheit," p. 371. The authors identified a latency period of ten to eighteen years.

112. Körbler, *Strahlen*, p. 76. The *Latenzzeit* between exposure to chromium and the development of lung cancer was "between twenty and forty years" according to official commentaries on Germany's occupational health legislation; see the *Monatsschrift für Krebsbekämpfung* 7 (1940): 215.

113. Pfeil, "Lungentumoren." Tobacco dust inhalation in cigar and cigarette factories was another early worry, one that looks somewhat odd in retrospect, given how slowly the medical profession responded to the much larger threat posed by cigarettes themselves (see chapter 6).

114. Richard Fischer, *Die industrielle Herstellung und Verwendung der Chromverbindungen, die dabei enstehenden Gesundheitsgefahren für die Arbeiter und die Massnahmen zu ihrer Bekämpfung* (Berlin: A. Seydel, 1911); also "Die Gefährlichkeit der Chromatbetriebe—eine Sage?" *Beilage zum Proletarier*, May 18, 1912.

115. W. Alwens, E.-E. Bauke, and W. Jonas, "Auffallende Häufung von Bronchialkrebs bei Arbeitern der chemischen Industrie," *Münchener medizinische Wochenschrift* 83 (1936): 485–87.

116. John A. Paris, *Pharmacologia*, 5th ed. (London, 1822), p. 208; compare also Ernest L. Kennaway, "A Contribution to the Mythology of Cancer Research," *Lancet* 243 (1942): 769–72, for a refutation of the Paris report.

117. Jonathan Hutchinson, "Arsenic Cancer," *British Medical Journal* 2 (1887): 1080–81; James Whorton, *Before Silent Spring: Pesticides and Public Health in Pre-DDT America* (Princeton: Princeton University Press, 1974), pp. 52–53, 262n36. In 1898, physicians discovered a high rate of tumors among the inhabitants of Reichenstein, a Silesian town whose water supply became contaminated with arsenic as it filtered through mine tailings (Hueper, *Occupational Tumors*, p. 40).

118. Hien, *Chemische Industrie*, pp. 309–11.

119. Pein, "Über die Ursachen."

120. Fritz Curschmann, "Die Anzeigepflicht von Berufskrankheiten," *Medizinalarchiv für das Deutsche Reich* 4 (1913): 1–6.

121. Ina Wagner, *Die gewerbehygienische Diskussion während der Weimarer Republik auf dem Weg zur 1. Berufskrankheitenverordnung von 1925* (Berlin: Med. diss., 1990). Certain worm diseases of miners were also compensable, as was the *Schneeberger Krankheit*.

122. The history of occupational arsenic cancer is discussed in Hien, *Chemische Industrie*, pp. 305–48; compare also Hueper, *Occupational Tumors*, pp. 33–48 and 406–8.

123. Pein, "Über die Ursachen," p. 295; Georg Rodenacker, *Die chemischen Gewerbekrankheiten und ihre Behandlung* (Leipzig: J. A. Barth, 1940), p. 142.

124. See the Partei-Kanzlei's *Verfügungen/Anordnungen, Bekanntgaben*, vol. 3 (Munich: Zentralverlag der NSDAP, 1943), p. 46.

125. "Vorsichtsmassregeln zur Verhütung von Unglücksfällen beim Gebrauch von arsenhaltigen Pflanzenschutzmitteln," *Arbeitsschutz* 3 (1942): 244.

126. Sources can be found in the extensive reviews of current literature in the *Monatsschrift für Unfallheilkunde und Versicherungsmedizin* in the mid-1930s.

127. Schulz, "Gesundheitliche Schäden."

128. Ibid., pp. 57–62.

129. "Die Berufskrankheiten im Jahre 1935," pp. 258–59.

130. Waniek, "Verhütung der Staublungenkrankheiten," p. 288.

131. On the Deutscher Ausschuss für Staubschutzmasken, see Arnold Lämmert, "Über die Aufgaben der Staubbekämpfungsstelle beim Verband der deutschen gewerblichen Berufsgenossenschaften, Berlin," *Staub: Reinhaltung der Luft* 2 (1937): 365–71.

132. Kurt Kollmeier, *Silikose und Lungenkrebs* (Bonn: Med. diss., 1934); Teleky's 1938 review ("Beruflicher Lungenkrebs") also failed to find a link.

133. Paul Weiland, "Die schädigende Wirkung von Sericit und Stahlschleifstaub," *Archiv für Gewerbepathologie* 8 (1937): 412–25.

134. Holtzmann, "Staublunge durch Glaswolle," *Ärztliche Sachverständigen-Zeitung* 44 (1937): 263 ff.

135. Pliny the Elder is often said to have recorded that slaves working with asbestos came down with lung disease, but this seems to be based on a mistranslation; see Kevin Browne and Robert Murray, "Asbestos and the Romans," *Lancet* 336 (1990): 445.

136. Schulz, "Gesundheitliche Schäden," p. 62. The earliest recorded German cases of asbestosis were apparently those identified in Saxony by Büttner-Wobst and Trillitzsch; later work was done by Erich Saupe, the mineralogist Paul J. Beger, Fritz Stroebe, and H.-W. Wedler; see Hans-Wilfrid Wedler, "Über den Lungenkrebs bei Asbestose," *Archiv für klinische Medizin* 191 (1943): 189–209; also his "Asbestose und Lungenkrebs," *Deutsche medizinische Wochenschrift* 69 (1943): 575–76.

137. Martin Nordmann, "Der Berufskrebs der Asbestarbeiter," *Zeitschrift für Krebsforschung* 47 (1938): 288–302; Franz Koelsch, "Lungenkrebs und Beruf," *Acta Unio Internationalis Contra Cancrum* 3 (1938): 243–51; Friedrich Hornig, "Klinische Betrachtungen zur Frage des Berufskrebses der Asbestarbeiter," *Zeitschrift für Krebsforschung* 47 (1938): 281–87; Teleky, "Beruflicher Lungenkrebs."

138. See, for example, Kenneth M. Lynch and W. A. Smith, "Pulmonary Asbestosis III: Carcinoma of the Lung in Asbestos Silicosis," *American Journal of Cancer* 24 (1935): 56–64; also S. Roodhouse Gloyne, "Two Cases of Squamous Carcinoma of the Lung Occurring in Asbestosis," *Tubercle* 17 (1935): 4–10. An excellent bibliography of early asbestos health research can be found in Otto Lemke, "Asbestose und Lungenkrebs. Zur dritten Verordnung über Ausdehnung der Unfallversicherung auf Berufskrankheiten vom 16. Dezember 1936," *Arbeitsschutz* 3 (1943): 8–15.

139. See Philip E. Enterline's insightful "Changing Attitudes and Opinions regarding Asbestos and Cancer 1934–1965," *American Journal of Industrial Medicine* 20 (1991): 685–700; also the commentaries responding to this article in 22 (1992): 259–80.

140. For Teleky it was "in höchstem Grade wahrscheinlich, dass Asbestosis für Ca Entwicklung disponiert" ("Beruflicher Lungenkrebs," p. 259).

141. Nordmann is cited in Lemke, "Asbestose und Lungenkrebs," p. 12; compare also Hermann Gerbis, "Ein weiterer Fall von schwerer Lungenasbestosis mit ausgedehnter Krebsbildung," *Arbeitsblatt* 3 (1943): 315–16. Nordmann's CV and *Lebenslauf* are preserved in the NSDAP's Partei-Korrespondenz, National Archives, College Park, Maryland.

142. Arthur Böhme, "Untersuchungen an den Arbeitern einer Asbestfabrik," *Archiv für Gewerbepathologie und Gewerbehygiene* 11 (1942): 433–52.

143. Joachim Kühn, "Übermikroskopische Untersuchungen an Asbeststaub und Asbestlungen," *Archiv für Gewerbepathologie und Gewerbehygiene* 10 (1941): 473–85. Serpentine, rather than hornblende, was suggested as the most deadly form of the fiber at this point.

144. Ehrhardt, "Der heutige Stand," p. 193.

145. *Reichsarbeitsblatt* 3 (1940): 263. The "Richtlinien für die Bekämpfung der Staubgefahr in Asbest verarbeitenden Betrieben" are also discussed in Ehrhardt, "Der heutige Stand," pp. 191–93.

146. Alfred Welz, "Weitere Beobachtungen über den Berufskrebs der Asbestarbeiter," *Archiv für Gewerbepathologie und Gewerbehygiene* 11 (1942): 536–50.

147. Wedler, "Über den Lungenkrebs bei Asbestose," pp. 189–209. Wedler joined the Nazi party on May 1, 1937 (BDC).

148. Hans-Wilfrid Wedler, *Klinik der Lungenasbestose* (Leipzig: Georg Thieme, 1939), p. 68.

149. Martin Nordmann and Adolf Sorge, "Lungenkrebs durch Asbeststaub im Tierversuch," *Zeitschrift für Krebsforschung* 51 (1941): 168–82.

150. Welz, "Weitere Beobachtungen," p. 537.

151. Nordmann and Sorge, "Lungenkrebs," p. 169.

152. Hueper, *Occupational Tumors*, pp. 399–405; Barry I. Castleman, "Asbestos and Cancer: History and Public Policy," *British Journal of Industrial Medicine* 48 (1991): 427–30. Asbestos-induced lung cancer was actually officially recognized in 1940, in one of the *Merkblatt* commentaries on compensable occupational illnesses; see the *Monatsschrift für Krebsbekämpfung* 7 (1940): 214–15.

153. David Ozonoff, "Failed Warnings: Asbestos-Related Disease and Industrial Medicine," in *The Health and Safety of Workers*, ed. Ronald Bayer (New York: Oxford University Press, 1988), p. 140.

154. Eberhard Gross, "Das Carcinom vom Standpunkt des Gewerbetoxikologen," in Adolf Butenandt et al., *Chemie und Krebs* (Berlin: Chemie, 1940), pp. 101–2.

155. Franz Koelsch, *Was weisst Du von Berufskrankheiten und Gewerbehygiene?* (Berlin: Arens, 1944), p. 25.

156. Enterline, "Changing Attitudes," p. 691; "German writers had made up their minds about the relationship between asbestos and lung cancer by 1943" (ibid.).

157. References can be found in ibid., pp. 692–93. Richard Doll by this time had already given solid epidemiologic evidence for the link; see his "Mortality from Lung Cancer in Asbestos Workers," *British Journal of Industrial Medicine* 12 (1955): 81–82.

158. Richard Doll, personal comunication.

159. Sellers, "Discovering Environmental Cancer," pp. 1824–35; compare also Harry M. Marks, *The Progress of Experiment: Science and Therapeutic Reform in the United States* (New York: Cambridge University Press, 1977), pp. 136–63.

160. Lothar Horbach and Hans Loskant, *Berufskrebsstudie: Forschungsbericht, Deutsche Forschungsgemeinschaft* (Boppard: Bold, 1981). Horbach and Loskant estimated that as many as 20 percent of all cancers in the general population were of occupational origins.

161. Hien, *Chemische Industrie*, pp. 213–71.

162. Oswald Bumke, *Erinnerungen und Betrachtungen: Der Weg eines deutschen Psychiaters* (Munich: Pflaum, 1952), p. 145.

163. *Trials of War Criminals*, 8:577.

164. Rehn, "Blasengeschwülste," pp. 588–600; David Michaels, "Waiting for the Body Count: Corporate Decision Making and Bladder Cancer in the U.S. Dye Industry," *Medical Anthropology Quarterly*, n.s., 2 (1988): 215–32.

165. Hueper, *Occupational Tumors*, pp. 470–71. Fritz Curschmann as early as 1920 noticed that bladder cancers usually developed "only after many years of work" with aniline dyes; see his "Statistische Erhebungen über Blasentumoren bei Arbeitern in der chemischen Industrie," *Zentralblatt für Gewerbehygiene* 8 (1920): 145–49.

166. "Verordnung über Ausdehnung der Unfallversicherung auf gewerbliche Berufskrankheiten," *Reichsgesetzblatt* 1 (1925): 69–70. Germany modified its occupational health legislation in 1929 and again in 1936; the 1936 law increased the number of compensable illnesses but made it more difficult for workers to obtain compensation for work-related injuries; see "Dritte Verordnung über Ausdehnung der Unfallversicherung auf Berufskrankheiten vom 16. Dezember 1936," *Reichsgesetzblatt* 1 (1936): 1117; also "Die entschädigungspflichtigen Berufskrankheiten," *Arbeitsschutz* 3 (1940): 19–29.

167. Staemmler, "Beruf und Krebs," p. 122.

168. Hueper, *Occupational Tumors*, p. 474.

169. B(etina?) Ewerbeck, "Ein Gang durch das Werk," *Gesundheitsführung*, November 1940, p. 429, cited in Hien, *Chemische Industrie*, pp. 224–25. Hien notes that I. G. Farben in 1939 published an article on "the myth of aniline dyes being poisonous" (p. 257).

170. L. Simon, "Dauererfolge der operativen Behandlung von Anilintumoren," *Zentralblatt für Gewerbehygiene* 7 (1930): 78–80; also his "Prognose und Behandlung der sogenannten Anilintumoren der Blase," in *Verhandlungen der Deutschen Gesellschaft für Chirurgie* (Berlin: J. Springer), pp. 709–11. Both articles are cited in Hien, *Chemische Industrie*, p. 220. Curschmann in 1920 failed to produce bladder tumors in experiments using dogs; see his "Statistische Erhebungen," pp. 145–46. Wilhelm Hueper eventually succeeded where Curschmann failed; see his paper with F. H. Wiley and H. D. Wolfe, "Experimental Production of Bladder Tumors in Dogs by Administration of Beta-Naphthylamine," *Journal of Industrial Hygiene and Toxicology* 20 (1938): 46–84.

171. Ernst W. Baader, "Berufskrebs," in Adam and Auler, *Neuere Ergebnisse*, pp. 104–28.

172. Koelsch was a Prussian conservative along the lines of the Deutschnationale Partei; he developed an exhibit on industrial hygiene for Dresden's Hygiene Museum and authored an influential textbook on occupational disease that went through several editions from 1937 through 1966 (*Lehrbuch der Arbeitshygiene*, published by Enke of Stuttgart).

173. There are other reasons to doubt the accuracy or completeness of cancer registries. Falling between the cracks were workers who left a carcinogenic line of work and later developed cancer, and no one knows how many of the German soldiers who died in the war (five to six million) might have eventually developed cancer.

174. Gine Elsner, "Die Betriebsärzte der IG Farben-Werke," in *Pax Medica: Stationen ärztlichen Friedensengagements und Verirrungen ärztlichen Militarismus*, ed. W. Beck, G. Elsner, and H. Mausbach (Hamburg: VSA, 1986), pp. 42–62; Hien, *Chemische Industrie*, pp. 233–38.

175. Brooks, *Hitler's Nuclear Weapons*, p. 123.

176. Hermann Kaienburg, *"Vernichtung durch Arbeit": Der Fall Neuengamme* (Bonn: J.H.W. Dietz, 1990).

177. Hans Reiter, "Arbeitshygiene und Vierjahresplan," in his *Das Reichsgesundheitsamt, 1933–1939: Sechs Jahre nationalsozialistische Führung* (Berlin:

Springer, 1939), p. 251. Reiter also pointed out that lead shortages had prompted the use of substitutes in many industries—printing and painting, for example—reducing the health risks in those industries (ibid.).

178. Götz Aly, Peter Chroust, and Christian Pross, *Cleansing the Fatherland: Nazi Medicine and Racial Hygiene* (Baltimore: Johns Hopkins University Press, 1994), pp. 1–98.

179. In one of his Hauptquartier conversations, Hitler entertained the rather cryptic idea that people with heart and lung disease "nicht mehr in der Öffentlichkeit bleiben können und dürfen ebenfalls keine Nachkommen mehr erzeugen"; these were measures "die nach siegreichem Kriegsende schnellstens durchgeführt werden müssen." See the memo authored by Hessen-Nassau Gauleiter Jakob Sprenger to an unnamed Kreisleiter, preserved in the Archiv der sozialen Demokratie der Friedrich-Ebert-Stiftung, Nachlass Fritz Henssler, Mappe 2, Az. I/B/37869/8, published in *Utopie Kreativ* 55 (1995): 36–37. Ernst Haeckel had proposed making voluntary euthanasia available to terminally ill cancer patients: see his *Die Lebenswunder: Gemeinverständliche Studien über biologische Philosophie* (Stuttgart: Kröner, 1904), pp. 131–35. The psychiatrist E. Wauschkuhn, anticipating the implementation of the euthanasia plans of Karl Binding and Alfred Hoche, as early as 1922 warned that it was "only a matter of time" before cancer patients, along with the blind and the deaf, tubercular, war-wounded, and persons unable to work would be put to death; see his "Die Freigabe der Vernichtung lebensunwerten Lebens," *Psychiatrisch-Neurologische Wochenschrift* 24 (1922): 217. There is no evidence that cancer patients were ever singled out for euthanasia in the Nazi period.

180. On the German euthanasia program, see Michael Burleigh, *Death and Deliverance: "Euthanasia" in Germany, 1900–1945* (Cambridge: Cambridge University Press, 1995); Henry Friedlander, *The Origins of Nazi Genocide: From Euthanasia to the Final Solution* (Chapel Hill: University of North Carolina Press, 1995); and Ernst Klee, *"Euthanasie" im NS-Staat, die "Vernichtung lebensunwerten Lebens"* (Frankfurt: S. Fischer, 1983). On parallel U.S. initiatives, see Ezekiel J. Emanuel, "The History of Euthanasia Debates in the United States and Britain," *Annals of Internal Medicine* 121 (1994): 793–802; also Martin S. Pernick, *The Black Stork: Eugenics and the Death of "Defective" Babies in American Medicine and Motion Pictures since 1915* (New York: Oxford University Press, 1996).

181. Advocates of organic medicine espoused similar views: Karl Kötschau in 1939, for example, argued that people had to work, even if it cost them some of their health. The choice, as he put it, was between performance and elimination ("entweder Leistungsfähigkeit oder natürliche Ausmerze"); see his *Kämpferische Vorsorge statt karitative Fürsorge* (Nuremberg: Deutsche Volksgesundheit, 1939), p. 177; also Hien, *Chemische Industrie*, pp. 146–57.

182. Hermann Hebestreit, "Bedeutung und Zukunftsaufgaben der Arbeitsmedizin," *Zentralblatt für Gewerbehygiene* 18 (1941): 154–64.

183. Sepp Graessner, "Neue soziale Kontrolltechniken durch Arbeits- und Leistungsmedizin," in Baader and Schultz, *Medizin und Nationalsozialismus*, p. 149. The elderly for Haubold were "für das Gesamtvolk nicht mehr direkt nützliche[s] Leben"; see his "Statistik," p. 150.

CHAPTER 5
THE NAZI DIET

1. Cancer was already being blamed on improper diet during the First World War; see David Paul von Hansemann, "Beeinflusst der Krieg die Entstehung oder das Wachstum von Geschwülsten?" *Zeitschrift für Krebsforschung* 15 (1916): 492–516. Nutrition was a feature of Germany's otherwise Taylorist labor physiology in the 1920s; see Dietrich Milles, "Working Capacity and Calorie Consumption: The History of Rational Physical Economy," in *The Science and Culture of Nutrition, 1840–1940*, ed. Harmke Kamminga and Andrew Cunningham (Amsterdam: Rodopi, 1995), pp. 82–87.

2. Virchow, *Krankhafte Geschwülste*, 1:81–82.

3. Dormanns, "Die vergleichende geographisch-pathologische Reichs-Carcinomstatistik."

4. "Mitteilungen," *Monatsschrift für Krebsbekämpfung* 5 (1938): 328.

5. The SS paper *Schwarzes Korps* complained about German tourists "wolfing down whipped cream" in Viennese coffeehouses after the annexation of Austria; a pro-militarist slogan urged a choice between "Fighting Power" and "Whipped Cream" (*Schlagkraft oder Schlagobers!*); see George Davey Smith, S. A. Ströbele, and M. Egger, "Reply," *Journal of Epidemiology and Community Health* 51 (1997): 209.

6. Reichsjugendführung, *Du hast die Pflicht, gesund zu sein!*, Heft 3, *Gesund durch richtig Ernährung* (n.p.: Gesundheitsaktion der Hitler-Jugend, 1939), p. 22.

7. Kitzing, *Erziehung*, p. 220.

8. Liek, *Der Kampf*, p. 22.

9. Franz G. M. Wirz, *Gesunde und gesicherte Volksernährung* (Dresden: Müllersche Verlagshandlung, 1938), pp. 1–16.

10. Ibid.; compare Gumpert, *Heil Hunger!*, pp. 22–23.

11. See my *Racial Hygiene*, pp. 235–37. Mussolini was a bread enthusiast: a 1941 Hitler Youth health handbook recites several lines of doggerel from the Duce, praising bread as "das Herz des Hauses, den Duft des Tisches, das Freudezeichen des Herdes"; see Kitzing, *Erziehung*, p. 187.

12. Wirz, *Gesunde und gesicherte Volksernährung*, p. 17. The Weltmilch-Kongress, meeting in Berlin, had recently endorsed the consumption of skim milk (ibid.).

13. Will Kraft, *Deutschlands Nahrungsfreiheit* (Dresden: Müllersche Verlagshandlung, 1937).

14. Kortenhaus, "Krebs," p. 426. A number of influential "orthodox" physicians joined in this critique of the (Virchowian) idea of cancer as the product of local irritation, favoring instead the hypothesis of damage to the entire organism; see Ferdinand Sauerbruch and E. Knake, "Die Bedeutung von Sexualstörungen für die Entstehung von Geschwülsten," *Zeitschrift für Krebsforschung* 44 (1936): 223.

15. Friedrich Kortenhaus argued that replacing animal fats with plant oils would help prevent cancer; see his "Krebs," p. 441.

16. Reichsjugendführung, *Gesund durch richtige Ernährung*, vol. 3 of the *Gesundheitsaktion der Hitler-Jugend* (n.p., n.d.), pp. 15–18, 22–23.

17. The rise of Nazism complicated German vegetarianism: Nazism came under attack at the summer 1933 meeting of the International Vegetarian Union in Switzerland, prompting the German participants to withdraw from the international body. Ragnar Berg, a natural foods advocate at Dresden's Rudolf Hess Hospital, was invited to participate in the union's 1935 meeting in Denmark but refused, protesting its anti-German stance. Berg's protest reached Franz Wirz in Hess's office, who asked the police to detain two German delegates—both physicians—wanting to travel to the meeting. In July of that year, P. Orlowsky of the NSDAP's Hauptamt für Volksgesundheit traveled to the Stettiner Bahnhof to make the arrests, accompanied by two Kriminalbeamte. In his report, Orlowsky characterized the delegates as "eine negative Auslese . . . Männlein und Weiblein in phantastischen Aufzügen, mit Pappschachteln und Paketen beladen, der offizielle grüne Lodenmantel nicht zu vergessen. . . . Schillerkragen und lange Mähne taten das übrige, um zu zeigen, dass hier 'Urnatürliches Leben' am Werke ist" (Orlowsky to Wirz, July 7, 1935, Box 323 Folder 7, Deutsche Kongress-Zentrale, Hoover Institution Archives, hereafter DKZ, HIA). Germany's Verband deutscher Vegetarier-Vereine e.V. was headed by Karl Bartes of Eden bei Oranienburg; vegetarian literature was published by the Vegetarische Presse in Dresden.

18. Anna Goldfeder, "Ist Tomatensaft als krebserzeugender Faktor anzusehen?" *Zeitschrift für Krebsforschung* 40 (1934): 181–85.

19. Schüller, "Gibt es eine Prädisposition?" pp. 826–27; George H. Fink, *Cancer and Precancerous Changes* (London: Lewis, 1903); Hoffman, *Cancer and Diet*, p. 84.

20. Fritz Bodinus, *Der Schlüssel zur wirksamen Krebsbekämpfung* (Cologne: Ernst Stauf, 1937), pp. 60–82.

21. "Mitteilungen," *Monatsschrift für Krebsbekämpfung* 10 (1942): 99–100. Høgaard figured that the cancer-free Eskimos of Angmagssalik consumed a daily average of 300 grams of protein, 170 grams of fat, and less than 22 grams of carbohydrates (ibid.). Johannes Kretz's *krebsfeindliche Diät* advised the consumption of easily digestible proteins like fish, along with vitamins and few carbohydrates, while cautioning against animal fats, artificially colored or preserved foods, and coffee, alcohol, tobacco, and foods that are too hot or highly spiced; see his "Krebsfeindliche Diät," *Monatsschrift für Krebsbekämpfung* 9 (1941): 161–72.

22. Hans Truttwin, "Fleischerprophylaxe," *Monatsschrift für Krebsbekämpfung* 9 (1941): 57. The original French source is Jules Blier, "Une croyance populaire à propos du cancer," *Presse médicale* 43 (1935): 1514.

23. Hans Truttwin, "Krebs und Geschlechtlichkeit," *Wiener klinische Wochenschrift* 56 (1943): 28–31 and 49–54.

24. Victor E. Mertens, "Krebs der Fleischer," *Monatsschrift für Krebsbekämpfung* 10 (1942): 219–21. Mertens pointed out that the Arabs had once used meat as a form of cancer therapy, pressing raw chicken meat onto tumors as a compress (p. 219).

25. Druckrey, "Ergebnisse," p. 116.

26. Kitzing, *Erziehung*, p. 182.

27. Schenck, *Patient Hitler*, p. 27; the view was not uncommon in the organic medical community; see Werner Kollath, "Grundlagen einer dauerhaften Ernährungslehre," *Wiener medizinische Wochenschrift* 91 (1941): 158.

28. Paul Adloff, "Über die ursprüngliche Lebensweise des Menschen," *Deutsche zahnärztliche Wochenschrift* 43 (1940): 293–94.

29. Wirz, *Gesunde und gesicherte Volksernährung*, pp. 24, 11–13.

30. Cited in Gumpert, *Heil Hunger!*, p. 81, translation slightly modified.

31. Cited in ibid., p. 81.

32. Ibid., p. 77; the original source is Gertraud Fieck, "Vorratswirtschaft, eine ernährungspolitische Notwendigkeit," *Ärztin* 15 (1936): 204 ff.

33. Gumpert, *Heil Hunger!*, p. 83.

34. Goebbels, *Diaries*, p. 81 (entry for February 12, 1942).

35. Ada Petrova, "Tales from the 'Myth File,'" *Newsweek*, May 8, 1995, pp. 52–53.

36. Otto D. Tolischus, "At Home with the Führer," *New York Times*, May 30, 1937.

37. There is no mention of Hitler in Rynn Berry's *Famous Vegetarians and Their Favorite Recipes* (New York: Pythagorean Publishers, 1993).

38. Rudolf Diels, *Lucifer ante Portas* (Stuttgart: Deutsche Verlags-Anstalt, 1950), p. 84.

39. Schenck, *Patient Hitler*, pp. 27–28.

40. Diels, *Lucifer*, p. 82.

41. Robert G. L. Waite, *The Psychopathic God, Adolf Hitler* (New York: Basic Books, 1977), p. 19.

42. Cited in Arnold Arluke and Boria Sax, "Understanding Nazi Animal Protection and the Holocaust," *Anthrozoös* 5 (1992): 18.

43. Peter Viereck, *Metapolitics: The Roots of the Nazi Mind* (New York: Capricorn, 1961), p. 119.

44. Waite, *Psychopathic God*, p. 26.

45. Walter C. Langer, *The Mind of Adolf Hitler: The Secret Wartime Report* (New York: Basic Books, 1972), pp. 49–57; Arluke and Sax, "Understanding Nazi Animal Protection," p. 29 n. 6.

46. Langer, *Mind*, p. 170; Arluke and Sax, "Understanding Nazi Animal Protection," p. 29 n. 6; also Arnold Arluke and Boria Sax, "The Nazi Treatment of Animals and People," in *Reinventing Biology*, ed. Lynda Birke and Ruth Hubbard (Bloomington: Indiana University Press, 1995), pp. 228–60.

47. Picker, *Hitlers Tischgespräche*, pp. 438–39.

48. Thomas Fuchs, "Adolf's Rules," *Los Angeles Times*, December 21, 1986.

49. Waite, *Psychopathic God*, p. 19.

50. Hedwig Winzen to E. M. Hoppe, July 14, 1936, Reel 30, #383, United States Holocaust Museum Research Institute Archives.

51. Gustav Freiherr von Pohl, "Krankheiten durch Erdausstrahlungen: I. Mitteilung, Krebs," *Zeitschrift für Krebsforschung* 32 (1930): 597–604.

52. John Toland, *Adolf Hitler* (Garden City, N.Y.: Doubleday, 1976), p. 277. Hitler personally intervened on at least one occasion—in 1940—to support a scholar's (Gerhard Seeger's) work on the role of follicle hormones in the devel-

opment of cancer. We do not know why Seeger's research caught his eye (it involved the use of the newly invented electron microscope), but his offer of 500 RM per month does suggest he was paying some attention to cancer research. See Karl Brandt to Hans-Heinrich Lammers, 4.2.3.40 R43 II/1226b, Bundesarchiv Potsdam (hereafter BAP). We also have the testimony of the SS doctor Wilhelm Keppler in the Foreign Office, who on October 14, 1944 wrote to Himmler, "I know that the Führer is especially interested in the question of how to combat cancer" (Grawitz file, BDC).

53. The psychohistorian Rudolf Binion is the author of this oft-repeated speculation; see Schenck, *Patient Hitler*, pp. 518–24.

54. Felix Kersten, *The Kersten Memoirs: 1940–1945*, trans. C. Fitzgibbon and J. Oliver (New York: Macmillan, 1957), pp. 41–42, 294.

55. Schenck, *Patient Hitler*, p. 30.

56. Ernst-Günther Schenck, *Ich sah Berlin Sterben* (Herford: Nicolaische Verlagsbuchhandlung, 1970), p. 18.

57. Ibid., pp. 43–44.

58. Ibid., p. 44.

59. Ibid., pp. 44–45.

60. Schenck, *Patient Hitler*, p. 29.

61. Roger Manvell and Heinrich Fraenkel, *Hess: A Biography* (New York: Drake Publishers, 1973), pp. 64–65.

62. Helmut Heiber, *Goebbels*, trans. J. K. Dickinson (New York: Hawthorn, 1972), p. 232.

63. "Kleine Mitteilungen," *Vertrauensarzt und Krankenkasse* 5 (1937): 96.

64. The archives of the Deutscher Verein gegen den Missbrauch geistiger Getränke, later renamed the Deutscher Verein gegen den Alkoholismus, were destroyed by fire in 1944 or 1945. The best bibliography of early alcohol research is Mark Keller, ed., *International Bibliography of Studies on Alcohol* (New Brunswick, N.J.: Rutgers Center of Alcohol Studies, 1966). An earlier bibliography assembled by Emil Abderhalden (*Bibliographie der gesamten wissenschaftlichen Literatur über den Alkohol und den Alkoholismus* [Berlin: Urban & Schwarzenberg, 1904]) contains several dozen entries on the topic of human "spontaneous combustion."

65. "1883–1933: 50 Jahre Deutscher Verein gegen den Alkoholismus," *Auf der Wacht* 50 (1933): 18–20.

66. Geoffrey J. Giles, "Student Drinking in the Third Reich," in *Drinking: Behavior and Belief in Modern History*, ed. Susanna Barrows and Robin Room (Berkeley and Los Angeles: University of California Press, 1991), pp. 132–43.

67. Robert J. Karp et al., "Fetal Alcohol Syndrome at the Turn of the Twentieth Century," *Archives of Pediatrics and Adolescent Medicine* 149 (1995): 45–48.

68. See Brian Katcher, "The Post-Repeal Eclipse in Knowledge about the Harmful Effects of Alcohol," *Addiction* 88 (1993): 729–44; also Philip J. Pauly, "How Did the Effects of Alcohol on Reproduction Become Scientifically Uninteresting?" *Journal of the History of Biology* 29 (1996): 1–28.

69. Hermann Häberlin, "Ueber Verbreitung und Aetiologie des Magenkrebses," *Deutsches Archiv für klinische Medizin* 44 (1889): 475–76 and 496–99; a

good review is Christoph Ludewig, *Beiträge zur Statistik des Speiseröhrenkrebses* (Göttingen: Med. diss., 1905).

70. Karl B. Lehmann, *Kurzes Lehrbuch der Arbeits- und Gewerbehygiene* (Leipzig: S. Hirzel, 1919), pp. 58–59.

71. Staemmler, "Beruf und Krebs," p. 122.

72. Schüller, "Gibt es eine Prädisposition?" p. 829.

73. Hans Doerfler, "Zur Frage der Vererbbarkeit des Krebses," *Monatsschrift für Krebsbekämpfung* 10 (1942): 45.

74. Liek, *Der Kampf*, p. 21.

75. "Stand im Zeichen des Alkoholverbotes," *Auf der Wacht* 50 (1933): 38 and 77; Giles, "Student Drinking," p. 134.

76. Werner Bracht and Wilhelm Messer, *Alkohol Volk Staat*, 3d ed. (Berlin: Reichsgesundheitsverlag, 1941), p. 34. Hitler's remarks were first published in the *Völkischer Beobachter* on March 31, 1926. Commenting on his speech, the editors noted that the Führer had not intended to deny a comrade his occasional glass of beer but simply wanted to indicate "how easily a man forgets his duty under the influence of alcohol." Hitler once claimed to have given up alcohol in 1905, after drinking himself into a stupor celebrating his Realschule graduation; during the Second World War he sometimes drank beer to put himself to sleep, though he apparently worried that this would make him fat (Schenck, *Patient Hitler*, p. 33).

77. Prof. Dr. Immanuel Gonser, "Zeitwende!" *Auf der Wacht* 50 (1933): 37. Gonser had directed the Antialcoholism Association for more than thirty years; he was replaced in 1937 by Ernst Bauer.

78. "Von der goldenen Jubiläumsfeier unseres Vereins," *Auf der Wacht* 50 (1933): 78–80. The "Führer" of the new organization was Fritz Bartels; the chair was Immanuel Gonser; see *Vertrauensarzt* 1 (1933): 72. The Reichsstelle gegen die Alkohol- und Tabakgefahren, based in Berlin-Dahlem, grew out of the older Deutscher Verein gegen den Alkoholismus; the new organization eventually swallowed up most of Germany's religious temperance organizations. The Reichsstelle was organized in typical Nazi fashion, with a Gaustelle in all Gauen and a Kreisstelle in all Kreisen; the leaders in each region are listed in "Gaue der Reichsstelle gegen die Alkohol- und Tabakgefahren," *Auf der Wacht* 57 (1940): 60–62. The bureau was mainly involved in propaganda but was also involved in coordinating distribution of alcohol-free drinks, supervising ads, administering the state's three hundred Trinkerberatungsstelle and three hundred Trinkerfürsorgestelle, and so forth. On pre-Nazi organizations, see Christian Stubbe, "Deutscher Verein gegen den Alkoholismus 1883–1933," *Auf der Wacht* 50 (1933): 1–3 and 18–20.

79. Max Fischer, "Die Alkoholgefahr," *Öffentlicher Gesundheitsdienst* 1 (1935): 202–4.

80. "Berichte," *Öffentlicher Gesundheitsdienst* 1 (1935): 202–4; *Die Genussgifte* 35 (1939): 57, 65.

81. "Stand im Zeichen des Alkoholverbotes," *Auf der Wacht* 50 (1933): 38, 77.

82. Bracht and Messer, *Alkohol Volk Staat*, pp. 26–28.

83. Ibid., pp. 14–16. There were 266,400 traffic accidents in Germany in 1937, and 10,014 traffic deaths in 1935. According to police records, 5,600 of the

nation's 8,000 annual traffic fatalities were associated with alcohol in the period 1934–1937 (ibid.).

84. *Auf der Wacht* 54 (1937): 54.

85. "Mitteilungen," *Öffentlicher Gesundheitsdienst* 7 (1941): 336.

86. Kitzing, *Erziehung*, pp. 194–95; compare Heinrich Hunke, "Rede des Präsidenten des Werberates der deutschen Wirtschaft," in *Volksgesundheit und Werbung*, ed. Werberat der deutschen Wirtschaft (Berlin: Carl Heymanns, 1939), pp. 42–43.

87. Hans Reiter and Wilhelm Heupke, *Obst und flüssiges Obst in der Volksernährung und Krankenbehandlung* (Berlin: Wacht-Verlag, 1938).

88. Jeremy Noakes, "Nazism and Eugenics: The Background to the Nazi Sterilization Law of 14 July 1933," in *Ideas into Politics*, ed. R. J. Bullen, H. Pogge von Strandmann, and A. B. Polonsky (Totowa, N.J.: Humana, 1984), p. 80.

89. Ernst Sprungmann, "Die Bedeutung der Neuregelung des staatlichen Gesundheitswesens," *Öffentlicher Gesundheitsdienst* 1 (1935): 578.

90. Verschuer, *Erbpathologie*, p. 178.

91. "Bierverbrauch im Deutschen Reich," *Vertrauensarzt* 6 (1938): 157.

92. Gumpert, *Heil Hunger!*, pp. 33–37.

93. Arthur Gütt, "Öffentliches Gesundheitswesen und Vierjahresplan," *Öffentlicher Gesundheitsdienst* 3 (1937): 211–12.

94. Werberat, *Volksgesundheit und Werbung*, p. 9. Insurance officials pointed out that drinkers cost much more to insure than nondrinkers, owing to their increased risk from heart disease (*Bierherz*), cancer, diabetes, and many other ailments; see Ferdinand Sauerbruch, Fritz Lickint, and Ernst Gabriel, *Arzt, Alkohol und Tabak* (Berlin: Reichsgesundheitsverlag, 1940), pp. 14–15.

95. Kitzing, *Erziehung*, p. 232.

96. Kleine, *Ernährungsschäden als Krankheitsursachen*, p. 34.

97. Gumpert, *Heil Hunger!*, p. 36.

98. Bracht and Messer, *Alkohol Volk Staat*, pp. 31–32.

99. Cited in ibid., p. 34.

100. Friedlander, *Origins of Nazi Genocide*; Wolfgang Ayass, *"Asoziale" im Nationalsozialismus* (Stuttgart: Klett-Cotta, 1995).

101. Gumpert, *Heil Hunger!*, p. 38.

102. In 1938, Hermann Göring sold his Four-Year Plan to Bavarians by promising a "considerable increase in beer production"; see ibid., p. 40.

103. Goebbels, *Diaries*, pp. 64, 82.

104. Kitzing, *Erziehung*, pp. 230–31.

105. George Reid, "Die Bedeutung der Genussgifte Alkohol und Nikotin für den menschlichen Körper," in *Die Gesundheitsführung der Jugend*, ed. Robert Hördemann and Gerhard Joppich (Munich: Lehmann, 1939), p. 314.

106. Kitzing, *Erziehung*, pp. 231–32.

107. Hermann Druckrey, "Kaffeeröstprodukte und Krebs," *Medizinische Klinik* 35 (1939): 614–15. Similar objections had been raised against Roffo's claims to have proven the carcinogenicity of tobacco tars in laboratory experiments: Ernest Kennaway of England charged that Roffo had burned his tobacco at too high a temperature, producing tars that would never have been produced through the ordinary act of smoking.

108. Sauerbruch, Lickint, and Gabriel, *Arzt, Alkohol und Tabak*, p. 11.

109. Karl Heinz Roth, "Leistungsmedizin: Das Beispiel Pervitin," in *Ärzte im Nationalsozialismus*, ed. Fridolf Kudlien (Cologne: Kiepenheuer & Witsch, 1985).

110. C. Püllen, "Bedeutung des Pervitin für die Chirurgie," *Chirurg* 13 (1939): 485 ff.

111. *Trials of War Criminals*, 1:633.

112. Hans Zimmermann, *Zur Frage der Wirkung von Pervitin auf Konzentrationsleistungen* (Dortmund: Med. diss., 1946).

113. "Berliner Medizinische Gesellschaft," *Klinische Wochenschrift* 23 (1944): 178. Interest in these particular experiments—conducted at Buchenwald—seems to have been generated by suspicion that an SS officer by the name of Koehler had died from a deliberate act of poisoning. One theory was that a South American poison had been used (curare?); another was that Pervitin in combination with a narcotic had been used. Experiments were undertaken to determine whether taking both drugs in combination could be fatal; see *Trials of War Criminals*, 1:691–92.

114. Martin Lee, *Acid Dreams: The CIA, LSD, and the Sixties Rebellion* (New York: Grove Weidenfeld, 1987), p. 17.

115. Gerhard Kärber, "Schlafmittelmissbrauch," *Reichs-Gesundheitsblatt* 14 (1939): 537–39.

116. Hans F. Michaelis, "Über die Wirkung einer warmen Mahlzeit auf die Leistungsfähigkeit von Frauen bei Nachtarbeit," *Arbeitsphysiologie* 12 (1942): 134–41.

117. Bernhard Schlegel and Heinrich Böttner, "Experimenteller Beitrag zur Ernährung bei Hitzeeinwirkung auf den menschlichen Organismus," *Die Ernährung* 6 (1941): 177–85.

118. Konrad Lang, "Ernährung," in Ernst Rodenwaldt et al., *Hygiene. Part I: General Hygiene* (Wiesbaden: Dieterich'sche Verlagsbuchhandlung, 1948), pp. 121–23.

119. Ibid., pp. 121–22.

120. Heinrich Kraut and Herbert Bramsel, "Der Calorienbedarf der Berufe," *Arbeitsphysiologie* 12 (1942): 197–221.

121. Lang, "Ernährung," p. 123.

122. Eduard Schratz, " 'Deutscher Tee': Was er sein sollte und was er ist," *Die Deutsche Heilpflanze* 6 (1940): 112 ff.

123. Hans Geith, "Ratschläge für das Heilkräutersammeln mit Schulkinder," *Die Deutsche Heilpflanze—Beilage*, March 1936, p. 53.

124. Andreas Hock, "Die Zusammensetzung des Kaninchendepotfettes nach Verfütterung eines gesättigen Fettes mit teilweise ungerader Kohlenstoffatomzahl," *Die Ernährung* 6 (1941): 278–81; Lang, "Ernährung."

125. Lang, "Ernährung," pp. 129–31.

126. Karl Glässer, "Die möglichst restlose Verwertung des Schlachttierblutes zur menschlichen Ernährung," *Berliner und Münchener Tierärztliche Wochenschrift*, July 12, 1940, pp. 333–36.

127. Henry Huttenbach, "The Myth of Nazi Human Soap," *Holocaust and Genocide Newsletter*, February 1995, pp. 1–2.

128. E. W. Hope et al., *Industrial Hygiene and Medicine* (London: Ballière, 1923).

129. This list derives partly from a paper read by Alfred Neumann of Vienna at the 1933 International Cancer Congress in Madrid, cited in Hoffman, *Cancer and Diet*, p. 100.

130. Hoffman, *Cancer and Diet*. By 1942, German insurance officials recognized dietary therapy as a compensable form of cancer therapy.

131. Felix Mandl, *Theorie und Praxis der Krebskrankheit* (Vienna: Wilhelm Maudrich, 1932); Otto Buchinger, *Das Heilfasten und seine Hilfsmethoden als biologischer Weg*, 2d ed. (Stuttgart: Hippokrates, 1935).

132. Liek, *Der Kampf*, p. 204; Hoffman, *Cancer and Diet*, pp. 393–400.

133. Hoffman, *Cancer and Diet*, pp. 70–90; a good German review is Carl Lewin, *Die Ätiologie der bösartigen Geschwülste* (Berlin: Springer, 1928).

134. Hoffman, *Cancer and Diet*, pp. 81–86, 245. The allergy theory is developed by G. Hager in his "Krebsentstehung," *Medizinische Welt* 12 (1938).

135. Hoffman, *Cancer and Diet*, pp. 79–93.

136. Hans Auler, "Über die Wartung und Behandlung Krebskranker," *Monatsschrift für Krebsbekämpfung* 1 (1933): 28–30, 61–63, 101–5, 160–65, 208–11, 261–66. Auler claimed that the salt-free diet popularized by Max Gerson actually promoted tumor growth. Gerson's diet involved eating lots of raw fruits and vegetables; in the 1930s it also became known as the Sauerbruch-Herrmannsdorfer-Gerson diet.

137. Max Rubner did not even mention vitamins in his 1916 review of Germany's wartime nutritional situation; see his *Deutschlands Volksernährung im Kriege* (Leipzig: Naturwissenschaften, 1916).

138. John R. Loofbourow, "Vitamin D," *Bulletin of Basic Science Research* 3 (1931): 101 ff.

139. Joachim Kühnau, "Probleme der Vitamin-Terminologie," *Zeitschrift für Vitaminforschung* 1 (1932): 184–91.

140. Arthur Scheunert, "Gemüse als Vitaminquelle," *Deutsche medizinische Wochenschrift* 57 (1931): 835.

141. Soer, *Wieviel Vitamin D ist zur Heilung und zur Vorbeugung von Rachitis notwendig* (Leiden: Med. diss., 1931).

142. E. Glanzmann and T. Gordonoff, "Zur Einführung," *Zeitschrift für Vitaminforschung* 1 (1932): 1.

143. A 1939 article in the Swiss medical weekly showed that cancer patients suffered deficits of vitamin C; the conclusion drawn from this was that vitamin supplements should be given to anyone suffering from the disease; see Silvio Antes and Clemente Molo, "Zur C-Bilanz bei Geschwulstkranken," *Schweizerische medizinische Wochenschrift* 69 (1939): 619–23.

144. Wilhelm Caspari, "Hormone, Vitamine und Krebs," *Arbeiten aus dem Institut für experimentelle Therapie* 27 (1933): 13 ff.

145. Wilhelm Caspari, "Über Ernährung der Krebskranken," *Fortschritte der Therapie* 9 (1933): 129.

146. Fränkel and Gereb, "Wachstumstendenz maligner Tumoren und Vitamin," *Zeitschrift für Krebsforschung* 38 (1933); 524 ff.; Leo von Gordon, "Vitamine und Krebs," *Zeitschrift für Krebsforschung* 38 (1933): 398–408.

147. Borst, *Streiflichter*, p. 7. Official skepticism did little, however, to stop the vitamin craze: during the war, vitamins were distributed at schools and factories, and Robert Ley launched a "vitamin operation" to improve the performance of workers on the job.

148. Scott Podolsky, "Cultural Divergence: Elie Metchnikoff's *Bacillus bulgaricus* Therapy and His Underlying Concept of Health," *Bulletin of the History of Medicine* 72 (1998): 1–27.

149. Friedrich Burgkhardt, "Die zusätzliche biologische Behandlung des Krebses mit hochwertigen Kolistämmen (Mutaflor) und Leberextrakten," *Monatsschrift für Krebsbekämpfung* 9 (1941): 98. Burgkhardt's "cancer-fighting diet" barred heavy animal fats, along with alcohol, salt, nicotine, and hot spices. Butter, milk, and plant fats were permitted, however (p. 109).

150. See, for example, Hugo von Tietzen und Hennig, "Eine Lanze für Mutaflor," *Hippokrates* 8 (1937): 495–96.

151. Martin Weiser, "Mutaflor und Karzinom," *Monatsschrift für Krebsbekämpfung* 10 (1942): 101–9.

152. Wilhelm Heupke, *Die Faeces des Menschen* (Dresden: Steinkopff, 1939).

153. Tomizo Yoshida, "Experimenteller Beitrag zur Frage der Epithelmetaplasie," *Archiv für pathologische Anatomie und Physiologie* 283 (1932): 29–40; Takaoki Sasaki and Tomizo Yoshida, "Experimentelle Erzeugung des Leberkarcinoms durch Fütterung mit o-Amidoazotoluol," *Archiv für pathologische Anatomie und Physiologie* 295 (1935): 175–200; also Bauer, "Fortschritte," pp. 158–60.

154. Riojun Kinosita, "Studies on the Cancerogenic Chemical Substances," *Transactions of the Japanese Pathology Society* 27 (1937): 665–727.

155. Norbert Brock, Hermann Druckrey, and Herwig Hamperl, "Die Erzeugung von Leberkrebs durch den Farbstoff 4-Dimethylamino-azobenzol," *Zeitschrift für Krebsforschung* 50 (1940): 431–56.

156. There is extensive documentation on Druckrey's work in R73/10785–10787, Bundesarchiv Koblenz (hereafter BAK). As late as July 1944 Druckrey was awarded RM 12,000 for his research on experimental carcinogenesis (Mentzel and Blome to Druckrey, July 28, 1944, R73/10787, BAK); after the war, he headed up the DFG's Farbstoffkommission, established in 1949 to explore the carcinogenicity of food dyes (Wagner and Mauerberger, *Krebsforschung*, p. 230).

157. Adolf Butenandt, "Neuere Beiträge der biologischen Chemie zum Krebsproblem," in Butenandt et al., *Chemie und Krebs*, pp. 36–37.

158. V. Bülow-Schwarte to Auswärtiges Amt, July 25, 1939, R18/3656, BAK.

159. René Reding, "Des dangers de cancérisation résultant de l'emploi de colorants dans l'alimentation et en thérapeutique," *Acta Unio Internationalis Contra Cancrum* 4 (1939): 735–53.

160. Hermann Druckrey, "Bericht an das Reichsgesundheitsamt," September, 13, 1939; and Reiter to Reichsminister des Innern (hereafter RMI), October 21, 1939, R18/3656, BAK. The *Lebensmittelgesetze* (Food Laws) of 1927 and 1936 had limited hazardous colorings in foods but made no mention of cancer; see *Reichsgesetzblatt* 1 (1927): 134–37 and *Reichsgesetzblatt* 1 (1936): 18–22.

161. Wiedel to Volksgesundheitsamt, August 6, 1941, R18/3656, BAK.

162. Reiter to RMI, January 6, 1943, R18/3656, BAK.

163. K. H. Bauer to RMI, January 26, 1943, R18/3656, BAK.

164. Reiter's letter is mentioned in I. G. Farben to Melior, November 19, 1939, BAK, R18/3656. Farben sold dyes worth seven million reichsmarks in 1942; see K. H. Bauer to RMI, January 26, 1943, R18/3656, BAK.

165. Eberhard Gross, *Berufskrebs und Krebsforschung* (Cologne: Westdeutscher Verlag, 1955), p. 34.

166. Reiter to RMI, February 28, 1941, R18/3656, BAK. By 1940, twelve different I. G. Farben dyes were under study at Reiter's request; researchers included the staff at Druckrey's laboratory in Berlin, but also Robert Bierich at the Institut für Krebsforschung in Hamburg, Prof. Richard Labes at Jena's Pharmakologische Anstalt, Prof. Karl Zipf at the Pharmakologisches Institut of Königsberg, and several others (Reiter to RMI, January 10, 1940, R18/3656, BAK).

167. On June 19, 1944, for example, the Hauptvereinigung der Milch-, Fett- und Eierwirtschaft issued regulations on colorings in cheese; see the *Reichs-Gesundheitsblatt* 19 (1944): 373.

168. Reiter to RMI, February 20, 1943, R18/3656, BAK.

169. Reiter to RMI, June 30, 1943, R18/3565, BAK.

170. Baumgartner to RMI, December 8, 1941, R18/3656, BAK.

171. Johannes Kretz, "Gegen die missbräuchliche Verwendung krebsgefährlicher Teerfarbstoffe (Azofarbstoffe) in den Lebensmitteln," *Hippokrates* 15 (1944): 127–28. Kretz and others assumed that the harmful effects of the dyes came from their disruption of protein metabolism; DNA was not yet recognized as the molecular basis of heredity, and many people assumed that proteins would turn out to be the key regulators of carcinogenesis. Carcinogens like butter yellow were often said to work by impairing cellular respiration, and it was not until the 1950s that this theory was replaced by the DNA mutation theory.

172. K. H. Bauer to Paul Rostock, Reichskommissar des Führers für das Sanitäts- und Gesundheitswesen, November 9, 1944, R18/3656, BAK.

173. Theodor J. Bürgers, "Wasserhygiene," in Rodenwaldt et al., *Hygiene*, pp. 89–94.

174. Ordinances of February 1, 1939, and February 27, 1939, barred the use of saccharine in foods unless special permission was obtained from the Interior Ministry. Food products containing the artificial sweetener also had to be clearly labeled to that effect; see *Reichsgesetzblatt* 1 (1939): 111 and 336; Walther Fromme, "Öffentlicher Gesundheitsdienst," in Rodenwaldt et al., *Hygiene*, p. 27. Eberhard Schairer, a leading pathologist and tobacco researcher (see chapter 6), during the war began an effort to explore the cancer-causing potency of saccharine, though it is not clear what conclusions were reached (George Davey Smith, personal communication).

175. Gumpert, *Heil Hunger!*

176. Heinz Faulstich, *Von der Irrenfürsorge zur "Euthanasie": Geschichte der badischen Psychiatrie bis 1945* (Freiburg: Lambertus, 1993), pp. 206–7.

177. Horst Dickel, "Alltag in einer Landesheilanstalt im Nationalsozialis-

mus: das Beispiel Eichberg," in *Euthanasie in Hadamar: Die nationalsozialistische Vernichtungspolitik in hessischen Anstalten*, ed. Landeswohlfahrtsverband Hessen (Kassel: LWV, 1991), p. 106.

178. Burleigh, *Death and Deliverance*, pp. 240–47.

179. Gumpert, *Heil Hunger!*, pp. 13, 54–57, 77.

180. Terry Charman, *The German Home Front 1939–1945* (London: Barrie & Jenkins, 1989), p. 47.

181. Goebbels, *Diaries*, pp. 145–46.

182. George Davey Smith, S. A. Ströbele, and M. Egger, "Reply," *Journal of Epidemiology and Community Health* 51 (1997): 209; John Ardagh, *Germany and the Germans*, 3d ed. (London: Penguin, 1995), p. 212.

CHAPTER 6
THE CAMPAIGN AGAINST TOBACCO

1. This chapter is a revised version of my article "The Nazi War on Tobacco: Ideology, Evidence, and Public Health Consequences," *Bulletin of the History of Medicine* 71 (1997): 435–88.

2. Daniel J. Kevles, "Blowing Smoke," *New York Times Book Review*, May 12, 1996, p. 13; Richard Kluger, *Ashes to Ashes: America's Hundred-Year Cigarette War, the Public Health, and the Unabashed Triumph of Philip Morris* (New York: Alfred A. Knopf, 1996). The most commonly cited studies are four published in 1950: Ernst L. Wynder and Evarts A. Graham, "Tobacco Smoking as a Possible Etiologic Factor in Bronchiogenic Carcinoma," *JAMA* 143 (1950): 329–336; Richard Doll and A. Bradford Hill, "Smoking and Carcinoma of the Lung. Preliminary Report," *British Medical Journal* 2 (1950): 739–48; Robert Schrek et al., "Tobacco Smoking as an Etiologic Factor of Disease. I. Cancer," *Cancer Research* 10 (1950): 49–58; and Morton L. Levin, Hyman Goldstein, and Paul R. Gerhardt, "Cancer and Tobacco Smoking. A Preliminary Report," *JAMA* 143 (1950): 336–38. These are followed by Ernst Wynder's animal experimental work and the large prospective studies by E. Cuyler Hammond of the American Cancer Society in the United States and by Richard Doll and A. Bradford Hill of Oxford and London: see Ernst L. Wynder et al., "Experimental Production of Carcinoma with Cigarette Tar," *Cancer Research* 13 (1953): 855–64; E. Cuyler Hammond and Daniel Horn, "Smoking and Death Rates—Report on Forty-four Months of Follow-up of 187,783 Men," *JAMA* 166 (1958): 1159–72; Richard Doll and A. Bradford Hill, "Lung Cancer and Other Causes of Death in Relation to Smoking," *British Medical Journal* 2 (1956): 1071–81.

3. Edgar Bejach, *Die tabakgegnerische Bewegung in Deutschland mit Berücksichtigung der ausserdeutschen Tabakgegnerbewegungen* (Berlin: Med. diss., 1927), pp. 3–4. Tobacco had been peddled as a therapeutic agent in Braunschweiger pharmacies as early as 1598, and Bejach records an advertisement for the herb as a "Wunderkraut" at a Frankfurt trade fair of 1582 (p. 3).

4. Henner Hess, *Rauchen: Geschichte, Geschäfte, Gefahren* (Frankfurt: Campus, 1987), p. 20. Hess notes that the world's first known tobacco ban, enacted in 1575, prohibited smoking in Mexican churches (p. 23).

5. Bejach, *Die tabakgegnerische Bewegung*, pp. 1–7. Eugen Dühring, Engels's antisemitic nemesis, opposed tobacco as "unclean"; see Frederick Engels, *Anti-Dühring* (New York: International Publishers, 1939), p. 130.

6. The Bund Deutscher Tabakgegner, publisher of *Der Tabakgegner*, was established in Dresden-Bühlau in 1912; that same year an Alkohol- und Tabakgegnerverein was established in Hanover, headed by Hermann Stanger; the Graz organization was headed by a Dr. Meister. In May of 1914 an "Internationale Anti-Tabak-Liga" was founded with German, Austrian, Danish, and Swedish representation; the league organized antitobacco congresses after the war. See Bejach, *Die tabakgegnerische Bewegung*, pp. 3–4; Egon Caeser Conte Corti, *Die trockene Trunkenheit: Ursprung, Kampf und Triumph des Rauchens* (Leipzig: Insel, 1930); and Richard Bretschneider, ed., *Der Weltbund der Tabakgegner (Internationale Anti-Tabak Liga): Vorgeschichte, Gründung und Entwicklung* (Dresden: Emil Pahl, 1939). The Bund Deutscher Tabakgegner was moved to Berlin in 1936 and renamed the Deutscher Bund zur Bekämpfung der Tabakgefahren, where it was attached to the Reichsarbeitsgemeinschaft für Rauschgiftbekämpfung.

7. John C. Burnham, *Bad Habits: Drinking, Smoking, Taking Drugs, Gambling, Sexual Misbehavior, and Swearing in American History* (New York: New York University Press, 1993).

8. *Die Genussgifte*, for example, was published from 1904 to 1938 under the title *Die Alkoholfrage*; after 1940, the journal was titled *Die Volksgifte*. *Auf der Wacht* was subtitled *Amtliche Organ der Reichsstelle gegen Alkohol und Tabakgefahren*, combining both alcohol and tobacco temperance. This last-named journal was published by the Wacht Verlag, which also published the *Wacht-Zeitschrift: Kampfblatt gegen den Missbrauch des Alkohols*; *Garungslose Früchteverwertung*; and the *Blätter für praktische Alkoholgefährdeten-Arbeit*. In 1937, the print run for Wacht Verlag journals was 310,000. In 1940, the publishing house became a division of the Reichsgesundheitsverlag.

9. Robert E. Gaupp, Emil Kraepelin, Emil Abderhalden, and Adolf von Strümpell, "An die Deutsche Ärzteschaft," *Münchener medizinische Wochenschrift* 68 (1921): 832.

10. Bejach, *Die tabakgegnerische Bewegung*, p. 6.

11. Louis Lewin, *Phantastica: Die betäubenden und erregenden Genussmittel* (Berlin: Georg Stilke, 1924), pp. 320–21.

12. Hofstätter, *Die rauchende Frau*; compare his equally paternalistic *Die arbeitende Frau: Ihre wirtschaftliche Lage, Gesundheit, Ehe und Mutterschaft* (Vienna: M. Perles, 1929).

13. Gilman, *Freud*, p. 176.

14. Boehncke, "Tabak und Volksgesundheit," pp. 625–30.

15. See my *Racial Hygiene*, pp. 228, 239–40.

16. Corti, *Die trockene Trunkenheit*; Walter Hermannsen, "Erzieher und Erzieherin! Ein Wort an Euch!" *Die Genussgifte* 35 (1939): 74–75; Fritz Lickint, "Nikotinmissbrauch und Nikotinismus," *Zahnärztliche Mitteilungen* 30 (1939): 306–9. Otto Neustätter, an Austrian socialist, characterized smoking as "lung masturbation" in his "Zur Frage des Lungenrauchens," *Münchener medizinische Wochenschrift* 78 (1931): 794. The expression "dry drunkenness" dates from the

NOTES TO PAGES 179–81   327

satire of the Jesuit poet (and smoker) Jakob Balde: *Truckene Trunkenheit: Straff-rede wider den Missbrauch des Tabaks* (Nuremberg: Michael Endter, 1658); for background, see Sigmund von Birken, *Die Truckene Trunkenheit*, ed. Karl Pörnbacher (Munich: Köel, 1967).

17. Conti's words were spoken at a May 25, 1939, Berlin meeting sponsored by the Werberat der deutschen Wirtschaft; see *Volksgesundheit und Werbung*, pp. 7–10.

18. Blaich, "Nazi Race Hygiene," p. 15.

19. John Hill, *Cautions against the Immoderate Use of Snuff* (London, 1761), pp. 27–38; Samuel T. von Soemmerring, *De morbis vasorum absorbentium corporis humani* (Frankfurt, 1795), p. 109. Joannes Jacobus Holland appears to have been the first to propose a link between smoking and cancer, in his *Dissertatio inauguralis medico-chirurgica sistens carcinoma labii inferioris absque sectione persanatum* (Rinteln, 1739).

20. Juraj Körbler, "Thomas Harriot (1560–1621), fumeur de pipe, victime du cancer?" *Gesnerus* 9 (1952): 52–54.

21. Etienne-Frédéric Bouisson, *Tribut à la chirurgie*, vol. 1 (Paris: Baillière, 1858), pp. 259–303. A good early statistical review of the role of tobacco in cancers of the mouth, lips, and esophagus is Hugo H. Ahlbom's "Prädisponierende Faktoren für Plattenepithelkarzinom in Mund, Hals und Speiseröhre: Eine statistische Untersuchung am Material des Radiumhemmets, Stockholm," *Acta Radiologica* 18 (1937): 163–85. Sigmund Freud, who contracted cancer of the mouth in 1923 and eventually died of the disease, in 1924 and again in 1939 attributed his malady to his fondness for cigars; see Gilman, *Freud*, pp. 175 and 177.

22. Friedrich Tiedemann, *Geschichte des Tabaks* (Frankfurt: H. L. Brönner, 1854), p. 371.

23. Michael Kaminsky, *Ein primäres Lungencarcinom mit verhornten Plattenepithelien* (Greifswald: Med. diss, 1898).

24. Isaac Adler, *Primary Malignant Growths of the Lungs and Bronchi* (New York: Longmans, Green, and Co., 1912), p. 3.

25. Georg A. Brongers, *Nicotiana Tabacum: The History of Tobacco and Tobacco Smoking in the Netherlands* (Amsterdam: H.J.W. Becht's, 1964), pp. 228–29. At the Paris World Exhibition of 1867, a machine capable of rolling 3,600 cigarettes per hour was exhibited; see Paul Seufert, *Der Feldzug gegen die Zigarette* (Basel: Ernst Reinhardt, 1964), p. 33. By 1933, a high-speed rolling machine in Dresden operated by only three or four workers could produce 400,000 cigarettes per day; see "Allgemeine Tabakgegner-Umschau," *Deutscher Tabakgegner* 17 (1935): 17. The Philip Morris factory in Concord, North Carolina, today produces more than twice that many cigarettes *every hour*; see Christian Tenbrock, "Glimmstengel mit Batterie," *Die Zeit*, March 31, 1995, p. 39.

26. "Rauchen: Wie Gut," *Der Spiegel*, January 22, 1964, p. 63.

27. Hess, *Rauchen*, p. 49.

28. Anton Bock, "Das Lungenrauchen," *Vertrauensarzt* 6 (1938): 155–56.

29. See, for example, Kurt Wolf, "Der primäre Lungenkrebs," *Fortschritte der Medicin* 13 (1895): 725–38, and the references cited in my "Nazi War on Tobacco," pp. 444–45. The turning point in the acceptance of an increase was the

1923 congress of the German pathological society, where several participants (Berblinger, Teutschlaender, Askanazy, Fahr, Kraus, Mathias, Mönckeberg, and Versé) conceded the reality of the increase; see the *Verhandlungen der deutschen pathologischen Gesellschaft* 19 (1923): 190–92. On Leipzig's increase, see Carly Seyfarth, "Lungenkarzinome in Leipzig," *Deutsche medizinische Wochenschrift* 50 (1924): 1497–99; and more generally, Milton B. Rosenblatt, "Lung Cancer in the Nineteenth Century," *Bulletin of the History of Medicine* 38 (1964): 412–13.

30. A good review can be found in Hueper's *Occupational Tumors*, pp. 369–468. On the gas warfare theory, see Fritz Reiche, "Zur Genese der Bronchialkrebse und ihre Beziehungen zu Kampfgasschädigungen," *Medizinische Welt* 6 (1932): 1013–14; on the street dust and road tar inhalation theory, see P. Hampeln, "Häufigkeit und Ursache des primären Lungenkarzinoms," *Mitteilungen aus den Grenzgebieten der Medizin und Chirurgie* 36 (1923): 145–50. For the racial mixing thesis, see Jens Paulsen's correspondence as cited in Hildebrandt's *Rassenmischung*, p. 102. Walter Kikuth claimed that X-rays might be responsible for the increase; see his "Über Lungencarcinom," pp. 107–28. Schönherr believed that increasing automobile traffic was responsible for the growing lung cancer rates in Chemnitz; see his "Beitrag," p. 450, also pp. 443–44 for his discussion of the malnutrition hypothesis. Walther Berblinger in Jena in 1925 discussed mine gases, chemo-toxic inflammation, and smoking, but decided that irritating influenza germs from the recent pandemic were the most likely cause of the increase; he therefore predicted that lung cancer rates would eventually decline. See his "Die Zunahme des primären Lungenkrebses in den Jahren 1920–1924," *Klinische Wochenschrift* 4 (1925): 913–16. Edgar Bejach did not mention lung cancer in his 1927 survey of German antitobacco movements (*Die tabakgegnerische Bewegung*).

31. Franz Herz, "Hat das Lungenkarzinom an Häufigkeit zugenommen?" *Medizinische Klinik* 26 (1930): 1666–69. Pfeil endorsed Herz's view in his 1935 "Lungentumoren," pp. 1198–99.

32. Hintze, "Kultur und Krebs," p. 62.

33. Cigarettes began to come under suspicion in the mid-1920s; see, for example, Robert Probst, "Die Häufigkeit des Lungencarcinoms," *Zeitschrift für Krebsforschung* 25 (1927): 431. A good overview of tobacco hazards research circa 1930 is Friedrich Schmetz, *Das Tabakrauchen im Lichte der öffentlichen Gesundheitspflege* (Berlin: Schoetz, 1930). A brilliant early critique of nontobacco explanations for the rise of lung cancer, based on experience from Cracow, is Adam Syrek, "Zur Häufigkeitszunahme des Lungenkrebses," *Zeitschrift für Krebsforschung* 36 (1932): 409–15.

34. Hermann Tillmanns does not mention lung cancer in his "Ueber Theer-, Russ- und Tabakkrebs," *Deutsche Zeitschrift für Chirurgie* 13 (1880): 519–35; nor does Hans Pässler in his "Ueber das primäre Carcinom der Lunge," *Archiv für pathologische Anatomie und Physiologie* 145 (1896): 191–278.

35. Joseph Cortyl, *Du cancer des fumeurs* (Paris: Med. diss., 1897). The expression *cancer des fumeurs* was borrowed from Bouisson's 1861 *Tribut*.

36. Hermann Rottmann, *Über primäre Lungencarcinome* (Würzberg: Med. diss., 1898), pp. 29, 52. Härting and Hesse failed to mention tobacco as a pos-

sible cause of the *Schneeberger Krankheit* (uranium miners' lung cancer), favoring arsenic, instead, as the guilty party (radiation is now the recognized culprit).

37. Fritz Lickint, "Tabak und Tabakrauch als ätiologischer Factor des Carcinoms," *Zeitschrift für Krebsforschung* 30 (1929): 349–65; compare also the fascinating review and response by Victor E. Mertens, "Zigarettenrauch eine Ursache des Lungenkrebses? (Eine Anregung)," *Zeitschrift für Krebsforschung* 32 (1930): 82–91. Herbert L. Lombard and Carl R. Doering independently of Lickint documented a high proportion of smokers among U.S. lung cancer patients in their "Cancer Studies in Massachusetts," *New England Journal of Medicine* 198 (1928): 481–87.

38. Adler, *Primary Malignant Growths*, p. 22; a connection is also posited in Theodor Fahr's discussion of the paper by Otto Teutschlaender in the *Verhandlungen der deutschen Gesellschaft für Pathologie* 19 (1923): 192, and in Schönherr, "Beitrag," p. 443. Carly Seyfarth in 1924 pointed to the high proportion of tobacco workers, innkeepers, and bartenders among Leipzig's lung cancer victims, suggesting that exposure to "tobacco particles" (including smoke) might account for that city's rising lung cancer rates; see his "Lungenkarzinome," p. 1499.

39. Fritz Lickint, *Tabakgenuss und Gesundheit* (Hanover: Bruno Wilkens, 1936), pp. 83–84. Frederick L. Hoffman was one of the first Americans to take Lickint seriously; see his "Cancer and Smoking Habits," in *Cancer . . . Comprising International Contributions to the Study of Cancer*, ed. Frank E. Adair (Philadelphia: Lippincott, 1931), pp. 62–66; also his *Cancer and Diet*, p. 489. Jesse M. Gehman was another; see his *Smoke over America* (East Aurora, N.Y.: The Roycrofters, 1943), pp. 180–84. The Viennese clinician Franz Högler in 1941 noted that 82 percent of his lung cancer patients were male and that all were heavy smokers; he also recognized that the removal of tar from cigarettes was as important as the elimination of nicotine. See his "Welche Erkrankungen sind auf Nikotinschäden zurückzuführen?" *Wiener klinische Wochenschrift* 50 (1941): 1016.

40. Fritz Lickint, *Tabak und Organismus: Handbuch der gesamten Tabakkunde* (Stuttgart: Hippokrates, 1939); compare also his "Die Bedeutung des Tabaks für die Krebsentstehung," *Deutscher Tabakgegner* 17 (1935): 27–30. Some brief notes on Lickint's biography can be found in Wilhelm C. Crecelius, "In memorium Fritz Lickint," *Deutsches Gesundheitswesen* 15 (1960): 2283–84, and in Werner Schüttmann, "Ein Jubiläum im Kampf gegen den Tabakmissbrauch," *Münchener medizinische Wochenschrift* 131 (1989): 966–68. Lickint in 1939 was appointed a member of the Führerrat of the Deutschen Bundes für Lebensreform; see *Reine Luft* 21 (1939): 2.

41. Other German terms used at this time to designate nicotine addiction include: *Nicotismus* (Bamberger), *Nicotianismus* (Krafft-Ebing), *Nicotinsucht* (Lickint), *Fumigatismus* (Werner Kautzsch), and *Kapnomanie* (J. Stein); see Lickint, "Nikotinmissbrauch," pp. 306–9. *Tabakismus* was a German rendition of John Harvey Kellogg's "tobaccoism." The concept of "chronischer Nikotinismus" dates back at least to Leo Fürst's "Zur Prophylaxe des Coffeinismus und Nikotinismus," *Die ärztliche Praxis* 14 (1901): 351–54.

42. Lickint first uses the term "Passivrauchen" in his 1936 *Tabakgenuss und Gesundheit*, p. 26, though his 1935 article in the *Münchener medizinische Wochenschrift* notes that three of the seven women in his lung cancer series had lived in "smoke-saturated rooms" fouled by their smoking husbands ("Der Bronchialkrebs der Raucher," vol. 82, pp. 1233–34). Tobacco critics prior to this time had spoken about the dangers of "Aufenthalt in rauchigen Räumen" (e.g., Bejach, *Die tabakgegnerische Bewegung*, p. 11), and Frederick Hoffman in 1931 had speculated that female cancer of the lung might well stem from exposure to "air pollution" caused by "almost universal smoking habits"; see his "Cancer and Smoking Habits," p. 67. Lickint himself identified passive smoking with Julius Fink's concept of *Nicotinismus innocentium*; see *Tabak und Organismus*, p. 269.

43. Lickint, *Tabakgenuss und Gesundheit*, p. 85. Angel H. Roffo used Lickint's notion of cancers lining the *Rauchstrasse* in his "Krebserzeugende Tabakwirkung," *Monatsschrift für Krebsbekämpfung* 8 (1940): 97.

44. Fritz Lickint, Nazi party membership records, National Archives. In March of 1935 Lickint had had to resign as chairman of the Bund Deutscher Tabakgegner; he was replaced by Georg Boehncke; see "Bundes-Umschau," *Deutscher Tabakgegner* 17 (1935): 20. Lickint continued to write for the journal, however.

45. "Volksgesundheit und Genussgifte," *Deutsches Ärzteblatt* 69 (1939): 196.

46. Georg Boehncke, *Die gesetzlichen Grundlagen der Bekämpfung des Tabakmissbrauches in Deutschland* (Berlin: Wacht-Verlag, 1937), p. 12.

47. Heinrich Lottig, "Über den Einfluss von Alkohol, Nikotin und Schlafmangel auf die Höhenfestigkeit," *Luftfahrtmedizinische Abhandlungen* 13 (1938): 218–33. Otto Schmidt, director of the Danzig Academy's Gerichtsärztliches Institut, found elevated levels of carbon monoxide in the blood of smokers many hours after they had last smoked; see his "Der Kohlenoxydgehalt des Blutes bei Rauchern," *Reichs-Gesundheitsblatt* 4 (1940): 53–58. Schmidt also worried about indoor air pollution from other sources—the carbon monoxide threat to housewives from gas ovens, for example, and the similar threat posed by gas heaters; see his "Über den Kohlenoxydgehalt des Blutes bei chronischer Kohlenoxydvergiftung," *Volksgesundheit im Reichsgau Danzig-Westpreussen* 1 (1939/40): 323–30.

48. "Berlin: Control of the Use of Alcohol and Tobacco," *JAMA* 113 (1939): 2163–64.

49. Rudolf Friedrich, "Das Nicotin in der Ätiologie und in der postoperativen Nachbehandlung der Ulcuskrankheit," *Archiv für klinische Chirurgie* 179 (1934): 9–28.

50. Karl E. Westphal and Hans Weselmann, "Über Nikotinschädigungen des Magens," *Die Genussgifte* 36 (1940): 1–12; also their *Magenerkrankungen durch Tabakmissbrauch* (Berlin: Reichsgesundheitsverlag, 1940). Compare Franz Reichert's opinion that deaths from stomach perforation (ulcer) were three times more common in men than in women owing to "the alarming increase of cigarette smoking"; see his *Über die Häufigkeit von Krankheiten: Tuberkulose, Ulkuskrankheit und Krebs* (Leipzig: Georg Thieme, 1941), p. 26.

51. Theodor Deneke of Hamburg claimed that 75 percent of all early-onset

angina, and half of all late-onset angina, could be attributed to tobacco; see his "Tabak und Angina pectoris," *Zeitschrift für ärztliche Fortbildung* 33 (1936): 573–76; H. Reindell and R. Winterer, "Untersuchungsergebnisse über die Wirkung des Rauchens auf den Kreislauf," *Die Tabakfrage* 24 (1942): 84–88.

52. Walther Kittel, "Hygiene des Rauchens," in *Wehrhygiene*, ed. Siegfried Handloser and Wilhelm Hoffmann (Berlin: Springer, 1944), p. 242; Paul Laurentius, "Über Herzschäden durch Tabakmissbrauch bei Wehrmachtangehörigen," *Der Deutsche Militärarzt* 11 (1941): 633–40.

53. Alfred Goedel, "Kriegspathologische Beiträge," in *Kriegschirurgie*, ed. Arnold Zimmer (Vienna: Franz Deuticke, 1944), 1:45 and 51–52. The volume was part of the series *Wehrmedizin: Kriegserfahrungen 1939–1943*, edited by Zimmer.

54. Boehncke, *Die gesetzlichen Grundlagen*, p. 6.

55. Werner Hüttig, "Der Einfluss der Genussgifte auf das Erbgut und seine Entwicklung (Alkohol, Nikotin)," *Öffentlicher Gesundheitsdienst* 1 (1935): 171.

56. Paul Bernhard, "Über die Ursachen der Sterilität der Frau," *Zentralblatt für Gynäkologie* 67 (1943): 793; also his *Der Einfluss der Tabakgifte auf die Gesundheit und die Fruchtbarkeit der Frau* (Jena: G. Fischer, 1943).

57. Agnes Bluhm, *Die rassenhygienischen Aufgaben des weiblichen Arztes* (Berlin: A. Metzner, 1936).

58. Kitzing, *Erziehung*, pp. 225–26; the proposal was by D(esiré?) Demeaux.

59. Boehncke, "Tabak und Volksgesundheit," p. 627.

60. George Boehncke in 1939 asserted that "there is no doubt that a large proportion of both smokers and chewers of tobacco should be regarded as addicted (*tabaksüchtig*)"; see his *Die Bedeutung der Tabakfrage für das deutsche Volk* (Berlin: Reichsausschuss für Volksgesundheitsdienst, 1939), p. 14. Leonardo Conti in 1939 affirmed that alcohol and nicotine, like morphine and opium, cause "a chronic addiction"; see his *Zur Gründung der Reichsstelle gegen die Alkohol- und Tabakgefahren* (Berlin: Reichsgesundheitsverlag, 1939), p. 3. Nicotine addiction (*Nikotinsucht*) in at least one case was blamed for the commission of a murder; see "Aus dem Gerichtssaal," *Reine Luft* 20 (1938): 48.

61. Irmgard Hanselmann, *Zigaretten, Ärzteschaft und Sucht im Spannungsfeld von Politik und Krieg (1900–1950)* (Tübingen: Med. diss., 1991), pp. 49–118.

62. Boehncke, *Die gesetzlichen Grundlagen*, p. 4.

63. "Kleine Mitteilungen," *Vertrauensarzt* 9 (1941): 128. The office in question was the Reichsmeldestelle für Suchtgiftbekämpfung.

64. Kittel, "Hygiene des Rauchens," p. 243.

65. Cited in William B. McAllister, *A Limited Enterprise: The History of International Efforts to Control Drugs in the Twentieth Century* (Ph.D. diss., University of Virginia, 1996), p. 214.

66. Angel H. Roffo, "Durch Tabak beim Kaninchen entwickeltes Carcinom," *Zeitschrift für Krebsforschung* 33 (1931): 321–32; also his "Der Tabak als Krebserzeugendes Agens," *Deutsche medizinische Wochenschrift* 63 (1937): 1267–71, and his "Krebserzeugende Tabakwirkung," pp. 97–102. T. Chikamatsu, about the same time as Roffo, demonstrated the carcinogenic agency of tobacco tars in experimental animals; see his "Künstliche Erzeugung des Krebses durch Tabakteer bei Kaninchen und Maus," *Transactions of the Japanese Pathology Society*

21 (1931): 244 ff. The first efforts to induce cancer using tobacco tars seem to have been those of the military physician Anton Brosch of Vienna, who painted guinea pigs with "the well-known carcinogens" tar, paraffin, soot, and tobacco juice, with unclear results; see his "Theoretische und experimentelle Untersuchungen zur Pathogenesis und Histogenesis der malignen Geschwülste," *Archiv für pathologische Anatomie und Physiologie* 162 (1900): 32–84. Otto Schürch and Alfred Winterstein in the early 1930s performed experiments suggesting that tobacco tars induced tumors only in individuals possessing a certain "predisposition"; see their "Experimentelle Untersuchungen zur Frage Tabak und Krebs," *Zeitschrift für Krebsforschung* 42 (1935): 76–92. Victor Mertens in 1930 was apparently the first to conduct experiments to determine whether mice breathing cigarette smoke developed lung cancers (see his "Zigarettenrauch"); he later pointed out that E. von Zebrowski of Kiev in 1908 had exposed rabbits to tobacco smoke to study its health effects, though no mention was made of cancer. See E. von Zebrowski, "Zur Frage vom Einfluss des Tabakrauches auf Tiere," *Centralblatt für allgemeine Pathologie* 19 (1908): 609–17; Victor E. Mertens, "Noch einmal Zigarettenrauch und Lungenkrebs," *Zeitschrift für Krebsforschung* 51 (1941): 183–92.

67. Lickint, "Die Bedeutung," p. 30; also his *Tabakgenuss und Gesundheit*, pp. 84–85. Fr. Thys of the Fondation Médicale Reine Elisabeth in Brussels was another who claimed that too much attention was being given to nicotine and too little to tar in the genesis of lung cancer; see his "Note sur l'étiologie du carcinome bronchique," *Revue belge des sciences médicales* 7 (1935): 640–44. Mertens by 1941 could claim that nicotine was "seldom blamed" for carcinogenesis; see his "Noch einmal Zigarettenrauch," p. 183.

68. Richard Doll, personal communication, October 30, 1996.

69. Neumann Wender, "Eine neue Gefahr für den Raucher," *Münchener medizinische Wochenschrift* 80 (1933): 737–38.

70. Enrico Ferrari, "Tabakrauch und Lungenkarzinom," *Münchener medizinische Wochenschrift* 80 (1933): 942.

71. Klarner, *Vom Rauchen*, p. 22.

72. Rudolf Fleckseder, "Ueber den Bronchialkrebs und einige seiner Entstehungsbedingungen," *Münchener medizinische Wochenschrift* 83 (1936): 1585–88. Aaron Arkin and David H. Wagner in the United States found that 90 percent of their lung cancer patients were heavy smokers; see their "Primary Carcinoma of the Lung," *JAMA* 106 (1936): 587–91. Roffo gave a figure of 95 percent ("Krebserzeugende Tabakwirkung," p. 97). Franz Strnad at Nonnenbruch's clinic in Prague in 1938 found that the proportion was just under 50 percent, and concluded that smoking probably played a role in the onset of the disease; he also observed that the tobacco explanation of the lung cancer rise was "particularly popular among southern Slavic authors"—apparently referring to his colleagues in Prague ("Der Lungenkrebs," p. 309).

73. Franz Hermann Müller, "Tabakmissbrauch und Lungencarcinom," *Zeitschrift für Krebsforschung* 49 (1939): 57–85. A brief abstract of Müller's paper was translated into English and published in the September 30, 1939, issue of *JAMA* (p. 1372).

74. Müller, "Tabakmissbrauch," p. 59.

75. Ibid., p. 57. Walther Reinhard in his "Der primäre Lungenkrebs," *Archiv der Heilkunde* 19 (1878): 385 was one of the first to note this sexual asymmetry (there were 16 male and 11 female lung cancers in his sample); Walter H. Walshe in the fourth edition of his *Practical Treatise on the Diseases of the Lungs* (London: Smith, Elder, 1871) had also noted the inequality. Hans Pässler's 1896 review included 50 men and 18 women ("Ueber das primäre Carcinom der Lunge," p. 246); Adler's 1912 sample of 374 cases was 72 percent male (*Primary Malignant Growths*, p. 22). Seyfarth's 1924 review of 307 cases autopsied at Leipzig's university pathology institute included 258 males ("Lungenkarzinome," p. 1498); for Seyfarth, this sexual asymmetry was "undoubtedly" due to higher male occupational exposures, an attribution curiously at odds with his recognition that tobacco might play a role in the increase of cancer. For Wilhelm Hueper in 1942, by contrast, the discrepancy most likely occurred because men were much heavier smokers (see his *Occupational Tumors*, p. 426); Hueper's conclusion is especially noteworthy given his subsequent distrust of the "cigarette theory."

76. Müller, "Tabakmissbrauch," pp. 62–63.

77. Ibid., p. 78. Müller does not say much about how the healthy controls were chosen; nor does he say why he ignores the female smokers. All 96 individual cases are discussed, however, including details on occupational exposures, age, type and quantity of tobacco smoked, kind and location of lung malignancy, and previous medical history, especially of lung disease.

78. Ibid.

79. Doll and Hill, "Smoking," pp. 739–48.

80. Wynder and Graham, "Tobacco Smoking," p. 329.

81. Müller, "Tabakmissbrauch," pp. 79–82.

82. See, for example, Wynder and Graham, "Tobacco Smoking," pp. 329–36; Richard Doll and A. Bradford Hill, "A Study of the Aetiology of Carcinoma of the Lung," *British Medical Journal* 2 (1952): 1271–86. Willem F. Wassink cited both Lickint and Müller in his "Ontstaansvoorwaarden voor Longkanker," *Nederlands Tijdschrift voor Geneeskunde* 4 (1948): 3732–47.

83. Prof. Berthold Ostertag in 1942 asserted that "the increase of lung tumors among smokers is well known and undisputed" (hinreichend bekannt und unumstritten); he added that it was vital for physicians "to help free tobacco addicts from their addiction." See his "Krebsbekämpfung, Krebsbehandlung," *Medizinische Klinik* 38 (1942): 281; compare Prof. Wolfgang Denk's assertion: "We must reckon with the possibility that the inhalation of *cigarette smoke* has something to do with the extremely high incidence of lung cancer among men," in his "Der Krebs des Mannes," *Wiener klinische Wochenschrift* 56 (1943): 2.

84. Lickint, "Der Bronchialkrebs," pp. 1232–34.

85. De Crinis's remarks, originally published in the *Deutsches Ärzteblatt*, are reported in "Mitteilungen," *Monatsschrift für Krebsbekämpfung* 9 (1941): 197.

86. By "consensus" I mean the dominant or majority opinion, not that everyone agreed. A 1939 article in Germany's journal of continuing medical education conceded that German lung cancer rates had risen to 20–25 times the levels of only two decades previously, but denied that tobacco was the

primary cause (Hintze, "Kultur und Krebs," pp. 61–76). A 1941 article on Stettin's skyrocketing lung cancer rates conceded that "numerous authors" blamed tobacco but suggested that "contact with animal products" (e.g., among butchers and leather workers) might be a cause; see (Gerhard?) v. Glinski, "Über die Zunahme des primären Lungenkrebses," *Hippokrates* 12 (1941): 829–34. A 1944 text on diseases of the lung listed tar, dust, automotive exhaust, "chronic catarrh," and congenital malformation as possible contributors to the increase—ignoring tobacco altogether—but concluded that the true causes were "unknown"; see Adolf Sylla, *Lungenkrankheiten* (Berlin: Urban & Schwarzenberg, 1944), p. 619. Tobacco was the most-discussed theory in a postwar Viennese surgical text on lung cancer, whose authors nonetheless concluded that the cause of the disease's increased incidence "has not yet found a truly satisfactory explanation"; see Georg Salzer et al., *Das Bronchuscarcinom* (Vienna: Springer, 1952), p. 6. Hans Stroink, however, recalls that during his residency at Munich's Pathology Institute in 1947, when shown a lung cancer, institute director Ludwig Burkhardt would ask "what did he smoke?" (personal communication, May 5, 1998).

87. In Austria, the Nazi-minded citizens of Tyrol, Vorarlberg, and Styria organized a tobacco boycott in 1933–1934 as part of an effort to bring down the government (by depriving the state treasury of tax revenues). Styria's anti-Nazi Sicherheitskommissar ordered all tobacco salesmen to hand over lists of customers who had stopped purchasing cigars and cigarettes, the goal presumably being to identify and punish supporters of the Nazi cause. Uncooperative tobacco shops were threatened with loss of their license, and the abstaining customers were threatened with a fine of a thousand schillings or imprisonment for up to three weeks; see "Behördlicher Kampf gegen Tabakabstinenz in Deutsch-Oesterreich," *Ärztliche Sachverständigen-Zeitung* (1934): 200.

88. Boehncke, *Die Bedeutung*, pp. 11–12. The ministry's Erlass was dated March 21, 1938.

89. Sauerbruch, Lickint, and Gabriel, *Arzt, Alkohol und Tabak*. This second Reichstagung Volksgesundheit und Genussgifte was sponsored by the Nazi party's Hauptamt für Volksgesundheit; a summary of the proceedings can be found in "Berlin: Stimulants Endanger Public Health," *JAMA* 112 (1939): 2339–40. On March 6, 1939, Reiter had issued a call to Germany's leading medical, pharmacological, and nutritional societies to investigate the public health impact of nicotine; see his "Aufruf an die deutsche medizinische Wissenschaft!" in his *Reichsgesundheitsamt*, pp. 262–63.

90. See, for example, Hermann Stanger, *Ethik, Weltanschauung und Tabak* (1937), and Johannes Ude, *Rauchsklaverei und Kultur* (1937), both published in Vienna by the Reichsstelle gegen die Alkohol- und Tabakgefahren. The journal *Reine Luft* was published from 1938 to 1941 by the Berlin-based Deutscher Bund zur Bekämpfung der Tabakgefahren e.V. Following the annexation of Austria, *Reine Luft* absorbed *Tabakfreie Kultur*, the organ of the Austrian and Czechoslovakian antitobacco leagues. On October 4, 1940, the Reich interior minister asked all public health offices to display the journal in their waiting rooms; see "Runderlass des Reichsministers des Innern," *Reichs-Gesundheitsblatt* 15 (1940): 950. Other journals publishing antitobacco literature included

Die Volksgesundheit (People's health), *Volksgesundheitswacht* (Guarding the people's health), *Gesundes Volk* (Healthy people), and *Gesundes Leben* (Healthy life).

91. Bretschneider's *Der Weltbund* has Georg Bonne's remarks on tobacco as a *Feind des Weltfriedens* (p. 16); the term *Tabakterror* was originally used by the Stockholm antitobacco activist J. L. Saxon (ibid., p. 11).

92. Klarner, *Vom Rauchen*, p. 28.

93. "Erkennung und Bekämpfung," p. 183, reporting on the April 5–6, 1941, meeting in Weimar of the Wissenschaftliche Tagung zur Erforschung der Tabakgefahren, to which Hitler sent a telegram of greetings. Julius Streicher several years previously had asserted that nicotine was "das grösste Gift für unser Volk"; see Erich Bruns and Robert Ley, *Partei, Volksgesundheit, Genussgifte. 2. Reichstagung Volksgesundheit und Genussgifte* (Berlin: Wacht-Verlag, 1939), p. 9.

94. Boehncke, *Die Bedeutung*, pp. 11–13; "Erkennung und Bekämpfung," pp. 183–85.

95. Kitzing, *Erziehung*, pp. 225–26; Charman, *German Home Front*, pp. 53–56.

96. Ferdinand Goebel, *30 Experimente mit Alkohol und Tabak* (Berlin: Reichsgesundheitsverlag, 1940).

97. Klarner, *Vom Rauchen*, p. 45. The July 3, 1934, "Gesetz über die Vereinheitlichung des Gesundheitswesens" assigned to physicians the task of combating "abuse of alcohol, tobacco, sleeping pills, and opiates and similar poisons"; the methods specified to combat such ills included genetic and racial hygiene, marital counseling, and public health education (Boehncke, *Die Bedeutung*, pp. 10–15; also his *Die gesetzlichen Grundlagen*).

98. "Das Haus ohne Aschenbecher," *Die Tabakfrage* 24 (1942): 91.

99. Richard Kissling, *Der Tabak im Lichte der neusten naturwissenschaftlichen Forschungen* (Berlin: Paul Parey, 1893), p. 65. The first known efforts to develop low-nicotine tobacco products were those by Karl A. Mündner (1835–1891) of Brandenburg, a tobacco manufacturer and colleague of Otto Unverdorben, the first to identify nicotine in pipe residues. Mündner developed a low-nicotine *Gesundheitszigarre* using selective breeding techniques and new chemical extraction methods; his son Richard went on to develop filter-tipped cigars—the filters being made from wool and cork. Paul Koenig, director of the Reichsanstalt für Tabakforschung in Forchheim, characterized Mündner as the "erster Bekämpfer des Nikotins durch Entdeckung der Entnikotinisierung des Tabaks," offering this as evidence of the social responsibility of the German tobacco industry; see his *Die Entdeckung des reinen Nikotins* (Bremen: Arthur Geist, 1940), pp. 21–22 and plate 10.

100. Franz K. Reckert, *Tabakwarenkunde: Der Tabak, sein Anbau und seine Verarbeitung* (Berlin: Max Schwalbe, 1942), p. 31.

101. Germany was never a major grower of tobacco, though in 1938 it did produce about 35,500,000 kg—less than Greece (42,000,000 kg), Italy (42,000,000 kg), or Japan (65,400,000 kg). The United States at this time was the world's largest producer (624,400,000 kg), followed by British India (510,000,000 kg) and the Soviet Union (about 200,000,000 kg); see "Der Welt-Tabakanbau," *Chronica Nicotiana* 1 (Heft 2, 1940): 131.

102. Moritz to Lammers, October 7, 1941, R43 II/1226b, BAP.

103. Wilhelm Preiss, *Verordnung über nikotinarmen und nikotinfreien Tabak* (Berlin: Von Decker, 1939).

104. Klarner, *Vom Rauchen*, pp. 43–44.

105. Ibid., pp. 39–41.

106. Else Pappenheim and Erwin Stengel, "Zur Psychopathologie der Rauchgewohnheiten," *Wiener klinische Wochenschrift* 37 (1937): 354–56.

107. "Professor Dr. Schlick ermordet," *Tabakfreie Kultur* 25 (1936): 8.

108. "Berlin," pp. 2163–64; *Reichs-Gesundheitsblatt* 14 (1939): 323, 511–12, 550.

109. Wilhelm Spengler, *Genuss?—Ja! Genussgifte?—Nein!* (Dresden: Müllersche Verlagshandlung, 1939), p. 53.

110. Kurt Friebe, *Eisenbahn-Verkehrsordnung* (Leipzig: Verkehrswissenschaftliche Lehrmittelgesellschaft, 1938), p. 29.

111. "Anordnung," *Reichs-Gesundheitsblatt* 14 (1939): 550; "Rauchverbot für die Polizei auf Strassen und in Diensträumen," *Die Genussgifte* 36 (1940): 59.

112. "Berlin: Alcohol, Tobacco and Coffee," *JAMA* 113 (1939): 1144–45.

113. "Kleine Mitteilungen," *Vertrauensarzt* 9 (1941): 196; "Mitteilungen," *Öffentlicher Gesundheitsdienst* 7 (1941): 488.

114. Charman, *German Home Front*, p. 56; Christoph M. Merki, "Die nationalsozialistische Tabakpolitik," *Vierteljahrshefte für Zeitgeschichte* 46 (1998): 36.

115. Walther Fromme, "Öffentlicher Gesundheitsdienst," in Rodenwaldt et al., *Hygiene*, p. 36.

116. *Informationsdienst des Hauptamtes für Volksgesundheit der NSDAP*, April/June 1944, pp. 60–61; Martin Bormann to Hans-Heinrich Lammers, March 4, 1944, R43 II/1226b, BAP.

117. *Reichsgesetzblatt* 1 (1940): 742 and 814.

118. "Rauchverbot," *Arbeitsschutz*, May 15, 1943, p. 136. Prior even to the war, some tobacco bans had little to do with health. Smoking was not allowed in hospital wards and on German U-boats, for example, though in the latter case ten-minute smoking breaks were sometimes allowed when a submarine had surfaced. Smoking was also often banned in factory bathrooms, because urinals kept clogging up from the discarded butts; see Klarner, *Vom Rauchen*, pp. 29–31.

119. "Todesstrafe für verantwortungsloses Rauchen," *Die Tabakfrage* 24 (1942): 89.

120. "Bestimmung des Werberates," *Wirtschaftswerbung*, December 1941, pp. 396–97; "Berlin: The Nicotine Content of Tobacco Products," *JAMA* 113 (1939): 1145–50.

121. "Werberat," *Chronica Nicotiana* 3 (Heft 1, 1942): 91–92.

122. Rath to Astel, February 25, 1942, Bestand L 512, Universitätsarchiv Jena.

123. Klarner, *Vom Rauchen*, p. 7.

124. Walther Funk to Partei-Kanzlei, May 20, 1941, R43 II/1226b, BAP.

125. Bormann to Lammers, April 16, 1941, R43 II/1226b, BAP. Hitler's order was issued April 23, 1941.

126. Walther Funk to Partei-Kanzlei, May 20, 1941, R43 II/1226b, BAP.

127. "Erkennung und Bekämpfung," pp. 183–85. Hitler contributed RM

100,000 from his Reichzkanzlei; Frau Alfred Ploetz, wife of the deceased racial hygienist, also contributed RM 500; see Bestand L 510, Universitätsarchiv Jena. By 1944 this institute was sometimes called the Institut zur Bekämpfung der Tabakgefahren; this is the name printed, for example, on the title page of Erich Schöniger's medical dissertation; see his *Lungenkrebs und Tabakverbrauch* (Jena: Med. diss., 1944).

128. Lickint to Astel, April 21, 1941, Bestand L 512, Universitätsarchiv Jena.

129. "Erkennung und Bekämpfung," pp. 183–85.

130. Ibid. Compare Klarner's characterization of the tobacco industry as "stark mit jüdischen Elementen durchsetzt" (*Vom Rauchen*, p. 46).

131. "Why has the struggle against tobacco arisen in Thuringia? Because in Thuringia we have eliminated one enemy of the people [*Volksfeind*] after another (most recently, tuberculosis)"; see "Auszugsweise Abschrift," May 5, 1941, R43 II/1226b, BAP. Saxony's Gauleiter Martin Mutschmann was another antitobacco activist; by 1939 he had barred smoking in all government office buildings (Sauerbruch, Lickint, and Gabriel, *Arzt, Alkohol und Tabak*, p. 13).

132. Klee, *"Euthanasie"*, pp. 341–42 and 425.

133. "Erkennung und Bekämpfung," p. 183. Astel had joined the anticommunist Freikorps shortly after the First World War; he was named president of Thuringia's Landesamt für Rassewesen on September 1, 1933, and director of Jena's Anstalt für Menschliche Züchtungslehre und Vererbungsforschung in June of 1934 (in 1935 renamed the Institut für Erbforschung und Rassenpolitik). He was awarded the NSDAP's Goldenes Ehrenzeichen in January of 1939.

134. Weindling, *Health*, p. 529.

135. "Die einzelnen wissenschaftlichen Bearbeiter dürfen, damit sie in Blick, Urteil und Haltung unbefangen und unabhängig sind, nicht tabaksüchtig sein. Nichtrauchen is daher für die Mitarbeit an der Erforschung und Bekämpfung der Tabakgefahren genau so Voraussetzung wie arische Abstammung für die Eignung zu völkischem Kampfe, der zum Siege führen soll"; see Fritz Sauckel, "Abschrift," March 20, 1941, R43 II/745b, BAP. Sauckel's proposal was apparently conveyed to Hitler by Reichsleiter Martin Bormann, who approved the funds. Reichsstatthalter and Gauleiter Fritz Sauckel (sometimes derisively remembered as "Sauleiter Gauckel") launched an antitobacco campaign for Thuringia about this time, involving measures such as the barring of women under the age of twenty-five from smoking in public; see NS 18/22 and 18/1826, BAK.

136. Goebbels, *Tagebücher*, p. 714. In February of 1939 *Reine Luft* announced the decision of a "major film company" to make an antitobacco film in collaboration with the German Antitobacco League (21 [1939]: 2); it is not clear whether this was the same as the film mentioned by Goebbels.

137. Bestand L510, Universitätsarchiv Jena; compare also Roth, "Filmpropaganda," in *Reform und Gewissen: "Euthanasie" im Dienst des Fortschritts*, ed. Götz Aly et al. (Berlin: Rotbuch, 1985), pp. 125–93; and Michael Burleigh's 1993 film, *Selling Murder: The Killing Films of the Third Reich*. After the war, on December 1, 1945, Skramlik filed a petition to be considered "a victim of fascism"; see Susanne Zimmermann, *Die medizinische Fakultät der Universität Jena während der Zeit des Nationalsozialismus* (Jena: Med. diss., 1994), p. 96. Skramlik was named

president of the University of Jena after his predecessor, Karl Astel, committed suicide.

138. Zimmermann, *Die medizinische Fakultät*, p. 97.

139. Horst Wüstner, *Eine Krebsstatistik mit besonderer Berücksichtigung des Bronchialcarcinoms* (Jena: Med. diss., 1941).

140. Eberhard Schairer and Erich Schöniger, "Lungenkrebs und Tabakverbrauch," *Zeitschrift für Krebsforschung* 54 (1943): 261–69.

141. Personalakten Eberhard Schairer, D-2487, Universitätsarchiv Jena; George Davey Smith, personal communication. Davey Smith met with Schairer's daughter-in-law in 1994; she refused to grant an interview with the eighty-seven-year-old physician. She did say, however, that her father-in-law was disappointed he had not received more credit for his tobacco work.

142. Schairer and Schöniger, "Lungenkrebs," p. 263.

143. George Davey Smith, Sabine A. Ströbele, and Matthias Egger, "Smoking and Health Promotion in Nazi Germany," *Journal of Epidemiology and Community Health* 48 (1994): 220.

144. Schairer and Schöniger, "Lungenkrebs," pp. 263–66.

145. Albert Dietrich, "Krebs als Kriegsfolge," *Zeitschrift für Krebsforschung* 54 (1944): 198–99.

146. The *Science Citation Index* reveals that Schairer and Schöniger's paper is cited three or four times in the 1960s, only once in the 1970s, and then not again until 1988, when Ernst Wynder cited it in an article in *Public Health Reports*. Among sixty-five citations of papers by Schairer in the period 1965–1984, only two are to the 1943 paper with Schöniger. The paper simply does not figure in the canonical histories of smoking and health.

147. Myroslaw Nawrockyj, *Tabak und Krebs: Eine Literaturzusammenstellung* (Heidelberg: Med. diss., 1953); Colin White, "Research on Smoking and Lung Cancer: A Landmark in the History of Chronic Disease Epidemiology," *Yale Journal of Biology and Medicine* 63 (1990): 29–46.

148. *Smoking and Health: Report of the Advisory Committee to the Surgeon General of the Public Health Service* (Washington, D.C.: U.S. Government Printing Offfice, 1964).

149. *Smoking and Health: A Report of the Royal College of Physicians of London on Smoking in Relation to Cancer of the Lung and Other Diseases* (London: Pitman Medical Publishing, 1962). The report lists only six German-language sources among 216 references, and all but three date from after the Second World War. Twelve separate papers by Richard Doll are cited.

150. Richard Doll, personal communication.

151. Paul Reckzeh, "Chronische Tabakvergiftung und Lebenserwartung," *Medizinische Klinik* 35 (1939): 1169–71. Reckzeh reported that 14 among 1,700 deaths covered by a leading life insurance company in 1938 were listed as due in whole or in part to nicotine abuse (p. 1170).

152. Grüneisen, "Krebsbekämpfung," p. 1499.

153. Westphal and Weselmann, "Über Nikotinschädigungen," p. 14. Westphal at this time was head of internal medicine at Berlin's City Hospital. He joined the NSDAP and SS in 1937, and by 1939 was an SS Rottenführer. Excessive drinkers were treated far more harshly than excessive smokers: in

1934, for example, the NSDAP Kreisleitung for the city of Ulm announced that unemployed men who used their welfare money to become drunk would be confined to a concentration camp; see "Konzentrationslager für Trinker," *Vertrauensarzt* 1 (1934): 71. There is no evidence that smokers were ever treated so harshly, though Boehncke in 1939 did recommend "productive and useful work"—e.g., road construction or farm work—as an appropriate therapy for tobacco addicts. Boehncke also proposed that in extreme cases, such persons could be deprived of their civil rights and placed under the guardianship of the state (*Die Bedeutung*, p. 14). Compare his 1937 remark that such persons should be "forcibly separated" (*zwangsweise abgesondert werden*) from the rest of society (*Die gesetzliche Grundlagen*, p. 15); also Wilhelm Messer, "Zur Entmündigung von Tabaksüchtigen," *Reine Luft* 24 (1942): 36–40.

154. Kortenhaus, "Krebs," p. 425.

155. See Charlotte Lickint, "Wir deutschen Frauen rauchen nicht!" *Deutscher Tabakgegner* 16 (1934): 1–2.

156. Sauerbruch, Lickint, and Gabriel, *Arzt, Alkohol und Tabak*, p. 13.

157. Gabriele Schulze and Käte Dischner, *Die Zigarettenraucherin* (Jena: Med. diss., 1942); compare also Bernhard's *Einfluss der Tabakgifte*.

158. Jill Stephenson, *The Nazi Organisation of Women* (London: Croom Helm, 1981), p. 188.

159. Hess, *Rauchen*, p. 45; compare also Mark W. Rien and Gustaf Nils Dorén, *Das Neue Tabago Buch* (Hamburg: Reemtsma, 1985), p. 124. Tobacco imports cost Germany about 400 million reichsmarks in 1940; see Klarner, *Vom Rauchen*, p. 48.

160. Merki, "Nationalsozialistische Tabakpolitik," p. 28.

161. Picker, *Hitlers Tischgespräche*, pp. 327–28. Hitler on July 18, 1942, characterized tobacco as "die Rache des Roten Mannes (Indianers) dafür, dass der Weisse ihm den Schnaps gebracht und dadurch ihn zugrunde gerichtet habe" (ibid., p. 439). In January of that year he said that smoking "gehöre zu den widerwärtigsten Dingen"; he also blamed smoking for the undoing of Dietrich Eckart, Paul Ludwig Troost, and his own father; smoking was also about to undo his friend and photographer, Heinrich Hoffmann (Schenck, *Patient Hitler*, p. 32).

162. Klarner, *Vom Rauchen*, p. 31.

163. John C. Burnham, "American Physicians and Tobacco Use: Two Surgeons General, 1929 and 1964," *Bulletin of the History of Medicine* 63 (1989): 10–15.

164. "Hitler's Attitude toward Alcohol," *Scientific Temperance Journal*, Spring 1933, p. 18.

165. Medizinalrat Dr. (Friedrich?) Pfeuffer, "Gesundheitliche Gefahren des Tabakgebrauchs," *Öffentlicher Gesundheitsdienst* 7 (1941): 515.

166. Klarner, *Vom Rauchen*, p. 33.

167. Hans Reiter characterized nicotine as the "grösste Schädling der Volksgesundheit" and "grösste Schädling der deutschen Wirtschaft" at a May 25, 1939, meeting sponsored by the Werberat der deutschen Wirtschaft; see *Volksgesundheit und Werbung*, p. 17.

168. Walter Naasner, *Neue Machtzentren in der deutschen Kriegswirtschaft, 1942–1945* (Boppard am Rhein: Boldt, 1994).

169. Wolfgang Cyran, *Genuss mit oder ohne Reue? Eine medizinische Analyse über die Gefahren des Rauchens* (Reinbek: Rowohlt, 1968), p. 34. Lickint's postwar publications include: *Tabakgenuss und Gesundheit* (Hanover: Wilkens, 1936; rev. ed., 1951); *Die Zigarette, dein Schicksal; Die Zigarette—des Menschen Feind* (Wiesbaden: Walther, 1951); *Ätiologie und Prophylaxe des Lungenkrebses als ein Problem der Gewerbehygiene und des Tabakrauches* (Dresden: Steinkopff, 1953); *Wem schaden Alkohol, Tabak und Kaffee* (Berlin: Volk und Gesundheit, 1953); *Alkohol und Gesundheit* (Hanover: Wilkens, 1954); and *Arbeitshygiene* (Berlin: Technik, 1955).

170. Peter N. Lee, ed., *Tobacco Consumption in Various Countries*, 4th ed. (London: Tobacco Research Council, 1975), p. 28.

171. This argument is briefly suggested in Davey Smith et al., "Smoking," p. 222; compare also George Davey Smith, Sabine Ströbele, and Matthias Egger, "Smoking and Death," *British Medical Journal* 310 (1995): 396.

172. See, for example, Hermannsen, "Erzieher und Erzieherin!" p. 78.

173. Boehncke, *Die Bedeutung*, p. 10.

174. Helmut Heiber, *Goebbels* (New York: Hawthorn Books, 1972), p. 233.

175. Zimmermann, *Die medizinische Fakultät*, pp. 95–96; BAK NS 18/226. Goebbels smoked thirty to fifty cigarettes a day from the 1920s through the 1940s.

176. "Antinikotin-Propaganda," in *Verfügungen/Anordnungen/Bekanntgaben*, ed. Partei-Kanzlei, vol. 1 (Munich: Zentralverlag der NSDAP, 1943), p. 408.

177. Walther Funk to Stellvertreter des Führers, May 5, 1941, R43 II/1226b BAP.

178. "Form der Propaganda gegen den Tabakmissbrauch," May 22, 1941, R43 II/1226b, BAP.

179. Hans-Heinrich Lammers to Walther Funk, June 10, 1941, R43 II/1226b, BAP.

180. Klarner, *Vom Rauchen*, pp. 29–30.

181. Walther Kittel, "Alkohol und Wehrmacht," in *Wehrhygiene*, ed. Siegfried Handloser and Wilhelm Hoffmann (Berlin: Springer, 1944), p. 241.

182. Kittel, "Hygiene des Rauchens," p. 244.

183. "Zur Tabakwarenversorgung," *SD-Berichte zu Inlandsfragen*, September 9, 1943, R58/188, BAP.

184. "Versorgung mit Tabakwaren," March 28, 1944, R43 II/1226b, BAP.

185. See, for example, Reid's "Weltanschauung, Haltung, Genussgifte," p. 64. Reiter's words are in Werberat, *Volksgesundheit und Werbung*, p. 17.

186. Reckert, *Tabakwarenkunde*, p. 236.

187. "Erkennung und Bekämpfung," p. 184.

188. Klarner, *Vom Rauchen*, p. 46. According to the *Statistisches Jahrbuch für das Deutsche Reich*, there were 638,339 Germans involved in the tobacco trade in 1936/37. Most of these were employees of hotels, coffee shops, or food stores carrying tobacco products; only about 53,000 were exclusively involved in tobacco production or sales (ibid., p. 234). The best history of German tobacco industry finances is still Kurt Pritzkoleit's *Auf einer Woge von Gold: Der Triumph der Wirtschaft* (Vienna: Kurt Desch, 1961), pp. 181–244.

189. *Die Malerei der Gotik und Frührenaissance* (Hamburg, 1938) had sold 700,000 copies by 1938.

190. Waldorf-Astoria, *Uniformen der Marine und Schutztruppen* (Munich, n.d. [1932]), Vorwort; Kosmos, *Bild-Dokumente unserer Zeit* (Dresden, 1933).

191. Pritzkoleit, *Auf einer Woge von Gold*, pp. 215–18.

192. Conan Fischer, *Stormtroopers: A Social, Economic and Ideological Analysis, 1929–1935* (London: Allen & Unwin, 1983), pp. 128–29.

193. "Kritische Umschau," *Deutscher Tabakgegner* 15 (1933): 11. The SPD's "Freiheit" cigarette was advertised as "tied to our struggle": "Zigaretten aber auch, und das ist das Wesentliche, die verbunden sind mit unserer Kampfbewegung" ("Tausend in der Minute," *Hamburger Echo*, January 1, 1933).

194. Diels, *Lucifer*, p. 299.

195. Pritzkoleit, *Auf einer Woge von Gold*, pp. 215–17.

196. The Internationale Tabakwissenschaftliche Gesellschaft was established in March of 1938 with separate sections for History, Chemistry, Technical Affairs (including breeding and cultivation), Economics, and Finance. The idea was to bring together tobacco experts in meetings timed to coincide with tobacco trade fairs, where the latest farming and manufacturing equipment could be displayed. A Central Tobacco Office (Zentralstelle für Tabak) based in Rome was established at this same time; the office was to coordinate the agricultural and packaging aspects of the industry, while the association would handle the technical and scientific aspects; see "Die Entwicklung der Internationalen Tabakwissenschaftlichen Gesellschaft," *Chronica Nicotiana* 1 (Heft 3, 1940): 25–32. The association was supposed to have a "purely German membership" (*rein deutsches Gremium*), and General Secretary Helmuth Aschenbrenner worked to ensure that none of the foreign section heads were Jews (Magyars, however, were fine). The Hungarian Janos Bodnar, director of Debreczen's Chemical-Medical Institute, was suspected at one point of being Jewish; the DKZ report found that he was a full-blooded Magyar (as was his wife) but had admitted more Jews than were allowed according to that university's *numerus clausus* during his tenure as dean of the medical school; see Aschenbrenner to DKZ, April 29, 1939, and DKZ to Aschenbrenner, June 16, 1939, DKZ, HIA.

197. See, for example, *Tabak und Neurose*, vol. 2 of the *Monographiae Nicotianae* (Bremen: Arthur Geist, 1942), p. 144, cited in Merki, "Nationalsozialistische Tabakpolitik," p. 32.

198. *Chronica Nicotiana* 3 (Heft 1, 1942): 71–74.

199. Margarete Focken, "Über ambulante Behandlung des Ulcus ventriculi und duodeni in der Allgemeinpraxis mit Sexualhormonen," *Deutsche medizinische Wochenschrift* 67 (1941): 1118–21; R.G.J.P. Huisman, "Tabak und Ulkus," *Chronica Nicotiana* 3 (Heft 1, 1942): 71–72.

200. *Chronica Nicotiana* 1 (Heft 2, 1940): 70; the psychiatric judgment was that of Johannes Lange.

201. *Chronica Nicotiana* 1 (Heft 2, 1940): 48.

202. The president of the *Tabacologia medicinalis* was a Prof. Dr. Andriska of Budapest, with a Prof. Dr. Baglioni of Rome as vice president, though the

commission was clearly a puppet project of the German tobacco industry. Some records of the commission are preserved in the Deutsche Kongress-Zentrale, Hoover Institution Archives.

203. Aschenbrenner was obviously already nervous in March of 1939, when he wrote the German Congress Board to inquire about an upcoming meeting of the International Antitobacco League (Weltbund gegen die Tabakgefahren): preparations were underway for the International Tobacco Congress scheduled for later that year in Bremen, and Aschenbrenner wanted to make sure the pro- and antitobacco meetings did not coincide (this was to be "avoided at all costs"); see Aschenbrenner to Deutsche Kongress-Zentrale, March 10, 1939, DKZ, HIA.

204. DKZ to Aschenbrenner, September 12, 1941, DKZ, HIA.

205. Conti to Internationale Tabak Gesellschaft, August 26, 1941, DKZ, HIA.

206. Aschenbrenner to Reichswirtschaftsministerium (hereafter RWM), September 1, 1941, DKZ, HIA.

207. Aschenbrenner to RWM, September 1, 1941, DKZ, HIA. Aschenbrenner claimed that an effort had been made to protest the ban, including a threat by some doctors to boycott the 1939 meeting—which Aschenbrenner cautioned against (ibid.). The threat was of little consequence, since the meeting never took place.

208. Aschenbrenner to RWM, October 4, 1941, DKZ, HIA. Aschenbrenner protested Conti's ban on the society as a violation of the "great tradition of international physicians' organizations"; see Aschenbrenner to RWM, September 9, 1941, DKZ, HIA. Bresler had authored a book with the title *Tabakologia medizinalis: Literarische Studie über den Tabak in medizinischer Beziehung* (Halle: Marhold, 1911), though a Prof. Mayer Gmelin was also sometimes called the "Nestor der Tabakforschung."

209. Aschenbrenner to Schweig, December 24, 1941, DKZ, HIA.

210. Aschenbrenner to Reichsstelle, November 1, 1941, DKZ, HIA.

211. See my *Cancer Wars*, pp. 106–10.

212. "Rauchen: Wie Gut," p. 64.

213. Reichswirtschaftsminister to Lammers, February 24, 1944, R43 II/1226b, BAP.

214. Charman, *German Home Front*, p. 53. The Reich Health Office spent a lot of time in 1943 and 1944 evaluating tobacco substitutes; see R86/4041, BAK. A list of more than a dozen legal substitutes—including lavender, thyme, thistle leaves, and lemon peels—can be found in the *Reichs-Gesundheitsblatt* 14 (1939): 491. Allied airplanes dropped propaganda leaflets over Germany in January of 1945, making fun of Germany's tobacco shortages and tobacco substitutes, including marijuana (*Hanfblätter*); German authorities wondered if this might be part of a subtle ploy to get people to try the drug and poison themselves in the process (Hudolin to Brendemühl, January 13, 1945, R86/4041).

215. Kittel, "Hygiene des Rauchens," p. 245. The order in question was H.Dv. 86/1 Nr. 17 of 20.6.1940.

216. Pritzkoleit, *Auf einer Woge von Gold*, pp. 221–22. Allied occupation authorities after the war lowered the tax to 60 percent, and subsequent German legislation lowered it into the 42–56 percent range. Cigarettes manufactured in

Berlin were not taxed at all, which is the main reason production in that city grew from 168 million in 1953 to 18.8 *billion* in 1960 (ibid.). The Social Democratic Party opposed postwar tobacco taxes as unfair to workers; see "Der teure Tabak," *Der Sozialdemokrat*, October 17, 1946.

217. Kittel, "Hygiene des Rauchens," p. 245. The Russian POW figures were reportedly gathered by Prof. Arnold Loeser of Freiburg, a consulting pharmacologist for the army (ibid.).

218. Seufert, *Der Feldzug*, p. 31.

219. In the summer of 1946, Germany's six largest cigarette companies in the British zone of occupation were producing only 10 million cigarettes per day, compared to ten times this amount for the years prior to 1939. In 1947, 14.8 million cigarettes were being manufactured daily in the British, French, and American zones of occupation; one year later, production had still risen only to 24.3 million per day in the western zone. Contrast this with the year 1979, when West German manufacturers produced 370 million cigarettes per day. See Friedheim Merz, *Die Stunde Null—Eine Sonderdokumentation* (Bonn: Neuer Vorwärts, 1981), pp. 62–64. Merz estimates a ratio of illegal to legal production of cigarettes in the immediate postwar years of about two to one. This would mean a German postwar production on the order of 30 percent of prewar levels, assuming no illegal production in prewar years.

220. Merz, *Stunde Null*, p. 66.

221. Richard Doll et al., "Lung Cancer Mortality and the Length of Cigarette Ends: An International Comparison," *British Medical Journal* 1 (1959): 322–25; Cyran, *Genuss*, pp. 20–21 and 34–35.

222. One can refine such estimates for later periods, when statistical data are presumably more reliable and when occupational factors may have played a lesser role in the genesis of lung cancers—making cigarettes the more exclusive cause of the disease. The 3,958 cigarettes smoked per person in the United States in 1962, for example, yielded a male lung cancer death rate of about 72 per 100,000 in 1984, meaning that (given the above assumptions) it still takes about five or six million cigarettes to produce a lung cancer. In Germany the yield is still somewhat higher, though the gap has narrowed: 1,640 cigarettes were smoked per adult in 1960, producing a male lung cancer mortality of 42 per 100,000 in 1980, which means that it took about four million cigarettes to cause a given cancer.

223. Paul Koenig, *Tabakkleinanbau* (1944), 2d ed. (Hanover: M. & H. Schaper, 1946), p. 7. There were only 6,000 to 10,000 home growers in Germany prior to 1939, concentrated in the northeastern parts of Germany. Home growers were allowed to cultivate up to 50 square meters, or a maximum of 200 plants, from which 10–12 kg of dried tobacco could be produced. Up to 25 plants could be grown tax free. The same regulations were preserved by Allied authorities after the war, though the tax-exempt amount was reduced to 15 plants (ibid.).

224. Daily tobacco rations in the early war years for males included 5 cigarettes (or 1–2 cigars) for males and half this amount for women. Rations in the later years of the war were smaller. In the early postwar years, men were allotted between 0.9 and 1.3 cigarettes per day, while women were allotted only half this amount. See ibid., p. 63. Rations for Waffen-SS men were increased to

10 cigarettes per day in the middle of the war; see Ernst G. Schenck, *Zur Frage der Sonder- und Konzentrat-Verpflegung der Waffen-SS* (n.p.: SS-Wirtschafts-Verwaltungshauptamt, n.d. [1944?]), p. 17. One of the curious contradictions of the era is that Jews and political prisoners in concentration camps, like upstanding German women outside the camps, received half rations throughout the war. There is an interesting logical oddity here: "healthy" German women received half rations because tobacco was known to be bad for you; Jews and concentration camp prisoners received half rations because tobacco was also viewed as precious and in short supply. See Dr. Kreitmair of Vienna to the Reichsstelle für Kaffee und Tabak, August 19, 1944, R8 XII/53, BAK.

CHAPTER 7
THE MONSTROUS AND THE PROSAIC

1. An indoor domestic radon hazard was identified in Germany as early as 1907, and then periodically rediscovered in the 1930s, 1950s, and 1970s, before political events drew attention to the hazard—especially the Arab oil crisis and the subsequent insulation of homes, but also the accident at Three Mile Island; see my *Cancer Wars*, pp. 197–216.

2. Richard Walther Darré, *Das Schwein als Kriterium für nordische Völker und Semiten* (Munich: Lehmann, 1933).

3. Fr. W. Landgraeber, "Radium-Mineralien und Lagerstätten auf der Erde," *Wiener klinische Wochenschrift* 52 (1939): 777.

4. Deaths caused by human experimentation were actually a minuscule fraction of the total medical murders committed during the Nazi era: roughly 1,000 people died from the effects of human experimentation, whereas 200,000 people were killed in the "euthanasia operation"; see my "How Many People Died from Nazi Human Experiments?" unpubl. MS.

5. Fritz Lickint, "Die konservative Behandlung des Krebses," *Hippokrates* 7 (1936): 668.

6. Karl H. Bauer et al., "Weitere Erfahrungen mit cancerogenen Stoffen," *Langenbecks Archiv* 193 (1938): 499–502; Bauer to Deutsche Forschungsgemeinschaft, July 13, 1938, R73/10179, BAK.

7. Liek, *Der Kampf*, pp. 19–20.

8. In Hanover in 1937, for example, a naturopathic healer treated a woman complaining of stomach pains with homeopathic remedies; he also found a lump in her breast that he identified as cancerous, yet continued to treat her with homeopathic preparations. The healer advised the woman to have an operation, but she refused. In April of 1939 the tumor ulcerated; the woman went to a licensed physician who ordered her into a hospital, but it was too late for surgery. She was treated with radium but died in June of 1940. The naturopathic healer was convicted of "negligent manslaughter" (*fahrlässige Tötung*) and sentenced to four months in prison "for having failed to insist that the woman submit to an operation." See Bruno Steinwallner, "Zur fahrlässigen Behandlung von Krebskranken," *Monatsschrift für Krebsbekämpfung* 10 (1942): 160–61. In a similar case in 1941, a Gräfelfing woman was convicted of manslaughter for the death of a cancer patient under her care; the woman was

declared "a danger to the community" and sentenced to six months in prison. The *Monatsschrift für Krebsbekämpfung* ridiculed the punishment, asking, "Why only six months?" ("Mitteilungen," 9 [1941]: 179). Additional cases can be found in Nagel to Reichsärztekammer, April 27, 1937, E 1496, THW.

There are other cases where cancer literature was suppressed for the criminal activities of its authors. In 1936, for example, a physician by the name of Josef Wetterer, editor of *Kampf dem Krebs*, was sentenced to two and a half years in prison for fraud and profiteering. (Auler to Landesausschuss, December 15, 1936, E 1493, THW.) Wetterer was barred from the German Radiological Society, his journal was banned, and his book, *Heraus aus der Krebsnot*, for which he had won the Cadilhac Prize, was confiscated by the Gestapo. The court ordered a psychiatric evaluation (by euthanasia experts Schneider and Schwenniger), which found him suffering from "grotesque greed" and "a pathologic drive for profit and power"; see "Mitteilungen," *Monatsschrift für Krebsbekämpfung* 5 (1937): 29.

9. It is not obvious to me that the level of fraud or dishonesty was higher in the Nazi era than in most other periods of history. One rarely hears stories of plagiarism, or falsification of data, or other kinds of "misconduct" in the narrow definition of this term sometimes worried about in governmental research institutions; see, however, Robert L. Berger, "Nazi Science—The Dachau Hypothermia Experiments," *New England Journal of Medicine* 322 (1990): 1435–40.

10. Hans Stroink, "Borst and the Von Brehmer Incident," *American Journal of Dermatopathology* 8 (1986): 522–24. Stroink threw out the only known copy of Borst's speech in the spring of 1998, two months before I contacted him.

11. Documentation can be found in E 1496, THW. Military authorities about this time asked the Reich Health Office to conduct a separate investigation; see G. Zeugerle to Reichsgesundheitsamt, March 4, 1936, and the undated review by H. Dieckmann, "Zusammenfassender Bericht über die amtliche Nachuntersuchung der v. Brehmerschen Krebsdiagnostik," R86 2764, BAK. Reiter's office concluded that the technique had "no diagnostic or therapeutic value."

12. David J. Hess, *Can Bacteria Cause Cancer? Alternative Medicine Confronts Big Science* (New York: New York University Press, 1997), p. 41.

13. Brehmer headed the Paracelsus Institut at the Theresien Hospital in Nuremberg from 1935 to 1937; in a postwar text he says that Hitler dissolved the institute in 1937, but he does not mention that it was Streicher who brought him there in the first place. He does say that he came under Gestapo surveillance and was "silenced" after 1937, though he was able to continue his research at a tumor research laboratory in Berlin. See Wilhelm von Brehmer, *"Siphonospira polymorpha v.Br."* (Haag/Amper: Linck-Verlag, 1947), p. 170.

14. Wolfgang Weyers, *Death of Medicine in Nazi Germany: Dermatology and Dermatopathology under the Swastika* (Philadelphia: Promethean Medical, 1996), p. 138. Erik Enby presents similar misrepresentations in his *Hidden Killers: The Revolutionary Medical Discoveries of Gunther Enderlein* (Saratoga: S & G Communications, 1990), pp. 5–9.

15. Hermann Druckrey evaluated Brehmer's claims and found them "völlig haltlos" (totally without merit); he also cautioned that the refutation of Brehmer's therapy "should teach us not to undertake therapeutic experiments

on humans without first checking and rechecking the results in animal tests" ("Ergebnisse," p. 113). Brehmer after the war claimed that his life had been threatened, his speeches and publications banned, and that he had been put under Gestapo surveillance; see his *"Siphonospira"*, p. 170.

16. Borst and Gruneisen, "Niederschrift über die Mitgliederversammlung des Reichsausschusses für Krebsbekämpfung am 1.Dezember 1933," E 1498, THW.

17. "Geschäftsbericht," R86 2764, BAK; A. Rothacker and H. Degler, "Das magische Reis und seine Probleme," *Hippokrates* 8 (1937): 331–58.

18. "Mitteilungen," *Monatsschrift für Krebsbekämpfung* 5 (1937): 116. The court also ruled that it was the duty of every German to alert the police to anyone's trying to sell such devices.

19. "Mitteilungen," *Monatsschrift für Krebsbekämpfung* 9 (1941): 159.

20. Goebbels, *Tagebücher*, p. 651 (entry for May 20, 1941).

21. "Mitteilungen," *Monatsschrift für Krebsbekämpfung* 9 (1941): 219.

22. See Albert Hellwig, "Keine Krebsbehandlungen durch Nichtärzte," *Ärzteblatt für das Sudetenland*, no. 13 (1941), reporting on a three-year sentence imposed on a quack healer.

23. Werberat, *Volksgesundheit und Werbung*, p. 28.

24. Auler, *Der Krebs und seine Bekämpfung*, p. 4.

25. Werberat, *Volksgesundheit und Werbung*, pp. 7–10.

26. Ibid., p. 33; the words are those of Heinrich Hunke.

27. Hans Auler and Heinrich Martius, *Diagnostik der bösartigen Geschwülste* (Munich: Lehmann, 1943), preface.

28. See my *Cancer Wars*, pp. 36–48.

29. "Referate: Geschwulst," *Monatsschrift für Unfallheilkunde* 46 (1939): 280–81; Dietrich, "Krebs als Kriegsfolge."

30. Deichmann, *Biologen unter Hitler*, pp. 126–29. This ruse of using cancer research to obtain military deferment was apparently practiced often enough to raise some eyebrows: Richard Kuhn in October of 1942 informed the Reich Research Council that "work in the cancer area . . . should not automatically disqualify one from military service" (ibid., p. 126).

31. Himmler pointed out that as of February 20, 1945, there were 28,145 KZ prisoners over the age of fifty and 4,898 over the age of sixty (it is clear he is talking only about camps on German soil—though he does point out that the recent "clearing" of Auschwitz and Monowitz may have elevated the German figures). Himmler in January of 1945 had asked Grawitz to test certain cancer chemotherapeutic agents at Joachim Mrugowski's Hygiene Institut der Waffen-SS; Grawitz had already had Hermann Druckrey test a bismuth compound known as "del Franco" in 1944. Druckrey tested dozens of other substances in his capacity as senior adviser on toxicology for the Wehrmacht; see Grawitz file, BDC. I would like to thank Ulf Schmidt for drawing these files to my attention.

32. Himmler to Grawitz, n.d. (after February 20, 1945), Grawitz file, BDC.

33. Blome was a doctoral student under Reich Health Office chief Hans Reiter and, like Reiter, sported dueling scars from his student days. Blome also

was an ardent antisemite and friendly with Weimar foreign minister Walther Rathenau's murderers; ten years prior to the *Machtergreifung* he was already distributing Nazi propaganda in his office for his patients to read; see his *Arzt im Kampf—Erlebnisse und Gedanken* (Leipzig: Barth, 1942), pp. 25, 130, 220, 242; Peter-Ferdinand Koch, *Menschenversuche* (Munich: Piper, 1996), pp. 206–26. Ferdinand Lönne suggested to Blome the need for a centralized institute in 1938; see Blome, "Krebsforschung," p. 411. The Reich Institute for Cancer Research was administered by the Kaiser Wilhelm Gesellschaft and included on its board of directors, apart from Mentzel and Blome: Prof. Erich Schumann, head of the Abteilung Wissenschaft im Oberkommando der Wehrmacht; C. H. Lasch, deputy director of the Landesverbände für Geschwulstforschung in Berlin; Ernst Telschow, general director of the Kaiser Wilhelm Gesellschaft; Kurt Huchzermeyer of the NSDAP's Public Health Office for the Reichsgau Wartheland; and Hanns Streit, Kurator der Reichsuniversität, Posen ("Satzung des Zentralinstituts für Krebsforschung e.V." June 18, 1942, R2/12540 BAK). Keitel approved the facility (Klee, *Auschwitz*, pp. 87–93). Hermann Göring named Kurt Blome Bevollmächtigter für Krebsforschung in April of 1943. For further background, see Deichmann's excellent *Biologen*, pp. 211–24.

34. Ramm, "Systematische Krebsbekämpfung."

35. Joan Austoker, *A History of the Imperial Cancer Research Fund 1902–1986* (Oxford: Oxford University Press, 1988).

36. Friedrich Hansen, *Biologische Kriegsführung im Dritten Reich* (Frankfurt: Campus, 1993).

37. Götz Aly, "Die schwarze Ratte im U-Boot," *Frankfurter Allgemeine Zeitung*, March 9, 1994; Klee, *Auschwitz*, pp. 87–93.

38. Other scientists appointed to the institute included Dr. (Bodo?) Trappe, as Oberassistent, and a Dr. Dehn, responsible for animal experiments. Not everyone at the institute had suspicious origins—Friedrich Holtz, for example, had been head of the physical chemistry laboratory of Berlin's Allgemeines Institut gegen die Geschwulstkrankheiten (from 1935 to 1938) prior to being named director of the Nesselstedt facility in 1943; his primary research focus in the 1930s was on cancers caused by ultraviolet light (Hansen, *Biologische Kriegsführung*, pp. 141–52).

39. Ibid., pp. 158–61.

40. Klee states that experiments on Russian POWs "probably were performed" at Nesselstedt (*Auschwitz*, p. 88). Blome was recruited in 1951 to work for the U.S. Army Chemical Corps under its secret "Project 63"; he had been acquitted of wrongdoing in Nuremberg (his incriminating interrogation by U.S. intelligence officials had not been admitted as evidence), but the U.S. consul in Frankfurt ruled him inadmissible for immigration on the basis of the intelligence report. Blome eventually agreed to work as a Project 63 physician at Camp King; see Linda Hunt, *Secret Agenda: The United States Government, Nazi Scientists, and Project Paperclip, 1945 to 1990* (New York: St. Martin's, 1991), pp. 180–81. Blome helped with Himmler's plan to develop a vaccine against the rinderpest virus at the Reich Research Institute on the island of Riems; Riems was captured by the Russians in 1945 and reestablished as a biowarfare

laboratory that operated until 1948 (ibid., p. 186). Koch notes that some of Blome's bacterial cultures were captured by the Russians at Alt-Rehse's Doctors' Führer School (*Menschenversuche*, p. 264).

41. Hansen suggests that the 500,000 RM allocated for Nesselstedt in December of that year actually went to the construction of the Geraberg facility, which was never completed. American soldiers discovered the unfinished buildings, along with bacterial flasks and other laboratory equipment, when they captured Geraberg in April of 1945 (*Biologische Kriegsführung*, p. 141). It would be interesting to explore the extent to which Japanese-German medical contacts during the war were organized to further collaboration in the field of biowarfare; Hansen points out that Dr. Enryo Hojo lectured on the topic at the Military Medical Academy of Berlin in October of 1941 (ibid., p. 87). See also Hellmut Haubold, "Deutschlands und Japans Zusammenarbeit im Gesundheitswesen," *Die Gesundheitsführung*, March–April 1944, pp. 54–56.

42. Walter Vöcking, "Die Entwicklung des Heil- und Gewürzpflanzenanbaues im Deutschen Reich," *Die Deutsche Heilpflanze—Beilage*, July 1939, p. 30.

43. Ludwig Lendle, "Über Vergiftungsmöglichkeiten bei Anbau, Sammeln und Verarbeitung einheimischer Arzneipflanzen," *Die Deutsche Heilpflanze—Beilage*, November 1934, pp. 11–12.

44. Walter Wuttke-Groneberg, *Medizin im Nationalsozialismus: Ein Arbeitsbuch* (Tübingen: Schwäbische Verlagsgesellschaft, 1980), pp. 188–202.

45. Enno Georg, *Die wirtschaftlichen Unternehmungen der SS* (Stuttgart: Deutsche Verlags-Anstalt, 1963), pp. 62–65.

46. Groening and Wolschke-Bulhman, "Some Notes," pp. 120–23. Early American eugenicists regarded the magnificent redwoods of California as Aryans of the forest; the "Save-the-Redwoods League" established in 1918 counted at least eleven eugenicists among its members, including Madison Grant, Henry Fairfield Osborn, and Vernon Kellogg. See Susan R. Schrepfer, *The Fight to Save the Redwoods: A History of Environmental Reform 1917–1978* (Madison: University of Wisconsin Press, 1983), pp. 43–44.

47. Walther Schoenichen, *Naturschutz als völkische und internationale Kulturaufgabe* (Jena: Gustav Fischer, 1942), pp. 405–10. Schoenichen cited the words of Paul Sarasin at the First International Nature Protection Congress in Geneva that "the most important task of world nature protection must be to protect the last remnants of primitive human races from extermination, and to preserve them as undisturbed as possible for future generations" (pp. 406–7). Schoenichen added that it was important to make such demands in the name of biology and anthropology, and not some mushy humanitarianism (*verwaschenen Menschlichkeitsidee*) that throws "Hottentots, Jews, and Aryans all into one pot" (p. 408).

47. Ibid., pp. 406–18, and for background, see Raymond H. Dominick, *The Environmental Movement in Germany: Prophets and Pioneers, 1871–1971* (Bloomington: Indiana University Press, 1992), pp. 85–115.

49. Mervyn Susser, "Timing in Prenatal Nutrition: A Reprise of the Dutch Famine Study," *Nutrition Reviews* 52 (1994): 84–94.

50. J. M. Winter, "The Impact of the First World War on Civilian Health in

Britain," *Economic History Review*, 2d ser., 30 (1977): 487–507; Marks, *Progress of Experiment*, pp. 164–228.

51. Nikolaus Becker, Elaine M. Smith, and Jürgen Wahrendorf, "Time Trends in Cancer Mortality in the Federal Republic of Germany: Progress against Cancer?" *International Journal of Cancer* 43 (1989): 247; personal communication, Nikolaus Becker.

52. German women were often employed in weapons work during the war, though more often in supervisory positions; see Angelika Ebbinghaus, *Opfer und Täterinnen: Frauenbiographien des Nationalsozialismus* (Nordlingen: F. Greno, 1987).

53. There is indirect evidence that military men were more likely to smoke than civilians. A 1944 survey showed that lung cancer was the most common cause of cancer death among soldiers in the early years of the Second World War. In the German male population as a whole, by contrast, stomach cancers still outnumbered lung cancers by more than two to one. This peculiarity in the military was not due to its younger population, as shown by the fact that lung cancer was the most common cause of cancer death even after age-adjustment of the data (11 soldiers over 45 died of lung cancer; 10 soldiers over 45 died of stomach cancer); see Dietrich, "Krebs als Kriegsfolge," pp. 198–99. Given its long latency, many of these lung cancers would have begun to grow prior even to 1933, reflecting smoking patterns before the Nazi seizure of power.

54. Michael Burleigh, *Ethics and Extermination: Reflections on Nazi Genocide* (Cambridge: Cambridge University Press, 1997), pp. 4 and 150–51; Arthur L. Caplan, "The Doctors' Trial and Analogies to the Holocaust in Contemporary Bioethical Debates," in Annas and Grodin, *Nazi Doctors*, pp. 258–75.

55. Carey Goldberg, "Massachusetts Man's Goal Is to Rid Town of Tobacco," *New York Times*, October 7, 1997.

56. Rosie DiManno, "The New Rednecks: NicoNazis Pushing Bigotry's Borders," *Toronto Star*, March 10, 1997, p. A7.

57. For sources, see Arthur L. Caplan: *When Medicine Went Mad: Bioethics and the Holocaust* (Totowa, N.J.: Humana, 1992).

58. Barry M. Katz, *Foreign Intelligence: Research and Analysis in the Office of Strategic Services, 1942–1945* (Cambridge: Harvard University Press, 1989).

59. Mark Walker, *Nazi Science: Myth, Truth, and the German Atomic Bomb* (New York: Plenum, 1995).

60. See chap. 1, n. 9.

61. Eduard Pernkopf, *Topographische Anatomie des Menschen: Lehrbuch und Alas der regionär-stratigraphischen Präparation*, vols. 1–3 (Berlin: Urban & Schwarzenberg, 1937, 1943, and 1952, plus subsequent editions and translations). For background, see Jonathan Broder, "The Corpses That Won't Die," *Jerusalem Post*, February 22, 1996, pp. 24–25.

62. Carl Schoettler, "Is Lifesaving Tool a Product of Evil?" *Baltimore Sun*, August 1, 1997.

63. David J. Williams, "The History of Eduard Pernkopf's *Topographische Anatomie des Menschen*," *Journal of Biomedical Communication* 15 (1988): 2–12.

64. The two reviews are Malcolm H. Hast's in *JAMA* 263 (1990): 2115–16, and Richard S. Snell's in the *New England Journal of Medicine* 323 (1990): 205.

65. Howard A. Israel and William E. Seidelman, "Nazi Origins of an Anatomy Text: The Pernkopf Atlas," *JAMA* 276 (1996): 1633.

66. Richard S. Panush, "Nazi Origins of an Anatomy Text: The Pernkopf Atlas, *JAMA* 276 (1996): 1633–34.

67. Elisabeth Young-Bruehl, *Hannah Arendt: For Love of the World* (New Haven: Yale University Press, 1982), pp. 443 ff.

68. Paul Feyerabend, *Killing Time: The Autobiography of Paul Feyerabend* (Chicago: University of Chicago Press, 1994), pp. 42–53.

69. See my *Racial Hygiene*, pp. 179–180 and 380 n. 11.

70. Seidelman, "Mengele Medicus."

71. Robert Koenig, "Watson Urges 'Put Hitler Behind Us,'" *Science* 276 (1997): 892.

72. Jacob Sullum, *For Your Own Good: The Anti-Smoking Crusade and the Tyranny of Public Health* (New York: Free Press, 1998).

73. Max Horkheimer and Theodor W. Adorno, *Dialectic of Enlightenment* (1944) (New York: Herder and Herder, 1972), p. xi.

BIBLIOGRAPHY

ARCHIVES

Bundesarchiv Berlin, formerly the Berlin Document Center (BDC), housing some ten million Nazi party membership records, copies of which are now also accessible in the National Archives in College Park, Maryland.

Bundesarchiv Koblenz (BAK): R2, R8, R18, R21, R73, R86.

Bundesarchiv Potsdam (BAP): Reichsministerium für Wissenschaft; Reichsministerium des Innern.

Deutsches Hygiene-Museum, Dresden.

Friedrich Schiller Universität Jena, Universitätsarchiv: Personalakten; Akten des "Wissenschaftlichen Instituts zur Erforschung der Tabakgefahren": L-510, L-512.

Geheimes Staatsarchiv, Preussischer Kulturbesitz, Berlin-Dahlem: Rep. 76 Va Sekt.1 Tit. IV, no. 5, vol. 27, pp. 19–27v, 89, 89v.

Hamburger Institut für Sozialforschung, Reemtsma Family Archives.

Hoover Institution Archives (HIA), Deutsche Kongress-Zentrale (DKZ).

Mugar Memorial Library, Special Collections, Alexander papers, Boston University, Boston, Massachusetts.

National Archives, Washington, D.C.: T-175 #87, folder 193, Captured German Documents, plus Nazi party and SS membership rolls.

Rockefeller Foundation Archives, Warren Weaver's dairy, 4263–64.

Thüringisches Hauptstaatsarchiv, Weimar (THW): E 663, E 1493–1498.

United States Holocaust Museum Research Institute Archives, Washington, D.C.

JOURNALS (SELECTED)

Arbeitsmedizin: Abhandlungen über Berufskrankheiten und deren Verhütung (1935–1944), series edited by Ernst W. Baader, M. Bauer, and E. Holstein in cooperation with the Deutsche Gesellschaft für Arbeitsschutz. Published after the war as the *Abhandlungen über Arbeitsmedizin*.

Arbeitsphysiologie (1928–1954); suspended 1945–1948; merged with *Luftfahrtmedizin* in 1955 to form the *Internationale Zeitschrift für angewandte Physiologie einschliesslich Arbeitsphysiologie*.

Arbeitsschutz: Unfallverhütung, Gewerbehygiene (1925–1944), issued as a supplement of the *Reichsarbeitsblatt*, edited by the Deutsche Gesellschaft für Arbeitsschutz and, during the war, by the Generalbevollmächtigten für den Arbeitseinsatz.

Archiv für Gewerbepathologie und Gewerbehygiene (1930–1944), Berlin; resumed publication in 1954. A leading journal of industrial medicine.

Ärztliche Sachverständigen-Zeitung (1895–1944), edited by Ernst W. Baader; a leading organ of occupational and insurance medicine. Resumed publication in 1954 as the *Medizinische Sachverständige* (Berlin).

Auf der Wacht (1939–1942), official publication of the Reichstelle gegen die Alkohol- und Tabakgefahren, Nazi Germany's leading antialcohol and antitobacco organization.

Balneologe: Zeitschrift für die gesamte physikalische und diätetische Therapie (1934–1944), published by the Deutsche Gesellschaft für Bäder- und Klimaheilkunde, edited by H. Vogt. Germany's foremost journal on "spa science."

Chronica Nicotiana (1940–1942), published by the Internationale Tabakwissenschaftliche Gesellschaft, Bremen, edited by Helmuth Aschenbrenner. A pro-tobacco journal, continued after the war by *Tabacologia*.

Deutscher Tabakgegner (1919–1935), published in Dresden by the Verlag des Bundes deutscher Tabakgegner, edited by Richard Bretschneider, with Fritz Lickint as chairman; published 1938–1942 as *Reine Luft*.

Gasmaske: Zeitschrift für Atemschutz (1929–1941), published by the Auergesellschaft, a rare metal producer, in Berlin.

Die Genussgifte (1939–1941), published from 1904 to 1938 as *Die Alkoholfrage* and from 1941 to 1944 as *Die Volksgifte*.

Monatsschrift für Krebsbekämpfung (1933–1944), published by the Reichsausschuss für Krebsbekämpfung, edited by Victor Mertens. The leading Nazi-era cancer combat journal.

Öffentlicher Gesundheitsdienst (1935–1945), mouthpiece for the Interior Ministry's health policy, published by the Reichsausschuss für Volksgesundheitsdienst and edited by Fritz Cropp.

Praktische Karzinom-Blätter (1933–1938), edited by Alfred Neumann in Vienna, succeeded by *Radiologia Clinica*.

Radiologische Rundschau: Röntgen, Radium, Licht (1933–1938), published in Berlin by Karger as the official organ of the Bayrische Gesellschaft für Roentgenologie und Radiologie.

Reine Luft (1938–1941), published 1919–1935 as *Deutscher Tabakgegner* and 1941–1942 as *Die Tabakfrage: Zeitschrift zur Bekämpfung der Tabakgefahren* in Berlin. Official organ of the Reichsstelle gegen die Alkohol- und Tabakgefahren, also the official organ of Jena's Institut zur Erforschung der Tabakgefahren, edited by Ernst Lindig.

Staub: Reinhaltung der Luft (1936–1965), published by the Staubbekämpfungsstelle of the Verband der Deutschen Gewerblichen Berufsgenossenschaften.

Strahlentherapie (1912–1985), published by the Deutsche Röntgengesellschaft and the Gesellschaft für Lichtforschung, edited by Hans Meyer.

Süddeutsche Tabakzeitung (1891–1952), Germany's leading tobacco industry journal, printed in Mannheim-Mainz. Published beginning in 1952 as *Tabakzeitung* with a supplement, *Tabakforschung* (1949–) issued by the Bundesanstalt für Tabakforschung Forchheim bei Karlsruhe.

Der Tabakgegner (1912–1932), published in Trautenau from 1912 to 1916 by Schürer von Waldheim, and from 1916 until 1932 by Hermann Stanger; later published as *Tabakfreie Kultur* in Vienna (1935–37), absorbed by *Reine Luft* in 1938.

Zeitschrift für Krebsforschung (1904–1944), published by the Reichsausschuss für Krebsbekämpfung, edited by Albert Dietrich. Germany's foremost cancer research journal in the first half of the century.

Zentralblatt für Gewerbehygiene und Unfallverhütung (1913–1943), published by the Institut für Gewerbehygiene, Frankfurt, and the Deutsche Gesellschaft für Gewerbehygiene. Published after the war as the *Zentralblatt für Arbeitsmedizin und Arbeitsschutz* (1951–1975).

BOOKS AND ARTICLES

Adam, Curt, and Hans Auler, eds. *Neuere Ergebnisse auf dem Gebiete der Krebskrankheiten.* Leipzig: S. Hirzel, 1937.

Adler, Isaac. *Primary Malignant Growths of the Lungs and Bronchi.* New York: Longmans, Green, and Co., 1912.

Aly, Götz, and Karl Heinz Roth. *Die restlose Erfassung: Volkszählen, Identifizieren, Aussondern im Nationalsozialismus.* Berlin: Rotbuch, 1984.

Annas, George J., and Michael A. Grodin, eds. *The Nazi Doctors and the Nuremberg Code: Human Rights in Human Experimentation.* New York: Oxford University Press, 1992.

Arluke, Arnold, and Boria Sax. "Understanding Nazi Animal Protection and the Holocaust." *Anthrozoös* 5 (1992): 6–31.

"Die Aufgabe." *Monatsschrift für Krebsbekämpfung* 1 (1933): 2.

Auler, Hans. *Der Krebs und seine Bekämpfung.* Berlin: Reichsdruckerei, 1937.

Baader, Ernst W. "Berufskrebs." In *Neuere Ergebnisse auf dem Gebiete der Krebskrankheiten,* edited by Curt Adam and Hans Auler, pp. 104–128. Leipzig: S. Hirzel, 1937.

Baader, Gerhard, and Ulrich Schultz, eds. *Medizin und Nationalsozialismus: Tabuisierte Vergangenheit—Ungebrochene Tradition?* 2d ed. Berlin: Verlagsgesellschaft Gesundheit, 1983.

Bauer, Karl Heinrich. *Rassenhygiene: Ihre biologischen Grundlagen.* Leipzig: Quelle und Meyer, 1926.

———. *Mutationstheorie der Geschwulst-Entstehung.* Berlin: Springer, 1928.

———. "Fortschritte der experimentellen Krebsforschung." *Archiv für klinische Chirurgie* 189 (1937): 123–84.

———. "Krebs und Vererbung." *Münchener medizinische Wochenschrift* 87 (1940): 474–80.

Bauman, Zygmunt. *Modernity and the Holocaust.* New York: Oxford University Press, 1989.

Becker, Nikolaus, Elaine M. Smith, and Jürgen Wahrendorf. "Time Trends in Cancer Mortality in the Federal Republic of Germany: Progress Against Cancer?" *International Journal of Cancer* 43 (1989): 245–49.

Bejach, Edgar. *Die tabakgegnerische Bewegung in Deutschland mit Berücksichtigung der ausserdeutschen Tabakgegnerbewegungen.* Berlin: Med. diss., 1927.

Berblinger, Walther. "Die Zunahme des primären Lungenkrebses in den Jahren 1920–1924." *Klinische Wochenschrift* 4 (1925): 913–16.

"Berlin: Control of the Use of Alcohol and Tobacco." *JAMA* 113 (1939): 2163–64.

Bernhard, Paul. *Der Einfluss der Tabakgifte auf die Gesundheit und die Fruchtbarkeit der Frau.* Jena: G. Fischer, 1943.

"Die Berufskrankheiten im Jahre 1935." *Arbeitsschutz* 3 (1936): 257–63.

Biagioli, Mario. "Science, Modernity, and the 'Final Solution.'" In *Probing the Limits of Representation: Nazism and the "Final Solution",* edited by Saul Friedlander, pp. 185–205. Cambridge: Harvard University Press, 1992.

Blaich, Roland. "Nazi Race Hygiene and the Adventists." *Spectrum* 25 (September 1996): 11–23.

Blome, Kurt. "Krebsforschung und Krebsbekämpfung." *Ziel und Weg* 10 (1940): 406–12.

Blumenthal, Ferdinand. "Zum 25-jährigen Bestehen des Deutschen Zentralkomitees." *Zeitschrift für Krebsforschung* 22 (1925): 97–107.

Bock, Anton. "Das Lungenrauchen." *Vertrauensarzt* 6 (1938): 155–56.

Bock, Gisela. *Zwangssterilisation in Nationalsozialismus: Studien zur Rassenpolitik und Frauenpolitik.* Opladen: Westdeutscher Verlag, 1986.

Boehncke, Georg. "Tabak und Volksgesundheit." *Öffentlicher Gesundheitsdienst* 1 (1935): 625–30.

———. *Die gesetzlichen Grundlagen der Bekämpfung des Tabakmissbrauches in Deutschland.* Berlin: Wacht-Verlag, 1937.

———. *Die Bedeutung der Tabakfrage für das deutsche Volk.* Berlin: Reichsausschuss für Volksgesundheitsdienst, 1939.

Bonne, Georg. "Nachbehandlung nach Krebsoperation." *Hippokrates* 9 (1938): 612–13.

Borst, Max. *Streiflichter über das Krebsproblem.* Munich: Lehmann, 1941.

Bouisson, Etienne-Frédéric. *Tribut à la chirurgie.* Vol. 1. Paris: Baillière, 1858.

Boveri, Theodor H. *Zur Frage der Entstehung maligner Tumoren.* Jena: G. Fischer, 1914.

Bracht, Werner, and Wilhelm Messer. *Alkohol Volk Staat,* 3d ed. Berlin: Reichsgesundheitsverlag, 1941.

Brandt, Arthur. "Bericht über die im Schneeberger Gebiet auf Veranlassung des Reichsausschusses für Krebsbekämpfung durchgeführten Untersuchungen." *Zeitschrift für Krebsforschung* 47 (1938): 108–11.

Brehmer, Wilhelm von. "*Siphonospira polymorpha v.Br.*" Haag/Amper: Linck-Verlag, 1947.

Bretschneider, Richard, ed. *Der Weltbund der Tabakgegner (Internationale Anti-Tabak Liga): Vorgeschichte, Gründung und Entwicklung.* Dresden: Pahl, 1939.

Brooks, Geoffrey. *Hitler's Nuclear Weapons: The Development and Attempted Deployment of Radiological Armaments by Nazi Germany.* London: Cooper, 1992.

Bruns, Erich, and Robert Ley. *Partei, Volksgesundheit, Genussgifte. 2. Reichstagung Volksgesundheit und Genussgifte.* Berlin: Wacht-Verlag, 1939.

Burleigh, Michael. *Death and Deliverance: "Euthanasia" in Germany c. 1900–1945.* Cambridge: Cambridge University Press, 1995.

Burnham, John C. "American Physicians and Tobacco Use: Two Surgeons General, 1929 and 1964." *Bulletin of the History of Medicine* 63 (1989): 1–31.

Butenandt, Adolf, et al. *Chemie und Krebs.* Berlin: Chemie, 1940.

Charman, Terry. *The German Home Front 1939–1945.* London: Barrie & Jenkins, 1989.

Chiurco, Giorgio A. "Krebsbekämpfung im faschistischen Italien." *Deutsche medizinische Wochenschrift* 59 (1933): 1499–1502.

Clemmesen, Johannes. *Statistical Studies in the Aetiology of Malignant Neoplasms.* Copenhagen: Munksgaard, 1965.

Corti, Egon Caeser Conte. *Die trockene Trunkenheit: Ursprung, Kampf und Triumph des Rauchens.* Leipzig: Insel, 1930.

Curschmann, Fritz. "Statistische Erhebungen über Blasentumoren bei Arbeitern in der chemischen Industrie." *Zentralblatt für Gewerbehygiene* 8 (1920): 145–49.

Cyran, Wolfgang. *Genuss mit oder ohne Reue? Eine medizinische Analyse über die Gefahren des Rauchens.* Reinbek: Rowohlt, 1968.

Davey Smith, George, Sabine A. Ströbele, and Matthias Egger. "Smoking and Health Promotion in Nazi Germany." *Journal of Epidemiology and Community Health* 48 (1994): 220–23.

Deichmann, Ute. *Biologen unter Hitler: Vertreibung, Karrieren, Forschung.* Frankfurt: Campus, 1992.

Diels, Rudolf. *Lucifer ante Portas.* Stuttgart: Deutsche Verlags-Anstalt, 1950.

Dietrich, Albert. "Krebs als Kriegsfolge." *Zeitschrift für Krebsforschung* 54 (1944): 196–208.

Doll, Richard, and A. Bradford Hill. "Smoking and Carcinoma of the Lung. Preliminary Report." *British Medical Journal* 2 (1950): 739–48.

Dormanns, Ernst. "Beitrag zur Frage der Zunahme der Krebskrankheit." *Zeitschrift für Krebsforschung* 39 (1933): 40–53.

———. "Die vergleichende geographisch-pathologische Reichs-Carcinomstatistik 1925–1933." *Referate des II. Internationalen Kongresses für Krebsforschung und Krebsbekämpfung* 1 (1936): 460–79.

Druckrey, Hermann. "Ergebnisse der experimentellen Krebstherapie." *Zeitschrift für Krebsforschung* 47 (1938): 112–25.

Ehrhardt. "Der heutige Stand der Asbestosebekämpfung." *Arbeitsschutz* 3 (1940): 191–93.

Elsner, Gine. "Die Entwicklung von Arbeitsmedizin und Arbeitsschutzpolitik nach 1933." In *Arbeitsschutz und Umweltgeschichte,* edited by Hamburger Stiftung, pp. 85–100. Cologne: Volksblatt, 1990.

Enterline, Philip E. "Changing Attitudes and Opinions regarding Asbestos and Cancer 1934–1965." *American Journal of Industrial Medicine* 20 (1991): 685–700.

"Erkennung und Bekämpfung der Tabakgefahren." *Deutsches Ärzteblatt* 71 (1941): 183–85.

Fischer, Eugen. "Strahlenbehandlung und Nachkommenschaft." *Deutsche medizinische Wochenschrift* 55 (1929): 89–91.

———. "Erbschädigung beim Menschen." *Das kommende Geschlecht* 5 (1930): 1–19.

Fischer, Wolfram, et al., eds. *Exodus von Wissenschaften aus Berlin: Fragestellung, Ergebnisse, Desiderate.* Berlin: de Gruyter, 1994.

Fischer-Wasels, Bernhard. "Die experimentelle Erzeugung atypischer Epithelwucherungen und die Entstehung bösartiger Geschwülste." *Münchener medizinische Wochenschrift* 53 (1906): 2041–47.

———. "Die Bedeutung der besonderen Allgemeindisposition des Körpers für die Entstehung der Krebskrankheit." *Strahlentherapie* 50 (1934): 5–78.

———. "Bekämpfung der Krebskrankheit durch Erbpflege." *Deutsches Ärzteblatt* 64 (1934): 92–95.

Fleckseder, Rudolf. "Ueber den Bronchialkrebs und einige seiner Entstehungsbedingungen." *Münchener medizinische Wochenschrift* 83 (1936): 1585–88.

Forschungsinstitut der Friedrich-Ebert-Stiftung. *Wismut und die Folgen des Uranbergbaus.* Bonn: Friedrich-Ebert-Stiftung, 1992.

Friedlander, Henry. *The Origins of Nazi Genocide: From Euthanasia to the Final Solution.* Chapel Hill: University of North Carolina Press, 1995.

Giles, Geoffrey J. "Student Drinking in the Third Reich." In *Drinking: Behavior and Belief in Modern History*, edited by Susanna Barrows and Robin Room, pp. 132–43. Berkeley and Los Angeles: University of California Press, 1992.

Gilman, Sander L. *Freud, Race, and Gender.* Princeton: Princeton University Press, 1993.

Gimbel, John. *Science, Technology, and Reparations: Exploitation and Plunder in Postwar Germany.* Stanford: Stanford University Press, 1990.

Goebbels, Joseph. *The Goebbels Diaries: 1942–1943*, edited by Louis P. Lochner. Garden City, N.Y.: Doubleday, 1948.

———. *Die Tagebücher von Joseph Goebbels: Sämtliche Fragmente*, edited by Elke Fröhlich. Part 1, vol. 4, *Aufzeichnungen 1924–1941.* Munich: K. G. Saur, 1987.

Graessner, Sepp. *Leistungsmedizin während des Nationalsozialismus.* Hamburg: Med. diss., 1990.

Groening, Gert, and Joachim Wolschke-Bulmahn. "Some Notes on the Mania for Native Plants in Germany." *Landscape Journal* 11 (1992): 116–26.

Gross, Eberhard. *Berufskrebs und Krebsforschung.* Cologne: Westdeutscher Verlag, 1955.

Grüneisen, Felix. "Krebsbekämpfung im nationalsozialistischen Staat." *Deutsche medizinische Wochenschrift* 59 (1933): 1498–99.

Gumpert, Martin: *Heil Hunger! Health under Hitler.* New York: Alliance Book Corp., 1940.

Hanselmann, Irmgard. *Zigaretten, Ärzteschaft und Sucht im Spannungsfeld von Politik und Krieg (1900–1950).* Tübingen: Med. diss., 1991.

Hansemann, David Paul von. "Beeinflusst der Krieg die Entstehung oder das Wachstum von Geschwülsten?" *Zeitschrift für Krebsforschung* 15 (1916): 492–516.

Hansen, Friedrich. *Biologische Kriegsführung im Dritten Reich.* Frankfurt: Campus, 1993.

Harrington, Anne. *Reenchanted Science: Holism in German Culture from Wilhelm II to Hitler.* Princeton: Princeton University Press, 1996.

Härting, Friedrich H., and Walter Hesse. "Der Lungenkrebs, die Bergkrankheit in den Schneeberger Gruben." *Vierteljahrsschrift für gerichtliche Medizin* 30 (1879): 296–309, and 31 (1879): 102–32, 313–25.

Haubold, Hellmut. "Statistik und volksbiologische Bedeutung des Krebses." In *Neuere Ergebnisse auf dem Gebiete der Krebskrankheiten*, edited by Curt Adam and Hans Auler, pp. 143–50. Leipzig: Hirzel, 1937.

Hellner, Hans. "Experimentelle Knochensarkome und ihre Beziehungen zu allgemeinen Geschwulstproblemen." *Bruns' Beiträge zur klinischen Chirurgie* 168 (1938): 538–53.

Helmreich, Jonathan E. *Gathering Rare Ores: The Diplomacy of Uranium Acquisition, 1943–1954*. Princeton: Princeton University Press, 1986.

Herf, Jeffrey. *Reactionary Modernism: Technology, Culture, and Politics in Weimar and the Third Reich*. New York: Cambridge University Press, 1984.

Hermannsen, Walter. "Erzieher und Erzieherin! Ein Wort an Euch!" *Die Genussgifte* 35 (1939): 69–86.

Hess, Henner. *Rauchen: Geschichte, Geschäfte, Gefahren*. Frankfurt: Campus, 1987.

Hien, Wolfgang. *Chemische Industrie und Krebs*. Bremerhaven: Wirtschaftsverlag, 1994.

Hildebrandt, Wilhelm. *Rassenmischung und Krankheit: Ein Versuch*. Stuttgart: Hippokrates, 1935.

Hinselmann, Hans. "14 Jahre Kolposkopie. Ein Rückblick und Ausblick." *Hippokrates* 9 (1938): 661–67.

Hintze, Arthur. "Kultur und Krebs." *Jahreskurse für ärztliche Fortbildung* 7 (1939): 61–76.

Hoffman, Frederick L. *The Mortality from Cancer throughout the World*. Newark: Prudential, 1915.

———. "Cancer and Smoking Habits." In *Cancer . . . Comprising International Contributions to the Study of Cancer*, edited by Frank E. Adair, pp. 50–67. Philadelphia: Lippincott, 1931.

———. *Cancer and Diet*. Baltimore: Williams & Wilkins, 1937.

Hofstätter, Robert. *Die rauchende Frau: Eine klinische, psychologische und soziale Studie*. Vienna: Hölder-Pichler-Tempsky, 1924.

———. "Über die Notwendigkeit der periodischen Gesunden-Untersuchung und der allgemeinen Meldepflicht zur Bekämpfung der Krebskrankheit bei der Frau." *Wiener medizinische Wochenschrift* 89 (1939): 931–34.

Hofstätter, Robert, and Johannes Kretz. "50 Jahre Österreichische Krebsgesellschaft." *Der Krebsarzt* 15 (1960): 433–88.

Hohendorf, Gerrit, and Achim Magull-Seltenreich, eds. *Von der Heilkunde zur Massentötung: Medizin im Nationalsozialismus*. Heidelberg: Wunderhorn, 1990.

Holfelder, Hans. "Einsatz und Tätigkeit der Röntgenreihenbildnertruppe der SS in Mecklenburg." *Zeitschrift für Tuberkulose* 83 (1939): 257–64.

Holthusen, Hermann, and K. Englmann. "Die Gefahr des Röntgenkarzinoms als Folge der Strahlenbehandlung." *Strahlentherapie* 42 (1931): 514 ff.

Hubenstorf, Michael, and Peter Th. Walther. "Politische Bedingungen und allgemeine Veränderungen des Berliner Wissenschaftsbetriebes." In *Exodus von Wissenschaften aus Berlin: Fragestellung, Ergebnisse, Desiderate*, edited by Wolfram Fischer et al., pp. 5–100. Berlin: Walter de Gruyter, 1994.

Hueper, Wilhelm C. *Occupational Tumors and Allied Diseases*. Springfield, Ill.: Charles C. Thomas, 1942.

Hunt, Linda. *Secret Agenda: The United States Government, Nazi Scientists, and Project Paperclip, 1945 to 1990*. New York: St. Martin's, 1991.

Hüttig, Werner. "Der Einfluss der Genussgifte auf das Erbgut und seine Entwicklung (Alkohol, Nikotin)." *Öffentlicher Gesundheitsdienst* 1 (1935): 171.

Jagič, Nikolaus von, et al. "Blutbefunde bei Röntgenologen." *Berliner klinische Wochenschrift* 48 (1911): 1220–22.

Janker, Robert. "Die Röntgenreihenuntersuchung in Betrieben." *Arbeitsschutz* 3 (1942): 319–21.

Jehs, Michael. *Erwin Liek: Weltanschauung und standespolitische Einstellung im Spiegel seiner Schriften*. Frankfurt: Mabuse, 1994.

Jüngling, Otto. "Polyposis intestini." *Beiträge zur klinischen Chirurgie* 143 (1928): 476–83.

Kahlau, Gerhard, and A. Schraub. "Krebserzeugung durch Strahlung, insbesondere Schneeberger Lungenkrebs." In *Biophysics: Part I*, edited by Boris Rajewsky and Michael Schön, pp. 132–66. Wiesbaden: Office of Military Government, 1948.

Karbe, Karl-Heinz. "Das nationalsozialistische Betriebsarztsystem während des Zweiten Weltkrieges—Ein Instrument arbeitsmedizinischer Praxis?" In *Medizin für den Staat—Medizin für den Krieg: Aspekte zwischen 1914 und 1945*, edited by Rolf Winau and Heinz Müller-Dietz, pp. 66–81. Husum: Matthiesen, 1994.

Kater, Michael H. *Doctors under Hitler*. Chapel Hill: University of North Carolina Press, 1989.

Kikuth, Walter. "Über Lungencarcinom." *Archiv für pathologische Anatomie und Physiologie* 255 (1925): 107–28.

Kittel, Walther. "Hygiene des Rauchens." In *Wehrhygiene*, edited by Siegfried Handloser and Wilhelm Hoffmann, pp. 242–48. Berlin: Springer, 1944.

Kitzing, Wolfgang E. *Erziehung zur Gesundheit*. Berlin: Reichsgesundheitsverlag, 1941.

Klarner, Wolfgang. *Vom Rauchen: Eine Sucht und ihre Bekämpfung*. Nuremberg: Rudolf Kern, 1940.

Klee, Ernst. *"Euthanasie" im NS-Staat, die "Vernichtung lebensunwerten Lebens"*. Frankfurt: S. Fischer, 1983.

———. *Auschwitz, die NS-Medizin und ihre Opfer*. Frankfurt: S. Fischer, 1997.

Kleine, Hugo O. *Ernährungsschäden als Krankheitsursachen: Versuch einer Darstellung der gesundheitsschädlichen Folgen zivilisationsbedingter Fehlernährung*. Stuttgart: Hippokrates, 1940.

Koch, Peter-Ferdinand. *Menschenversuche: Die tödlichen Experimente deutscher Ärzte*. Munich: Piper, 1996.

Koelsch, Franz. "Lungenkrebs und Beruf." *Acta Unio Internationalis Contra Cancrum* 3 (1938): 243–51.

———. *Was weisst Du von Berufskrankheiten und Gewerbehygiene?* Berlin: Arens, 1944.

Konjetzny, Georg Ernst. "Chronische Gastritis und Magenkrebs." *Monatsschrift für Krebsbekämpfung* 2 (1934): 76–78.

Körbler, Juraj. *Geschichte der Krebskrankheit: Schicksale der Kranken, der Ärzte und der Forscher.* Vienna: Ranner, 1973.

———. *Strahlen: Heilmittel und Gefahr, Eine Geschichte der Strahlen in der Medizin.* Vienna: Ranner, 1977.

Kortenhaus, Friedrich. "Krebs." In *Deutsches Gold: Gesundes Leben—Frohes Schaffen,* edited by Hans Reiter and Johannes Breger, pp. 417–41. Munich: Carl Röhrig, 1942.

Kötschau, Karl. "Über Umweltschädigungen." *Hippokrates* 9 (1938): 1282–83.

Kranz, Heinrich. "Tumoren bei Zwillingen." *Zeitschrift für induktive Abstammungs- und Vererbungslehre* 62 (1932): 173–81.

Krug, Gerhard. *Die Organisation des Kampfes gegen den Krebs in wissenschaftlicher und sozialer Hinsicht.* Marburg: Med. diss., 1938.

Kudlien, Fridolf, ed. *Ärzte im Nationalsozialismus.* Cologne: Kiepenheuer & Witsch, 1985.

Lacassagne, Antoine. *Les cancers produits par les rayonnements électromagnétiques.* Paris: Hermann & Cie, 1945.

Lang, Konrad. "Ernährung." In *Hygiene. Part I: General Hygiene,* edited by Ernst Rodenwaldt, pp. 118–39. Wiesbaden: Dieterich'sche Verlagsbuchhandlung, 1948.

Langer, Walter C. *The Mind of Adolf Hitler: The Secret Wartime Report.* New York: Basic Books, 1972.

Lasch, Carl H. "Krebskrankenstatistik: Beginn und Aussicht." *Zeitschrift für Krebsforschung* 50 (1940): 245–98.

Lemke, Otto. "Asbestose und Lungenkrebs. Zur dritten Verordnung über Ausdehnung der Unfallversicherung auf Berufskrankheiten vom 16. Dezember 1936." *Arbeitsschutz* 3 (1943): 8–15.

Lenz, Fritz. *Menschliche Erblichkeitslehre.* Munich: Lehmann, 1921.

Lenzner, Curt. *Gift in der Nahrung,* 2d ed. Leipzig: Dykschen Buchhandlung, 1933.

Lickint, Fritz. "Tabak und Tabakrauch als ätiologischer Factor des Carcinoms." *Zeitschrift für Krebsforschung* 30 (1929): 349–65.

———. "Die Bedeutung des Tabaks für die Krebsentstehung." *Deutscher Tabakgegner* 17 (1935): 27–30.

———. "Der Bronchialkrebs der Raucher." *Münchener medizinische Wochenschrift* 82 (1935): 1232–34.

———. *Die Krebsfrage im Lichte der modernen Forschung.* Berlin: F. A. Herbig, 1935.

———. *Tabakgenuss und Gesundheit.* Hanover: Bruno Wilkens, 1936.

———. "Nikotinmissbrauch und Nikotinismus." *Zahnärztliche Mitteilungen* 30 (1939): 306–9.

———. *Tabak und Organismus: Handbuch der gesamten Tabakkunde.* Stuttgart: Hippokrates, 1939.

———. *Aetiologie und Prophylaxe des Lungenkrebses als ein Problem der Gewerbehygiene und des Tabakrauches.* Dresden: Steinkopff, 1953.

Liek, Erwin. *Krebsverbreitung, Krebsbekämpfung, Krebsverhütung.* Munich: Lehmann, 1932.

———. *Die Welt des Arztes: Aus 30 Jahren Praxis.* Munich: Lehmann, 1933.

———. *Der Kampf gegen den Krebs.* Munich: Lehmann, 1934.

Lifton, Robert Jay. *The Nazi Doctors.* New York: Basic Books, 1986.

Löwy, Julius. "Über die Joachimstaler Bergkrankheit; vorläufige Mitteilung." *Medizinische Klinik* 25 (1929): 141–42.

Macrakis, Kristie. *Surviving the Swastika: Scientific Research in Nazi Germany.* New York: Oxford University Press, 1993.

Marcuse, Julian. "Geschlecht gegen Rasse." *Sozialistischer Arzt*, February/March 1932, pp. 54–55.

———. "Nationalsozialistische Rassenexperimente." *Sozialistischer Arzt*, April/May 1932, pp. 76–78.

Marks, Harry M. *The Progress of Experiment: Science and Therapeutic Reform in the United States.* New York: Cambridge University Press, 1997.

Marx, Erich. "Die Radiumgefahr in Deutschland." *Neue Freie Presse*, September 25, 1932, p. 25, and September 27, 1932, p. 9.

Meinel, Christoph, and Peter Voswinckel, eds. *Medizin, Naturwissenschaft, Technik und Nationalsozialismus: Kontinuitäten und Diskontinuitäten.* Stuttgart: Geschichte der Naturwissenschaften, 1994.

Merki, Christoph M. "Die nationalsozialistische Tabakpolitik." *Vierteljahrshefte für Zeitgeschichte* 46 (1998): 19–42.

Mertens, Victor E. "Zigarettenrauch eine Ursache des Lungenkrebses? (Eine Anregung)." *Zeitschrift für Krebsforschung* 32 (1930): 82–91.

———. "Noch einmal Zigarettenrauch und Lungenkrebs." *Zeitschrift für Krebsforschung* 51 (1941): 183–92.

Merz, Friedheim. *Die Stunde Null—Eine Sonderdokumentation.* Bonn: Neuer Vorwärts, 1981.

Meyer, George. "Verhandlungen der Internationalen Konferenz für Krebsforschung vom 25.–27. September 1906 zu Heidelberg und Frankfurt a. Main." *Zeitschrift für Krebsforschung* 5 (1907): vii–xxxvi.

Meyer, Maximilian. "Schicksal der Krebskranken." *Reichs-Gesundheitsblatt* 15 (1940): 177–93.

Missriegler, Anton. "Die Krebsangst." *Hippokrates* 9 (1938): 469–71.

"Mitteilungen des Deutschen Reichsausschusses für Krebsbekämpfung." *Zeitschrift für Krebsforschung* 41 (1935): 525–38.

Müller, Franz Hermann. "Tabakmissbrauch und Lungencarcinom." *Zeitschrift für Krebsforschung* 49 (1939): 57–85.

Neitzel, Erich. "Berufsschädigungen durch radioaktive Substanzen." *Arbeitsmedizin: Abhandlungen über Berufskrankheiten und deren Verhütung* 1 (1935): 6–46.

Nordmann, Martin. "Der Berufskrebs der Asbestarbeiter." *Zeitschrift für Krebsforschung* 47 (1938): 288–302.

Nordmann, Martin, and Adolf Sorge. "Lungenkrebs durch Asbeststaub im Tierversuch." *Zeitschrift für Krebsforschung* 51 (1941): 168–82.

Pässler, Hans. "Ueber das primäre Carcinom der Lunge." *Archiv für pathologische Anatomie und Physiologie* 145 (1896): 191–278.

Paulsen, Jens. "Konstitution und Krebs." *Zeitschrift für Krebsforschung* 21 (1924): 126–28.

Pein, Heinz von. "Über die Ursachen der chronischen Arsenvergiftung der Weinbauern." *Medizinische Klinik* 37 (1941): 293–95.

Peller, Sigismund. "Über Krebssterblichkeit der Juden." *Zeitschrift für Krebsforschung* 34 (1931): 128–47.

———. *Not in My Time: The Story of a Doctor*. New York: Philosophical Library, 1979.

Pfeil, E. "Lungentumoren als Berufserkrankung in Chromatbetrieben." *Deutsche medizinische Wochenschrift* 61 (1935): 1197–1200.

Picker, Henry. *Hitlers Tischgespräche im Führerhauptquartier, 1941–42*. Bonn: Athenäum, 1951.

Pritzkoleit, Kurt. *Auf einer Woge von Gold: Der Triumph der Wirtschaft*. Vienna: Kurt Desch, 1961.

Proctor, Robert N. "From *Anthropologie* to *Rassenkunde*: Concepts of Race in German Physical Anthropology." In *Bones, Bodies, Behavior: Essays on Biological Anthropology*, edited by George W. Stocking, Jr., pp. 138–79. Madison: University of Wisconsin Press, 1988.

———. *Racial Hygiene: Medicine under the Nazis*. Cambridge: Harvard University Press, 1988.

———. *Cancer Wars: How Politics Shapes What We Know and Don't Know about Cancer*. New York: Basic Books, 1995.

———. "Gesundes Brot und Leibesübungen: Hat die ideologisch begründete Krebspräventionspolitik im Nationalsozialismus zu geringeren Krebsraten beigetragen?" *Einblick: Zeitschrift des Deutschen Krebsforschungszentrums* 9 (1995): 7–11.

———. "The Anti-Tobacco Campaign of the Nazis: A Little Known Aspect of Public Health in Germany, 1933–1945." *British Medical Journal* 313 (1996): 1450–53.

———. "Nazi Medicine and Public Health Policy." *Dimensions: A Journal of Holocaust Studies* 10 (1996): 29–34.

———. "The Nazi War on Tobacco: Ideology, Evidence, and Possible Cancer Consequences." *Bulletin of the History of Medicine* 71 (1997): 435–88.

Rajewsky, Boris, A. Schraub, and G. Kahlau. "Experimentelle Geschwulsterzeugung durch Einatmung von Radiumemanation." *Naturwissenschaften* 31 (1943): 170–71.

Ramm, Rudolf. "Systematische Krebsbekämpfung." *Die Gesundheitsführung*, November 1942, pp. 265–72.

"Rauchen: Wie Gut." *Der Spiegel*, January 22, 1964, pp. 60–68.

Reckert, Franz K. *Tabakwarenkunde: Der Tabak, sein Anbau und seine Verarbeitung*. Berlin-Schöneberg: Max Schwalbe, 1942.

Reckzeh, Paul. "Chronische Tabakvergiftung und Lebenserwartung." *Medizinische Klinik* 35 (1939): 1169–71.

Rehn, Ludwig. "Blasengeschwülste bei Fuchsin-Arbeitern." *Archiv für klinische Chirurgie* 50 (1895): 588–600.

Reiche, Fritz. "Zur Genese der Bronchialkrebse und ihre Beziehungen zu Kampfgasschädigungen." *Medizinische Welt* 6 (1932): 1013–14.

Reichsjugendführung. *Du hast die Pflicht, gesund zu sein!* Heft 3: *Gesund durch richtig Ernährung.* N.p.: Gesundheitsaktion der Hitler-Jugend, 1939.

Reid, George. "Weltanschauung, Haltung, Genussgifte." *Die Genussgifte* 35 (1939): 55–68.

Reiter, Hans. *Das Reichsgesundheitsamt, 1933–1939: Sechs Jahre nationalsozialistische Führung.* Berlin: Springer, 1939.

Reiter, Hans, and Johannes Breger, eds. *Deutsches Gold: Gesundes Leben—Frohes Schaffen.* Munich: Röhrig, 1942.

Reiter, Hans, and Günther Hecht. *Genussgifte Leistung Rasse.* Berlin: Reichsgesundheitsverlag, 1940.

Renneberg, Monika, and Mark Walker, eds. *Science, Technology and National Socialism.* Cambridge: Cambridge University Press, 1994.

Rodenwaldt, Ernst, et al. *Hygiene. Part I: General Hygiene.* Wiesbaden: Dieterich'sche Verlagsbuchhandlung, 1948.

Roffo, Angel H. "Der Tabak als Krebserzeugende Agens." *Deutsche medizinische Wochenschrift* 63 (1937): 1267–71.

———. "Krebserzeugende Tabakwirkung." *Monatsschrift für Krebsbekämpfung* 8 (1940): 97–102.

Rosenblatt, Milton B. "Lung Cancer in the Nineteenth Century." *Bulletin of the History of Medicine* 38 (1964): 395–425.

Rostoski, Kurt, Erich Saupe, and Georg Schmorl. "Die Bergkrankheit der Erzbergleute in Schneeberg in Sachsen." *Zeitschrift für Krebsforschung* 23 (1926): 360–84.

Rowntree, Cecil W. "Contribution to the Study of X-Ray Carcinoma and the Conditions which Precede Its Onset." *Archives of the Middlesex Hospital* 13 (1908): 182–205.

Rückert, Ernst, and Heinz Kleeberg. *25 Jahre Krebsforschung im deutschsprachigen Schrifttum: Eine Auswahl von Buch- und Zeitschriftenliteratur aus den Jahren 1931–1955.* Berlin: Volk und Gesundheit, 1961.

Salazar, Evelyn H. *Krebsforschung und Krebsbekämpfung in Berlin bis zum Jahre 1945.* Berlin: Med. diss., 1986.

Sauerbruch, Ferdinand, Fritz Lickint, and Ernst Gabriel. *Arzt, Alkohol und Tabak.* Berlin: Reichsgesundheitsverlag, 1940.

Schairer, Eberhard, and Erich Schöniger. "Lungenkrebs und Tabakverbrauch." *Zeitschrift für Krebsforschung* 54 (1943): 261–69.

Schenck, Ernst G. *Patient Hitler: Eine medizinische Biographie.* Dusseldorf: Droste, 1989.

Schinz, Hans R., and Adolf Zuppinger. *Siebzehn Jahre Strahlentherapie der Krebse: Zürcher Erfahrungen 1919–1935.* Leipzig: Georg Thieme, 1937.

Schmid, Ekkehard. "Messungen des Radium-Emanationsgehaltes von Kellerluft." *Mitteilung aus dem physikalischen Institut der Universität Graz* 82 (1932): 233–42.

Schmid, Wolfgang. *Die Bedeutung Erwin Lieks für das Selbstverständnis der Medizin in Weimarer Republik und Nationalsozialismus.* Erlangen-Nuremberg: Med. diss., 1989.

Schönbauer, Leopold, and Erna Ueberreiter. "Erlaubt das vorliegende statistische Material ein Urteil über eine Zunahme der Krebskrankheit?" *Wiener medizinische Wochenschrift* 100 (1950): 554–56.

Schönherr, Ernst. "Beitrag zur Statistik und Klinik der Lungentumoren." *Zeitschrift für Krebsforschung* 27 (1928): 436–50.

Schöniger, Erich. *Lungenkrebs und Tabakverbrauch.* Jena: Med. diss., 1944.

Schüller, Max. "Gibt es eine Prädisposition für Krebs und worin besteht sie?" *Archiv für Rassen- und Gesellschaftsbiologie* 1 (1904): 822–39.

Schulz, Otto. "Gesundheitliche Schäden durch gewerblichen Staub." *Die Gasmaske* 11 (1939): 57–66.

Seidelman, William E. "Mengele Medicus: Medicine's Nazi Heritage." *Milbank Quarterly* 66 (1988): 221–39.

Sellers, Christopher. "Discovering Environmental Cancer: Wilhelm Hueper, Post–World War II Epidemiology, and the Vanishing Clinician's Eye." *American Journal of Public Health* 87 (1997): 1824–35.

Seufert, Paul. *Der Feldzug gegen die Zigarette.* Basel: Ernst Reinhardt, 1964.

Seyfarth, Carly. "Lungenkarzinome in Leipzig." *Deutsche medizinische Wochenschrift* 50 (1924): 1497–99.

Staemmler, Martin. "Beruf und Krebs." *Münchener medizinische Wochenschrift* 85 (1938): 121–25.

Strnad, Franz. "Der Lungenkrebs." *Monatsschrift für Krebsbekämpfung* 6 (1938): 297–311.

Syrek, Adam. "Zur Häufigkeitszunahme des Lungenkrebses." *Zeitschrift für Krebsforschung* 36 (1932): 409–15.

Teleky, Ludwig. "Der berufliche Lungenkrebs." *Actio Unio Internationalis Contra Cancrum* 3 (1938): 253–73.

Teutschlaender, Otto. "Die Berufskrebse (mit besonderer Berücksichtigung der in Deutschland vorkommenden." *Zeitschrift für Krebsforschung* 32 (1930): 614–27.

———."Arbeit und Geschwulstbildung." *Monatsschrift für Krebsbekämpfung* 1 (1933): 30–304.

Thom, Achim. "Zur Entwicklung, staatlichen Förderung und Wirksamkeit der ausseruniversitären Krebsforschungszentren in Deutschland zwischen 1900 und 1945." Unpub. MS.

Thom, Achim, and Genadij I. Caregorodcev, eds. *Medizin unterm Hakenkreuz.* Berlin: Volk und Gesundheit, 1989.

Thomalla, Curt. *Gesund sein—Gesund bleiben.* Berlin: F. W. Peters, 1936.

Thys, Fr. "Note sur l'étiologie du carcinome bronchique." *Revue belge des sciences médicales* 7 (1935): 640–44.

Tiedemann, Friedrich. *Geschichte des Tabaks.* Frankfurt: H. L. Brönner, 1854.

Trials of War Criminals before the Nuernberg Military Tribunals. 15 vols. Washington, D.C.: U.S. Government Printing Office, 1949–1953.

Uehlinger, Erwin A., and Otto Schürch. "Über experimentelle Erzeugung von Sarkomen mit Radium und Mesothorium." *Deutsche Zeitschrift für Chirurgie* 251 (1939): 12–33.

Unna, Paul G. *Die Histopathologie der Hautkrankheiten.* Berlin: A. Hirschwald, 1894.

Verschuer, Otmar Freiherr von. *Erbpathologie, Ein Lehrbuch für Ärzte und Medizinstudierende*. Munich: Lehmann, 1937.

————. *Leitfaden der Rassenhygiene*. Leipzig: Georg Thieme, 1941.

Virchow, Rudolf. *Die krankhafte Geschwülste*. 3 vols. Berlin: August Hirschwald, 1863–1867.

"Vorwort zur neuen Folge." *Zeitschrift für Krebsforschung* 40 (1934): 1–2.

Wagner, Gustav, and Andrea Mauerberger. *Krebsforschung in Deutschland*. Berlin: Springer, 1989.

Waite, Robert G. L. *The Psychopathic God, Adolf Hitler*. New York: Basic Books, 1977.

Waniek, Hans. "Die Verhütung der Staublungenkrankheiten, insbesondere der Silikose." *Klinische Wochenschrift* 23 (1944): 288–89.

Wassink, Willem F. "Ontstaansvoorwaarden voor Longkanker." *Nederlands Tijdschrift voor Geneeskunde* 4 (1948): 3732–47.

Wedler, Hans-Wilfried. "Über den Lungenkrebs bei Asbestose." *Archiv für klinische Medizin* 191 (1943): 189–209.

Weindling, Paul. *Health, Race and German Politics between National Unification and Nazism 1870–1945*. Cambridge: Cambridge University Press, 1989.

Welz, Alfred. "Weitere Beobachtungen über den Berufskrebs der Asbestarbeiter." *Archiv für Gewerbepathologie und Gewerbehygiene* 11 (1942): 536–50.

Werberat der deutschen Wirtschaft. *Volksgesundheit und Werbung*. Berlin: Carl Heymanns, 1939.

Westphal, Karl E., and Hans Weselmann. "Über Nikotinschädigungen des Magens." *Die Genussgifte* 36 (1940): 1–14.

Winter, Georg. "Die erste Krebsbekämpfung, ihre Erfolge und Lehren." *Monatsschrift für Krebsbekämpfung* 1 (1933): 3–10.

Wirz, Franz G. M. *Gesunde und gesicherte Volksernährung*. Dresden: Müllersche Verlagshandlung, 1938.

Woitke, Ronald. *Zur Entwicklung der Krebserfassung, -behandlung und -fürsorge im "Dritten Reich"*. Leipzig: Med. diss., 1993.

Wüstner, Horst. *Eine Krebsstatistik mit besonderer Berücksichtigung des Bronchialcarcinoms*. Jena: Med. diss., 1941.

Wynder, Ernest L., and Evarts A. Graham. "Tobacco Smoking as a Possible Etiologic Factor in Bronchiogenic Carcinoma." *JAMA* 143 (1950): 329–36.

Yamagiwa, Katsusaburo, and Koichi Ichikawa. "Experimentelle Studie über die Pathogenese der Epithelialgeschwülste." *Mitteilungen aus der medizinischen Fakultät der kaiserlichen Universität zu Tokyo* 15 (1916): 295–344.

Zimmermann, Susanne. *Die medizinische Fakultät der Universität Jena während der Zeit des Nationalsozialismus*. Jena: Med. diss., 1994.

ACKNOWLEDGMENTS

I'D like to thank the following people for commenting on drafts or helping me sort through various ideas: Jim Adler, Keith Barbera, Iain Boal, Charles Fergus, George Davey Smith, Richard Doll, Lynne Fallwell, Fritz Hansen, Wolfgang Hien, Michael Hubenstorf, Michael Kater, Claudia Koonz, Nancy Krieger, Peter Martin, David Ozonoff, Brigitta van Rheinberg, Ulf Schmidt, Bill Seidelman, and Mark Walker. Michael Berenbaum in 1994 invited me to serve as the J. B. and Maurice C. Shapiro Senior Scholar-in-Residence at the U.S. Holocaust Memorial Museum in Washington, D.C., where with the assistance of my prodigious research assistant, Matthias Leitner, I was able to track down many of the more arcane sources of Nazi cancer research and policy. I'd also like to acknowledge a debt to Regine Kollek and Jan Philipp Reemtsma of the Hamburger Institut für Sozialforschung, who invited me to spend a wonderful eight months at the Institute doing research and writing. Additional support was made available from the National Library of Medicine and Penn State's Institute for Arts and Humanities.

I owe a special thanks to my unflagging companion of two decades, Londa Schiebinger.

Last but not least (as the Germans say), I'd like to mention the quadrumvirate of Harvard biologists with whom I had the fortune of teaching (and learning) "Biology and Social Issues" in the late 1970s and early 1980s. The course has evaporated with the passage of time, but they have continued their quest for "roots," and it is to them and others touched by their teaching that I have dedicated this book.

INDEX

70; cautions frantic pace of industry is causing new hazards, 118; declares cider "official people's drink," 147; opposes tobacco, 198, 208, 232; postwar career, 227. *See also* Reich Health Office

retinoblastoma, 68–69, 299n43

rhetoric: antitobacco, 179, 239; apocalyptic, 42, 170; campaign against foreign words, 46–47, 291n39; enlightenment, 8, 248; "euthanasia," 45; of "final solutions," 8, 44, 47–48, 106, 292n46, 292n48, 299n49; Germanized, 46–47; of impossibility, 27; of Jews as tumors, tumors as Jews, 46; medico-political euphemisms, 45; militaristic, 292n44; murderous euphemisms, 45–46; of nicotine addiction, 329n41; Nietzschean, 48; of "one in eight," 29; of performance, 77, 314n181; problem-solving, 292n48, 299n49; of quackery, 57

Ritter, Robert, 67

ritual scarring, 65

Roffo, Angel H., 184–85, 191–92, 195, 215, 320n107, 330n43, 331n66, 332n72

Röhm, Ernst, 234

Roosevelt, Franklin D., 10, 101

Rössle, Robert, 53, 279n1, 294n64, 298n25

Rostock, Paul, 170

Rostoski, Kurt, 97, 103, 282n21, 299n48

Rowntree, Cecil W., 103

Royal College of Physicians (London), 217, 338n149

Rubner, Max, 162

Rüdin, Ernst, 148

Rudolf Hess Hospital (Dresden), 55, 207n, 284n47, 316n17

Rudolf Virchow Hospital (Berlin), 35, 65, 288n4, 298n27

Rust, Bernhard, 13–14, 300n55

SA (Storm Troopers), 206, 234–35

saccharine, 170, 214, 324n174

Sachs, Hans, 36

Sagan, Carl, 16

Sarasin, Paul, 348n47

sarin, 16

Sauckel, Fritz: executed at Nuremberg, 81, 227; organizes five million foreign workers, 78–81; pushes for tobacco conversion, 207; spearheads Thuringia's

antitobacco campaign, 208–9, 227, 337n135; writes proposal for Jena's antitobacco institute, 209, 337n135

Sauerbruch, Ferdinand, 199, 232, 287n2, 315n14

Save-the-Redwoods League, 348n46

Sax, Boria, 136

scarlet red, 166, 169, 291n40

Schairer, Eberhard: citation history, 198, 338n146; Davey Smith's meeting with, 338n141; Doll unfamiliar with work of, 217; early career, 213–14; equates nicotine damage with rheumatism, 213; explores carcinogenicity of saccharine, 324n174; joins Nazi party, 214; proves cancer-tobacco link, 194, 215–17

Schenck, Ernst Günther, 22, 165

Schlick, Moritz, 202

Schmeling, Hans, 201

Schmidt, Otto, 209, 330n47

Schmidt, Ulf, 287n74, 346n31

Schneeberger Krankheit, 64, 97–101, 282n21, 299n48, 307n84–88, 310n121, 329n36

Schoenichen, Walther, 266–67, 348n47

Schönherr, Ernst, 283n32, 328n30

Schöniger, Erich, 194, 198. *See also* Schairer, Eberhard

Schopenhauer, Arthur, 177

Schultze, Walter, 22

Schulz, Otto, 106

Schumann, Erich, 347n33

Schumann, Horst, 90

Schürch, Otto, 332n66

Schwarz, Hans, 53

secondhand tobacco smoke. *See* passive smoking

Seeger, Gerhard, 317n52

Seidelman, William E., 279n2, 289n14, 350n65

Selektionsmedizin, 9, 77, 116–17

Sellers, Christopher, 113, 280n2, 312n159

Seventh-Day Adventists, 26, 179, 227

Seyfarth, Carly, 197, 329n38, 333n75

"sickness funds" (Krankenkassen), 76–77

Siemens company, 109–10

Silent Spring, 14–15. *See also* Carson, Rachel

silicosis, 40, 88–89, 101–2, 105–7

skim milk, 126, 315n12